Jenny Parsons

with Damian Williams

speakout

Elementary
Teacher's Resource Book

TEACHER'S RESOURCE BOOK CONTENTS

STUDENTS' BOOK CONTENTS

LISTENING/DVD	SPEAKING	WRITING
listen to short conversations showing different ways to introduce people	introduce people; do a quiz	improve your use of capital letters
	identify objects	
listen to conversations in various tourist places; learn to listen for key words; listen to prices and numbers	give information for numbers, prices, etc; make simple requests	
BBC **Fawlty Towers:** watch an extract from a sitcom about a hotel	arrival and check in at a hotel	complete a hotel registration form; write an email to book a hotel room
listen to a conversation between two friends choosing the right online group for them	talk about activities; talk about a group/team	
listen to people describing their jobs; listen and identify a variety of jobs	talk about routines; describe other people's routines	learn how to use linkers: *and*, *but* and *or*
learn to get a speaker to slow down and grade their language	learn to show you don't understand; ask questions at a tourist information centre	
BBC **Holiday: Fasten Your Seatbelt:** watch an extract from a reality programme about a difficult job	talk about life at home: likes and dislikes	write an internet posting to a penpal describing yourself
listen to people describing their friends	describe personality; do a quiz and find out what kind of friend you are	
	talk about your family	improve your use of apostrophe *'s*; write about your family
learn to show interest when you listen	make arrangements to meet friends	
BBC **Francesco's Mediterranean Voyage:** watch an extract from a documentary about a special occasion	talk about a special occasion	write an invitation
listen to a conversation between two people talking about a special flat	describe your home	improve your use of commas; write an email about your home
	talk about things you can do in towns; describe a favourite place in your town/city	
learn to say *no* politely in a shop; listen to various shopping conversations	have a conversation in a shop	
BBC **50 Places To See Before You Die:** watch an extract from a documentary about some amazing places	describe your favourite place of all	write a blog about your favourite place
listen to people talk about food	talk about your eating and drinking habits	learn to use paragraphs and write a short report
	talk about diets and lifestyle	
understand fast speech; listen to a man ordering in a fast food restaurant	order a meal in a restaurant	
BBC **Rick Stein's Seafood Odyssey:** watch an extract from a cookery programme about a famous chef	describe a special dish	write a recipe
listen to peple describing famous people's favourite things	talk about people's favourite things; describe your favourite childhood things	
	talk about your life/past events	link sentences with *because* and *so* and write your life story
learn to keep a conversation going; listen to someone describing their weekend	describe a perfect/terrible weekend	
BBC **The Culture Show:** watch an extract from a documentary about a famous dancer	interview a special person	write a profile essay about a special person

COMMUNICATION BANK page 160   AUDIO SCRIPTS page 167

STUDENTS' BOOK CONTENTS

LISTENING/DVD	SPEAKING	WRITING
listen to people discuss how they like to travel	talk about how you like to travel; compare places and holidays	
	plan and talk about a long journey	learn to check and correct information; write about a holiday
understand directions; learn to check and correct directions	give directions in the street	
BBC **Holiday 10 Best:** watch an extract from a travel show about Buenos Aires	describe a town/city you know	write a short article about a town/city
	talk about taking photos; talk about what people are doing	write a blog entry about what you are doing
listen to a radio programme about ideas of beauty	discuss what you know about various film stars; describe people's appearance	
learn to link words to speak faster	ask and answer a questionnaire about films; ask for and give recommendations	
BBC **Inside Out:** watch an extract from a documentary about an English music festival	describe an event	write a review of an event
listen to a guide giving a tour around a transport museum	talk about types of transport	
	talk about ways to travel around towns/cities	
listen to a man talk about his problems getting to work	apologise for being late; tell a long story	learn to use linkers and write a story
BBC **Airport:** watch an extract from a documentary about a day at Heathrow airport	deal with problems when flying	write an email about an experience at an airport/on a plane
listen to a radio interview with lottery winners	talk about your future plans/wishes	
	make predictions about situations	improve your use of linkers: *too*, *also* and *as well* and write a short story
learn to respond to suggestions; listen to people discussing which activities they want to do	make some suggestions and invite your friends to join you	
BBC **Wild Weather:** watch an extract from a documentary about the wettest place in Europe	talk about weather and how it makes you feel	write a message board notice about your country
listen to a radio programme about colds and flu	talk about what to do when you don't feel well and give advice; discuss cures for the common cold	
	do a quiz about your fitness; talk about healthy weekends	learn to use adverbs in stories and how to make stories more interesting
listen to different scenarios of people needing help and thanking someone	give advice and offer help; thank someone	
BBC **The Two Ronnies:** watch an extract from a sitcom about an unusual shopping experience	ask for help in a pharmacy	write some advice for a health message board
listen to people talking about their experiences	talk about unusual experiences	learn to use postcard phrases and write a postcard
	describe movement from one place to another; talk about past experiences	
listen to different scenarios on the phone	describe difficult situations/problems; say telephone numbers; phone someone about a problem	
BBC **Shark Therapy:** watch an extract from a documentary about sharks	describe an exciting/frightening experience	write a story about an exciting/frightening experience

COMMUNICATION BANK page 160   AUDIO SCRIPTS page 167

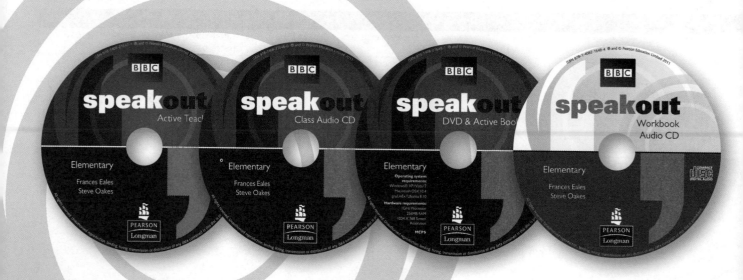

Before we started writing *Speakout*, we did a lot of research to find out more about the issues that teachers and students face and how these can be addressed in a textbook for the 21st century. The issues that came up again and again were motivation, authentic content and the need for structured speaking and listening strategies.

As English teachers, we know how motivating it can be to bring the real world into the classroom by using authentic materials. We also know how time consuming and difficult it can be to find authentic content that is truly engaging, at the right level and appropriate for our students. With access to the entire archive of the BBC, we have selected some stunning video content to motivate and engage students. We have also created tasks that will encourage interaction with the materials while providing the right amount of scaffolding.

We realise that the real world is not just made up of actors, presenters and comedians, and 'real' English does not just consist of people reading from scripts. This is why *Speakout* brings real people into the classroom. The Video podcasts show people giving their opinions about the topics in the book and illustrate some of the strategies that will help our students become more effective communicators.

Speakout maximises opportunities for students to speak and systematically asks them to notice and employ strategies that will give them the confidence to communicate fluently and the competence to listen actively. While the main focus is on speaking and listening, we have also developed a systematic approach to reading and writing. For us, these skills are absolutely essential for language learners in the digital age.

To sum up, we have tried to write a course that teachers will really enjoy using; a course that is authentic but manageable, systematic but not repetitive – a course that not only brings the real world into the classroom, but also sends our students into the real world with the confidence to truly 'speak out'!

From left to right: Frances Eales, JJ Wilson, Antonia Clare and Steve Oakes

STUDENTS' BOOK

- Between 90 and 120 hours of teaching material
- Language Bank with reference material and extra practice
- Photo Bank to expand vocabulary
- Audioscripts of the class audio

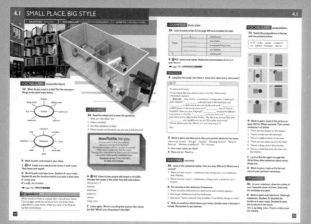
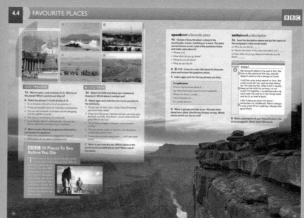

CLASS AUDIO CDs

- Audio material for use in class
- Test audio for the Mid-course and End of Course Tests

DVD & ACTIVE BOOK

- DVD content
- Digital Students' Book
- Audio, video and Video podcasts

WORKBOOK

- Grammar and vocabulary
- Functional language
- Speaking and listening strategies
- Reading, writing and listening
- Regular review and self-study tests

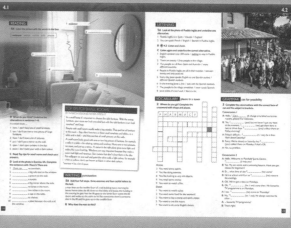

AUDIO CD

- Audio material including listening, pronunciation and functional practice

MYSPEAKOUTLAB

- Interactive Workbook with instant feedback
- Unit tests and Progress Tests
- Mid-course and End of Course Tests
- Test generator
- Streaming and downloadable Video podcasts
- Interactive Video podcast worksheets

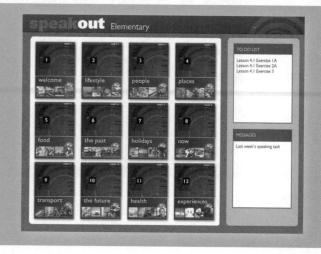

TEACHER'S RESOURCE BOOK

- Teaching notes
- Integrated key and audioscript
- Four photocopiable activities for every unit
- Mid-course and End of Course Test

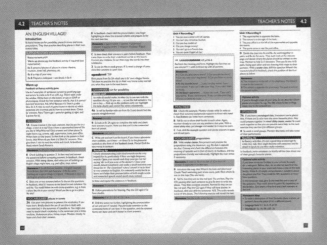
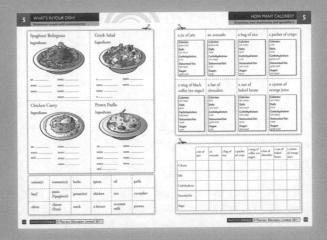

SPEAKOUT ACTIVE TEACH

- Integrated audio and video content
- Video podcasts
- Test master containing all course tests
- Answer reveal feature
- Grammar and vocabulary review games
- A host of useful tools
- Large extra resources section

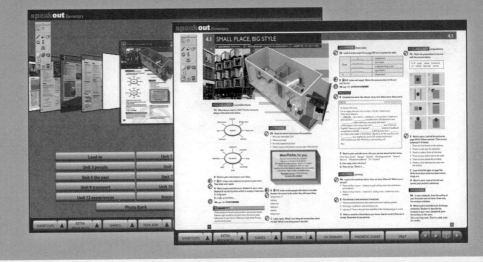

SPEAKOUT WEBSITE

- Information about the course
- Sample materials from the course
- Free downloadable worksheets
- Teaching tips
- Placement test
- A range of useful resources
- Video podcasts

A UNIT OF THE STUDENTS' BOOK

UNIT OVERVIEW

Every unit of Speakout starts with an Overview, which lists the topics covered. This is followed by two main input lessons which cover grammar, vocabulary and the four skills. Lesson three covers functional language and focuses on important speaking and listening strategies. Lesson four is built around a clip from a BBC programme and consolidates language and skills work. Each unit culminates with a Lookback page, which provides communicative practice of the key language.

INPUT LESSON 1

Lesson one introduces the topic of the unit and presents the key language needed to understand and talk about it. The lesson combines grammar and vocabulary with a focus on skills work.

> The target language and the CEF objectives are listed to clearly show the objectives of the lesson.

> Clear grammar presentations are followed by written and oral practice as well as pronunciation work.

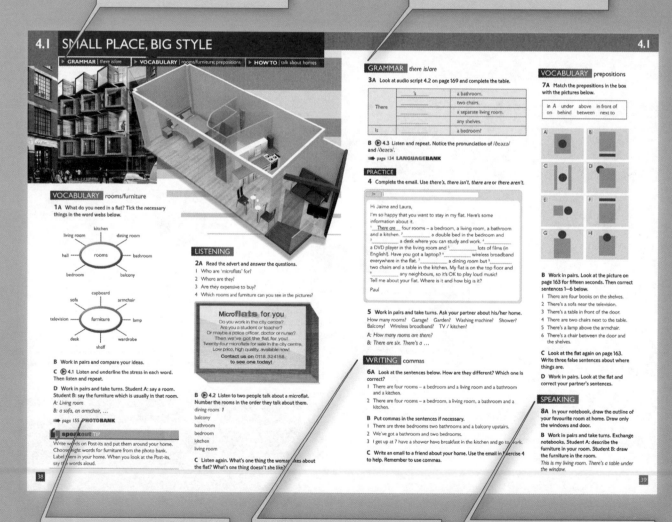

> Lexical sets are often expanded in the full colour Photo bank at the back of the Students' Book.

> Every pair of input lessons includes at least one writing section with focus on a variety of different genres.

> All lessons include a focus on speaking where the emphasis is on communication and fluency building.

INPUT LESSON 2

Lesson two continues to focus on grammar and vocabulary while extending and expanding the topic area. By the end of the second lesson students will have worked on all four skill areas.

Lexical sets are introduced in context. Practice of new words often includes pronunciation work.

Grammar and vocabulary sections often include a listening element to reinforce the new language.

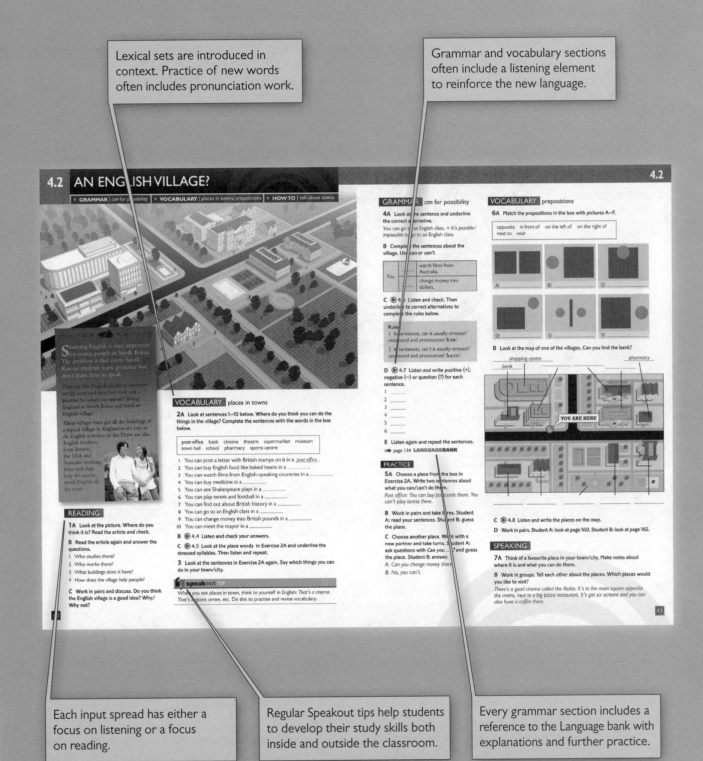

Each input spread has either a focus on listening or a focus on reading.

Regular Speakout tips help students to develop their study skills both inside and outside the classroom.

Every grammar section includes a reference to the Language bank with explanations and further practice.

FUNCTIONAL LESSON

The third lesson in each unit focuses on a particular function, situation or transaction as well as introducing important speaking and listening strategies.

The target language and the CEF objectives are listed to clearly show the objectives of the lesson.

Students learn a lexical set which is relevant to the function or situation.

Students learn important speaking and listening strategies which can be transferred to many situations.

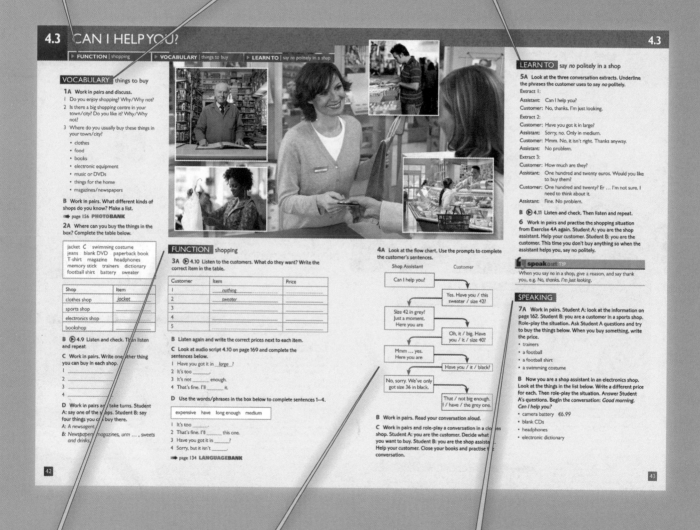

The functional language is learnt in context, often by listening to the language in use.

Conversation flow charts provide scaffolding that allows students to explore the new language.

The lesson ends with a speaking activity which gives students the chance to practise the new language.

DVD LESSON

The fourth lesson in each unit is based around an extract from a real BBC programme.
This acts as a springboard into freer communicative speaking and writing activities.

A preview section gets students thinking about the topic of the extract and introduces key language.

A series of different tasks helps students to understand and enjoy the programme.

The Speakout task builds on the topic of the extract and provides extended speaking practice.

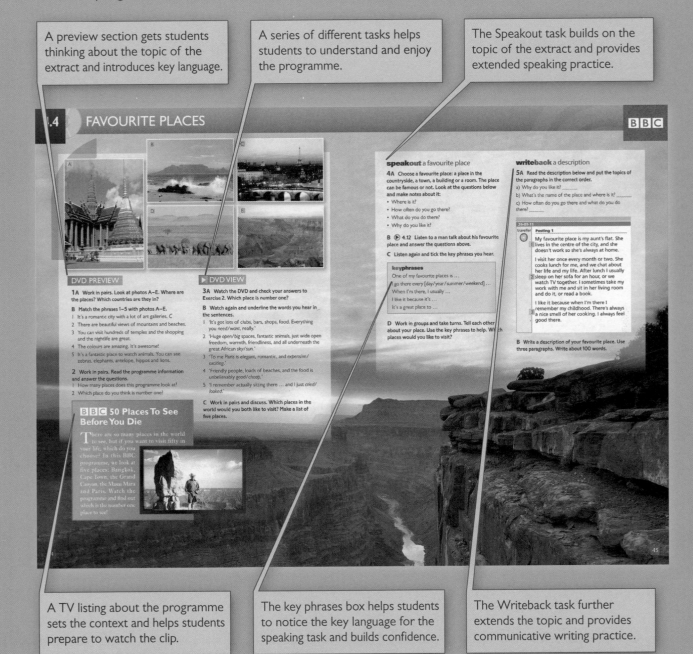

A TV listing about the programme sets the context and helps students prepare to watch the clip.

The key phrases box helps students to notice the key language for the speaking task and builds confidence.

The Writeback task further extends the topic and provides communicative writing practice.

LOOKBACK PAGE

Each unit ends with a Lookback page, which provides further practice and review of the key language covered in the unit. The review exercises are a mixture of communicative activities and games. Further practice and review exercises can be found in the Workbook. The Lookback page also introduces the Video podcast, which features a range of real people talking about one of the topics in the unit.

WORKBOOK

The Workbook contains a wide variety of practice and review exercises and covers all of the language areas studied in the unit. It also contains regular review sections as well as self-study tests to help students consolidate what they have learnt.

The Workbook features extensive practice of vocabulary, grammar, reading, writing and listening.

The Workbook contains regular listening practice using the accompanying audio CD.

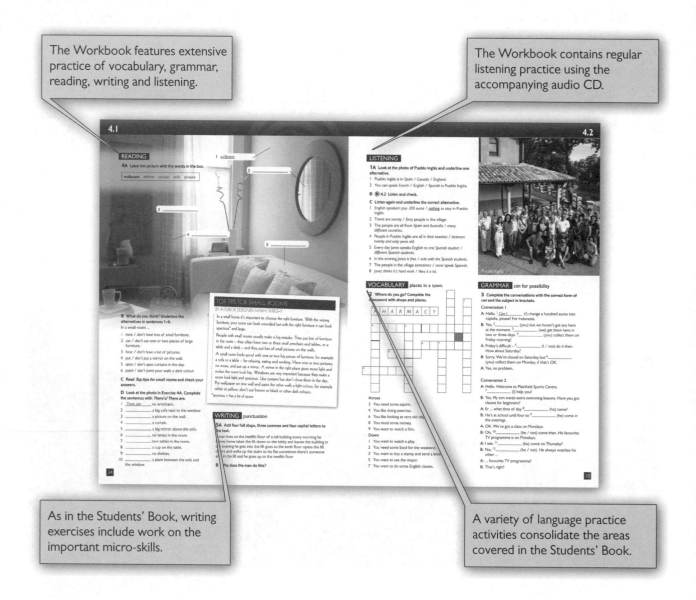

As in the Students' Book, writing exercises include work on the important micro-skills.

A variety of language practice activities consolidate the areas covered in the Students' Book.

MYSPEAKOUTLAB

MySpeakoutLab provides a fully blended and personalised learning environment that benefits both teachers and students. It offers:

- an interactive Workbook with instant feedback and automatic grade book.
- professionally written Unit Tests, Progress Tests, Mid-course and End of Course tests that can be assigned at the touch of a button.
- tools to create and assign your own tests or edit the Word versions to print out and use in class.
- interactive Video podcast worksheets with an integrated video player so students can watch while they do the exercises.
- tools to upload audio and video podcasts so speaking tasks can be assigned for homework.

ACTIVE TEACH

Speakout Active Teach contains everything you need to make the course come alive in your classroom.
It includes integrated whiteboard software which enables you to add notes and embed files.
It is also possible to save all of your work with the relevant page from the Students' Book.

All audio and video content is fully integrated and includes subtitles as well as printable scripts.

An answer reveal function lets you show the answers to an exercise at the touch of a button.

Shortcuts to the relevant pages of the Language bank and the Photo bank make navigation easy.

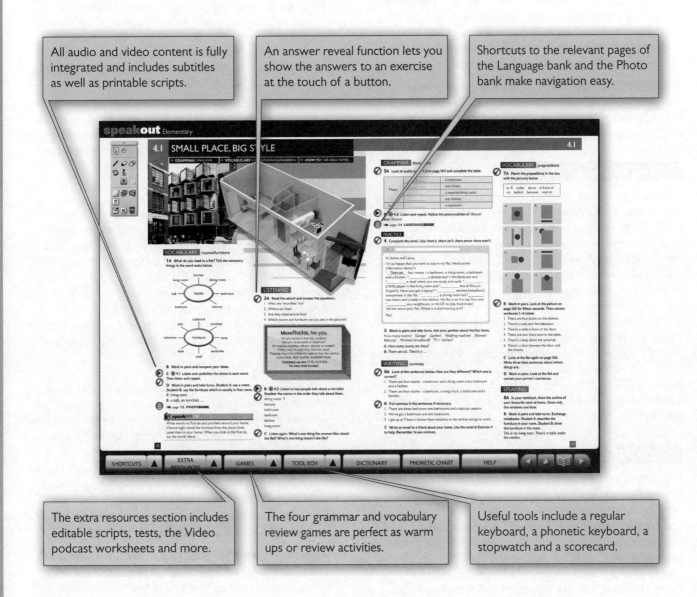

The extra resources section includes editable scripts, tests, the Video podcast worksheets and more.

The four grammar and vocabulary review games are perfect as warm ups or review activities.

Useful tools include a regular keyboard, a phonetic keyboard, a stopwatch and a scorecard.

WEBSITE

The Speakout website will offer information about the course as well as a bank of useful resources including:

• information about the course, its components and the authors.

• introductory videos by the authors of the course.

• sample materials and free downloadable worksheets.

• teaching tips.

• placement test.

• editable audio and video scripts, word lists and CEF mapping documents.

• Video podcasts for all published levels – both streaming and downloadable.

speakout is designed to satisfy both students and teachers on a number of different levels. It offers engaging topics with authentic BBC material to really bring them to life. At the same time it offers a robust and comprehensive focus on grammar, vocabulary, functions and pronunciation. As the name of the course might suggest, speaking activities are prominent, but that is not at the expense of the other core skills, which are developed systematically throughout.

With this balanced approach to topics, language development and skills work, our aim has been to create a course book full of 'lessons that really work' in practice. Below we will briefly explain our approach in each of these areas.

TOPICS AND CONTENT

In *Speakout* we have tried to choose topics that are relevant to students' lives. Where a topic area is covered in other ELT courses we have endeavoured to find a fresh angle on it. It is clear to us that authenticity is important to learners, and many texts come from the BBC's rich resources (audio, visual and print) as well as other real-world sources. At lower levels, we have sometimes adapted materials by adjusting the language to make it more manageable for students while trying to keep the tone as authentic as possible. We have also attempted to match the authentic feel of a text with an authentic interaction. Every unit contains a variety of rich and authentic input material including BBC Video podcasts (filmed on location in London, England) and DVD material, featuring some of the best the BBC has to offer.

GRAMMAR

Knowing how to recognise and use grammatical structures is central to our ability to communicate with each other. Although at first students can often get by with words and phrases, they increasingly need grammar to make themselves understood. Students also need to understand sentence formation when reading and listening and to be able to produce accurate grammar in professional and exam situations. We share students' belief that learning grammar is a core feature of learning a language and believe that a guided discovery approach, where students are challenged to notice new forms works best. At the same time learning is scaffolded so that students are supported at all times in a systematic way. Clear grammar presentations are followed by written and oral practice. There is also the chance to notice and practise pronunciation where appropriate.

In *Speakout* you will find:

- **Grammar in context** – We want to be sure that the grammar focus is clear and memorable for students. Grammar is almost always taken from the listening or reading texts, so that learners can see the language in action, and understand how and when it is used.

- **Noticing** – We involve students in the discovery of language patterns by asking them to identify aspects of meaning and form, and complete rules or tables.

- **Clear language reference** – As well as a summary of rules within the unit, there is also a Language bank which serves as a clear learning reference for the future

- **Focus on use** – We ensure that there is plenty of practice, both form and meaning-based, in the Language bank to give students confidence in manipulating the new language. On the main input page we include personalised practice, which is designed to be genuinely communicative and to offer students the opportunity to say something about themselves or the topic. There is also regular recycling of new language in the Lookback review pages, and again the focus here is on moving learners towards communicative use of the language.

VOCABULARY

Developing a wide range of vocabulary is key to increasing communicative effectiveness; developing a knowledge of high-frequency collocations and fixed and semi-fixed phrases is key to increasing spoken fluency. An extensive understanding of words and phrases helps learners become more confident when reading and listening, and developing a range of vocabulary is important for effective writing. Equally vital is learner-training, equipping students with the skills to record, memorise and recall vocabulary for use.

In *Speakout* this is reflected in:

- **A prominent focus on vocabulary** – We include vocabulary in almost all lessons whether in a lexical set linked to a particular topic, as preparation for a speaking activity or to aid comprehension of a DVD clip or a listening or reading text. Where we want students to use the language actively, we encourage them to use the vocabulary to talk about their own lives or opinions. At lower levels, the Photo bank also extends the vocabulary taught in the lessons, using memorable photographs and graphics to support students' understanding.

- **Focus on 'chunks'** – As well as lexical sets, we also regularly focus on how words fit together with other words, often getting students to notice how words are used in a text and to focus on high-frequency 'chunks' such as verb-noun collocations or whole phrases.

- **Focus on vocabulary systems** – We give regular attention to word-building skills, a valuable tool in expanding vocabulary. At higher levels, the Vocabulary plus sections deal with systems such as affixation, multi-word verbs and compound words in greater depth.

- **Recycling and learner training** – Practice exercises ensure that vocabulary is encountered on a number of occasions: within the lessons, on the Lookback page, in subsequent lessons and in the Photo bank/Vocabulary bank at the back of the book. One of the main focuses of the Speakout tips – which look at all areas of language learning – is to highlight vocabulary learning strategies, aiming to build good study skills that will enable students to gain and retain new language.

FUNCTIONAL LANGUAGE

One thing that both teachers and learners appreciate is the need to manage communication in a wide variety of encounters, and to know what's appropriate to say in given situations. These can be transactional exchanges, where the main focus is on getting something done (buying something in a shop or phoning to make an enquiry), or interactional exchanges, where the main focus is on socialising with others (talking about the weekend, or responding appropriately to good news). As one learner commented to us, 'Grammar rules aren't enough – I need to know what to say.' Although it is possible to categorise 'functions' under 'lexical phrases', we believe it is useful for learners to focus on functional phrases separately from vocabulary or grammar.

The third lesson in every unit of *Speakout* looks at one such situation, and focuses on the functional language needed. Learners hear or see the language used in context and then practise it in mini-situations, in both a written and a spoken context. Each of these lessons also includes a Learn to section, which highlights and practises a useful strategy for dealing with both transactional and interactional exchanges, for example asking for clarification, showing interest, etc. Learners will find themselves not just more confident users of the language, but also more active listeners.

SPEAKING

The dynamism of most lessons depends on the success of the speaking tasks, whether the task is a short oral practice of new language, a discussion comparing information or opinions, a personal response to a reading text or a presentation where a student might speak uninterrupted for a minute or more. Students develop fluency when they are motivated to speak. For this to happen, engaging topics and tasks are essential, as is the sequencing of stages and task design. For longer tasks, students often need to prepare their ideas and language in a structured way. This all-important rehearsal time leads to more motivation and confidence as well as greater accuracy, fluency and complexity. Also, where appropriate, students need to hear a model before they speak, in order to have a realistic goal.

There are several strands to speaking in *Speakout*:

- **Communicative practice** – After introducing any new language (vocabulary, grammar or function) there are many opportunities in *Speakout* for students to use it in a variety of activities which focus on communication as well as accuracy. These include personalised exchanges, dialogues, flow-charts and role-plays.

- **Focus on fluency** – In every unit of *Speakout* we include opportunities for students to respond spontaneously. They might be asked to respond to a series of questions, to a DVD, a Video podcast or a text, or to take part in conversations, discussions and role-plays. These activities involve a variety of interactional formations such as pairs and groups.

- **Speaking strategies and sub-skills** – In the third lesson of each unit, students are encouraged to notice in a systematic way features which will help them improve their speaking. These include, for example, ways to manage a phone conversation, the use of mirror questions to ask for clarification, sentence starters to introduce an opinion and intonation to correct mistakes.

- **Extended speaking tasks** – In the *Speakout* DVD lesson, as well as in other speaking tasks throughout the course, students are encouraged to attempt more adventurous and extended use of language in tasks such as problem solving, developing a project or telling a story. These tasks go beyond discussion; they include rehearsal time, useful language and a concrete outcome.

LISTENING

For most users of English (or any language, for that matter), listening is the most frequently used skill. A learner who can speak well but not understand at least as well is unlikely to be a competent communicator or user of the language. We feel that listening can be developed effectively through well-structured materials. As with speaking, the choice of interesting topics and texts works hand in hand with carefully considered sequencing and task design. At the same time, listening texts can act as a springboard to stimulate discussion in class.

There are several strands to listening in *Speakout*:

- **Focus on authentic recordings** – In *Speakout*, we believe that it is motivating for all levels of learner to try to access and cope with authentic material. Each unit includes a DVD extract from a BBC documentary, drama or light entertainment programme as well as a podcast filmed on location with real people giving their opinions. At the higher levels you will also find unscripted audio texts and BBC radio extracts. All are invaluable in the way they expose learners to real language in use as well as different varieties of English. Where recordings, particularly at lower levels, are scripted, they aim to reflect the patterns of natural speech.

- **Focus on sub-skills and strategies** – Tasks across the recordings in each unit are designed with a number of sub-skills and strategies in mind. These include: listening for global meaning and more detail; scanning for specific information; becoming sensitised to possible misunderstandings; and noticing nuances of intonation and expression. We also help learners to listen actively by using strategies such as asking for repetition and paraphrasing.

- **As a context for new language** – We see listening as a key mode of input and *Speakout* includes many listening texts which contain target grammar, vocabulary or functions in their natural contexts. Learners are encouraged to notice this new language and how and where it occurs, often by using the audio scripts as a resource.

- **As a model for speaking** – In the third and fourth lessons of each unit the recordings serve as models for speaking tasks. These models reveal the ways in which speakers use specific language to structure their discourse, for example with regard to turn-taking, hesitating and checking for understanding. These recordings also serve as a goal for the learners' speaking.

READING

Reading is a priority for many students, whether it's for study, work or pleasure, and can be practised alone, anywhere and at any time. Learners who read regularly tend to have a richer, more varied vocabulary, and are often better writers, which in turn supports their oral communication skills. Nowadays, the Internet has given students access to an extraordinary range of English language reading material, and the availability of English language newspapers, books and magazines is greater than ever before. The language learner who develops skill and confidence in reading in the classroom will be more motivated to read outside the classroom. Within the classroom reading texts can also introduce stimulating topics and act as springboards for class discussion.

There are several strands to reading in *Speakout*:

- **Focus on authentic texts** – As with *Speakout* listening materials, there is an emphasis on authenticity, and this is reflected in a number of ways. Many of the reading texts in *Speakout* are sourced from the BBC. Where texts have been adapted or graded, there is an attempt to maintain authenticity by remaining faithful to the text type in terms of content and style. We have chosen up-to-date, relevant texts to stimulate interest and motivate learners to read. The texts represent a variety of genres that correspond to the text types that learners will probably encounter in their everyday lives.

- **Focus on sub-skills and strategies** – In *Speakout* we strive to maintain authenticity in the way the readers interact with a text. We always give students a reason to read, and provide tasks which bring about or simulate authentic reading, including real-life tasks such as summarising, extracting specific information, reacting to an opinion or following an anecdote. We also focus on strategies for decoding texts, such as guessing the meaning of unknown vocabulary, understanding pronoun referencing and following discourse markers.

- **Noticing new language** – Noticing language in use is a key step towards the development of a rich vocabulary and greater all-round proficiency in a language, and this is most easily achieved through reading. In *Speakout*, reading texts often serve as valuable contexts for introducing grammar and vocabulary as well as discourse features.

- **As a model for writing** – In the writing sections, as well as the Writeback sections of the DVD spreads, the readings serve as models for students to refer to when they are writing, in terms of overall organisation as well as style and language content.

WRITING

In recent years the growth of email and the internet has led to a shift in the nature of the writing our students need to do. Email has also led to an increased informality in written English. However, many students need to develop their formal writing for professional and exam-taking purposes. It is therefore important to focus on a range of genres, from formal text types such as essays, letters and reports to informal genres such as blog entries and personal messages.

There are four strands to writing in *Speakout*:

- **Focus on genres** – In every unit at the four higher levels there is a section that focuses on a genre of writing, emails for example. We provide a model to show the conventions of the genre and, where appropriate, we highlight fixed phrases associated with it. We usually then ask the students to produce their own piece of writing. While there is always a written product, we also focus on the process of writing, including the relevant stages such as brainstorming, planning, and checking. At Starter and Elementary, we focus on more basic writing skills, including basic written sentence patterns, linking, punctuation and text organisation, in some cases linking this focus to a specific genre.

- **Focus on sub-skills and strategies** – While dealing with the genres, we include a section which focuses on a sub-skill or strategy that is generally applicable to all writing. Sub-skills include paragraphing, organising content and using linking words and pronouns, while strategies include activities like writing a first draft quickly, keeping your reader in mind and self-editing. We present the sub-skill by asking the students to notice the feature. We then provide an opportunity for the students to practise it.

- **Writeback** – At the end of every unit, following the DVD and final speaking task, we include a Writeback task. The idea is for students to develop fluency in their writing. While we always provide a model, the task is not tied to any particular grammatical structure. Instead the emphasis is on using writing to generate ideas and personal responses.

- **Writing as a classroom activity** – We believe that writing can be very usefully employed as an aid to speaking and as a reflective technique for responding to texts – akin to the practice of writing notes in the margins of books. It also provides a change of pace and focus in lessons. Activities such as short dictations, note-taking, brainstorming on paper and group story writing are all included in *Speakout*.

PRONUNCIATION

In recent years, attitudes towards pronunciation in many English language classrooms have moved towards a focus on intelligibility: if students' spoken language is understandable, then the pronunciation is good enough. We are aware, however, that many learners and teachers place great importance on developing pronunciation that is more than 'good enough', and that systematic attention to pronunciation in a lesson, however brief, can have a significant impact on developing learners' speech.

In *Speakout*, we have taken a practical, integrated approach to developing students' pronunciation, highlighting features that often cause problems in conjunction with a given area of grammar, particular vocabulary items and functional language. Where relevant to the level, a grammatical or functional language focus is followed by a focus on a feature of pronunciation, for example, the weak forms of auxiliary verbs or connected speech in certain functional exponents. Students are given the opportunity to listen to models of the pronunciation, notice the key feature and then practise it.

TEACHING ELEMENTARY LEARNERS

Teaching any particular level of language learner presents the teacher with a unique set of challenges and rewards. Some are particular to that level only, while others are applicable to a number of levels. Here we will try to offer a few thoughts and guidelines for teaching elementary learners.

The first thing to bear in mind is that labels for levels can be very broad and any elementary class will probably consist of individuals with a range of different learning experiences, styles and preferences. Some learners may have studied a considerable amount of English already, perhaps many years ago, while others may have come straight from a starter/beginner class. Some may be highly communicative and be able to get across a great deal with few words and a little grammar, while others may be above 'level' in their ability to do written grammar exercises or read a text but lack confidence when asked to speak as they feel their knowledge isn't enough to accurately convey what they want to say.

Many elementary students will be fairly new to language learning and may be relatively unfamiliar with the classroom practices and characteristics of a communicative language classroom, for example, pair work, mingling and less-controlled activities. These students will therefore need more orientation and explanation than higher level students. They may also find it difficult to understand classroom instructions and won't understand the metalanguage that teachers sometimes use to talk about grammar.

However, a class of elementary learners can be incredibly rewarding to teach. Progress is often fast and measurable and most elementary students thoroughly enjoy the interactivity of a modern language classroom as well as the camaraderie of the group. As regards level, we can generalise that the 'average' elementary student can already do a certain number of basic things in English, and could probably survive in an English speaking environment using a number of words and phrases, albeit quite inaccurately and with many gaps in their knowledge.

Here are our Top Tips to help at this level:

- When giving instructions, use gestures and always demonstrate an activity rather than explaining it; do it with a student yourself or ask two students to do it in front of the class.

- Grade your language so that it is easy to understand.

- Use gestures, visuals, real objects and concept questions when introducing language.

- Provide plenty of pair work for speaking activities or for checking answers after a listening or reading activity so that students can build up their confidence.

- Try to provide a good balance of communicative activities and more controlled accuracy building ones. Elementary students need both.

- Don't expect freer activities to sustain themselves for very long. It's common for lower level learners to shut down, get confused or feel unsure about a task.

- Remember to praise learners – insecurity is a major factor in inhibiting lower level learners and a bit of encouragement from the teacher can go a long way.

Antonia Clare, Frances Eales, Steve Oakes and JJ Wilson

TEACHER'S NOTES INDEX

OVERVIEW

NICE TO MEET YOU

Introduction

Ss get to know each other. They learn/revise the verb *be* and the names of countries and nationalities. They also practise greeting people and making introductions.

SUPPLEMENTARY MATERIALS

Resource bank p146

Photo bank p152

Warm up extra activity: bring a tennis ball/orange/ball of paper or similar.

Ex 4A: a map of the world (e.g. from Google Earth)

Ex 7A: pictures of famous places and food

Warm up

Your Ss may or may not know each other already but either way, you'll probably want to break the ice in the first lesson with a 'getting to know you' activity such as the *Meet and greet* worksheet on p146 of the **Resource bank** or a similar activity of your choice. This will also help you to assess your Ss' language level, especially their speaking skills.

Optional extra activity

If you are teaching a *multilingual class*, Ss may find the pronunciation of their classmates' names difficult. If so, you could follow up with a memory activity: organise Ss into a large circle, (if you have a *large class*, break the Ss into two or three smaller circles) and demonstrate the activity. Throw a ball (or similar) to a student, saying his/her name at the same time. The student then does the same to a different person in the circle. Ss continue this activity until they can remember their classmates' names fairly confidently.

VOCABULARY greetings

1A Ss match the photos to the places alone and check in pairs. N.B. It's a good idea for Ss to check their answers in pairs with most exercise types as it promotes Ss–Ss cooperation and builds their confidence. Elicit the answers and check/teach the meaning of any new words. Drill the pronunciation chorally (i.e. with the whole class repeating the words together) and then individually. Highlight the stress on the 2nd syllable in *hotel*.

Answers: B street C classroom D airport E office

B The aim of this exercise is to teach/revise Ss' knowledge of common everyday greetings and contextualise the use of the verb *be* via listening.

Teaching tip

While listening, Ss often miss the most important information because they try to understand every single word. After a while, this can make them get too confused so they stop listening. Tell Ss not to worry about words they don't understand and just concentrate on the task.

Check answers in feedback but don't explain new words yet.

Answers: 1D 2B 3C 4A 5E

C Play the CD again. Ss complete the answers and then check in pairs.

Teaching tip

At this stage, if Ss don't manage to write down all of the answers, play the CD again. The important thing is to build Ss' confidence with listening, not 'test' or demotivate them.

Check any new words/phrases in the conversations, e.g. *Nice to meet you, same (class), welcome, BBC News, Can I help you?, Please take a seat.* If you have a **strong class**, ask *Which is more polite: Hi or Good evening/afternoon?*

Answers: 1 Nice, you 2 How, you, you 3 Hi, Nice, meet 4 afternoon 5 Good afternoon

GRAMMAR present simple: *be*

2 Encourage Ss to try to work things out for themselves. They can do the exercise alone/in pairs and then check their answers in section 1.1 of the **Language bank** on p128.

Answers: is, 'm, Are, are, Is, isn't

Watch out!

Contractions: Ss often use the full form of the verb because it's easier, e.g. *I am Pedro.* To help Ss sound natural, encourage them to use contracted forms from the start. Model and drill the contracted forms of new verb forms thoroughly and correct the use of full forms when appropriate.

⟶ LANGUAGEBANK 1.1 p128–129

Read the notes with the Ss. Check understanding and highlight the alternative negative forms: *you're not, he's not,* etc. Model and drill sentences with contractions in each box. Elicit more examples for each use of *be*, e.g. *She's Marta. It's a pencil.* Ss can then ask and answer personalised questions in open pairs across the class, e.g. *Is Marcia a tourist? Are Boris and Hiroko students? Are you married?*

Answers:
A 1 'm 2 're 3 's 4 's 5 're 6 're
B 1 Are 2 'm not 3 'm 4 Are 5 'm 6 Are 7 am
C 1 Debra isn't in the café. 2 Is your name Khan? 3 Mr and Mrs Cabrera aren't at the airport. 4 This is my friend Paolo. 5 What are their names? 6 Where's the health centre?

speakout TIP

Read the tip with Ss. Explain that this will help them remember the new language. Elicit some examples to the board. Ss write their own sentences in their notebooks. Monitor to check they do it correctly.

Teaching tip

This is a good opportunity to focus on the importance of keeping organised records. Ss should have a notebook/file for their English classes. They could write their grammar notes in the front and new vocabulary in the back (see notes on recording vocabulary later).

PRACTICE

Culture notes
Greetings: In Britain, it's becoming more common for friends to kiss each other on the cheek when they meet. However, it's still normal for people to shake hands when they are introduced, particularly in formal situations.

3A Give Ss 3 mins to complete the conversation and check it in pairs. In feedback, check answers. Model and drill the conversation chorally. Ss then practise reading/memorising the conversation in groups of three. Monitor and help them with pronunciation. Finally, invite two stronger Ss to act out the introductions to the class with you as student A. Ss B and Ss C should shake hands. With **stronger classes**, teach a few useful phrases: *He's a friend of mine. She's my sister. He's a colleague.*

Answers: 2 's 3 to 4 you 5 Are 6 am

B After working in groups, Ss could then move round the class, introducing their partners to other Ss.

VOCABULARY countries and nationalities

4A If you have a map of the world, ask Ss to locate the countries in the table on the map. (Or use the one in the **photo bank** on p152.) Elicit/Teach the nationalities. Model and drill the pronunciation. In feedback, check the spelling and write it on the board. Ask Ss to notice the endings of each nationality: *-ish, -an/-ian, -ese.* Point out that *-an/-ian* is the most common ending. *French* is an exception (as are *Germany/ German, Greece/Greek, Thailand/Thai*). Ss should copy the table into their Vocabulary notebooks.

Answers:
1st row: British
2nd row: Italian, Brazilian
3rd row: Chinese, Japanese
4th row: French, American

B Do this with the whole class. If you have a *multilingual class*, elicit new countries and nationalities and write them on the board.

C Write the example words on the board and elicit the stressed syllable. Ss then do the exercise and check their answers in pairs. Play the CD again if necessary. In feedback, invite Ss to write the answers on the board: the class can agree/disagree. Check and drill problem words further.

Answers: Britain, British; Italy, Italian; Brazil, Brazilian; China, Chinese; Japan, Japanese; France, French; the USA, American

D Give Ss a time limit of 2 mins. Monitor and give feedback on pronunciation problems as needed.

Optional extra activity
As a light-hearted follow up, Ss work in small groups and take it in turns to mouth a country or nationality slowly and clearly (no sound must be made). The others have to say what it is.

⇒ PHOTOBANK p152

The **Photo bank** is a valuable resource and will enrich Ss' vocabulary. It is advised to do the exercises in class as the vocabulary is often necessary/useful for subsequent practice exercises.

1A Give Ss 2 mins to match the countries alone. The person with the most correct answers wins. Check/Drill the answers and prompt Ss to self-correct any pronunciation mistakes.

Answers: 2 C 3 L 4 R 5 K 6 A 7 P 8 B 9 N 10 F 11 H 12 E 13 D 14 O 15 Q 16 G 17 I 18 M

B Tell Ss to notice how the nationalities are organised according to their endings, This will help them remember the words. They could add the new words to the table (Ex 4A) in their Vocabulary notebooks.

Answers: 1 Egyptian 2 Argentinian 3 Indian 4 Australian 5 Russian 6 Canadian 7 Korean 8 Mexican 9 Malaysian 10 Scottish 11 Polish 12 Irish 13 Portuguese 14 Vietnamese 15 Japanese 16 German 17 Greek 18 Thai

PRACTICE

5A The aim of the quiz is to make the new language more memorable for Ss. N.B. Ss may have different preferred learning styles: the quiz helps both visual and auditory learners to remember new language because it uses picture and music prompts. First, check the meaning of the title of the quiz, and new words in the rubrics, e.g. *shapes, food*. However, don't teach the names of the dishes, etc yet as this is part of the quiz. Ss then do the quiz in pairs. Play the CD again if necessary.

B In feedback, check the answers and elicit/teach new food words, e.g. *pasta, sushi, curry, paella*. Then ask *Which music/country/shape/food do you like?* Ss can use other examples that aren't in the quiz in their answers if they want to.

Answers:
1 1 C (Russian folk music) 2 A (Irish jig)
3 D (Greek balalaika music) 4 B (Brazilian samba)
2 1 B 2 C 3 D 4 A
3 1 D (pasta) 2 C (sushi) 3 B (curry) 4 A (paella)

WRITING capital letters

6A In *weaker classes*, first check the meaning of the words in the box by eliciting/giving an example of each one, e.g. *city – London; famous place – Big Ben*. Ss could do the exercise in pairs/small groups. In feedback, discuss which rules are the same/different in their own language.

Answers: tick all categories except all nouns, jobs and food

B *Weaker Ss* could work in pairs for this exercise so that you can provide more support if needed. In feedback, nominate Ss to write the corrected sentences on the board. The other Ss check them and give the rule for each capital letter.

Answers: 1 The Eiffel Tower is in France. 2 'Buenos días!' is Spanish for 'hello'. 3 Sake is Japanese. 4 Spaghetti is food from Italy.

SPEAKING

7A Monitor closely and help Ss if necessary. If you've brought pictures of famous places/food and drink, give them out in order to motivate Ss and provide support for *slower Ss*.

B Do feedback in open pairs. Each pair reads out their information and the other pair guesses the country. Make notes on Ss' language problems and give feedback on these now or in the next lesson.

Homework ideas
- Ss learn ten new nationality/country words from this lesson for the next class.
- Language bank 1.1 Ex 1A–C, p129
- Workbook Ex 1–6, p5–6

TRAVEL LIGHT

Introduction

Ss learn/revise and practise *this/that*, *these/those*, possessive *'s* and *mine/yours* in the context of travelling.

SUPPLEMENTARY MATERIALS

Resource bank p145 and p148

Photo bank p152

Ex 1A: bring some of the items in the box to help teach meaning, e.g. sunglasses, a magazine, etc.

Warm up

Review of countries and nationalities: the alphabet game

The aim of the game is to activate and revise words Ss know in a particular category, in this case countries and nationalities. Demonstrate by saying the letter A. Ss must shout out the names of any countries/nationalities beginning with A: e.g. *Australian, Argentina*. Continue doing the same with the other letters of the alphabet: *B, C, D,* etc. If Ss can't think of a word for a specific letter, move on quickly to the next one to maintain the pace. In feedback, add/elicit any words Ss missed and correct pronunciation errors you noticed.

VOCABULARY objects

1A If you've brought photos to class, use them to elicit/ teach the words. Elicit one or two words Ss know before they complete the exercise. Check answers and teach any unknown words. The pronunciation is practised in Ex B.

Answers: B <u>watch</u> C <u>sung</u>lasses D <u>sweat</u>er
E <u>mag</u>azine F <u>news</u>paper G <u>lap</u>top H <u>di</u>ary I <u>tick</u>et
J <u>pass</u>port K <u>purse</u> L <u>keys</u> M <u>hair</u>brush N <u>MP3</u> player
O <u>mobile phone</u> **Missing object:** <u>tooth</u>brush

B Drill the example on the CD, highlighting the stress. Play the CD again to give Ss time to check their answers if necessary. In feedback, invite Ss to write the answers on the board, underlining the stress. Point out that most two-syllable nouns are stressed on the first syllable.

C Monitor closely to assess Ss' pronunciation. Also note how well Ss are using the articles *a/an* with singular countable nouns, and no article with plural nouns. In feedback, nominate Ss to ask/answer the questions in open pairs across the class. Correct/Teach the use of articles if necessary. N.B. There's more practice in Ex 1B of the **Photo bank** after Ex 7B.

D Give Ss 2 mins to write as many objects they can alone, and then check their answers in their books. In feedback, ask Ss how many words they remembered. Discuss which words they didn't write down, and possible reasons for it, e.g. *the pronunciation/spelling is difficult, they don't like the word or thing it relates to, they didn't have time to write it, they couldn't remember the meaning.* This will raise Ss' awareness of strategies that help them to learn new words. Finally, give Ss 4 mins to write the new words from Ex 1B in their notebooks.

speakout TIP

Read the tip with your Ss and elicit some examples from Ex 1D. Monitor to check how/where Ss are recording vocabulary in their notebooks, and if they're underlining the stressed syllables. Encourage Ss to write the singular words with *a/an* to get into the habit of using articles. Suggest Ss carry a vocabulary notebook in their bag/pocket so they can record and revise new words whenever they can.

READING

2A First, check the meaning of *bag* and *pocket* in the rubric. Then give Ss 2 mins to compare their answers to the question. Monitor closely and provide language Ss need if necessary. In feedback, elicit answers and write the names of any unusual objects/new words on the board.

Teaching tip

It's a good idea to activate Ss' knowledge of the topic of a reading or listening text with a discussion related to it. For this text, if you have a **stronger class**, ask questions like *Do you travel a lot? Where do you go? What do you usually take?*

B Lead in to the text. Elicit Ss' answers, or give them time to discuss them in pairs first. Then give Ss 2 mins to read the text and answer the questions alone, before checking in pairs. In feedback, check Ss' answers and point out the US spelling of *light* in *Travelite*. With a **stronger class**, teach new language, e.g. *intelligent travellers, cm, perfect, mine, of course, side pocket, to zip up, quick, easy.*

Answers: 1 Because it's small but you can carry a lot of things in it. 2 Yes, except for camera and watch.

GRAMMAR *this/that, these/those*

3A With **weaker classes**, look at the cartoon with Ss first. Ask *What are the people's names? Where are they? Are they happy?* Then Ss can discuss the problem in pairs/3s.

Answer: The three black bags look the same. Rob and Kate think they've got the wrong bags.

B Before listening, check the meaning of *Rob's bag* in the rubric. Tell Ss they'll learn the use of the apostrophe *'s* in Ex 5. Play the CD. Ss listen and then compare their answers. Monitor closely to see if all Ss agree or not. If the latter, then play the CD again. N.B. This is an important step because it gives Ss another chance to check and confirm their answers, which helps to build their confidence with listening.

Answer: A

Unit 1 Recording 5

M=Marco R=Rob K=Kate

M: Oh, that's my flight! Bye, Rob, Kate. I have to go!
R: OK. Bye, Marco. Have a good trip!
K: Yeah. Have a good trip, Marco!
M: Thanks. You, too. Bye!
R: He's a nice guy, Marco.
K: Yeah, he is. Wait a minute – is this my bag?
R: No, that's mine. This is your bag.
K: Wait, look. What are these?
R: Those? They're DVDs. But they aren't mine.
K: And they aren't mine.
R: What's that?
K: It's a book about Rome, but it isn't mine. Is it yours?
R: Oh no. That's Marco's …
K: And that bag?
R: Just a minute.
K: Oh good. Those are my sunglasses.
R: Oh, no …
K: And that's my laptop and my MP3 player.
R: So Marco's got my bag. Total disaster. Marco! Marco!!

C Give Ss time to read the questions. Then play the CD again. Ss listen and check their answers in pairs. Play the CD again if necessary before feedback.

Answers: 1 Marco's 2 Marco's 3 Kate's

D Play the CD again. Ss listen and write their answers. In feedback, elicit Ss' answers and check the meaning of *this/that, these/those*. Demonstrate using classroom objects, e.g. *books, pens, bags*. Point to them and say, e.g. *This is my pen. That's your pen. These are her books. Those are his books.* Model and drill the sentences.

Answers: 1 this 2 that 3 This 4 these 5 Those

E This exercise rechecks the concept of *this, that,* etc and provides an easy reference.

Answers: 1 those 2 these 3 this 4 that

F After Ss listen and repeat, drill individually to check if Ss can distinguish between the /ɪ/ and /iː/ in *this* and *these*. They might need some help. Demonstrate the long /iː/ sound by saying it and stretching your mouth into a smile, widening your hands at the same time. Then bring your hands together and round your lips, drop your jaw to demonstrate the short /ɪ/ sound.

▱ **LANGUAGEBANK** 1.2 p128–129

Check the language in the first table in section 1.2. Teach/ Demonstrate *near* and *far*. Ss then work in pairs. One student points to objects in the room and their partner says, e.g. *That's a bag. Those are books.*

A Ss could write and act out their own personalised dialogues based on the ones here.

Answers: 1 this, these, This, this 2 that 3 those, This, that

PRACTICE

4 First, model and drill the example questions/answers. Then you could extend the activity into a team game. Divide Ss into teams and number them A, B, C, etc. Then number the Ss in each group 1, 2, 3, etc. Student A1 asks Student B1 a question, e.g. *What's this/that in English?* Team B gets a point for the correct answer. Then Student B1 asks Student C1. Stop the activity when all Ss have had the chance to ask a question. The team with the most points wins.

GRAMMAR possessives

5 Ss should now be familiar with these forms. Use the exercise to check this before looking at the **Language bank**. Alternatively, Ss can check the answers themselves in **Language bank** 1.2, p128.

Answers: mine, yours, Marco's

Watch out!

The different uses of the apostrophe *'s* can be very confusing. Some Ss may translate from their L1 and say, e.g. *the car of my father* instead of *my father's car.* This is not grammatically incorrect but sounds very unnatural. Ss need a lot of practice of seeing the language in context and learning how to understand the different meanings.

▱ **LANGUAGEBANK** 1.2 p128–129

B Read and check the notes for possessive *'s*; *mine/yours*. Drill personalised questions and answers, e.g. *Is this Juan's book? No, it's Joanna's. Are these your pens? No, they're yours.*

Answers: 1 Megan's 2 your 3 yours 4 John's 5 my 6 Mine

C Check the meaning of *Thank you for coming* and *coat*.

Answers: 1 B *Yours* is over there. 2 B No, they aren't *Stefan's*. Maybe they're *Daniela's*. 3 B No, it's *Jason's. Mine's* black. 4 B No, it isn't *mine*. It's *Sam's*. This is *mine*.

PRACTICE

6 Check the example question. Monitor while Ss do the exercise to check they have understood what they have to do. Give them time to compare their answers before feedback. Invite pairs to act out their dialogues to the class. Invite other Ss to correct any problem answers.

Answers: 2 Ana's 3 mine 4 yours 5 your 6 mine 7 Ali's

SPEAKING

7A Check the example and then put Ss in small groups. Monitor while Ss identify the objects as they may need help with new vocabulary. With *stronger classes,* you could provide more vocabulary for this exercise by doing the exercises in the **Photo bank** on p152 now (see below).

B Number the Ss in each group from Ex 7A: 1, 2, 3, etc. Rotate Ss so that all the Ss 1 are working together, Ss 2 together, etc: each student must take two objects from their group with them (not their own) so they can do the activity. Then repeat, by renaming the Ss in each group: A, B, C, etc. Tell Ss A to regroup together, and so on, so they can redo the activity with different Ss. Monitor while Ss ask/answer questions and make notes of any problems. Give feedback by writing problem sentences on the board. Ask Ss to correct them in pairs/as a class.

▱ **PHOTOBANK** p152

1A Ss will know some of the words so use the exercises as a diagnostic tool. Ss work alone and then check in pairs. Check/Teach unknown words in feedback and drill the pronunciation. Elicit the main stress and ask Ss to write new words in their notebooks, underlining the stress.

Answers: 2 C 3 O 4 M 5 K 6 E 7 B 8 J 9 D 10 H 11 G 12 I 13 F 14 L 15 N

B First, elicit/check the rule for the use of articles: *a/an* with singular nouns and no article with plurals; *an* is used before vowels. In feedback, model and drill words Ss have problems with.

Answers: 3 an 4 – 5 a 6 – 7 an 8 – 9 a 10 a 11 a 12 – 13 – 14 – 15 a

Homework ideas
- Ss find a picture of a room/place with lots of objects in it and write a description of it as if they were talking to another person, e.g. *This is a table and that's a …*
- Language bank 1.2 Ex A–C, p129
- Workbook Ex 1A–5D, p7–8

CAN I HAVE A COFFEE?

Introduction

Ss learn and practise how to ask for and buy things in tourist places. They also practise the skill of listening for key words.

SUPPLEMENTARY MATERIALS

Resource bank p148

Ex 8: simple signs for places (café/shop) and props, e.g. white aprons/caps.

Warm up

Revision of possessions: memory game

Collect one item from every student in the class. It doesn't matter if some are the same as long as they *look* different, e.g. different watches, keys, etc. As you collect the items, elicit and drill: *That's Magda's pen. Those are Marc's keys.* Place all the objects where Ss can see them. Ask pairs of Ss to stand up in turn. Student A points to an object and asks e.g. *Is that Marc's pen?* Student B answers: *Yes, it is./No, it isn't. It's Magda's.*

VOCABULARY tourist places

1A Ss look at the photos. Elicit the names of the places if possible. Ss then match the photos to names 1–4. Check/ Drill the pronunciation of the places in feedback. With *strong classes*, ask *Where are the places? Do you have them in your town/city? Do you go to them? Why?*

Answers: 1 B 2 D 3 C 4 A

B Teach/Check the meaning of new words and drill them. Do the first word web as an example. Ss then work together in pairs and share their knowledge. The words will be checked in Ex C.

Answers:
souvenir shop: battery, souvenir
sandwich bar: cola, coffee, sandwich
money exchange: euros, money, exchange rate
train station: single ticket, return ticket, platform

Teaching tip

Ss should copy the word webs into their notebooks. They are a very effective way of recording vocabulary because the visual element helps Ss to revise and remember it more easily. Encourage them to use word webs whenever possible in their notebooks.

C Ss listen and compare their answers. Play the CD again if Ss don't agree. In feedback, recheck the meaning and pronunciation of the answers, and the words Ss added.

D Demonstrate the exercise, e.g. say *board, desk, chairs* and elicit *classroom*. Give Ss a min to look at the words in Ex B again and memorise them. *Stronger Ss* could use other places if they know any.

FUNCTION making requests

2A Check/Teach the meaning of *making requests* in the heading: *ask for something.* Remind Ss not to try to listen to every word and concentrate on doing the task. In feedback, ask Ss which words helped them to guess the place, e.g. *battery* and *sandwich.*

Answers: 1 In a souvenir shop 2 in a money exchange 3 in a sandwich bar 4 In a train station

---

Unit 1 Recording 9

Conversation 1

T=Tourist   S=Shop assistant

T: Excuse me. Do you speak English?
S: Yes. Can I help you?
T: Can I have one of those, please?
S: One of these batteries? For your camera?
T: Yes, that's right.
S: OK. That's eleven euros please.

Conversation 2

T=Tourist   C=Clerk

T: Excuse me. Do you speak English?
C: Yes. Can I help you?
T: Could I change this money, please?
C: Fine. That's four hundred and fifty pounds. Here you are – one hundred, two, three, four hundred. And ten, twenty, thirty, forty, fifty. Four hundred and fifty.
T: Thank you.
C: You're welcome.

Conversation 3

T=Tourist   W=Waiter

T: Can I have a sandwich and a cola, please?
W: That's six euros.
T: Ah, I only have five euros. How much is the sandwich?
W: Four euros fifty. And the cola is one-fifty.
T: OK. Could I have the sandwich, but no cola?
W: That's four-fifty.
T: Thank you.

Conversation 4

T=Tourist   TS = Ticket seller

TS: Can I help you?
T: Could I have a single to Sydney, please?
TS: Today?
T: Yes.
TS: That's twenty-five dollars.
T: Here you are. Which platform is it?
TS: Platform three.
T: Thanks

B Play the CD again. Ss listen and write their answers, and then compare them. Play the CD again if Ss still have some doubts. Check their answers and elicit the spelling. With *stronger classes*, elicit more detail from the conversations, e.g. *How much is the battery/ticket? Where does the man want to go?*

Answers: 1 a battery 2 £450 3 a sandwich 4 a single ticket (to Sydney)

Watch out!

The stress and intonation of polite requests can be hard for Ss to hear and produce. Model and drill the language clearly and thoroughly. Tell Ss that being polite is especially important in Britain and will make the difference between getting good or bad service!

3A Play the CD. Ss listen and write the answers. Play the CD again if necessary, pausing after each request. *Stronger classes* could try completing the requests before listening. In feedback, check answers and the reason we use Can/Could I … ? (It's polite.)

Answers: 2 Can I have 3 Could I have 4 Could I change

B Tell Ss to copy the question down and draw the stress and intonation pattern from the book. Then Ss listen and repeat.

Teaching tip

To help Ss understand intonation patterns use visuals or movement. Beat the stress with your hands while you model questions like these and illustrate the movement of the fall/rise intonation at the end of the request.

➡ LANGUAGEBANK 1.3 p128–129

Read and check the notes with your Ss. The important thing to stress here is the responses. Drill some requests and responses chorally and in open pairs across the class, e.g. *Can I have two coffees, please? Yes, of course.*

Show Ss how the exchange rates are pronounced: 0.651 = oh point six five one. 65.1 = sixty-five point one. Then ask Ss to complete the exercise.

Answers: 1 Can 2 could 3 euros 4 exchange 5 change 6 For 7 please 8 That's

4A Ss hear two versions of each of the requests in Ex 3A: one polite and one impolite. Play the first pair of sentences on the CD and ask *Which one is polite* and *Which is impolite? Why?* (The intonation of the first one is flat and the voice sounds bored/rude. The second speaker uses polite and friendly intonation.) Play the rest of the CD for Ss to note down their answers. In feedback, drill the polite requests.

Answers: 1 I 2 P 3 P 4 I 5 I 6 P 7 I 8 P

B Give Ss a few minutes to prepare and practise their questions. They could do this in pairs, and then ask/answer the questions with another partner. Monitor discreetly and give feedback on problem areas.

LEARN TO listen for key words

5A First, ask Ss to read the conversation. Check/Teach and drill questions with How much … ? Also explain the conventions for talking about euros, e.g. *four euros fifty* vs *one-fifty*. Model the example and read the **speakout tip** with Ss. Drill the example, exaggerating the stressed words to highlight the point here. Ss check their answers in Part B.

Teaching tip

Highlight the importance of sentence stress by explaining that stressed words are usually the *key* words in a sentence. Ss will be able to understand the main information when listening if they listen for the stressed words.

Unit 1 Recording 13

Conversation extract 1
How much is an orange juice?
It's two euros twenty.

Conversation extract 2
A single ticket is four euros eighty and a taxi is thirteen euros.

Conversation extract 3
That's two euros fifty for the coffee, and another three seventy-five for the sandwich and a bottle of water – that's one thirty. That's seven euros and fifty-five cents altogether.

B After listening and checking their answers, Ss can practise the conversation in pairs and act it out to the class.

Answers: B: That's <u>six</u> <u>euros</u>. A: <u>Ah</u>, I only have <u>five</u> euros. <u>How</u> much is the <u>sandwich</u>? B: <u>Four</u> euros <u>fifty</u>. And the <u>cola</u> is <u>one</u> <u>fifty</u>. A: <u>OK</u>. Could I have the <u>sandwich</u>, but <u>no</u> cola? B: That's <u>four</u> <u>fifty</u>.

6 Remind Ss to listen for the key, stressed words. Monitor while they check in pairs to see how well they've done with the pronunciation of *15* and *50*, *13* and *30*. Focus on this in feedback if necessary.

Answers: 1 c) 2 c) 3 a) 4 b) 5 c) 6 a)

7 First, put Ss in pairs, A and B, facing each other. Tell them *not* to show their books to their partners. N.B. The success of communicative activities like this depends largely on preparing and organising your Ss carefully. Model/Drill one or two examples if appropriate. Ss can then look at the relevant page in the back of their books. Tell Ss they're in a sandwich bar. They have similar items but different prices. Drill the examples: Ss write their answer in the grid. Give a time limit of 10 mins for this activity. Monitor closely to ensure they are doing the activity correctly, and make notes of any problems for feedback afterwards.

SPEAKING

8A Ss should write the prices in euros – or in their own currency if you have a *monolingual class*. Elicit some examples and write the prices on the board.

B Set the activity up carefully. Check the examples and elicit/drill some example requests/responses from the Ss. Also check the names of the food and drinks if necessary. With *monolingual classes*, Ss could design their own menus with food and drink prices from their country. This is especially appropriate if food and drinks are very different in a sandwich bar there.

Optional extension

To make the role-plays more realistic, put Ss in pairs and ask each pair to choose the place they want to work in. Then ask them to prepare shop signs, use realia (caps, aprons, etc) if you've got any, and decide on prices and things they sell if appropriate. Divide the pairs into two groups. Group A pairs are buyers and Group B pairs are sellers. They do the role-play for 5 mins. They then change roles and do another role-play. Monitor and take notes for feedback.

Monitor discreetly while Ss work, making notes of correct language as well as problems for feedback. In feedback, ask pairs to act out their role-plays to the class and invite comments. Then give feedback on Ss' performance.

Teaching tip

Feedback after a fluency activity can be dealt with in several different ways. It is important to bear in mind that the main focus does not always need to be on grammar mistakes. It can also focus on vocabulary, pronunciation and function. It's a good idea to balance your feedback with positive comments as well as things that could be improved. Task achievement is more important than errors of accuracy in a fluency activity. However, a focus on accuracy is always very useful for Ss, as long as the focus is on language that Ss should be familiar with and which is central to the task.

Homework ideas
- Ss write new dialogues set in the places in Ex 1. Each dialogue should include at least one request.
- Language bank 1.3 Ex A, p129
- Workbook Ex 1A–3B, p9

FAWLTY TOWERS

Introduction

In this lesson, Ss practise the four skills. First, they have the opportunity to watch an amusing excerpt from an authentic BBC sitcom of the 1970s, *Fawlty Towers*, set in a quirky British hotel. They then learn some basic language for hotel situations: checking into a hotel, filling in a registration form and writing an email to book a room.

SUPPLEMENTARY MATERIALS

Ex 6B: bring/download some hotel information with prices and booking forms

Warm up

Use the photos and the **Culture notes** to lead in to the lesson. First, write these words on the board: *hotel, manager, guest, waiter, waitress, animal, office, keys, reception desk*. Tell Ss not to worry if they don't know all of the words yet. Ss work in pairs. Give them 2 mins to find the people/objects in the photos. In feedback, elicit and check Ss' answers. They could stand up with their books and point to the people/things. Then use the photos to teach words Ss don't know, e.g. *animal/moose, guest, reception, manager*. Finally, ask *Do you know the people here/the TV programme* Fawlty Towers? Ss may recognise John Cleese. If so, elicit what Ss know about him. Otherwise tell them about him and the programme. Also introduce *the Major* – the older man with grey hair and a moustache.

Culture notes

Fawlty Towers is a legendary BBC sitcom. It's about a group of eccentric characters in a badly-run hotel who get involved in farcical situations. First broadcast on BBC1 in 1975, only twelve episodes were made. In spite of that, the sitcom is still very popular now, over 35 years later and reruns are played all over the world. In 2004, it was voted the top favourite BBC sitcom in an international poll. Basil Fawlty was played by the actor John Cleese, who is also known for his roles in the Monty Python films such as *The Life of Brian*, and as Q in some of the James Bond films.

▶ DVD PREVIEW

1 Check the instructions and remind Ss not to worry about unknown words at the moment. Give them 2 mins to read the text and then discuss their answers in pairs. In feedback, check answers. Ask further comprehension questions if it's appropriate to your Ss' needs. Also teach/check the meaning of *angry* for Ex 3A. With **stronger classes**, you could also teach, e.g. *comedy, terrible, staff*.

Answers: A Sybil Fawlty B Basil Fawlty C Manuel D Polly

2A Ss should be familiar with most of these icons/words so could do the exercise alone. Check pronunciation in feedback, highlighting the word stress. Ss copy the words into their notebooks, underlining the main stress.

Answers: A lift B stairs C restaurant D reception E keycard F room service G internet connection H car park

B Demonstrate the activity first. Then monitor closely to help Ss with pronunciation. Do feedback in open pairs across the class, e.g. Student A says *picture A*, and Student B responds with *lift*. Elicit corrections from the class when necessary.

C Give Ss 2 mins to answer the question in pairs, using the new vocabulary in Ex 2B. Monitor to check/teach other words they might want to use, e.g. *price, place, good food, comfortable beds, a good view, friendly staff*. In feedback, elicit and discuss Ss' opinions. Write new words on the board.

▶ DVD VIEW

3A Read the rubric and questions with Ss. Check *surprised* by miming it. Before Ss watch the DVD, tell them not to worry about words they don't understand: they only need to answer the four questions. Play the DVD. Ss compare their answers and if they don't agree, play it again. In feedback, elicit Ss' answers.

Answers: 1 T Manuel speaks English, but not very well. 2 F 3 T 4 F Basil is surprised by the Major's questions.

B Check new vocabulary in the questions, e.g. *cook, tired, remarkable, antique*, then play the DVD again. Ss underline the words they hear and compare answers. In feedback, play the DVD again to check answers. Tell Ss to say *stop!* when they hear each answer. Point out that *Samson's* is the name of a shop in the local town. If feasible, have a class discussion about the DVD. Ask *Did you like it? Did you think it was funny? Why/ Why not?*

Answers: 2 well 3 book 4 today 5 fine 6 animal 7 £12 8 Canadian

DVD 1 Fawlty Towers

Mn=Manuel M = Major BF=Basil Fawlty

Mn: How are you, sir? You see, I speak English well. I learn it from a book.
Hello, I am English. Hello. How are you, sir? I can speak English. Ah, hello, Major. How are you today?
M: Oh … I'm fine, thank you.
Mn: It's a beautiful day, today.
M: Is it? Oh … Yes, yes. I suppose it is.
Mn: Yes, I can speak English. I learn it from a book.
M: Did you, did you really? … Oh, there you are, Fawlty.
BF: Yes. I'm just going to open up, Major.
M: Oh, fine. I say, that, that's a remarkable animal you have there, Fawlty. Er … Where did you get it?
BF: Er … Samson's. In the town.
M: Really? Well, was, was it expensive?
BF: Er … 12 pounds, I think.
M: Good Lord! Japanese, was it?
BF: Canadian, I think, Major.
M: I didn't know the Canadians were as clever as that, by God!
BF: He's started early.

Optional extra activity

Exploit the DVD further by playing it again, pausing to ask comprehension questions, e.g. *Where is Manuel/the moose head? Why is the Major surprised? Why does the Major ask Fawlty about the moose?* The Major's language is particularly interesting. He's an old-fashioned Army officer and uses rather anarchic expressions such as *I say* and *Good Lord!*

speakout at a hotel

4A The **key phrases** are fairly simple but be prepared to teach/check them, especially *reservation*. Ss will check their answers in Ex B.

B Play the CD. Ss listen and check their answers in pairs. Monitor to see if they have many doubts. If so, play the CD again. In feedback, model and drill each answer chorally and individually, (see the answers in bold in the audio script below).

> **Answers:** G, R, R, R, R, R, G

C Ss listen again and check the spelling of the name and the phone number in pairs. Repeat the middle part of the CD if necessary. In feedback, check answers and elicit/drill the questions *Could you spell that? What's your phone number?*

> **Answers:** Mr Baumann, 212 4742 285

Unit 1 Recording 14

R=Receptionist G=Guest

R: **Good evening. Can I help you?**

G: Good evening. Yes, **I have a reservation.** My name's Baumann.

R: Ah, yes. Mr Baumann. **For two nights?**

G: That's right.

R: Could I ask you to complete this form?

G: Oh, I haven't got my glasses. Can you help?

R: Certainly. **What's your family name?**

G: Baumann.

R: **Could you spell that?**

G: B-a-u-m-a-n-n.

R: Is that double 'n'?

G: Yes, that's right.

R: Your first name?

G: Jeff.

R: And **what's your phone number?**

G: 212 4742 285.

R: OK. **You're in room 407.** That's on the fourth floor. The lift's over there.

G: Room 407?

R: Yes, and **this is your keycard.**

G: Thank you. **What time's breakfast?**

R: From seven to ten.

G: And where is it?

R: In the restaurant, over there.

G: Thank you.

R: **Have a good stay.**

G: Thanks.

> **Watch out!**
>
> The importance of setting up fluency and writing activities carefully should not be underestimated. The more time and support given to Ss during preparation time, the more accurate and confident their performance will be. The extra activity illustrates one way of setting up a role-play.

> **Optional extra activity**
>
> Prepare Ss for Ex 5. First, ask *Why does the receptionist read out the questions to the guest? Because he hasn't got his glasses.* Then write these prompts on the board: *Baumann, B-A-U-M-A-N-N, Jeff, 212 4742 285, room 407, from seven to ten, In the restaurant.* Elicit the questions the receptionist asked and write them on the board, e.g. *Your first name?*

5 First, write an email address on the board, e.g. *john.smith@ yahoo.co.uk* and check how to say it: *john-dot-smith-at-yahoo-dot-co-dot-uk*. Read and check the rubric with Ss. Then look at the registration form and example dialogue. Elicit Ss' ideas about who *Pirez* is and where he/she is from. Ss then work in pairs to check the questions they need to ask, if they didn't do the extra activity above. They must also invent the information about Pirez. Encourage them to be creative here.

Monitor and support Ss with spelling and grammar while they write. *Weaker Ss* can use the audio script for support if necessary. They can write out their conversation and rehearse it before the role-play. When this stage has been completed, Ss do the role-play with a different partner: they each ask/answer questions and complete the form. Monitor discreetly during this stage and take notes of both good language and problems for feedback later.

writeback an email to a hotel

6A First, check new words/phrases in the email, e.g. *I would like to, reply, Regards.* The latter is one of the conventions used to end a more formal or business letter, in the same way as *Yours sincerely* and *Yours faithfully*. Ss write the email in the correct order and check it in pairs. In feedback, show Ss on the board how to format the email, as shown below.

> **Answers:**
>
> 1 Dear Sir or Madam,
> 2 I would like to reserve a room 3 for one person
> 4 for two nights 5 from 15th November. 6 Please reply
> 7 to this email address.
> 8 Thank you in advance.
> 9 Regards,
> 10 Jamie McDonald

B First, check the cities/hotels and their pronunciation. Elicit some ideas about where Ss would like to stay. With *stronger classes*, you could ask *Why?* If you've brought some hotel brochures/information, distribute them amongst the Ss. Put Ss into small groups and give them time to discuss and decide on their choices. Monitor and provide help where necessary. Ss then write their email.

> **Teaching tip**
>
> To build Ss' confidence with their writing, and prevent them from becoming demotivated by too many errors of accuracy, encourage Ss to work collaboratively by using a process approach. Ss can ask you/each other questions about their doubts while they work. Once they've finished writing, Ss read each other's work and make supportive comments/suggestions. They then write the final draft in class or at home.

> **Homework ideas**
>
> - Ss write a final copy of their email from Ex 6B, or write a different one using another place on the list.
> - Workbook Ex 4, p9

LOOKBACK

Introduction

Lookback exercises can be used as extra practice or preparation for the next exercise in the Student's Book, e.g. a role-play.

SUPPLEMENTARY MATERIALS

Ex 4C: bring common everyday objects for Ss to use

PRESENT SIMPLE: *BE*

1A Ss should do the exercises alone. Check the answers to the gap fill but don't discuss the content. They'll check the answers in the next exercise.

Answers: 1 s 2 are 3 s 4 are 5 m, 's

B Ss answer the questions in pairs. They then work with another pair to compare/discuss their answers. Check answers in feedback and elicit anything else Ss know about these people/places.

Answers: 1 Malaysia 2 the USA, England, Japan, Portugal. 3 In Istanbul, Turkey. 4 Argentina, Brazil/Bolivia, Chile/Columbia. 5 Barack Obama (in 2010)

SPELLING AND COUNTRIES

2A Ss work alone to write the answers, and then check in pairs. *Fast finishers* can prepare other jumbled countries and write them on the board in feedback.

Answers: 1 Russia 2 Egypt 3 Spain 4 South Africa 5 Mexico 6 India

B Encourage *stronger Ss* to do this without looking back in their books.

C Ss work in pairs to spell each other's words. Monitor to assess how well they do this.

QUESTIONS WITH *BE*

3 First, check the rubric and example questions. Then divide the class into Ss A and B: Ss A work together in pairs; Ss B do the same. Each pair decides on their famous person and prepares information about him/her. Write prompts on the board to help, e.g. *man/woman, nationality, age, famous for films/books/music.* Give Ss 2 mins to prepare their questions. Then put Ss into A/B pairs. Give them 3–4 mins to ask/answer their questions. To make the game more competitive, restrict the number of questions Ss can ask to *ten*. If they don't guess the person, they lose. If time, Ss could repeat the game with new partners.

OBJECTS

4A Ss work alone. To provide more challenge, ask them to underline the stressed syllable in each noun.

Answers: 1 mobile phone 2 key 3 watch 4 purse 5 laptop 6 toothbrush

B Ss do the exercise alone and check their answers in pairs. Check answers in feedback. Ss can then practise reading the dialogues in pairs to prepare them for the next exercise. Monitor and check their pronunciation.

Answers: 1 A that 2 A these 3 A those

C If you have them, hand out common objects Ss know. This activity could be done as a class mingling activity. Ss take their objects(s) with them and ask/answer each other's questions.

WORD GROUPS

5A Check the rubric and examples. *Weaker Ss* can check back in their books if they need help. Monitor to support Ss and check their progress.

B First, read out your own words as an example for the class. Monitor while Ss do the activity and assess Ss' spelling. In feedback, Ss take it in turns to write two words from one word group on the board. Invite the class to correct spelling mistakes if necessary. They then have to guess the word group. With *stronger classes,* you could follow up with a more personalised activity. In small teams, Ss choose other word groups, e.g. *jobs, food, drinks,* and write three or four examples for each one. The teams then compete with each other to guess the word group.

Sample answers: 1 laptop, MP3 player, TV, battery, digital camera 2 glasses, hairbrush, office, credit (card), battery, euros, single, ticket, return, coffee, sandwich, Russia, Britain, Scotland, Poland, Ireland, Japan, Thailand 3 hotel, souvenir shop, café, restaurant, train station, sandwich bar, money exchange

POSSESSIVES

6A Check the meaning of *poem*. Elicit/Explain that the final word in each line of a poem often rhyme with each other. Ss check their answers in pairs before feedback. Model and drill the poem chorally.

Answers: 2 mine 3 my 4 fine 5 your 6 Ann's 7 yours 8 hands

B Ss practise reading the poem aloud until they can say it from memory. Invite them to say/read the poem to the class.

AT THE STATION

7A Check the example with Ss. Tell them they have to decide where to add a word from the box in each line. Ss work alone and then compare answers. *Weaker Ss* could work together. Monitor to assess their performance. Check answers in feedback. Prompt Ss to self-correct their mistakes, or invite other Ss to correct their classmates' mistakes if necessary.

Answers: B: A single or *return?* A: How much is *it?* A: And which platform *is* it? B: Over *there.* A: Thank *you.*

B Remind Ss that key words provide the main information in a sentence. Do the first one as an example. Ss make their list alone but provide support to *weaker Ss.*

Sample answers: A: ticket, Rome B: single, return, A: How much B: Twenty-five A: platform B: three, there A: Thank

C Ss compare their answers first. Then remind Ss that key words are usually stressed in a sentence. Monitor while Ss practise the conversation. Make notes on pronunciation and accuracy problems for feedback or assessment purposes. In feedback, invite pairs to act out the conversation.

OVERVIEW

2.1 JOIN US!

GRAMMAR | present simple: *I/you/we/they*

VOCABULARY | activities

HOW TO | talk about activities

COMMON EUROPEAN FRAMEWORK

Ss can take part in a conversation of a basic factual nature on a predictable topic, i.e. her/his school, etc; can ask and answer questions about pastimes; can make and respond to suggestions.

2.2 HIGH FLYERS

GRAMMAR | present simple: *he/she/it*

VOCABULARY | daily routines; jobs

HOW TO | talk about routines

COMMON EUROPEAN FRAMEWORK

Ss can describe his/her present or most recent job; can handle very short social exchanges about work and free time; can describe everyday aspects of his/her environment e.g. jobs; can form a series of simple phrases and sentences linked with simple connectors like *and*, *but* and *or*.

2.3 WHAT TIME DOES IT START?

FUNCTION | asking for information

VOCABULARY | the time

LEARN TO | show you don't understand

COMMON EUROPEAN FRAMEWORK

Ss can find specific, predictable information in simple everyday material such as information leaflets and timetables; can initiate, maintain and close simple, face-to-face conversations; can get all the information needed from a tourist office, as long as it is of a familiar, non-specialised nature.

2.4 CHALET GIRL ⊙ BBC DVD

speakout | life at home

writeback | an internet posting

COMMON EUROPEAN FRAMEWORK

Ss can describe himself/herself, what he/she does and where he/she lives.

2.5 LOOKBACK

Communicative revision activities

BBC VIDEO PODCAST

What's your daily routine?

In this video podcast, people talk about their jobs and daily routines, including what they like and don't like about them. It consolidates and extends language around the topics of work and lifestyle, including common verbs (present simple for routine) and time. The video podcast would work well at the end of lessons 2.2, 2.3 or at the end of unit 2 to provide further practice of the language learnt.

JOIN US!

Introduction

Ss learn/revise and practise the *I/you/we/they* forms of the present simple with verbs describing common activities. They read and listen to information about online special interest groups and create their own.

SUPPLEMENTARY MATERIALS

Resource bank p150

Ex 2A–B: pictures/photos of people showing the activity verbs, e.g. reading, listening to music, doing sport, eating junk food

Warm up

Revision of vocabulary: word dictation

Write the headings: *bag, sandwich bar, souvenir shop* across the board. Elicit/Check meanings and get Ss to copy down the words. Then dictate twelve nouns from Unit 1 that match one of the headings and may come up in Ex 2A, e.g. *a sandwich, an MP3 player, sweets, a newspaper, a book, coffee, DVDs, a magazine, water, a diary, hot chocolate, a menu.* Ss write the words under the correct heading and then compare their answers in pairs/teams. Some words could go under more than one heading, e.g. *a diary* (souvenir shop/bag). This doesn't matter as long as Ss can justify their answers. Pairs/Teams with the most correct answers win.

READING

1A Lead in. Ask *What are your favourite things/activities?* Ss' answers should indicate how well Ss know the present simple and common activity verbs. With *weaker classes*, elicit only nouns, e.g. *music, football, computer games.*

Teaching tip

Exploit the photos in the book whenever possible. They provide an excellent springboard for creating interest and exploiting Ss' knowledge of the world. Use them to teach/check vocabulary, practise descriptive language, give opinions, etc.

Use the photos to elicit/pre-teach vocabulary in the website extract, e.g. *like/watch films, eat popcorn, chat with people, travel, play tennis, do exercise, relax, listen to music.* Alternatively use your own pictures to pre-teach the verbs. Then check/teach vocabulary in the Ex 1A rubrics and questions, e.g. *website extracts, online groups, fast food.* Also ask *Who's Johnny Depp?* Remind Ss not to worry about words they don't know and to focus only on answering the questions. Give them a 1-min time limit to scan the texts quickly and answer.

B As Ss compare ideas, monitor closely. In feedback, ask Ss to justify their answers so that you can check their familiarity with the present simple and activity verbs further. Also check the meaning of *laid-back*.

Answers: 1 Four 2 Ss' own answers

VOCABULARY activities

2A First, check unknown vocabulary in the exercise, e.g. *junk food, running*. With a *mixed-ability class*, provide support for *weaker Ss* by putting them with *stronger ones*, or put *weaker Ss* together and give them extra support. Ask Ss to find and underline the verbs in the texts and then do the exercise.

Watch out!

Ss often make mistakes with **collocations, prepositions** and **articles** in English, e.g. *I make sport, We listen the music*. It's very important to encourage them to notice and record collocations as much as possible, e.g. verbs + nouns (see Ex 2 below), verb + prepositions (*write about, chat with*) and fixed phrases (*all the time, of course*).

In feedback, highlight the use of *go + running/swimming*. It would be useful to ask Ss *What tense are the verbs in the texts in?* Elicit/Tell Ss the name but don't explain further here. Ss study this later.

Answers: 2 watch 3 play 4 eat 5 read 6 listen to 7 go 8 do

B Check the words in the box first. *Fast finishers* could add other words that collocate with the verbs. In feedback, draw word webs on the board for each verb. Invite Ss to come to the board and write their answers in the correct place. They then copy the word webs into their notebooks, adding all the nouns from both Ex 2A and B.

Answers: 1 tea 2 DVDs 3 golf 4 a sandwich 5 newspapers 6 the teacher 7 swimming 8 nothing

C This could also be done in small groups or with the whole class. To change the pace and interaction pattern, Ss could test each other while walking around the room.

speakout TIP

Read the tip with Ss and refer back to the word webs in Ex 2 above. Invite Ss to explain why recording collocations is a good idea. To follow up, Ss underline all the verb + noun collocations in the text and write them down.

Answers: people, photos

LISTENING

3A Check instructions and remind Ss to concentrate on the task, not unknown vocabulary. Play the CD again if necessary after Ss have checked in pairs. In feedback, elicit the answers (see the bold sections in the audio script) but don't ask Ss for complete sentences: this would involve using the 3rd person. With *stronger classes*, ask further comprehension questions.

Answers:
like: films, (the idea of) travel, relaxing
don't like: sport

B If Ss can't answer this question, play the last part of the audio again.

Answer: the laid-back group

Unit 2 Recording 1

M=Man   W=Woman

W: Come on! You just sit around all day. Why don't you *do* something?
M: What?
W: I don't know – get an interest, go out, meet people …
M: Why?
W: It's good for you! Join a group … or something. Look, here are some interesting ones. The Film group, The Travel group, the Sport group and … the Laid-back group.
M: The Laid-back group?!
W: Yes, well. So which is the right group for you?
M: Oh, I don't know …
W: OK. Let's see. **Do you do a lot of sport?**
M: No, I don't. Not really. Well, not at all. **I don't like it.**
W: OK. **Do you like films?**
M: **Yes, I do.** Everyone likes films …
W: OK!
M: But I don't watch them very much.
W: Oh. Well, do you like meeting people then?
M: Ah, yes, I do.
W: OK!! And **do you travel a lot?**
M: Me – travel? **No, I don't** … but I like … the idea.
W: Well, do you take a lot of photos when you travel?
M: No, I don't. Hmm. Sorry.
W: Right. That's it!
M: That's it?
W: OK. One more question: **Do you relax a lot?**
M: That's a strange question! Of course I do. **I really like relaxing.**
W: Yes, that's true …
M: So, which group do you think is right for me?
W: Well, this one … of course!

GRAMMAR present simple: *I/you/we/they*

4A Ss read the table, then listen and complete the gaps. Monitor while they compare answers to check if they need to hear it again. *Stronger classes* could complete the table first, then listen and check their answers. In feedback, write the questions and short answers on the board and check the form: *Do + subject + verb, do not = don't.*

Answers: Do, do, don't

B Play the CD again two or three times and elicit the stressed words. Underline them on the board. N.B. This is an important exercise for Ss' pronunciation. If they can recognise the stressed words, it will be easier to recognise weak forms.

Answers: Do you like films? Yes, I do.
Do you <u>travel</u> a lot? <u>No</u>, I <u>don't</u>.

C Write the questions and phonemic symbols on the board. First, say *do you like* slowly, separating each word. Then repeat the phrase, getting faster until /duːjuː/ (do you) becomes /dʊjʊ/. Then drill the words chorally with the Ss in the same way. Play the CD again. Ss listen again and repeat the question.

Teaching tip

Strong and weak forms sometimes have an even weaker form in informal spoken English, e.g. for *do you* there is /duːjuː/, /dʊjʊ/ and /dʒʊ/. Elementary Ss are unlikely to be able to produce the weakest realisation so the middle one is more realistic and will help Ss produce more natural sounding English.

➠ **LANGUAGEBANK** 2.1 p130–131

Ss read the first language notes. Elicit/Check the question form and short answers again. Follow up with a personalised substitution drill in open/closed pairs, e.g. *Do you like films/music/football/books/junk food/magazines?* Ss respond with answers that are true for them.

Answers:
A 2 Do they go running every day? 3 Do you chat with friends a lot? 4 Do you like junk food? 5 Do they watch football on TV? 6 Do you go to the cinema a lot?
B 2 No, they don't. 3 Yes, we do. 4 No, I don't. 5 No, they don't. 6 Yes, we do.

PRACTICE

5A Check other verbs Ss might need from the texts, e.g. *take photos, post sth on a website, do nothing.* Give a time limit of 5 mins and monitor closely to check the accuracy of Ss' questions. *Fast finishers* could write more questions.

B Regroup Ss for this activity. Monitor carefully and take notes of Ss' problems for feedback. In feedback, elicit answers to the board (put a table on the board labelled *interest group 1, 2, 3 and 4,* etc and complete) to find the most popular group in the class. Give feedback on problems you noted down while monitoring.

Teaching tip

Monitoring is an essential part of the teaching and learning process. It helps you to assess how well Ss are coping with tasks. You can then adjust your expectations/approach in subsequent activities, especially feedback. It also gives Ss the chance to ask for help and clarification.

GRAMMAR present simple: *I/you/we/they*

6A In feedback, write the two sentences on the board and underline the verb forms: *read and don't read.*

B Elicit Ss' answers to the question and highlight the negative form on the board: We |don't| read books. Then check the full form: *do not.*

C Check the meaning of *regularly/at the moment of speaking.* Ask concept check questions: 1) *The laid-back group don't like work. Is this always true?* 2) *The Film group watch DVDs. Is this a habit/routine?* Elicit and drill personalised examples, e.g. *I love travel/films. I don't like sport/football.*

Answer: regularly

➠ **LANGUAGEBANK** 2.1 p130–131

Check the second language notes with Ss. Elicit more examples of things that are always true vs habits and routines, e.g. *I live in London, I don't eat junk food.*

Answers: C 2 watch 3 don't eat 4 don't work 5 read 6 don't drink 7 listen to

PRACTICE

7 Give Ss 1 min to read the last two website extract again. Ss then complete the text and check their answers in the texts. In feedback, tell Ss to cover their answers and look at you. Read out the extracts, pausing at each gap for Ss to answer.

Answers: 2 relax 3 do 4 play 5 go 6 do 7 don't eat 8 don't drink

Optional extra activity

To make this exercise more competitive, tell Ss that the first to finish with all the correct answers wins.

8A If Ss aren't keen on any of the groups here, brainstorm other ideas to the board. With *weaker classes,* also brainstorm possible activities, referring back to the lead in activity in Ex 1A. Pair/Group Ss according to their interests.

B Ss should take notes about the other group and prepare to present the information to the class.

Optional extra activity

This exercise could be extended into a *project.* If you have computers in your school, Ss could write up the information about their online group and download pictures to illustrate it. Otherwise they find pictures at home and bring them to the next class. They then create a poster with their texts and pictures. Display the posters around the classroom. Ss walk around and read about the other groups. In feedback, discuss which online group(s) they'd like to join, and why.

SPEAKING

9 If Ss don't belong to a team/group, they can use the online group they created in Ex 8, or invent one.

Homework ideas
* Ss write a paragraph about the online group they talked about in Ex 8.
* Language bank 2.1 Ex A–C, p131
* Workbook Ex 1–5, p10–11

HIGH FLYERS

Introduction

Ss learn/revise and practise the present simple 3rd person forms in the context of daily routines.

SUPPLEMENTARY MATERIALS
Resource bank p149 and p151
Photo bank p153
Warm up: a mingling activity (see notes below)
Ex 1A: pictures of everyday routines

Warm up

Revision of activities and the present simple

Before class, prepare a *Find someone who …* worksheet with ten questions. Use verbs from lesson 2.1, e.g. *Do you watch DVDs?* Make enough copies for all the Ss. They mingle and ask/answer the questions. If Ss answer *Yes*, the interviewer writes their name. He/She then moves on to another person until all the questions are answered, or a time limit of 5 mins is reached.

VOCABULARY daily routines

1A With *stronger classes*, Ss could cover the text in Ex 1A and look at the photos. They guess as many verbs as possible, e.g. *have breakfast*. They can then check with Ex 1A. *Weaker classes* will need more support. Use the photos/your own pictures to teach and drill the verb phrases.

Answers: B have breakfast C leave home D start work/school E have lunch F finish work/school G get home H have dinner I go to bed

B You may need to check the meaning of *early* and *late* and the form of *Wh-* questions in the exercise. While Ss check their answers in pairs, monitor closely for accuracy. In feedback, drill the questions using a rising intonation for *yes/no* questions and falling intonation for *Wh-* questions.

Answers: 2 have 3 leave 4 start 5 have 6 get 7 go

C Ss will need to answer with clock times for questions 3, 4 and 6. This will be covered in more detail in 2.3 so don't spend time on it here. With *weaker classes,* do an example: *What time do you start this class?* Elicit/Check answers, e.g. *At 9.*

WRITING *and, but* and *or*

2A Build on the sentences in feedback. Elicit/Drill more examples using prompts, e.g. *cereal, toast.* Ss say *I have cereal or toast for breakfast but I don't like it very much.*

Answers: 1 but 2 and 3 or

B Do some examples with Ss first, e.g. *In the week, I get up early <u>and</u> go running / <u>but</u> I don't have breakfast. In the week, I don't get up late <u>or</u> go to bed late.*

LISTENING

3 Lead in and create interest. Elicit details about the photo, e.g. *Which city is it? Where's the man? What's his job?* You could use the photo to teach/check *floor* and the ordinal numbers: *10th, 20th, 30th, 40th* for the listening below. N.B. *Window cleaner* is British English but in the US it's *window washer*. Brainstorm Ss' answers to the second question.

Answers: 1 window washer (Am Eng) 2 Ss' own answers

4A Remind Ss to focus only on the two questions. Elicit Ss' answers but don't play the CD again here.

Answers: 1 Yes, they do. 2 The pilot's family does. The window washer's wife thinks it's crazy, but his son wants to be one as well.

B If necessary, revise/teach the days of the week first then play the CD again.

Answers:
Daniel: 2 On a plane 4 On Monday morning
5 On Thursday
Ted: 1 On/Outside the 30th floor 2 On the 40th floor
3 At home 4 At six

Unit 2 Recording 3

I=Interviewer   P=Pilot   WW=window washer

I: And today on Radio 99 we talk to some high flyers – men and women who work in very high places around the world: high buildings or mountains or planes. Our first guest has breakfast with his family in London, lunch on a plane, and dinner in Singapore. **He leaves home on Monday morning** and only **gets home on Thursday.** Of course he's a pilot, and he flies the long-distance London to Singapore route for British Airways. Good morning, Daniel.

P: Good morning.

I: Well, you travel a lot … but do you actually like it?

P: Yes, yes I do.

I: And what does your family think about your job?

P: Well, they're OK about it. I mean, they think it's a good job. It's true that I'm not at home for three or four days a week. But I phone my family from the plane and from the airport in Singapore. Yes. They like my job and my routine, for them it's normal.

I: You have a boy and a girl, is that right?

P: Yes, that's right – six and eight years old. William and Sonia.

I: And William … does he want to be a pilot?

P: No, he doesn't! He doesn't want to fly. He wants to be a teacher. But Sonia wants to be a pilot like me.

I: OK. Thanks, Dan. Let's move on. Our next guest is also a high flyer – but of a very different kind. He's a window washer from New York. He washes windows on high-rise buildings in the city. He leaves home at six every day and starts work at seven. He has breakfast on the thirtieth floor – actually outside the thirtieth floor – he has lunch on the fortieth floor, and works all day in sun or rain. He finishes work at five and gets home for dinner. So why does someone become a window washer, Ted?

WW: Well, **my father washes windows,** my older brother washes windows … so I wash windows. I love it up high above the cars and the people. The only problem is the rain … and the cold.

I: What does your family think about your job?

WW: My wife doesn't like it. She thinks it's crazy. But she loves the money, it's very good money. And my son wants to be a window washer. It's normal in my family – it's a tradition.

I: So, you work all day outside the building.

WW: Yeah, that's right.

I: You eat there, you phone your wife from there …

WW: Yeah. Oh, and I even read my emails from there. It's my office.

I: Well then, I have a question. Where does a window washer, you know, urm … go to the bathroom?

WW: Oh, well … that's a window washer's secret!

GRAMMAR present simple: *he/she/it*

5A *Stronger Ss* may be able to do this without the audio script. Guide *weaker Ss* to the correct part of the script to make the task easier (see the bold sections in bold in the audio script).

Answers: 1 leaves 2 gets 3 washes

B Ss do this alone and check in pairs. In feedback, write the sentences on the board and elicit which final letters to underline in the verbs. Ss then copy them down.

Answer: s, es

Watch out!

The present simple 3rd person *-s* is late acquired and can still cause problems even for advanced learners. Constant correction, drills, etc are needed to prevent fossilisation of this common error. The same applies to *don't* and *doesn't*.

C In feedback, drill the pronunciation of the three verbs.

Answers: /z/ leaves, /ɪz/ washes

D You might want to teach Ss that 3rd person verbs ending in a voiced consonant add /z/, while those ending in an unvoiced consonant add /s/, e.g. *gets, leaves.*

Teaching tip

Demonstrate the difference between voiced and unvoiced sounds, e.g. /s/ and /z/, /t/ and /d/. Ask Ss to say the /s/ sound and put their hands on their throats: they won't feel a vibration. Then do the same for the voiced /z/ sound. This time they should feel a vibration.

Answers: /s/ works, starts, cooks, wants /z/ phones, reads, goes, loves /ɪz/ watches, teaches, relaxes, finishes

E Check Ss' answers, then drill the pronunciation of *doesn't*.

➡ LANGUAGEBANK 2.2 p130–131

Check the rules and elicit more examples of the 3rd person verb endings, e.g. *leaves, eats; washes.* With *weaker Ss*, use Ex A–C to check/reinforce 3rd person forms.

Answers:
A 2 studies 3 understands 4 takes 5 washes 6 chats
7 writes 8 has 9 plays 10 does
B 1 gets up 2 drinks 3 goes 4 studies 5 watches
6 listens 7 has 8 starts 9 reads 10 talks 11 works
12 meet 13 finishes 14 relaxes
C ... he *doesn't* like cats 2 ... he *doesn't* drink tea
3 ... she *doesn't read* books 4 ... she *doesn't* work on
Mondays 5 ... it *doesn't* have an internet connection

PRACTICE

6A Ss look at the photo and make predictions about Sian Williams's life before they read the text.

Answers: 2 doesn't have 3 leaves 4 goes 5 starts
6 leaves 7 gets 8 doesn't watch 9 listens to 10 cooks

B Teach/Check new vocabulary, e.g. *live on air, prepares for, next day's show.*

Answer: A TV presenter

7A For this activity, pair Ss with partners they know well.

B Monitor while Ss read their sentences and take notes on problems with accuracy.

GRAMMAR present simple: *he/she/it*

8A Write the sentences on the board with gaps for *does* and the verb. Elicit and underline the question forms. Ss then copy them down.

Answer: does

B Use the sentences on the board. Ss listen and tell you which words to stress.

Answers: Does he <u>want</u> to be a <u>pilot</u>?
<u>What</u> does your <u>family</u> think?

C When Ss repeat the sentence, beat the stress and show the intonation patterns with your hands.

➡ LANGUAGEBANK 2.2 p130–131

Ss can read the table and complete Ex D.

Answers: 1 Do 2 don't 3 does 4 does 5 teaches
6 does 7 does 8 doesn't 9 likes 10 do 11 watch
12 chat/talk 13 does 14 talks

PRACTICE

9 Write *flying doctor* and *circus acrobat* on the board. Brainstorm information about these jobs, and teach essential vocabulary for the task.

VOCABULARY jobs

10A If Ss don't know the job words, use the audio to teach them.

Answers: 1 chef 2 police officer 3 hairdresser 4 doctor
5 teacher 6 shop assistant

B With a *stronger class*, give Ss 3 mins to write their lists. They can look at the **Photo bank** to check if they have the same words. With *weaker classes*, brainstorm words Ss know and then do the exercise in the **Photo bank**.

➡ PHOTOBANK p153

1A Ss match the jobs they know. Teach those they don't. Elicit information about what each job involves, e.g. *A lawyer works in an office. He earns a lot of money.*

Answers: A doctor B nurse C politician D police officer E lawyer F sportsman/woman G business man/woman H actor/actress I accountant J shop assistant K waiter/waitress L teacher M hairdresser N personal assistant (PA) O receptionist P chef Q engineer

B Elicit the rule: *an* comes before a vowel sound.

Answers: All jobs take *a* except accountant, engineer, actor, actress.

SPEAKING

11 A light-hearted activity to round off the lesson. Do one or two examples to prepare Ss for it.

Homework ideas
- Ss write about the job of someone they know well.
- Language bank 2.2 Ex A–D, p131
- Workbook Ex 1A–7, p12–13

WHAT TIME DOES IT START?

Introduction

Ss learn how to ask for and buy things in tourist places. They also practise listening for key words and asking for clarification.

SUPPLEMENTARY MATERIALS

Resource bank p152

Ex 1: an imitation clock with moving hands

Ex 4A: a world map and photos of Hong Kong

Warm up

Revision of clock times and routine verbs

Write the following times on the board: *7.00, 8.00, 9.00, 12.00, 5.00, 7.00, 9.00, 11.00.* Then model/drill *What do you do at 7 o'clock every day?* Elicit Ss' answers, e.g. *I get up.* Ss then take it in turns to ask/answer the questions in pairs.

VOCABULARY the time

1A With *mixed ability classes*, put *stronger* and *weaker Ss* together. For a *weaker class*, present the language with clock drawings/imitation clock on the board.

Answers: 2 B 3 E 4 D 5 A 6 F

Watch out!

Ss can get confused with telling the time as there are several ways to do it. They often say *thirteen past/fifteen to* instead of *thirteen* **minutes** *past/fifteen* **minutes** *to/quarter to.* Explain that we can use *minutes* with all clock times except *half past.* We usually shorten it with *five/ten/twenty/twenty-five.* Drill and correct this error whenever necessary.

B First, check/drill the two ways of telling the time in question 3. Ss then do the exercise alone and check in pairs.

Answers: 2 ten 3 two 4 half 5 quarter 6 to

C First, model and drill the example question/answer in open pairs. Then monitor closely and give feedback on errors Ss make with telling the time.

2A Ss listen to the CD and compare their answers. Play the CD again if necessary. In feedback, play the CD again. Pause to elicit each answer. Ss then listen again and repeat the times.

Answers: 1 half past twelve/12.30 2 quarter past four/4.15 3 twenty to seven/6.40 4 twenty-five to five/4.35

B Divide the class into As and Bs and tell them to look at the relevant pages in the **Communication bank**. Give Ss 2 mins to practise saying the times shown on their clocks. Then put Ss into A/B pairs and give them 4 mins to ask/answer the questions. Monitor discreetly, taking feedback notes.

Answers:

A 2 half past nine 4 twenty past three 6 quarter past ten 8 twenty-five to two.

B 1 five o'clock 3 ten to eleven 5 quarter to eight 7 twenty-five past one

3 If necessary, drill the example questions first. Monitor and provide support to *weaker Ss. Fast finishers* could ask/answer more questions.

FUNCTION asking for information

Culture notes

Hong Kong is in SE Asia and consists of **Hong Kong Island**, **Kowloon**, the New Territories and 262 smaller islands. It's only 1,108 sq. km (428 sq miles) but has a population of 7 million which is mainly Chinese. The two official languages are English and Chinese.

Victoria Peak is 552 metres high with spectacular views of the city and its harbours.

Stanley and **Aberdeen** are areas on HK Island. **Stanley market** is famous for bargains of all kinds, especially silk clothes.

4A With Ss' books closed, create interest and activate Ss' knowledge of the world. Ask questions based on the **Culture notes** above, e.g. *Where's Hong Kong? Do you know it? Is it a city or a country? How many people live there?* Ss then open their books and look at the photos. Use them to check the meaning of new words in the leaflets: *island, harbour, port, night tour, tram ride, view, buildings, Chinese junk, city lights.* Give Ss 3–4 mins to read and underline the answers in the leaflets. Tell them to underline *only* the main information, not the detail, e.g. for question 3, *tram ride* not *start with a tram ride to Victoria Peak.* After reading, Ss compare and discuss their answers. In feedback, teach/check essential vocabulary in the answers. Elicit more detail if you have a *stronger class.*

Answers: 1 Hong Kong 2 The Hong Kong Island tour, the Harbour tour, the Night Tour. 3 Go on a tram ride, visit Aberdeen, go shopping at Stanley market, visit Repulse Bay; go round the harbour, relax in a café, enjoy the sun, see the city buildings, the mountains and the port; have dinner, walk in the night market, go on a Chinese junk, enjoy the city lights.

B Introduce the listening: tell Ss they'll hear a man and woman who want to book one of the tours. Remind Ss to focus on the questions and not worry about unknown language. After listening, Ss compare their answers and listen again if they have a lot of doubts.

Answers: 1 The Hong Kong Island tour. 2 No. 3 The man doesn't understand the tourist information woman. She speaks too fast and he feels very stupid.

Unit 2 Recording 9

A and B=Tourists   C=Tour Operator

A: Oh look, Tourist information. We can ask there.

B: OK … You ask.

A: No, you ask. My English isn't very good.

B: You speak English very well. You ask.

A: No, you ask.

B: No, *you* ask.

A: OK … Excuse me. Do you speak English?

C: Yes, can I help you?

A: Yes, thank you, my friend has a question.

B: Nooo … ohhh … uh … OK. We want to take a tour.

C: OK. Which tour is that? The Hong Kong Island tour, the Harbour tour, the Hong Kong by night tour?

B: Uhhh … I don't understand anything.

A: She asked which tour.

B: Oh, the Hong Kong Island tour.

C: Ah, the Island tour, good choice, and I think we have a couple of places left on the tour tomorrow morning if you're interested in that one …

B: Thank you, goodbye.

C: Oh. Goodbye.

A: What's the problem?

B: I don't understand her. She speaks too fast!

A: Oh, come on! Let's go back.

B: No, I don't want to. I feel sooo stupid!

A: Oh, come on.

5A Give Ss 3 mins to write the questions and compare answers.

B After Ss have listened and checked their answers, play the first question again. Write it on the board and elicit the stressed words. Then play the other questions. Nominate Ss to write them on the board and underline the stressed words. Also point out the position if the preposition *from* at the end of question 2. Give more examples: *What gym do you go to? Where does he come from?*

Answers: 1 What time does it start? 2 Where does it leave from? 3 When does the tour finish? 4 How much does it cost? 5 Do you take credit cards?

C Link the two words *does it* in each sentence on the board, and drill the sentences. Draw Ss' attention to pronunciation by beating the stress and moving your arms to illustrate the falling intonation at the end of the *Wh-* questions.

D Remind Ss to focus on answering the questions when listening. Play the CD again if necessary after Ss compare answers. In feedback, nominate Ss to ask and answer the questions across the class in open pairs (see questions in bold in the audio script below). Prompt Ss to self-correct or invite peer correction where needed.

Answers: 1 At 8 o'clock. 2 The front gate. 3 At 1p.m. 4 Six hundred and forty dollars for two. 5 Yes.

Unit 2 Recording 11

A and B=Tourists C=Tour Operator

A: Hello. We're back.

C: Hello again! So, do you want the Hong Kong Island tour?

A: Yes. Er. **Could you speak more slowly, please?**

C: Of course. Would you like to take the tour tomorrow morning or afternoon?

A: Tomorrow morning. **What time does it start?**

C: At eight o'clock exactly.

A: **Excuse me, eight o'clock …**

C: Yes, at eight.

A: And **where does it leave from?**

C: The bus leaves from the front gate here.

A: **Sorry, could you repeat that?**

C: The bus leaves from the front gate.

A: The front gate? Here? Outside?

C: Yes, just over there. Do you see the sign?

B: Yes, I can see the sign. I can see it!

A: And **when does the tour finish?**

C: The bus arrives back here at 1p.m.

A: 1p.m. OK. **How much does it cost?**

C: 320 dollars per person.

A: 320 dollars. So, 640 dollars for two.

C: That's right.

A: OK, that's good. So could we have two tickets for tomorrow morning, please?

B: Er, **do you take credit cards?**

C: Yes, of course …

⟶ LANGUAGEBANK 2.3 p130–131

A Refer Ss to the *Wh-* question table when they do Ex A.

Answers: 2 What time/When does the train arrive? 3 How much does it cost? 4 What time/When does the museum open? 5 What time/When does the museum close? 6 How much does it cost?

B Before looking at the table, write *in, at* and *on* across the board. Elicit short answers to suitable questions, using the prepositions, e.g. *When do you watch TV/play football? In the evening. At the weekend. On Sunday.* Ss then read and copy the table into their notebooks before doing Ex B.

Answers: *At* the weekend … a lot *on* Saturday but *on* Sunday … We get up *at* 10 o'clock *in* the morning … We have lunch *at* about … then *in* the afternoon … *In* the evening we watch … to bed *at* about 11.30 *at* night.

LEARN TO show you don't understand

6A Give Ss time to read the text before listening. Play the CD. Ss underline their answers and then compare them. In feedback, check answers and ask Ss if they've ever had a similar experience.

Answers: 1 Could you speak more slowly, please? 2 Excuse me, eight o'clock? 3 Sorry, could you repeat that?

B Ss could first listen and underline the stressed words as shown below. When they repeat the sentences, check that their intonation rises and falls in the same way as the recording: *Could you speak more slowly, please? Excuse me, eight o'clock? Sorry, could you repeat that?*

speakout TIP

Stress the importance of knowing how to say that you don't understand in a foreign language, and *how* to do it politely!

C First, demonstrate the activity with a *stronger student.* Mumble your address/phone number (or invented ones) very quickly. Encourage your Ss to say their own/invented addresses and phone numbers in a similar way. In feedback, invite Ss to act out their dialogues to the class.

SPEAKING

7A First, check the rubrics and put Ss in A/B pairs facing each other. Tell them not to show each other their books. Write $HK100 on the board and tell Ss it means 100 Hong Kong dollars. Ss A look at p161 and Ss B ask the questions to complete their notes. Monitor discreetly and take notes of good and problematic language/pronunciation.

B Ss change roles for the second role-play. Monitor closely to provide support but also continue to take notes of good and problematic language or pronunciation, particularly the use of the 3rd person verbs. Give Ss feedback on their performance at the end.

Homework ideas

- Ss write a paragraph about their partner's routines from Ex 3.
- Ss write a dialogue of a role-play from Ex 7.
- **Language bank** 2.3 Ex A–B, p131
- **Workbook** Ex 1–3B, p14

CHALET GIRL

Introduction

In this lesson, Ss watch an excerpt from a BBC travel programme 'with a difference'. They then learn/practise language to talk about their daily lives at home, and write an internet posting about themselves.

SUPPLEMENTARY MATERIALS

Ex 2: bring photos/pictures of daily tasks, e.g. cooking breakfast, washing floors, making the bed.

Warm up

Create interest and introduce some of the vocabulary from the DVD (in bold). Mime skiing and ask, e.g. *Do you like skiing? Why/Why not? When/Where do people/you go skiing? Do you know any famous ski resorts?* If you have a world map, use it to elicit places where people ski, including Verbier in Switzerland. Then Ss look at the photo on p24–25. Ask *Where do people stay when they go skiing?* Teach *In chalets* (or *hotels*). Ask *Do you watch TV holiday programmes? Why/Why not?* Tell Ss they'll watch a holiday programme later in the lesson.

Culture notes

Toyah Willcox is a well known British celebrity with a varied career. In the 1990s, she became a popular BBC presenter on programmes such as the long-running *Holiday* series.

The excerpt here is from another BBC holiday programme called *Holiday: Fasten Your Seatbelt* (1996–8). Each week, a BBC presenter tried out holiday-related jobs. Ss see some of Toyah's experiences as a chalet girl in the popular skiing resort of **Verbier**, in the southwest of Switzerland.

▶ DVD PREVIEW

1 Ss look at the photo of Toyah and make speculations. Ask *Where's she from? How old is she? What does she do?* Ss then read the text to check their predictions and answer the questions. In feedback, check *fasten your seatbelts* in the title and *chalet girl*. Elicit/Teach *she cleans and cooks, a cook*.

Answers: 1 She's a TV presenter, singer and actress. 2 A chalet girl in Switzerland.

2 Use the photos to check vocabulary in the list: *cook breakfast, go shopping for food, wash the floor*. Also check the meaning of *go out with, buy bread, make soup* and teach *(do the) housework*.

Answers:
Food: cook breakfast, go shopping for food, make a cake, buy bread, make soup
Cleaning: clean the rooms, wash the floors
People: meet the guests, go out with the guests

Optional extra activity

After feedback, reinforce the new vocabulary with a miming activity. In pairs/small groups, Ss take turns to mime an activity from the list. The others guess what it is, using the *verb + noun* not the present continuous.

▶ DVD VIEW

3A Remind Ss to concentrate on the task. Play the DVD again if necessary.

Answers: 1 go shopping 2 meet the guests 3 make soup 4 make a cake 5 buy bread 6 cook breakfast 7 clean the rooms 8 wash the floors 9 go out with the guests

Teaching tip

As an alternative approach to this, play the DVD with the sound turned down. Ss will be able to concentrate on the action in the programme and activate the vocabulary they know while doing the task at the same time.

B Check *salt, professional* and *francs* (the Swiss currency) first. Ss probably won't be able to answer in full sentences, the past tense, etc but it doesn't matter. If you have to replay the DVD, select the scenes related to the prompts. With a *stronger class*, elicit other jobs Toyah does in the chalet: *cleans the sink/mirror/bath, hoovers (vacuums) the rooms, makes the beds*.

Answers: 1 Toyah goes shopping and spends too much money: 174 francs instead of 100. 2 She puts too much salt in the soup. 3 She makes her first cake and is embarrassed because Rosemary, one of the guests, is a professional cook. 4 She wakes up the guests very early in the morning because she hasn't got her key. She forgot to take it when she went to buy bread. 5 She cooks eggs for breakfast but one of the guests didn't want/like them.

C Elicit an example first. Monitor closely to help Ss if necessary. In feedback, have a class discussion. Ask *Would you like this job? Why/Why not?*

Possible answers:
Good things: She gets free accommodation and ski pass. She's independent, can ski in the afternoons, meets people and goes out with the guests.
Bad things: She doesn't earn a good salary (£56 a week), she works very hard: she has to do the shopping, cook and clean the chalet.

DVD 2 Chalet Girl

V=Voice-over T=Toyah C=Clair G=Guest

V: On *Holiday: Fasten Your Seatbelt*, a number of famous people try different jobs. This job is for a chalet girl, for Crystal Holidays in the skiing resort of Verbier. And our applicant is:

T: Toyah Willcox.

V: Your job, please?

T: Chalet girl.

V: Essential?

T: Catering experience, outgoing personality and basic French.

V: And salary?

T: £56 a week, plus tips, accommodation, insurance and ski pass.

V: Applicant accepted.

V: Toyah Willcox works as a TV presenter, but this week she has a new job as a chalet girl in Switzerland. Toyah arrives at Verbier to start work and her boss shows her some of her jobs.

C: OK. In the bathroom, clean the sink, mirror, bath … OK?

T: OK.

V: Toyah starts her work with a trip to the supermarket to buy food for the week.

C: Erm, Toyah, how much did you spend?

T: Um … a hundred and seventy-four.

C: I was thinking more along the lines of … the list would cost perhaps a hundred francs.

T: Oh …

V: Two hours later the guests arrive.

T: Hello. Welcome!

V: Toyah welcomes them. They've travelled by plane and then by bus from England. They want to ski, relax and eat some very good food.

V: Toyah makes soup.

T: Just check that it's salt … yep. Uh! Oh no! Uh!

V: And a cake.

T: This is my first cake.

G: It looks good.

G: Did you know that Rosemary is a professional cook?

T: Oh, gosh oh … Oh no!

V: Early morning and Toyah is up to get fresh bread for breakfast, … but then there's a problem.

T: Mistake number three. I haven't got a key. Trish, Brian, it's Toyah. Sorry.

G: No, it's all right.

G: Don't apologise.

T: Go back to bed and I'll, I'll bring you a cup of tea.

V: A little later, Toyah makes breakfast for the guests.

T: Um … The plate's hot.

G: I don't … I won't have an egg.

T: Oh, sorry.

V: After breakfast, the guests go skiing, and Toyah is alone, … but there's no time to rest. Toyah hoovers the rooms, makes the beds, cleans the bath and washes the floor.

V: But it's not all housework for Toyah. She goes out with her guests, gives them a hot drink and tries out a new sport! Off she goes …

T: And I'm not coming back!

speakout life at home

4A Ss write their lists alone and then compare them in pairs/small groups. In feedback, brainstorm Ss' answers and write any new vocabulary on the board.

B After feedback, you could ask further comprehension questions if appropriate, e.g. *Why is the woman surprised? Why does the man like cleaning?*

Answers: 1 M 2 W 3 W

Unit 2 Recording 14

M=Man W=Woman

M: Oh no! Look at this mess. Where's the hoover?

W: Urm … Oh, here it is. I am surprised, Marc. **Do you like cleaning?**

M: **Yes, I love it!**

W: Uh, really?! Why?

M: Well, I study all week and by Friday my apartment looks terrible!

W: Right …

M: So on Saturdays I clean all morning. It makes me feel good. What about you? Do you like cleaning?

W: **No, I don't. I hate it.** I don't like cleaning or washing.

M: So … **what do you like doing?**

W: At home, I like doing nothing! Well, **I like playing video games and watching TV**, you know … just relaxing.

M: **Me, too.** But *after* the cleaning!

C First, drill the **key phrases** (in bold in the audio script) using the audio as a model. Encourage Ss to show strong emotions in *Yes, I love it! No, I don't. I hate it!* Monitor and make notes on examples of good language and problems for feedback later. To extend the activity, Ss swap groups and tell them about their initial partners.

D Ss discuss this in groups. Monitor carefully and encourage Ss to use the **key phrases** wherever possible.

E In feedback, get Ss to report back to the class. Ask who has similar lives.

writeback an internet posting

5A Give Ss 3 mins to read the posting and answer the question. Check/Teach new vocabulary, e.g. *law, active,* and ask simple comprehension questions. Write them on the board or ask Ss to write them.

Alternative activity
You could do this via a jigsaw activity. Divide the class into pairs/groups of As, Bs and Cs. Each group writes four questions; As do paragragh1, Bs do paragraph 2 and Cs do paragraph 3. You should monitor while they prepare. Then organise Ss into groups of 3, each with an A, B and C student. They ask and answer each other's questions.

B First, elicit some answers from Ss using the notes here. They should use Leona's posting as a model for their writing.

C Ss work in groups and read each other's postings. They then discuss which Ss would match. Give Ss feedback on their writing if necessary.

Homework ideas
- Ss write a paragraph about partner's opinions in Ex C.
- Ss write a final draft of the posting in Ex 5B.
- Workbook Ex 4, p14

LOOKBACK

Introduction

The **Lookback** exercises are very flexible and can be exploited in a variety of ways, e.g. as fillers if there's time at the end of the lesson or to boost Ss' energy levels between activities.

JOBS

1A Give Ss 1 min to circle the jobs. The first Ss to finish is the winner. To follow up, Ss underline the main stress in each word and check answers in pairs. The pair with the most correct answers wins.

> **Answers:** 1 nurse 2 teacher 3 waiter 4 hairdresser
> 5 receptionist 6 engineer 7 lawyer 8 actress
> 9 accountant 10 doctor 11 politician 12 chef

B Ss discuss and decide which jobs are right for the people. Ss should try to justify their answers, e.g. *A nurse works with people every day.*

> **Possible answers:** 1 nurse, teacher 2 hairdresser, politician 3 doctor, accountant 4 accountant, engineer 5 actress, waiter, sportsperson 6 chef, waiter

ACTIVITIES

2A In *mixed ability classes*, group *weaker Ss* together so that you can provide them with more support. *Stronger Ss* could do the exercise together and should try not to look back in their books for the answers.

> **Answers:** 2 watch 3 take 4 listen to 5 do 6 eat 7 read
> 8 go

B Ss ask/answer the questions in pairs and make notes of their partner's answers. They then write them in sentences to hand in for your assessment, e.g. *Michel reads sports magazines.*

PRESENT SIMPLE QUESTIONS

3A Ss should write about a person they know but not too well. Then they can speculate. It would be preferable for Ss to work with a different partner than in Ex 2A.

> **Answers:** 2 plays/doesn't play 3 goes/doesn't go
> 4 does/doesn't do 5 studies/doesn't study 6 watches/
> doesn't watch 7 goes/doesn't go 8 cooks/doesn't cook

B In feedback, ask the class how many correct sentences they had and whether there were any surprises.

DAILY ROUTINES

4A Monitor to help struggling Ss with this.

B Encourage Ss to extend the conversations by asking as many questions as possible, in preparation for the next activity. They should take notes of relevant information. Monitor and make notes of problems with the target language. You can then decide what language needs revising, which Ss are having problems, etc.

C Again, monitor and take notes as above.

ASKING FOR INFORMATION

> **Culture notes**
> **Malta** is a group of seven islands in the Mediterranean Sea, about 90km south of Sicily. Only the three largest islands, Malta Island, Gozo and Comino are inhabited. It has a vivid history due to its strategic history and is well known for its World Heritage sites. Valetta is the capital city.

5A If you have a map, elicit the location of Malta. Ask Ss *What do you know about Malta? Where is it? What do you know about it?* Ss then write questions using the information. Don't give any help with the questions – see what they can produce by themselves. However, monitor closely and make notes for feedback and assessment purposes.

> **Answers:** 1 What time/When does the tour start?
> 2 What time/When does it finish? 3 Where does it leave from? 4 How much is it? 5 Do you accept credit cards?

B Ss could swap roles after the first role-play. Monitor while Ss talk and assess their performance. You may want to keep records of their accuracy/fluency to compare with the results of more formal tests.

> **Optional extra activity**
> Revise time phrases with this activity.
>
> Prepare nine present simple questions using information Ss will know, e.g. *When do you have your English class? What time does the class start/finish? How much does a coffee cost? When do you relax/go to the cinema/do your homework/go out with friends?* In class, draw a large grid with nine squares on the board and number them 1–9. Ss copy it with squares large enough to write in. Start with square 1 and ask the questions in numerical order. Ss write their answers with time phrases, e.g. *On Wednesday. In the afternoon. At 5.15. At the weekend.*
>
> Ss swap books for feedback. Elicit answers, focussing on the prepositions. Ss tick the square if their partner has the correct one. The winners are those with the most correct answers.
>
> N.B. You can use a grid like this for any warm up involving words/short phrases.

OVERVIEW

This video podcast consolidates and extends Ss' vocabulary around the topic of friends and family. The material also encapsulates authentic usage of the modifiers and frequency adverbs presented in lesson 3.1 as well as recycling key vocabulary. The video podcast would work well at the end of lessons 3.1, 3.2 or at the end of unit 3.

JUST GOOD FRIENDS

Introduction

Ss practise using the present simple further with adverbs of frequency and modifiers. They learn adjectives to describe personality, and read and talk about themselves and friends.

SUPPLEMENTARY MATERIALS

Resource bank p153 and p154

Warm up: check/prepare the prompts (see below for details)

Warm up

Revision of question forms: team game

Organise Ss into teams: A, B, C, etc and give each student in each team a number: 1, 2, 3, etc. Give an example, e.g. *At 6.30 in the morning.* Elicit a question which matches this answer, e.g. *What time do you/does he/do they get up?* Team A starts. If Ss 1 gives a correct question, he/she gets 3 points. If he/she has to consult his team, he gets 2 points. If the team get it wrong, Team B can answer and get 1 point. Teams take it in turns to provide a question. Use these prompts to start with: *7.30 in the evening, an accountant, £350 a week, Paris, 7.15 in the morning, relax and play video games, at 11.30 at night, Australia, 1.30, $79 return, On Mondays and Fridays, at 9.15, at 10, 12 and 2 (times).*

Teaching tip

You can play team games like this with a variety of different language. People of all ages usually enjoy games: they provide motivation as well as memorable practice.

VOCABULARY personality

1A Ss look at the pictures. Check understanding, e.g. for picture 1, ask *Who/Where are the people? Does the man (woman?) talk a lot? Do the other people talk? No, because the man's very talkative.* Do the same with the other pictures.

Answers: 2 D 3 A 4 C 5 E

B First, check the example with Ss to make it clear what they have to do. Before checking the meaning of the opposites, allow Ss to try it themselves. Teach/Check new words in feedback.

Answers: 2 unkind 3 quiet 4 unfriendly 5 serious

C Ss listen to the words and mark the stress. Elicit the stress for, e.g. *intelligent.* Hold up the fingers of one hand. Ask *How many syllables?* Show four fingers. Ask *Where's the stress?* Point to the second finger. Ss then underline the stressed syllables.

Answers: 1 in**tel**ligent 2 **kind** 3 **tal**kative 4 **friend**ly 5 **fun**ny 6 **stu**pid 7 un**kind** 8 **quiet** 9 un**friend**ly 10 **se**rious

D Listen to Ss' answers and use the same technique as above to correct Ss' pronunciation if necessary.

E Give Ss time to think and note down adjectives to describe their friend. Encourage *fast finishers/stronger Ss* to use other descriptive adjectives they know. In feedback, invite Ss to tell the class about their partner's friends.

speakout TIP

Check Ss understand the tip and elicit two examples from the exercise above. Check/Teach new words here, e.g. *unwell*: used to describe people's health: *My grandfather is very unwell at the moment.*

LISTENING

2A Check the meaning of *close friends*. Ask *Is a close friend a good friend? Do you see him/her often? Do you tell him/her about your problems?* Remind Ss to focus on answering the questions and not get distracted by unknown language. Play the CD. Ss complete the answers and check in pairs. In feedback, ask Ss to justify their answers if they can.

Answers: 1 Yes. 2 She isn't sure.

B Ss listen again. While they check in pairs, monitor closely to decide if they need to hear the CD again. If you have a *stronger class*, Ss can check their answers in the audio script at the back of the book.

Teaching tip

Try to exploit the audio scripts for extra language practice and/or promoting learner autonomy. You will be able to use this one as a model for speaking and writing later on in the lesson.

Unit 3 Recording 2

Conversation 1

A: I don't like talkative people, and my friend José is usually very quiet. People think he's not very friendly because he's quiet and often serious, but in fact he's really friendly and he's sometimes very funny – not all the time, but sometimes. We don't like doing the same things, so we hardly ever do things together, maybe two or three times a year. For example, he likes computer games and staying at home and I go out a lot … but it's not a problem. When we meet, he always asks me how I am, and he really listens to me. And when he phones me with a problem, I always listen to him. He's a good friend, and we usually understand each other well.

Conversation 2

B: My friend Rosa is usually very funny – she makes jokes and we laugh a lot. We like the same things, we're always together. We often go out to clubs – two or three times a week – and to parties … She talks a lot, and she's a friendly person, but are we really close friends? I don't know … I think I'm a good friend to her, but she … when I have a problem, she hardly ever listens to me. So sometimes she's not very kind. She's an intelligent person, and I sometimes feel stupid around her. We don't always understand each other, but you know, she's a good friend … I think.

Optional extra activity

Do this as a whole-class activity. Write the first four sentences from conversation 1 on the board. Play the CD again, pausing for them to repeat it line by line. Then erase one or two words from each line on the board. Ss repeat the dialogue again, adding the missing words. Continue this procedure until all the words have been erased. Ss should now be able to act out the conversation from memory, either in pairs or to the class. N.B. Use this activity for any dialogue as long as it's not too long.

GRAMMAR frequency adverbs

3A With a *stronger* or *mixed ability class*, Ss can try to work things out for themselves. They do Ex 3A and B alone/in pairs, and check their answers in section 3.1 of the **Language bank** on p132. However, if you're sure your Ss aren't familiar with frequency adverbs, or you want to change the pace and interaction of the class, draw the line from the student page on the board with the percentages 0% and 100% marked. Read and check sentences 1–4. Ask Ss where you should write each adverb on the line, or invite Ss to come to the board and write the adverbs themselves.

Answers: 10% hardly ever 40% sometimes 60% often 80% usually

B Elicit more examples in feedback, using the information from the audio script.

Answers: 1 after 2 before

⟹ LANGUAGEBANK 3.1 p132–3

Recheck the rules and point out the two positions of *usually* and *sometimes* in a sentence. Ss can do Ex A and B in class or at home, depending on how much controlled practice they need. If time is limited, go to Ex 4 as this provides personalised practice.

Answers:
A 1 The Ss are never late. 2 They always do their homework. 3 It hardly ever rains here. 4 We don't usually watch TV in the morning. 5 I am sometimes very quiet. 6 The lesson is often funny.
B 2 I always have breakfast with my family. 3 My father usually reads the paper./Usually my father reads the paper. 4 We're often tired in the morning. 5 I hardly ever get up before 7a.m. 6 I never drink coffee. 7 He's sometimes late./Sometimes he's late.

PRACTICE

4A First, check the meaning of *each other* (question 6). Ss could look at the audio script or play the CD again: *He's a good friend and we usually understand each other well.* Check concept, e.g. *Does José understand his friend? Yes. Does José's friend understand him? Yes. So they understand … ?* Elicit *each other.* Check the example to introduce Ss to this kind of ordering exercise. Then elicit the word order for question 2 and write it on the board. Ss must give reasons for the order, e.g. *We are always = subject + verb + adverb of frequency.*

Answers: 2 We're always together. 3 I sometimes feel stupid around him/her. 4 My friend is usually very funny. 5 I always listen to him/her. 6 We don't always understand each other.

B First, do question 1 in Ex 4A as an example. If you have *strong class*, elicit questions they could ask each other while doing the exercise, e.g. *Are you usually very quiet? Is your friend usually very quiet?*

READING

5A Create interest in the quiz. Ss look at the photo and the title. Check *true* and *fair-weather friends*. (Use the definition of fair-weather friend in the last paragraph of the key to the quiz.) To prepare Ss for question 2 in the quiz, ask *How often do you see your friends? Every day? Once, twice, three times a week?* Check the meaning and use of *once* and *twice*. Also check/teach other words and phrases your Ss need, e.g. *together, make time, leave him/her alone, ready, have fun together.* Give Ss 5 mins to do the quiz and read the key. Monitor closely to make sure Ss are doing the quiz correctly and clarify vocabulary for them if necessary.

B Give Ss 2 mins to compare their answers and find out how close they are to the friend they chose. In feedback, invite Ss to tell the class about their findings.

GRAMMAR modifiers

6A In feedback, ask *What comes after these words? Verbs or nouns?* Meaning is checked in the next exercise.

Answers:
True friends: *very close, really good friends,*
Just good friends: *quite close*
Fair-weather friends: *aren't very close*

B Let Ss try this alone first, before checking in pairs. The ticks (✓✓) provide the clue to meaning.

Answers: 1 really good 2 good 3 quite good 4 not very good

C Do individual repetition to check that Ss are stressing the correct modifiers.

Answers: 1 We're <u>really</u> good friends. We're <u>very</u> good friends. 2 We're <u>good</u> friends. 3 We're <u>quite</u> good friends. 4 We're <u>not very</u> good friends.

> ⇒ **LANGUAGEBANK** 2.1 p132–3
>
> After looking at the box on p132, elicit statements about Ss in your class if appropriate, e.g. *Daniela and Yuki are good friends.* Ss could also find the modifiers in the audio script for Ex 2 above.
>
> **C** *Weaker Ss* could do the exercise in class if they need more guidance.
>
> **Answers:** 2 very/really funny 3 quite good 4 very/really intelligent 5 not very easy 6 very talkative 7 really/very good

PRACTICE

7A Do the example with Ss and check *laugh at my jokes* if necessary. In feedback, nominate Ss to read out the corrected sentences and invite peer-correction if necessary.

Answers: Sentences 3 and 5 correct. 2 I'm not very quiet. 4 I'm very funny. 6 I'm very serious.

B Monitor while Ss write their sentences and check their accuracy and spelling. In *mixed ability classes*, put *weaker Ss* together and give them extra help them. When Ss compare answers in pairs, encourage them to discuss and agree/disagree with their partners' statements. In feedback, ask Ss which sentences are true about them.

SPEAKING

8A Check instructions and give Ss 3 mins to decide who they'll choose and prepare notes to justify their choice. Monitor closely to provide help with language Ss need.

> **Teaching tip**
>
> It's important to be aware of the timing and pace in a class. Monitoring is one way of controlling this. *Fast finishers* often start chatting to their classmates and lose their concentration. Ss often haven't completed the task properly so check what they've done. Give *fast finishers* something else to do, e.g. more questions, helping slower Ss.

B While Ss compare their answers, encourage them to ask more questions, e.g. *Why are/aren't you very close?* Ss take notes about their partner's friends and report back to the class. Give feedback on Ss' performance.

> **Homework ideas**
> * Ss write about their friends from Ex 8.
> * Language bank 3.1 Ex A–C, p133
> * Workbook Ex 1A–5, p15–16

BIG HAPPY FAMILIES

Introduction

Ss learn/revise and practise *has/have got* and vocabulary to talk about their families.

SUPPLEMENTARY MATERIALS

Resource bank p155

Photo bank p154

Warm up: prepare wall prompts, (see below.)

Ex 5: ask Ss to bring photos of their family – in paper/electronic form

---

Warm up

Lead into the topic of family life using wall prompts in a mingling activity. Before class, write 8–10 prompts on A4 paper, e.g. *make breakfast, clean the house, cook dinner, go to the supermarket.* Stick the prompts around the classroom and model/drill an example: *Do you make breakfast at the weekend?* Elicit answers with a frequency adverb, e.g. *Yes, always. No, hardly ever.* Give Ss 3–4 mins to walk round asking and answering the questions in pairs/3s.

VOCABULARY family

1A The aim of the exercise is to activate family words that Ss know. With a *strong* or *mixed ability class*, ask *Have you got a big or small family?* Elicit answers and activate family words before they do the exercise. With *weaker classes*, use the photo to teach/elicit and drill the family words in the exercise. Ss should write the words in their notebooks in two columns: male and female.

Suggested answers: The parents are in the middle of the back row. There are 16 children in the photo. All the children are sons or daughters (Ss should identify at least one of each). There are 7 visible boys (not counting the baby) and 8 girls (Ss should identify at least one of each). The parents are also husband and wife.

B Elicit other male/female family words Ss know and write them on the board. They add them to their lists, underlining the main stress.

⟹ PHOTOBANK p154

1A Ss do the exercise alone and then compare answers. In feedback, check/drill the meaning of new words and elicit the main stress. Ss should add new words to their lists from Ex 1A and B on p30.

Answers: 1) A and B 2) C and D 3) F 4) C 5) I and J 6) G 7) I 8) E and F 9) G and H 10) I and J

B Before Ss do the exercise, model/drill the pronunciation of the family's first names, *Frank, Maggie,* etc. Elicit more information about Robert in the example to illustrate the activity, e.g. *He's Elizabeth's husband, Mark and Amy's father, Katy's uncle, Amy's his daughter, Mark's his son, Katy's his niece, Jake's his nephew.*

Monitor and check Ss' accuracy while they write. Ss can then read out their descriptions in groups. Other Ss listen and check if they're correct.

READING

2A With *strong classes*, divide the class into four groups for the discussion: A, B, C and D. Group A makes a list of good things about life in a big family; B, a list of bad things; C, a list of good things about a small family; D, a list of bad things. If more than four groups are needed, divide the class in half and organise two sets of four groups (A–D) with the same tasks. Give Ss 3 mins to make their lists. Monitor closely to help with vocabulary they need. Then regroup Ss with an A, B, C and D students in each. They read out their lists and agree/disagree. Then do feedback with the class. With *weaker classes*, have a brief discussion with the whole class before moving to Ex B.

Possible answers:
big family: **good** children always have company; they have to learn to share things/don't get spoilt; clothes/toys, etc are handed down and reused **bad** expensive; children don't have some many opportunities; don't have so much individual attention.
small family: **good** more money/attention; parents have closer contact **bad** spoilt/given too much attention; children can be lonely/fight each other more/be more competitive

B First, put Ss into A/B pairs, facing each other. Tell them not to show each other their books. Check the titles of both texts. Elicit where *Ukraine* is, using a map if you have one. Do the examples for both texts to show Ss what to do. Remind them that not all their numbers are in the texts. Also teach *bored* and *boring* as these words occur in both texts, and practise the pronunciation of *choir* /kwaɪə(r)/. Give Ss 2–3 mins to circle the numbers. Monitor closely to provide help with vocabulary but also remind Ss to focus on the task, not words they don't need.

C Elicit one or two examples before Ss exchange their information. Tell them to use notes as in the example in Ex B, not complete sentences. This will help to avoid the use of *has/have got*, which is taught in Ex 3. In feedback, check Ss' answers and ask them if their opinions of large families have changed.

Answers:
A 11: They've got 11 daughters. 1: They've only got one bathroom. 7: They drink 7 litres of milk for breakfast every day. 6: Six of the 12 children have breakfast from 6.30 to 7; the other six have breakfast from 7 to 7.30. 15: Their only son, Charles, is 15 years old.
B 8: There are eight girls in the family. 7: The house has got seven rooms. 9: There are nine boys. 15: Their car's got 15 seats.

D Tell Ss to show each other their texts when to confirm their answers. In feedback, focus on useful vocabulary from the texts, e.g. *noisy, normal, voices, cereal, packed lunches, lucky.*

Answers: The Chernenko family eat dinner together/don't all live together. The Lewis family all live together. Both families like their big family.

Optional extra activity
Exploit the text further: Ss work in pairs/small groups and write 4–6 questions about their text using the present simple. Reorganise Ss so that they work with groups who worked on the other text and tell them to take turns to ask/answer the questions.

GRAMMAR *have/has got*

Watch out!

Here Ss learn and practise the British use of *has/have got* for talking about possessions/families. *Has/have got* doesn't use the auxiliary *do*. However, the American usage of *do you have*, etc is acceptable. Ss can get confused and say, e.g. *Do you have got …* Clarify the difference early on: provide plenty of controlled practice and correct when necessary.

3A Ss find the sentences in the text and complete them. Check the meaning and form in feedback.

Answers: 1 have got 2 has got 3 haven't got

B Ss complete the table alone and compare answers. They can then check them in the first table in the **Language bank**, on p132. Recheck the concept and drill the pronunciation.

Answers: have, has, have, has

C Play the CD. Ss listen and underline the answers. In feedback, point out that it's important to use contracted forms to make their speaking more natural. The next exercise will focus on this.

Answers: 1 's 2 've 3 haven't 4 hasn't

D Use finger highlighting to illustrate the contracted forms. N.B. Use finger highlighting when you model/drill sentences with contractions. First, say the full form using two fingers, *has not*, and then put the fingers together for the contracted form, *hasn't* to show the merging of words.

⇒ LANGUAGEBANK 3.2 p132–3

Read the notes with Ss. If you have a *strong class*, they will be aware of the use of *any* in questions. If not, don't explain it here: Ss will study this form in the next unit. Ss have practised the question form yet but will do so in Ex 5. Check the form and read the notes with your Ss here to prepare them for this.

Answers:
A 1 Have 2 got 3 've got 4 haven't got 5 Have 6 got
7 have 8 've got 9 's got 10 have got 11 have got
12 has got 13 Has 14 got 15 's got
B 2 Have you got 3 has your classroom got 4 Is your best friend 5 Are you 6 Have you got 7 Are you
8 Is your brother

PRACTICE

4A Give Ss 15 seconds to look at the text and tell you what the topic is: a family. Do an extra example before Ss start. Ss compare answers before feedback. Nominate Ss to answer and encourage them to correct themselves when they make a mistake (self-correct).

Answers: 2 is 3 is 4 'm 5 is 6 've got 7 hasn't got 8 isn't 9 's got 10 'm 11 've got 12 're

B Check the examples in the family tree, including the ages. Ss then do the activity alone and compare their answers. In feedback, ask *What sort of words follow have got and be?* Family words; ages.

Answers: Andreas; Mark, 30; Marek; Eva; Vlad, 3; Henryk, 1

SPEAKING

5A Elicit the first answer as an example. Refer Ss back to the question form table in the **Language bank** if necessary. In feedback, drill the questions and elicit true answers if possible.

Answers: 1 Have, got 2 have, got 3 Has, got 4 has, got

B Demonstrate the activity. Draw a family tree with two members on the board: use your own/an invented family.

C First, model/drill the example questions. Ss then ask you the questions: add your answers to your family tree on the board. Ss then exchange their own family trees and ask/answer the questions in pairs. *Fast finishers* add more family members to their trees. Monitor and make notes on accuracy and pronunciation for feedback. N.B. If Ss have brought family photos, they can use them instead of/together with their family tree.

D Monitor while Ss check their family trees. In feedback, nominate Ss to tell the class/group about their partner's family.

WRITING apostrophe 's

6A Check the meaning of *first marriage* in the text and do another example. Ss then work alone. Do feedback after the next exercise.

Answers: sister's, name's, she's, Jane's, he's

B Do an example before Ss discuss their answers. In feedback, encourage them to do self and peer correction.

Answers:
has: Stuart's (has) got …
is: name's (is) …; she's (is) a doctor
's: sister's, Jane's

C Ss could add the apostrophes in their books or, if they need practice with writing, copy the corrected text in their notebooks. Check the meaning of *energetic, lively, married* and *single*.

Answers: I've got two brothers … He's an engineer … he's married to Katia. … They've got one daughter … She's at school … He's single.

D Ss could use the same people from Ex 5 or choose different ones. N.B. If you know that the subject of families is too sensitive for any of your Ss, or that they need a challenge, offer them an alternative: they write about an imaginary family or a family from the TV. If you have computer facilities, they could look online and find out about the family of a favourite singer/actor. Encourage Ss to use the text in Ex 6C as a model. They should also show their drafts to each other, and ask for advice and help if necessary.

Homework ideas
• Ss write a final draft of their family members from Ex 6D or make a poster and add photos.
• Language bank 3.2 Ex A–B, p133
• Workbook Ex 1A–6C, p17–18

ARE YOU FREE TONIGHT?

Introduction

Ss learn and practise time expressions. They then practise the skill of how to be a good listener and to show interest in what the other person is saying. Finally, they learn and practise useful phrases for making arrangements.

SUPPLEMENTARY MATERIALS

Resource bank p156

Ex 7: copies of local entertainment listings, e.g. from the cinema, theatre, clubs, etc (with times) from newspapers or the internet

Warm up

Lead in to the lesson: dictogloss

This isn't a traditional dictation. Read the following text at normal speed:

> My friend Jane's got a new job in an office. She really likes it because the job's interesting and the people are very friendly. The work's quite difficult, but Jane's intelligent and doesn't have any problems with it. She gets home late every night, but she doesn't work on Saturday. We usually go shopping in the afternoon and see a film in the evening.

Ss listen. Dictate it again with short pauses between each sentence. Tell Ss to make notes of key words, not write full sentences. Read it once more at normal speed for Ss to add to their notes. Ss work in pairs/3s to reconstruct the text, as closely as possible to the original, using their notes. It doesn't have to be exactly the same but Ss have to concentrate on making their text grammatically accurate with correct spelling. Distribute copies of your original text for Ss to compare, or invite Ss to take it in turns to write sentences on the board. Discuss them as a class. N.B. A dictogloss can be used with any short text.

VOCABULARY time expressions

1A Check that Ss know *months* and the meaning of *a.m.*, *p.m*, *first*. Model/Drill the time expressions in feedback.

Answers: 2 a) 3 e) 4 b) 5 d)

B Ask *How often do you go to a club?* and elicit some sample answers, e.g. *once a month/week, never*. Give Ss 1 min to note down their own answers for each activity.

C Ss compare their answers. Monitor and make notes for a correction slot.

Teaching tip

A correction slot is the stage when you give feedback and encourage Ss to notice and correct errors they made in a previous activity.

LISTENING

2A Check the rubric and pre-teach *interesting, difficult, busy*. Play the CD. Ss listen and compare their answers. Play the CD in feedback if Ss aren't sure of the answers.

Answers: work and the cinema

B Ss check their answers in the audio script at the back of their books. In feedback, ask Ss to justify their answers.

Answers: 2 F Ron doesn't like all the people in his office. 3 T 4 F They don't agree to meet.

C Ss discuss the answer in pairs before feedback.

Answers: No, because he never answers or responds to Ron's comments.

Unit 3 Recording 5

J=Jack   R=Ron
J: Hello?
R: Hi, Jack. It's Ron.
J: Oh, hi. How are you?
R: Fine, thanks. And you?
J: OK.
R: Uh, well, I'm at my new office, you know I've got a new job … Uh, the work's quite interesting and the people are very friendly … Hello, are you there?
J: Yes. Yes, I'm still here.
R: … and the work isn't too difficult … Hello, are you there?
J: Yes.
R: Oh … and, well, I haven't got my own office, and one of the people in my office is really unfriendly … Are you there?
J: Yes, I'm here.
R: Anyway, are you free tonight?
J: Yeah, I think I am. What do you want to do?
R: How about going to the cinema? I'd like to see the new Will Smith film.
J: Will Smith … ah, wait, I'm busy. Sorry.
R: Oh … OK, well, maybe next time.
J: Yeah, see you.
R: Bye.

3A With *weaker classes*, let Ss listen first. Ask *Is Denise unfriendly? Is she like Jack?* They then listen again and complete the notes. With *stronger classes*, Ss could listen and check their answers in the audio script.

Answers: 1 half past five 2 the ABC cinema 3 six o'clock

B Ss discuss the questions in pairs/groups.

Answers: Yes, because she asks Ron questions and responds to his comments in a friendly way. She shows interest in him (see the underlined sentences in the script).

Unit 3 Recording 6

D=Denise   R=Ron
D: Hello?
R: Hi, Denise. It's Ron.
D: Oh, hi. <u>How are you?</u>
R: Fine, thanks. And you?
D: I'm OK. <u>How's your new job?</u>
R: Good. The work's quite interesting and the people are quite friendly.
D: <u>Uh-huh.</u>
R: … and the work isn't too difficult.

D: <u>That's great!</u>
R: It's not perfect. I haven't got my own office, and one of the people in my room is really unfriendly …
D: <u>Oh, that's a shame!</u>
R: Yeah. Anyway, are you free tonight?
D: Yeah, I think so. What do you want to do?
R: How about going to the cinema? I'd like to see the new Will Smith film.
D: Sounds good. Where's it on?
R: At the ABC in town.
D: OK. What time do you want to go?
R: It's on at six o'clock and at half past eight. What's good for you?
D: I finish work at five. So six is good.
R: Right. How about meeting at … er … half past five at the cinema?
D: Yes, that's fine.
R: Great! See you there.
D: Yeah. Oh, how about inviting Jack?
R: Hmm. *You* call him!
D: OK. Bye.
R: Bye.

<hr>

LEARN TO   show interest

4A Play this part of the CD again while Ss read and underline the phrases. Teach *That's a shame!* Check the answers but don't focus on pronunciation at this point.

Answers: 1 Uh-huh 2 That's great! 3 Oh, that's a shame!

B Check *neutral* in the rubric. Elicit Ss' answers and play the CD again for them to listen and repeat the pronunciation of the three phrases.

Answers: Positive: That's great! Negative: Oh, that's a shame! Neutral: Uh-huh.

C Teach/Check and drill the adjectives *terrible, awful, fantastic* and *wonderful* by saying them with the appropriate emotion and facial expressions. Ss then complete the two lists.

Answers:
Positive: great, fantastic, wonderful.
Negative: terrible, awful

Watch out!

Ss are often too shy/reluctant to exaggerate their intonation and show strong emotion. It's useful to exaggerate your own model when drilling the target language. Physical movement can also help Ss to relax. Tell Ss to stand up as they say the stressed syllable, and then sit down. Standing up helps them to raise the pitch of their voice. Repeat this as many times as necessary, getting faster and faster.

D Model the stress and intonation of the examples with your hands/arms. Encourage Ss to show strong emotion when they repeat the phrases, as described above.

E With a *weaker class*, Ss can listen first without responding. Check *boyfriend, nice, rain* and then elicit their responses in open class. As a follow up, Ss work in pairs, taking it in turns to say their own sentences for their partner to respond to.

<hr>

Unit 3 Recording 8

2 I haven't got any money.
3 I've got a new boyfriend …
4 … but he's not a very nice person.
5 Oh, look – rain!
6 My English teacher is great!

<hr>

FUNCTION   making arrangements

5A Lead in to the topic. Ss look at the photos. Ask, e.g. *Do you like going to the theatre? How often do you go? What sort of plays do you like?* Check making arrangements. Ask *What do you do when you want to go to the cinema with a friend?* Ask/invite them. *And then/What else?* Talk about when/where to meet. Then elicit examples of questions Ss might ask when they invite a friend somewhere or arrange to go to the cinema. They could plan what to say in their L1 if this would help them. Ss then do the exercise and check in pairs before they listen/check in Ex B. Alternatively, if Ss need more support, play the CD first. Ss underline the correct answers.

Answers: 1 Are 2 do you want 3 How 4 it on 5 want 6 It's 7 What's 8 meeting

B Play the CD as many times as necessary until Ss are confident. Highlight the use of the verb + *ing* form after *How about* … Then drill the sentences in open/closed pairs.

⇒ LANGUAGEBANK 1.3 p132–3

Check the tables and notes. Emphasise how important the responses are. Model and drill the interactions in open/closed pairs, e.g. *How about going out tonight? That's a good idea./Mmm. That's a problem.*

Answers: 1 Are you free 2 how 3 good for 4 What do you want 5 How about going 6 time do you want 7 How about meeting

6 Ss should cover Ex 5A when they do this. Monitor closely to check/help with pronunciation and accuracy.

SPEAKING

7A Use authentic nightlife listings, e.g. *cinema/theatre/club listings* as prompts here if you have them. Encourage Ss to choose other places, not only the cinema.

B First, check the flowchart with your Ss. Then play the CD for Ex 3A again. Ss listen and tick the correct part of the flow chart as they hear it. With *weaker classes*, you could play each section again for Ss to repeat and to gain confidence. They could then write out their conversation and rehearse it before doing the role-play. In feedback, invite Ss to act out their conversations to the class. Do a correction slot as required.

Optional extra activity

When Ss have finished the first role-play, they could do it again or choose a different place to talk about with another partner, this time sitting back-to-back. You could give some feedback before this if necessary, to improve Ss' performance.

Homework ideas
• Ss write a different dialogue based on the one in Ex 7B.
• Language bank 3.3 Ex A, p133
• Workbook Ex 1–3, p19

A CELEBRATION IN CRETE

Introduction

In this lesson Ss practise the four skills in the context of how people celebrate special occasions. They watch an excerpt from the BBC programme *Francesco's Mediterranean Voyage* about a Greek wedding and practise talking about their own special occasions. Finally, they write an invitation to a celebration of their choice.

SUPPLEMENTARY MATERIALS

Warm up: a map of Greece and/or the Mediterranean

Ex 1 and/or 5: bring pictures/photos of special occasions (both you and Ss) – download multicultural occasions if possible

Ex 6: use computer facilities (if available)

Warm up

Culture notes
Crete is the largest island in Greece. It was the centre of Ancient Greek and Minoan culture, exemplified in the ruins of Knossos. It's now a very popular holiday destination.

Tell Ss they're going to watch a DVD programme about Greece. Show them a map of Greece and ask *What do you know about it? Which places/islands do you know?* Elicit information and places on the map, e.g. *Athens, Rhodes, Santorini, Crete*. Ss then open their books and look at the large photo of Crete. Ask *What can you see?* A white town, beautiful blue sea, high mountains. Elicit any other information Ss know about the country. Use the **Culture notes** for reference.

DVD PREVIEW

1 If you or the Ss have brought some pictures of special celebrations, use them to teach the names of celebrations and as prompts for this activity. If you have a *multilingual class*, Ss might have more to say. However, don't spend more than 4 mins on the lead in as they'll have the opportunity to talk a lot about celebrations throughout the lesson.

Possible answers: birthdays, weddings, Christmas, New Year's Eve, wedding anniversaries, graduation celebrations, housewarming parties

2A Check the meaning of *presents/gifts, give, wear, special clothes*. *Stronger Ss* can do the exercise in pairs. With *weaker/mixed ability classes* organise Ss appropriately. In feedback, recheck meaning. Ask, e.g. *When do you wear special clothes?*

Answers: 2 eat special food 3 go to a restaurant
4 sing 'Happy Birthday' 5 give presents/gifts to each other
6 watch football on TV 7 invite guests 8 dance to special music 9 wear special clothes

B Elicit/Give example, e.g. *give presents*. Monitor closely to provide help if needed. Elicit new phrases and write them on the board, then check meaning and pronunciation. Ss write the new words in their vocabulary notebooks.

3A Give Ss 30 seconds to read and answer the question. In feedback, ask what the photo shows.

Answers: A local (Greek) wedding.

Alternative approach

With books closed, lead in to the DVD programme. Play the introduction and freeze frame on the title *Francesco's Mediterranean Voyage*. Before Ss start watching, ask *What's the programme about? Which places does he visit? How does he travel?* In feedback, use a map if possible to elicit the places/countries: *Venice, Dubrovnik, Corfu, Athens, Rhodes, Istanbul*. Ask *Do you know these places?* Some Ss might have visited them and will able to say a few things. Then play the next frame with the tile *Crete*. Freeze frame again and ask Ss what they know about it. If they don't know it, tell them/show them the map. You can then turn down the sound (as in Unit 2) and Ss watch a silent version of the programme before they read the text. Or Ss read the text now and answer the question.

B If Ss have dictionaries, encourage them to look up the words themselves and find the correct meanings, either working alone/in pairs. If not, teach/check *architect, historian, bride, gorgeous, nervous bridegroom, reception, celebrate* (see the words in bold below).

DVD 3 Francesco's Mediterrean Voyage

F=Francesco T=Taxi driver M=Maria

F: *Kalimera.*

T: *Kalimera.*

F: Er … Can you show me around Crete?

T: Yes.

F: This is the biggest Greek island of all, so I've got a local guide for the next two days.

T: Francesco, do you want to see a Cretan wedding?

F: Oh, great! Traditional Cretan weddings can be incredible. Preparations often last days. Mamas is taking me to meet the **bride**, Maria Skula.

F: *Kalimera*, Francesco.

M: Welcome. Come in.

F: Congratulations!

M: Thank you.

F: Are you a little **nervous**?

M: A little.

F: All the women are helping prepare for the wedding feast. They're making decorations in dough for special wedding bread. How many guests for your wedding?

M: One thousand, five hundred, about.

F: Mama mia, it's a lot!

F: The whole of Maria's village has **turned out** to see her get married. The bride arrives with her father. She's **gorgeous**.

F: This is the **nervous bridegroom**, Jorgos. In a few minutes he and Maria will be man and wife.

M: I do!

F: And now we go to party.
It's certainly the largest wedding reception I've ever been to.
At Cretan weddings, guests give money as gifts.
And now the food is served. The meat of one hundred fifty **sheep** … and a whole lot more.
Maria and Jorgos' first dance as man and wife includes all their close family.

F: I'm destroyed! Ah, really.

▶ DVD VIEW

4A Check the instructions and play the DVD. Ss answer the questions and compare their answers. Play it again if necessary.

Answers: (they) have a party, eat special food, go to a restaurant, give presents/gifts, invite guests, dance to special music, wear special clothes

B Ss might know the answers if they've already watched the DVD two or three times. Ss answer the questions and compare their answers. If they have doubts about any of the answers, replay the relevant sections of the programme.

Answers: 2 F 3 T 4 F 5 T

C First, check new language in the exercise: *turned out (came to see), largest, ever been to, served, sheep, whole lot more.*

Answers: 2 man, wife 3 wedding 4 money 5 food 6 dance, family

D Play the DVD again, stopping at each answer. Replay the sentences from the programme if necessary. You could stop the DVD at different points and ask prediction questions, e.g. *What happens next? Stronger Ss* could describe scenes: *They're dancing, eating a lot of food, enjoying the reception.* Finally, ask *What do you think of the wedding? Is it the same/different to your country? How?* Ss discuss the questions in groups and feed back to the class.

Optional extra activity
The discussion above would also provide a basis for project work: weddings in my country/other countries.

speakout a special occasion

5A Check the instructions and elicit examples. Avoid weddings if you think the topic has been covered adequately. If you have a *multilingual class*, Ss from the same country/region might want to work together. Monitor and notice what kind of language Ss are using/problems they're having but don't help much at this stage. Ss will rework their notes in Ex D below.

B Write *Hogmanay* on the board and ask Ss what they know about it. If no one knows, then Ss look at the pictures and try to guess. Teach *shortbread, coal, duster* – but don't sing *Auld Lang Syne* yet … it's on the CD! Play the CD and follow procedures for listening.

Answers: 1 D 2 C 3 A 4 B

C Play the CD. Ss tick the **key phrases** and then compare their answers. In feedback, elicit the phrases and encourage Ss to add details they remember about Hogmanay. You could also play the CD again while Ss read the script.

Answers: ✓ happens in (Scotland) on (New Year's Day); on the day before we always (clean the house); We also have a special custom; I like it because

D It's important to give Ss time to look at their notes again and think about where/how they can use the **key phrases**, e.g. *I want to talk about Christmas in Hungary.* Monitor and support Ss while they do this. However, during the fluency activity which follows, monitor at a distance making notes on examples of good language and problems, especially with the **key phrases**, for feedback later.

Unit 3 Recording 10

M=Man W=Woman
W: What's a special occasion in your country?
M: Hogmanay.
W: Hog … er … man …?
M: Hog-man-ay. **Let me tell you about it.** OK … Hogmanay happens in Scotland on New Year's Day. In our families, **on the day before** Hogmanay, **we always** clean the house – all day –because it's important to start the New Year in a clean house. Then, in the evening, we usually have a big party with friends and family. At midnight we stand in a circle, join hands, sing 'Auld Lang Syne', you know. 'Should auld acquaintance be forgot.' I think people sing this in a lot of countries now. **We also have a special custom.** After midnight, the first person who visits the house gives presents to the family, usually shortbread or coal. This brings good luck. Then we eat and drink. The party often goes on all night. **I like it because** all our friends and family come together and it's a great start to the New Year!

writeback an invitation

6A Ask *Do you send/get invitations like this?* Discuss with the class. Ss then do the task. Check new language in feedback, e.g *RSVP (répondez s'il vous plaît* meaning 'please respond').

Answers: 1 A New Year party. 2 At 16A Abbey Street in Dublin. 3 On Saturday 31st December at 8p.m.

B Ss can write an invitation for the same occasion they talked about in Ex 5, or choose a new one. They can write it alone or in pairs. If you have computer facilities in your school, Ss could find an invitation site, write their invitation and print it out. They could also add drawings/pictures. Monitor and provide support to those who need it.

C To help Ss write their replies/emails, write this framework on the board:

Hi _____,
Thank you very much for your invitation to _____ on
_____.
I'd love to come. OR I'm sorry I can't come because
_____.
Do you want me to bring anything?
See you soon.
_____

Ss copy it and complete it with their replies. Monitor and check the accuracy of their writing. Ss then give their replies back to the Ss who invited them.

Homework ideas
• Ss write about a special celebration in their country/another country using information from Ex 5.
• Workbook Ex 4, p19

LOOKBACK

Introduction

As well as ideas mentioned in previous **Lookback** sections, the exercises here can be used for revision after the relevant lesson. They can of course also be used as a revision lesson at the end of each unit. The key is to vary the way the exercises are exploited in order to fulfil their original purpose – communicative practice.

SUPPLEMENTARY MATERIALS

Extra activity after Ex 5C: prepare the prompts for the mingling activity

PERSONALITY

1A Make this into a race. The first student to write all the correct answers wins.

> **Answers:** 2 talkative – quiet 3 friendly – unfriendly
> 4 serious – funny 5 kind – unkind

B Read and check the example with Ss and drill the responses *I agree. I don't agree.* Monitor and assess Ss' use of the adjectives, and provide new ones they might need. *Weaker Ss* could refer back to p28 if necessary. Pairs could then join with another pair and compare their opinions. Take notes on Ss' problems and do a correction slot in feedback.

> **Possible answers:** 1 doctor: friendly 2 parent: kind,
> intelligent 3 TV presenter: interesting, friendly, serious
> (depending on the programme)

C Put Ss in pairs and monitor while they work, noting problems with meaning, spelling and pronunciation for a correction slot in feedback.

FREQUENCY ADVERBS

2A Give Ss 1 min to write the adverbs and check in pairs.

> **Answers:** always, usually, often, sometimes, hardly ever,
> never.

B Check the example and position of the adverb. Give Ss 3–4 mins to write their sentences. Monitor and make notes on Ss' accuracy for feedback or assessment purposes. Check how well Ss are positioning the adverbs in their sentences.

C Once again, continue to monitor and make notes for feedback and assessment. In feedback, nominate pairs to tell the class about their similarities and differences.

FAMILY

3A Do an example with Ss. They compete the exercise alone and compare answers. Nominate Ss to come to the board and write the answers with the correct spelling.

> **Answers:** 1 grandfather 2 nephew 3 niece 4 aunt
> 5 father/uncle 6 parents

B Check the example and give Ss 2 mins to write four sentences alone. Monitor and help *weaker Ss* with spelling and pronunciation. Ss don't have to write true sentences – they can invent them.

C Put Ss in pairs and monitor while they work, noting problems with meaning, spelling and pronunciation for a correction slot in feedback.

HAVE/HAS GOT

4A Check the example and monitor while Ss prepare the questions. Check/Drill them in feedback to prepare for Ex B.

B Do this as a mingling activity. Ss stand and walk around asking/answering the questions. They write the name of the person who answers *yes.* Remind them to use a different name each time. To follow up, Ss work in groups to share their information and write a summary of their findings, e.g. *Naomi and Carla have got a cat.* They could put this information on a poster and display it on the classroom walls for other Ss to read and compare.

MAKING ARRANGEMENTS

5A Ss complete the verbs alone and compare answers. Check them before moving to Ex B.

> **Answers:** 2 go to 3 have 4 watch 5 play

B Elicit one or two examples and where to write them, e.g. *go running, Saturday or Sunday morning.* Give Ss 2 min to complete the diary. Monitor quickly to make sure all Ss are completing the task correctly.

C First, model and drill the example and alternative responses. Repeat the question again and elicit responses from the class, based on their diaries. Then put Ss into groups. They take turns to invite each other. If one Ss says *no,* they can ask another one. If nobody can accept, another Ss takes a turn. Monitor discreetly and make notes on Ss' performance. In feedback, write correct/incorrect sentences on the board. Ss work in pairs to decide which ones are correct and how to correct the mistakes.

> **Optional extra activity**
>
> Before class, write sentences on small pieces of paper, enough for one per student. Mix positive and negative statements like those in Ex 4C on p32, e.g. *I've got a new boyfriend/girlfriend. My dog's not well. It's my birthday today. My car doesn't work. Look! I've got a great new mobile. I've got a fantastic new job. I haven't got any money. My husband/ wife hasn't got a job. My boyfriend/girlfriend's got a job in Australia. My job's really boring. This lesson is quite difficult. I like him but he doesn't like me.*
>
> Demonstrate by reading a statement and eliciting a response, e.g. *I want to come with you but I'm really busy./ My husband's got a new job in New York!* Elicit *That's a shame!/That's fantastic!* with the appropriate intonation and energy. Ss mingle making/responding to the statements energetically!

PUNCTUATION

6A *Weaker Ss* could look back in their book if they need help.

> **Answers:** Hi! Are you free tonight? How about going
> to the TX club? How about meeting/Let's meet at eight
> o'clock outside.

B Collect Ss' replies and mark them.

> **Homework ideas**
> • **Workbook** Review and check 1, p20–21
> • **Workbook** Test 1, p22

OVERVIEW

BBC VIDEO PODCAST

Where do you live?

In this video podcast, people describe the place where they live and discuss what they like and don't like about it. The material extends Ss' descriptive vocabulary around the topics of accommodation, location and society. We recommend using the video podcast as an introduction to the unit or at the end of lesson 4.1 or unit 4 to recycle the language learnt.

SMALL SPACE, BIG STYLE

Introduction

Ss learn/revise the use of *there is/there are* with rooms and furniture. They then practise describing rooms and homes, including their own.

SUPPLEMENTARY MATERIALS

Resource bank p157 and p158

Photo bank p155

Ex 1A: pictures of rooms/furniture (in addition to the ones in the **Photo bank**) to present the vocabulary

Warm up

Lead in to the topic of the lesson. Dictate/Write on the board: *Where do you live; in a house or a flat? Is it big/small? How many rooms has it got? Where is it? Who do you live with? Do you like your home? Why/Why not?* Give Ss 2–3 mins to ask/answer the questions in pairs/small groups. Nominate Ss to describe their partner's houses to the class in feedback.

VOCABULARY   rooms/furniture

1A Ss look at the word webs and the picture of the interior of the microflat. Elicit rooms and furniture Ss know, using the vocabulary in the word webs, e.g. *bedroom* and *bed*. With *weaker classes*, teach the rooms and furniture vocabulary with your own pictures if you have some. Ss then tick the things they need in a flat. To avoid a situation where they say they need everything, tell them to make two lists: a) basics b) extras.

B Monitor closely while Ss compare their lists: check how well they're using the target language. In feedback, check *shelf* and *shelves*. Ss can copy the word webs into their notebooks and add to them later.

C Ss underline the words in their word webs as they listen, and check in pairs before repeating. In feedback, check the stress of each word again. Make sure Ss correct any words they've underlined wrongly.

Teaching tip

Use finger highlighting to correct/drill problem words. Hold up one hand in a fist. Open one finger for each syllable, e.g. di-ning-room. Ask *Where's the stress?* Elicit Ss' answers and show it with the first finger *di*.

Answers:

rooms: living room, kitchen, dining room, bathroom, balcony, bedroom, hall.

furniture: sofa, cupboard, armchair, lamp, wardrobe, shelf, desk, television

D Monitor closely again and do remedial work in feedback if needed. In a *mixed ability class*, put *weaker Ss* together so that you can provide more support.

▶ PHOTOBANK p155

The vocabulary here builds on what Ss have just practised. If you are short of time, Ss can do the exercises at home, using dictionaries to check. N.B. The photos can be used for later exercises in the lesson, describing rooms with *there is/are*.

1A In feedback, check answers, using finger highlighting to elicit the word stress.

Answers: 1 D 2 D 3 C 4 E 5 A 6 F 7 C 8 B 9 H 10 G 11 C 12 C

B

Answers: a) table b) desk c) rug d) sink e) cupboard f) lamp g) sofa h) plant i) armchair j) carpet k) washbasin l) bath m) shower n) bed o) wardrobe

2 Make this activity into a competition to vary the pace of the class. Give Ss another 30 seconds to check their lists in pairs. The winners are the pair with the most (correctly spelt) answers.

speakout TIP

This helps Ss to constantly review new words together with the items they represent – and remember them more easily. Check in the next lesson how many Ss have tried it.

LISTENING

Culture notes

Microflats were first launched in London in 2002, designed by architects Stuart Piercy and Richard Conner. The concept was based on the tiny 'pods' in overcrowded Tokyo where people have lived since the 1970s, and from traditional yacht design, where every inch of space is used.

The development of microflats has grown in response to the demand for cheap accommodation for young people, particularly students, young professionals and 'keyworkers' like teachers and nurses, who can't afford to buy or rent a flat of their own in large expensive cities.

2A Ss first look at the photo and check what *microflats* are. Ask *How big are they? How many rooms have they got?* In feedback, check new words, e.g. *high quality, available.*

Answers: 1 students, teachers, police officers, doctors, nurses 2 In the city centre 3 No, they aren't. 4 a bedroom, a bathroom, a kitchen, a living room and a balcony; a bed, a wardrobe, a table, a chair, a shower, cupboards, a cooker, a table, chairs, a sofa and a TV

B Follow procedures for listening. A *strong class* can check their answers in the audio script at the back of the book.

Answers: 2 living room 3 kitchen 4 bedroom 5 bathroom 6 balcony

C Play the CD again. Ss listen and compare their answers. In feedback, check the answers. Then ask Ss *Do you like the microflat? Why/Why not?*

Answers:
likes: the balcony
dislikes: everything else!

Unit 4 Recording 2

M=Man W=Woman

W: Hi! It's me.
M: Hi, Mum! Come on in.
W: Here, I brought you a plant. A small plant for your microflat!
M: Thanks, it's great! I'll put it here on the dining room table.
W: Oh, so this is the dining room.
M: Yes, well, this is where I eat.
W: There are only two chairs? It's good your father isn't here.
M: Mum, it's a microflat. There isn't a lot of furniture.
W: It's very … sweet. Now, is there a living room?
M: Well, there isn't a separate living room. This *is* the living room. Just here.
W: Oh, I see. Yes, there's a sofa and a TV … yes, it *is* a living room.
M: And here's the kitchen.
W: Oh, I see, three rooms in one – the dining room, the living room and the kitchen.
M: Mum, it's a microflat.
W: Is there a bedroom? Or do you sleep on the sofa?
M: Of course there's a bedroom. Come through here.
W: Yes.
M: Here it is.
W: This is nice – but there aren't any shelves. Where do you put your things?
M: There's a wardrobe here.
W: Oh, but look, there *is* a bathroom!
M: Mum.
W: … and a toilet!
M: Mum. Listen, do you want a drink? Let's go out to the balcony.
W: The balcony! Is there really a balcony?
M: Of course there's a balcony. It's a microflat.

GRAMMAR *there is/are*

Watch out!

Ss often leave out *there* in *there is* and say, e.g. *Is a sofa in the living room.* Or they might translate it from their L1, e.g. *It has a sofa in the living room.* It's important to highlight and check the form clearly, and give plenty of controlled practise and feedback.

3A With a *weaker* or *mixed ability class*, play the CD again: Ss listen and read the audio script. When they've completed the table, check the concept: we use *there is/are* to say something 'exists' in a place. Check further using objects in the classroom, e.g. *There's a table. Is there a cupboard?* Ss could then underline examples of *there is/there are* in the audio script (all underlined).

Answers: are, 's, aren't, there

B Write *there's a* and *there are* on the board with the phrases in phonemics under each one. Underline the weak /ə/ at the end of both phrases. Ss then listen and repeat the sentences from Ex 3A. Play the CD as many times as necessary to build Ss' confidence.

⟫⟫ **LANGUAGEBANK** 4.1 p134–5

Recheck the form and use of the target language if necessary. With a *weaker class* who need more controlled practice, do Ex A and B.

> **Answers:**
> A 2 There are four chairs in the living room. 3 There are two bedrooms in my flat. 4 There isn't a sofa in my living room. 5 There's a bathroom upstairs. 6 There aren't any shelves in the bedroom.
> B 1 are there 2 Is there 3 are there 4 Is there 5 Is there 6 are there

PRACTICE

4 Introduce and check the email briefly first. Ask e.g. *Who's the email to/from? How many rooms does the flat have? How many DVDs/DVD players has he got? Which floor is the flat on?* Give Ss 1 min to read and find the answers. Check new language: *wireless broadband, top floor, neighbours, loud music, how big is it? Fast finishers* could write questions to ask in feedback, e.g. *How many bedrooms are there? Is there a DVD player? Are there any neighbours?* In feedback, build on the *fast finisher* questions if you have them, in preparation for Ex 5.

> **Answers:** 2 There's 3 there's 4 There's 5 there are 6 There's 7 There isn't 8 there are 9 there aren't

5 Elicit and drill sample questions using the prompts. Give Ss time to prepare their questions. Make notes of their problems with the target language. In feedback, do a correction slot.

> **Teaching tip**
> Correction slots can be used for feedback or as warm ups in the next lesson. They're a very important part of the learning/teaching process: they tell you what Ss need help with. Write 4–6 sentences on the board. Include both correct and incorrect sentences that you note while monitoring. Ss correct the errors alone/in pairs. Then do feedback again.

WRITING commas

6A Ss check their answers in the email above. Point out that in a sentence with a list of more than two things, commas are essential to understanding.

> **Answers:** Sentence 2 is correct because there are commas between each item on the list, except the last one after *and*.

B In feedback, Ss write two sentences (with two or three nouns) about their homes. In feedback, invite Ss to write them on the board.

> **Answers:** 1 There are three bedrooms, two bathrooms and a balcony upstairs. 2 No commas. 3 I get up at 7, have a shower, have breakfast in the kitchen and go to work.

C Write the first sentence from paragraph 2 in the email on the board and use it to elicit information about Ss' homes: *There are … five rooms, two bedrooms, a living room, a kitchen and a bathroom.* (Alternatively, if they're still on the board, use Ss' sentences from Ex B above.) Ss then draft their own email. Monitor and encourage Ss to compare and help each other.

VOCABULARY prepositions

7A Alternatively, you could first present and give controlled practise of the prepositions using classroom objects, e.g. *The book's on the table. The pen's under the book,* etc. Then use the exercise to check further.

> **Answers:** B under C between D behind E next to F above G on H in front of

B Keep to the time limit: this will increase the challenge and raise adrenalin! In feedback, Ss look at the picture again and check their answers in pairs.

> **Answers:** 1 There aren't any books on the shelves. 2 There isn't a TV in the room. 3 There's a table in front of the window. 4 Correct but the chairs are on opposite sides of the table. 5 There's a lamp near the sofa/between the sofa and the table. 6 There's a chair between the door and the armchair.

C Elicit and write an example with Ss. Then give them 2–3 mins to write their sentences. Monitor and help Ss with accuracy and spelling.

D Ss correct each other's sentences, using the picture as a reference. As a follow up, Ss describe one of the rooms on p155. Their partner has to guess which room they're describing.

SPEAKING

8A Give Ss 3 mins to decide on their favourite room. They should use a piece of paper large enough to draw the furniture in.

B First, demonstrate the activity. Ss should face each other and not show the outline plans to each other. Monitor and take notes on examples of correct/incorrect language for a correction slot in the warm up for the next lesson.

> **Homework ideas**
> - Ss write an email about their homes. Suggest using the one in Ex 4 as a model.
> - Photo bank Ex 1A–C, p54
> - Language bank 4.1 Ex A–B, p135
> - Workbook Ex 1A–5B, p23–24

AN ENGLISH VILLAGE?

Introduction

Ss learn/revise *can* for possibility, places in towns and more prepositions. They then practise describing places in their own towns/cities.

SUPPLEMENTARY MATERIALS

Resource bank p159

Warm up: photocopy the feedback activity if required (see notes below)

Ex 2: pictures/photos of places in a town: theatre, museum, town hall, pharmacy, etc

Ex 6: a map of your area

Ex 8: Prepare a webquest – see details in Ex 8

Warm up

Feedback on fluency activity game

Use 6–7 examples of sentences containing good language and errors Ss made in Ex 8 on p39, e.g. *There's table under the window.* Write them on the board, or use an OHP or photocopies. Check the first sentence with Ss. Ask *Is it correct/incorrect?* Incorrect. Ask *Why?* Because it's *There's a table …* Give Ss 3–4 mins to work in pairs/teams to decide a) which sentences are incorrect and b) how to correct them. Check Ss' answers. Pairs/Teams get 1 point for getting a) right, and 2 points for b).

READING

1A Create interest in the topic and text. Ask *Do you live in a village, a town or a city? Does it have a supermarket/cinema? Do you like it? Why/Why not?* Elicit answers and other places Ss might know, e.g. *cinema, café, supermarket, bank, post office.* Write them on the board. Ss then look at the picture in their books. Ask *Where do you think it is?* Elicit Ss' answers. Then give them 1 min to read the article and check. In feedback, check where South Korea is.

Answers: An English village in South Korea.

B Check *buildings* in question 3. Ss then read and answer the questions before comparing answers. In feedback, check answers. With **strong classes**, elicit what sort of buildings an English village might have, e.g. *post office, shop, school.*

Answers: 1 South Korean students. 2 English teachers from Britain, the USA and Australia. 3 All the same buildings as a typical village in England. 4 Because it easy to do English activities all day.

C Elicit one or two answers before Ss discuss the questions. In feedback, elicit Ss' reasons to the board in two columns: *Yes* and *No*. You could follow on with more questions, e.g. *Is there a place like this in your country? Would you like to go to a place like this?*

VOCABULARY places in towns

2A Use your own pictures to present the vocabulary if you have them. Briefly check the use of *can* (this is dealt with next exercise) in the sentences: *it's possible to.* You might also need to teach/check vocabulary in the sentences: *post a letter, medicine, Shakespeare plays, history, mayor.* Monitor closely. Ss listen and check their answers.

B In feedback, check/drill the pronunciation. Use finger highlighting to show the stressed syllable and prepare Ss for the next exercise.

Answers: 2 <u>su</u>permarket 3 <u>ci</u>nema 4 <u>phar</u>macy 5 <u>the</u>atre 6 <u>sports</u> centre 7 mu<u>se</u>um 8 <u>school</u> 9 <u>bank</u> 10 town <u>hall</u>

C Ss then check their answers in pairs before feedback. Then invite them to write their underlined words on the board. Correct any mistakes. Ss can then copy the words into their notebooks.

3 Ss can do this in small groups. If Ss need a change of pace, elicit their answers in open class.

speakout TIP

Elicit places from Ex 2A which are in Ss' own villages/towns. Tell them to practise this tip on their way home today and tell you what they saw in the next lesson.

GRAMMAR *can* for possibility

Watch out!

As with all modal verbs, Ss often try to use **can** with the auxiliary *do*, e.g. *Do you can …* or use the full infinitive: *You can to buy …* Pick up on the problem early on: highlight the form clearly and correct the errors consistently.

4A Ss will be familiar with *can* from Ex 2 and should find this exercise straightforward.

Answer: possible

B Ss look at Ex 2A again to complete the table and check their answers in pairs. Point out that *can't* is the contracted form of *cannot*.

Answers: can, can't

C Write *can* and *can't* on the board. If you have a phonemic chart available, use it here – or direct Ss to the phonemic symbols to the front of the **Student's book**. Model/Drill the two words in isolation.

Teaching tip

Clearly demonstrating individual sounds can be very helpful for Ss, particularly if they are high-frequency sounds. Open your mouth and drop your jaw for /ɑː/ saying 'ah' as if you were at the doctor's. Close your mouth almost completely and make a small sound in your throat for /ə/. The unstressed 'schwa' sound /ə/ as in /kən/ is very common in English. It's extremely useful for Ss to know as it helps their pronunciation of both single words and connected speech sound much more natural.

Ss listen and repeat the sentences in feedback.

Answers: 1 unstressed 2 stressed

D Follow procedures for listening. Play the CD again if Ss have doubts.

Answers: 1 + 2 – 3 ? 4 ? 5 – 6 +

E Drill the sentences further, highlighting the pronunciation of *can* and *can't* if needed. Pay particular attention to the unstressed form of *can* /kən/ in the question, and the stressed forms *can* /kæn/ and *can't* /kɑːnt/ in short answers.

Unit 4 Recording 7

1 You can post a letter with UK stamps.
2 You can't play American football.
3 Can you buy medicine?
4 Can you change money?
5 You can't go to a French class.
6 You can speak English all day!

> ⟶ **LANGUAGEBANK** 4.2 p134–5
>
> Recheck the meaning and form. Highlight the fact that we use *can/can't* + verb (without *to*) with all persons.
>
> > **Answers:**
> > A 2 Can you play tennis there? 3 Can you smoke there? 4 Can you take your dog there? 5 Can you listen to music there?
> > B At the seaside hotel ... 2 you can play tennis. 3 you can't smoke 4 you can't take your dog. 5 you can't listen to music.
> > At the beach apartment ... 6 you can cook. 7 you can't play tennis. 8 you can't smoke. 9 you can take your dog. 10 you can listen to music.

PRACTICE

5A Check the example. Monitor closely while Ss write to check their accuracy and provide support to those who need it. *Fast finishers* can write more sentences.

B Tell Ss not to show their books to each other. Again, monitor closely to sort out any problems that arise. With a *mixed ability class*, put *stronger* and *weaker Ss* in separate pairs.

C First, drill the example question and *yes/no* answers in open and closed pairs.

VOCABULARY prepositions

6A With *weaker classes*, first present and practise the prepositions using the classroom, e.g. *My desk is opposite the door.* Convey and check the difference between the meaning of *opposite* and *in front of* clearly. In feedback, drill the prepositions chorally and individually. Highlight the main stress if necessary.

> **Answers:** A next to B on the left of C in front of D near E opposite F on the right

B Introduce the map. Ask *Where's the bank and pharmacy?* Check/Teach *swimming pool, tennis courts, park.* Elicit where Ss are on the map (You are here).

C Tell Ss that they are on the red spot: *You are here.* Play the CD, pausing after each sentence to give Ss time to write the places. They then compare answers. Remind Ss they are on the red spot. Play the CD again if they still have doubts. In feedback, elicit and drill the sentences. N.B. The audio reveals some of the places. The following exercise will reveal the rest.

> **Answers:** See the audio script below.

Unit 4 Recording 8

1 The supermarket is opposite the bank.
2 The cinema is on the right of the bank.
3 The post office is on the left of the supermarket and opposite the cinema.
4 The sports centre is near the post office.

D Divide the class into As and Bs. As work together in pairs, and Bs do the same. They each look at the relevant page and decide where the places should be written on the map. Monitor to help Ss if necessary. Then put Ss into A/B pairs, facing each other and not showing their maps to their partners. With a *weaker class*, drill the question *Where's the museum/school?* In feedback, check the position of the four places as below.

> **Answers:**
> A The museum is on the left of the pharmacy. The theatre is next to the museum.
> B The school is opposite the pharmacy. The park is behind the sports centre.

> **Optional activity**
> If you've brought maps of your area, Ss can describe where places are in pairs/3s, e.g. *The ABC cinema's here in Kings street, next to the sandwich bar.*

SPEAKING

7A If you have a *monolingual class*, brainstorm some places first. If there are Ss who have the same favourite place, they could prepare together. In *mixed ability classes*, weaker Ss could work together so that you can provide extra help. In the next exercise they can then join different groups.

B Ss work in small groups. Monitor discreetly and take notes of their performance.

> **Teaching tip**
> In fluency activities, it's not a good idea to interrupt Ss while they talk: they might become self-conscious and be afraid to speak in case they make mistakes.

In feedback, invite volunteers to briefly tell the class about one of their group's favourite places.

> **Optional extra activity**
> If you have computer facilities in your school, Ss could do a webquest. Before class, do an internet search of the interesting places in your town and make a note of the web link(s). Write 8–10 simple comprehension questions about the places you find. They could be *Wh-* questions or true/false questions.
>
> In the computer class, give Ss the web link and a copy of the questions. They work alone/in pairs/3s, depending on the facilities. Give them a time limit and check answers at the end.

> **Homework ideas**
> • Ss write a description of their favourite place in town, or partner's favourite place (if it's a different town).
> • Language bank 4.2 Ex A–B, p135
> • Workbook Ex 1A–5B, p25–26

CAN I HELP YOU?

Introduction

Ss learn and practise the names of shops and how to buy things in them. They also learn one of the most useful aspects of shopping: saying *no* politely.

SUPPLEMENTARY MATERIALS

Resource bank p160

Photo bank p156

Ex 1–2: pictures (or realia) of some things you can buy in a clothes shop, sports shop, electronic shop or bookshop

Warm up

Revision of prepositions: picture dictation

Draw the street plan below on the board but with only *cinema* filled in:

post office	bank	cinema	pharmacy	theatre
		Main Street		
town hall	café	museum	sports centre	supermarket

Then dictate the position of the other places, e.g. *The bank is on the left of the cinema. The café is opposite the bank.* Ss write the places in the correct spaces. In feedback, nominate Ss to come to the board. The class tells him/her where to write the names, e.g. *The pharmacy is on the right of the cinema.*

VOCABULARY things to buy

1A First, create interest and activate vocabulary Ss already know. Ss look at the photos. Ask *Where are the people? What kind of shops are they in?* If Ss know the present continuous, ask *What are the people doing/buying?* Ss can then discuss questions 1 and 2. Before they do question 3, check the vocabulary items by eliciting examples of each type, e.g. *clothes: jeans, trainers, tops, shoes.* **Weaker Ss** could give the trade names of shops if they don't know what type of shop it is. However, you could then teach/drill the name of each shop in feedback: *clothes shop, supermarket, bookshop,* etc.

B Give Ss 2 mins to write their lists. *Stronger Ss* could check them in the **Photo bank** on p156. Otherwise, elicit Ss' lists and write them on the board, or nominate Ss to come to the board and write their lists. Check meaning/pronunciation before moving on to the **Photo bank**.

> ⮞ **PHOTOBANK** p156
>
> **1** Ss work in pairs and match the photos. Check meaning/ pronunciation. Ask *What can you buy in this shop?*
>
> **Answers:** 1 B 2 L 3 E 4 F 5 G 6 I 7 H 8 M 9 J 10 K 11 D 12 N 13 C 14 A

2A Ss work alone and check in pairs. Ask them to try to pronounce and underline the stressed syllable in each word. They'll check their answers in the next exercise.

B Play the CD and allow Ss to repeat the words as many times as necessary. They can also correct any mistakes with their underlining.

Answers:
clothes shop: jeans, T-shirt, sweater
sports shop: swimming costume, trainers, football shirt
electronics shop: blank DVD, headphones, memory stick, battery
bookshop: paperback book, magazine, dictionary

C Give Ss 1 min to do this. *Fast finishers* can write more words. Check them all in feedback.

D *Weaker Ss* could use the **Photo bank** photos to help them, but covering the names of the shops. Give Ss extra practice by changing partners or doing a mingling activity to change the pace/interaction.

FUNCTION shopping

3A Before starting, remind Ss that they only need to focus on key information and not get distracted by unknown language. With *stronger classes*, you might find they've already written the prices, too. If so, check them and move to Ex 3C.

Answers: 3 battery 4 dictionary 5 trainers

B Remind Ss of how to say prices in English. Look back at p13 in the Student's book if necessary.

Answers: 2) 19.99 3) 8.99 4) 6.99 5) €120

Unit 4 Recording 10

A=Assistant C=Customer

Conversation 1
A: Can I help you?
C: No, thanks. I'm just looking.

Conversation 2
A: Can I help you?
C: Yes, how much is that?
A: 19.99.
C: OK. Where are the changing rooms?
A: Over there, next to the mirrors.
C: Thanks.
A: How is it?
C: Hmm. **It's too small. Have you got it in large?**
A: Sorry, no.
C: Mmm. **It's not big enough.** No, it isn't right. Thanks anyway.
A: No problem.

Conversation 3
C: Uhhh … Excuse me.
A: Yes, can I help you?
C: I need one of these for my camera. This one's dead.
A: Let's see. What type is that?
C: Uhh … let's see, the number is DLK-760.
A: Here you are. That's **8.99.**
C: That's fine. I'll take it.

Conversation 4
C: Excuse me?
A: Yes, can I help you?
C: Yes, how much is this?
A: Uh, let's see … it's 22.95.
C: Have you got it in paperback?

A: Er, yes, I think so. Here. It's **6.99**.

C: Oh good, but this is English–English. Have you got an English–Arabic one?

A: No, I'm sorry, we haven't.

C: All right. I'll have this one. The paperback.

Conversation 5

A: Can I help you?

C: Yes, can I try these trainers?

A: What size are you?

C: Thirty-eight.

A: These are size thirty-eight. How are they?

C: Yes … urm … good, thanks. How much are they?

A: **One hundred and twenty euros.** Would you like to buy them?

C: One hundred and twenty? Er … I'm not sure. I need to think about it. Thanks.

A: Fine. No problem.

C Guide Ss if necessary to the correct place in the audio script and play the CD again for these conversations. Ss listen, read and complete the gaps. Teach/Check the useful vocabulary: *changing rooms, mirrors*. In feedback, teach/check the meaning of *too small* and *not big enough*. Demonstrate with other examples: try to lift the table and say/elicit *It's too heavy. I'm not strong enough*. Model and drill the sentences. At this point, Ss could look at the first two tables in the **Language bank**, on p132. Or use the information there to check the concept of *too* and *not enough*. Then elicit/drill other words that could replace *large* in question 1, e.g. *small, medium, extra large, green, blue, paperback*. Finally, check/drill *I'll take it. It's the same as I'll have/buy it.*

Answers: 2 small 3 big 4 take

Optional extra activity

Stronger classes rehearse and act out one of the other conversations on the audio script. Teach/Check new language, e.g. *Can I try these trainers?*

D This exercise checks understanding of the language in Ex 3C. Ss do it alone and check in pairs.

Answers: 1 expensive 2 have 3 medium 4 long enough

⟹ LANGUAGEBANK 4.3 p132–3

Check the tables and notes in section 4.3. Ss could do Ex A now if they need more controlled practice before moving on; otherwise they can do it at home.

Answers: Have you got, in 2 Have you got, in 3 not, enough 4 How much 5 expensive

Culture notes

A comparison between British and European clothes sizes:

Men's clothes

British	36	38	40	42	44	46
European	46	48	51	54	56	59

Women's clothes

British	10	12	14	16	18	20
European	38	40	42	44	46	48

4A Ss now prepare for a role-play. First, check what type of sizes Ss are familiar with as they tend to vary from one country to another. Then Ss write the sentences. Monitor and do feedback to check for accuracy.

Answers: Have you got this sweater in size 42? Oh, it's too big. Have you got it in size 40? Have you got it in black? That's not big enough. I'll have the grey one.

B Ss rehearse and memorise the conversation together while you monitor and help. If necessary, play conversation 2 again and ask Ss to listen and repeat to build their confidence.

C Ss could change partners for this activity. To make it more realistic, ask them to stand up and imagine they're in a shop. *Stronger Ss* can do the role-play several times with different partners, using a different item, size, colour, etc each time.

LEARN TO say *no* politely in a shop

5A Do the first response as an example: *No, thanks. I'm just looking.* Ask *What do you say in your country? Is it the same/different?* Ss work alone/in pairs, and check their answers in the next exercise.

B When Ss repeat, listen carefully and correct their intonation if necessary.

Answers: 1 No, thanks. I'm just looking. 2 No, it isn't right. Thanks anyway. 3 I'm not sure. I need to think about it.

6 Ss do the same role-play except for the last line. Read and check the **speakout tip**, then give them time to prepare/decide what they're going to say. Invite Ss to act out their conversation to the class. Give feedback on their performance as required.

SPEAKING

7A First, Ss A look at p162 and check the instructions. Ss B do the same on this page. Check the meaning of *swimming costume*. Ss A write their prices for the items on p162, while Ss B prepare their questions, e.g. *Good morning. Have you got any trainers? How much are they?* etc, using the items here. Drill a sample question and answer before Ss work together. Tell Ss A to start with *Good morning. Can I help you?* Make notes on their performance for feedback later. N.B. Ss could put a really high price on some things so the customer might not buy them and has to say *no* politely.

B Ss now change roles. Ss B are the shop assistants and Ss A are the customers. Check the meaning of *blank CDs*. Ss A prepare their questions while Ss B write their prices. Then while Ss do the role-play, monitor and make notes on their performance. In feedback, invite Ss to act out their conversations to the class. Then give feedback and do any necessary remedial work.

Homework ideas

- Ss write a dialogue based on the role-play in Ex 6/7.
- Language bank 4.3 Ex A, p135
- Workbook Ex 1A–3, p27

FAVOURITE PLACES

Introduction

In this lesson Ss practise the four skills in the context of favourite places. They first watch a BBC TV travel programme about five of the top tourist destinations in the world. They then learn how to describe their own favourite places.

SUPPLEMENTARY MATERIALS

Warm up and Ex 1A: a map of the world

Warm up

Create interest in the lesson: spend about 10 mins on this lead in. Show/Give Ss a map of the world. Ask *What's the number 1 place to visit in the world?* Give Ss 1 min to decide and make notes/think about their reasons. They then talk about their place in pairs/3s and show their partners where it is on the map. They should give reasons for their choices if possible. In feedback, elicit Ss' answers and write the five most popular number 1 places on the board. Leave the list on the board to refer back to later.

DVD PREVIEW

1A Ss look at the photos and name them. Elicit places Ss know and teach the locations of the others using your own map if you have one. Drill the pronunciation of the place names but don't reveal too much information about the places yet because this will be covered in Ex 1B.

Answers: A Bangkok, Thailand B Cape Town, South Africa C Paris, France D the Masai Mara, Kenya E The Grand Canyon, USA

Culture notes

Bangkok is the capital of **Thailand**. 95% of the population is Buddhist and there are many beautiful temples to visit.

Cape Town is a city in the south of South Africa. It is famous for its unusual shaped mountain called Table Mountain.

Masai Mara is a national game reserve in the southwest of Kenya, and named after the famous African tribe, the Masai (or Massai).

Paris is considered to be the most romantic city in the world, especially the walks along the banks of the River Seine.

The Grand Canyon has almost 5 million visitors a year. It's 277 miles (446 km) long, from 4 to 18 miles (6.4 to 29 km) wide, and its deepest point is over a mile (1.83 km).

B Read and check new language in the sentences using the photos here: *romantic, art galleries, views, temples, awesome.* There's a photo of *elephants* in one of the photos: Ss will see the other animals in the DVD. Ss work alone and check in pairs. In feedback, check Ss' answers. If they know any of these places, elicit opinions/details of what they know briefly; more information will be revealed when they watch the DVD.

Answers: 2 B 3 A 4 E 5 D

2 Check the questions before Ss read the text. Give them 2–3 mins to do the exercise and discuss their number one place, giving reasons if they can. Ss work alone and check in pairs. Elicit, but don't confirm, their answers until they watch the DVD in Ex 3A.

► DVD VIEW

3A Remind Ss to concentrate on checking their answers from Ex 2 and not worry if they don't understand everything. Play the DVD. Ss watch and then compare their answers. If they still have doubts, play the DVD again. Give *stronger Ss* another task, e.g. *count the number of all the famous places you recognise/see.*

Answers: 1 Fifty 2 The Grand Canyon is number one.

B First, Ss read the sentences. Check/Teach the meaning of essential vocabulary: *huge, wide-open freedom, warmth, sky, sunset, cried.* Remind Ss to listen carefully for the correct word in each sentence, in italics. After watching, Ss check their answers in pairs. If they still have doubts, play the relevant sections of the DVD again. Give *stronger Ss* another task, e.g. *write one interesting thing in each place.* In feedback, check Ss' answers (see the underlined sentences in the audio script). Then refer back to the five places on the board from the warm up activity. Ask *Are any of the places on the DVD on your list? Do you think the Grand Canyon is the number one place? Is it awesome?* Have a brief discussion but don't prolong it as Ss will discuss this further in Ex 3C.

Answers: 1 need 2 open, sky 3 expensive 4 cheap 5 cried (answers in bold in the audio script)

C Check the rubric. Refer back to the places on the DVD and the five places on the board from the warm up. Ask *Do you still think these are the five number 1 places to visit?* Emphasise that now Ss have to decide on five places they *both* want to visit. As a starting point, Ss could write their own list and then compare it with their partner's. Give a time limit of 5 min. They have to keep suggesting places until they both agree on five. Each pair then writes the places on a piece of paper and puts it on the board/walls. Ss get up and read the lists to see how similar/different they are to theirs. Finally, discuss the lists and decide what the three most popular places are and why.

DVD 3 50 Places To See Before You Die

VO=Voiceover M=Marc W1=1st woman W2=2nd woman
W1=3rd woman JL=Joanna Lumley EH=Eamonn Holmes
LS=Lucy Sassoon AF=Alex Fraser M1=1st man
JP=John Palmer MJ=Melanie Jones

VO: There are so many amazing places to see around the world. Here are some of your favourites.
Welcome to Bangkok! With over 6 million people it's big, it's busy, and you love it! It's very good for shopping and the nightlife is great, too.

M: It's got lots of clubs, bars, shops, food … Everything you need, really.

VO: There are 400 temples in Bangkok, so Bangkok is an important place for Buddhists around the world and tourists love to visit the temples, too.

VO: You also love the Masai Mara in Kenya. It's a fantastic place to watch animals: zebras, elephants, antelope, hippos and lions. You can see them all. So, why is it so special?

JL: Huge open spaces, fantastic animals, just wide open freedom, warmth, friendliness, and all underneath the great African sky.

VO: Now a popular, romantic city ... the city of lights, Paris.

W1: <u>To me, Paris is elegant, romantic and expensive.</u>

W2: Go in the spring and enjoy the art galleries.

VO: And enjoy the views of the city from the top of the Eiffel Tower.

VO: Back to Africa now, South Africa. Yes, it's Cape Town. And behind Cape Town is the 1,000 metre high Table Mountain, with its fantastic views.

EH: Cape Town is one of my top three places on Earth.

W3: <u>Friendly people, loads of beaches and the food is unbelievably cheap.</u>

M1: We went there over New Year and it was lovely. I mean, just a lovely, lovely place.

EH: Great place, Cape Town.

VO: You love the mountains and beaches that make Cape Town so special. And these little guys – the penguins.

VO: This is the big moment: the number one place to see before you die. Your favourite is ... the Grand Canyon! The Grand Canyon is an amazing place. You can read about the Grand Canyon and you can look at photographs and videos, but nothing can prepare you for the real thing.

AF: There's so much to see that you never stop seeing something new.

JP: The colours are just so ... amazing

MJ: With every changing inch of the sunset, the colours in the canyon change.

LS: <u>I remember actually sitting there ... and I just cried.</u>

VO: But there's only one word that everyone says when they talk about the Grand Canyon.

Voices: It really is awesome ... Just completely awesome ... Awesome ... 'Awesome' is the word ... It was awesome ... Awesome ... Awesome ... 'Awesome''s the only word ... Truly awesome.

speakout a favourite place

4A Check the instructions and elicit examples. If you have a *multilingual class*, Ss from the same country/region might want to work together. Monitor and notice what problems Ss are having but don't help much at this stage. Ss will work on their notes again in Ex 4C.

B Write *Lake Titicaca* on the board. Ask *What do you know about it?* If no one does, ask *What would you like to know about it?* Elicit questions and write them on the board, e.g. *Where is it?* Play the CD. Ss listen for the answers to their questions. Check them in feedback. Then read the **key phrases**. Ss listen again and check their answers in pairs before feedback. You could also play the CD again while Ss read the script, to help them with Ex 4C.

> **Answers:** Tick all sentences except *I like it because it's ...* (see the underlined sentences in the audio script).

Unit 4 Recording 12

<u>One of my favourite places in the world is</u> Lake Titicaca. It's between Bolivia and Peru and is, urm, about 4,000 metres above sea level. The water is always very, very cold. <u>I go there every year</u> with my family and we stay in a small town near the lake. <u>When I'm there I usually</u> go out on the lake in a boat, and sometimes I visit one of the small islands. Sometimes there are big waves on the lake, but it's usually very quiet. So why do I like the lake? Well, I love its deep blue colour and <u>it's a great place to</u> relax.

C First, elicit some examples based on Ss' notes in Ex 4A, and the audio script above. Use the **key phrases**, e.g. *One of my favourite places is ...* Give Ss time to look at their notes again alone to think about where/how they can use the **key phrases**. Monitor and support them while they do this. In feedback, invite volunteers to tell the class about their favourite places.

writeback a description

5A First, give Ss 1–2 mins to read the model text and answer this question: *Who is the writer? What's his/her favourite place?* Then elicit answers to the class. Check the instructions and the meaning of *childhood*, *smell*. Ss check in pairs/3s before feedback.

> **Answers:** a) 3 b) 1 c) 2

B Ss use their notes from Ex 4 and the text in Ex 5 to help them write the first draft of their description. Monitor and provide support to those who need it. Also encourage them to show their drafts to other Ss to ask advice and build confidence.

> **Homework ideas**
> * Ss write a description of their favourite places, using the draft copy and notes from Ex 4/5.

LOOKBACK

Introduction

As well as providing communicative practice and revision activities, the **Lookback** exercises are designed to help you assess your Ss progress with the language they've learnt in the unit. The assessment is largely informal, as in monitoring and giving feedback on Ss' errors. This allows you to identify what Ss are having problems with and clarify them. However, you could also focus on individual Ss while they work on these activities and compare their performance with their results in more formal tests. Ss often perform better when they are not in a formal testing situation.

FURNITURE AND ROOMS

1A Ss do this activity alone and compare their answers. Tell them not to look back in their books while they do this. N.B. To change the pace of the class, you could make the exercise more competitive: the first pair to finish, and get all the correct answers, wins.

Answers: 1 armchair 2 bed 3 cupboard 4 shelves 5 sofa 6 wardrobe 7 lamp 8 desk

Optional extra activity
Ss work in pairs/teams. Give them 2–3 mins to look back in their books and prepare 8 more room/furniture words in the same way – without the vowels. They should write them on a piece of paper. Collect the papers when they've finished and redistribute them. The pairs/teams have to write the words correctly. Again, the first ones to finish, and get all the correct answers, win.

B Ss do this exercise alone. If necessary, use your own house as an example and put the sentence on the board as an extra model. *Weaker Ss* could look back in their books if they're not sure. Monitor closely to help and check they are writing the correct words.

C Monitor and check/drill their answers in feedback.

PLACES IN TOWNS

2 Check the meaning of *secret message* and the *hint*. Also check/teach new language in the phrases: *medicine, get (buy) some fruit,* and *get (have) a haircut.* Then do the first word as an example. You could make this activity more competitive in the same way as suggested in Ex 1.

Answers: 1 internet café 2 sports shop 3 pharmacy 4 greengrocer's 5 hairdresser's 6 bakers 7 supermarket 8 bookshop 9 electronics shop 10 clothes shop 11 dry cleaner's Secret message: no more money

THERE IS/THERE ARE AND PREPOSITIONS

3A Do an example with Ss. They then do the activity alone. In feedback, invite volunteers to come to the board and draw the picture.

B Tell Ss not to show their books to other Ss while they do the exercise.

C First, model and drill the example question and answer. Remind Ss they need to use prepositions here. Ss face each other in pairs. Tell them not to show their pictures to their partners. Monitor closely to assess how well Ss are using the prepositions and give feedback if necessary.

CAN FOR POSSIBILITY

4A Do the first question as an example. Then ask Ss to work alone while you monitor to assess how well they're using the question form. Check/Drill Ss' answers and give feedback as necessary.

Answers: 1 Where can I buy a battery for my camera? 2 Where can I smoke? 3 How can I say 'beautiful' in Italian? 4 Where can they watch the football match? 5 Can my friend come to the lesson? 6 What can we do in the sports centre?

B Ss do this exercise alone. Again, monitor and check/drill their answers in feedback.

C Monitor while Ss work and make sure they're taking it in turns to ask the questions. *Fast finishers* can give their own prompts: their partners have to think of the correct questions. Do feedback in open pairs across the class. Give feedback on problems Ss had with *can*, prepositions and other vocabulary.

SHOPPING

5A Ss could do this alone and check their answers in their books. Check/Drill the answers in feedback and do remedial teaching if necessary.

Answers: 1 Have you got *these* shoes in size 36? 2 They aren't *big enough.* 3 Have you got *them in* size 34? 4 How much *are they?* 5 That's too expensive. 6 *I'll* take them. 7 No, *it's* all right. Thanks anyway. 8 I'm not sure. I need *to* think about it.

B Ss could work with a different partner if appropriate. Point out that the sentences they choose will affect whether the customer buys the item or not. While Ss write their conversation, monitor and take notes on the writing ability of each individual student, if possible.

Teaching tip
Use this to assess their writing skills in terms of accuracy and add the information to your class assessment records.

C While Ss do the role-play, monitor and take notes on their speaking skills.

Teaching tip
Once again, use this to assess Ss' speaking skills in terms of accuracy and add the information to the records.

OVERVIEW

B|B|C **VIDEO PODCAST**

What's your favourite dish?

In this video podcast, people describe their favourite kind of food and a favourite dish. They also talk about their favourite place to eat and why they like it. The material consolidates and extends Ss' food and 'eating out' vocabulary in a fun, authentic way. The video podcast could work well as an introduction to the unit or at the end of the unit to recap/recycle the key vocabulary and language learnt.

MYFRIDGE.COM

Introduction

Ss learn/revise countable and uncountable nouns for food and drink and their containers; *some*, *any* and quantifiers. They learn and practise how to order a meal in a restaurant.

> **SUPPLEMENTARY MATERIALS**
>
> Resource bank p161 and p162
>
> Photo bank p157
>
> **Warm up:** write the sentences from the text on separate pieces of paper: one set for each group of Ss
>
> **Ex 2:** pictures of food/drink items (or realia)

Warm up

Introduction to the topic of the lesson: student dictation

Before class, write/print out each sentence separately from the text below. There are eleven sentences but the first one is the example.

> *Hi, I'm Susan.* I'm from Australia and Australians love barbecues. We have them in our gardens and on the beach. We have special places for barbecues in the parks, too. We always invite lots of people to our barbecues. We cook the burgers and fish. Our friends and family bring other things. They bring salads, beer, cola and fruit. We usually have barbecues in the afternoon. We talk and listen to music … and eat! It's great!

In class, put Ss into groups of 5–10, and ask them to stand up if possible. Give each student one or two sentences from the dialogue, *not* in the right order. Ss practise saying their sentence(s) to themselves. Provide help with pronunciation and vocabulary. Each student then reads out their sentence(s) to the group. Ss move around to stand (or sit) in the right order in their group. They may have to read out their sentences several times until they can do this. Ss then read out their sentences in the correct order. Ask them to do this several times until they can say it at normal speed, without looking at their papers if possible. As a follow up, Ss can dictate the sentences to each other in their groups, or you can hand out a photocopy for them to check it themselves. N.B. This activity can be used for any text. It works particularly well with narratives.

VOCABULARY food/drink

1A Lead in with a brief discussion. Ask Ss *What's your favourite food? What food/drink do you love/hate?* If you have pictures of food/drink items, use them here as prompts. Teach/Check and drill new words. Before Ss do the exercise, check *fridge* and *vegetarian*. Ask *What can you put in a fridge? Do vegetarians eat meat?* Monitor and notice how well they use food and drink vocabulary. In feedback, ask *stronger classes* to justify their answers. This will give you an idea of how well they can use *some* and *any*. N.B. Ss might be confused because of the *hot dog* in the vegetarian fridge, A. This is deliberate (see audio script). For the time being, ask *Do vegetarians eat hot dogs? Why is there a hot dog in fridge A?* Ss can speculate about this.

Answers: 1a) B b) A c) C 2 Ss' own answers.

2A With a *weaker class*, use the pictures here to present the nouns, or use your own pictures/realia. With a *mixed ability class*, put *stronger* and *weaker Ss* together to do the activity: the former can help the latter. In *strong classes*, Ss do the exercise alone and check their answers in pairs. Check/Drill pronunciation in feedback.

Answers:
Fridge A: carrots, water, a cucumber, yoghurt, cheese, milk, a hot dog
Fridge B: banana, cola, butter, bread, leftovers
Fridge C: apple, chicken, sardines, wine, grapes, fruit juice

B First, check the headings and elicit an example for each. Ss then complete the table alone, or in pairs. Tell them to write the table in their notebooks as a written record. In feedback, recheck the meaning/pronunciation of each word. Ss can underline the stress in words of more than one syllable.

Answers:
meat: a hot dog
fish: sardines
fruit: a banana, an apple, grapes
vegetables: carrots, a cucumber
drink: milk, cola, water, wine, fruit juice
other: butter, bread, yoghurt, leftovers, cheese

C Demonstrate the activity and then put Ss into pairs. Monitor closely: make a note of problems with meaning and/or pronunciation for feedback.

⤷ PHOTOBANK p157

1A–B With a *weaker class*, check Ss' understanding using the pictures. Otherwise, Ss work alone/in pairs to do the exercise. In feedback, check answers and use finger highlighting to elicit the main stress. Ss can then add the new words to their word tables from Ex B above.

Answers: 1–7 C, 8 U, 9–11 C, 12 U, 13–15 C, 16–25 U, 26 C

GRAMMAR countable and uncountable nouns

Watch out!

Many languages don't distinguish between countable and uncountable nouns and Ss tend to translate from their L1. It's important to clarify the difference and give sufficient controlled practice. Correct Ss, and encourage them to self-correct whenever possible to prevent fossilisation (i.e. becoming a habit which is difficult to change.)

3A With a *weaker class*, teach the concept of countable and uncountable. Show a picture of eggs for example. Ask *How many eggs are there? Six.* Ask *Can you count them? Yes. Are they singular or plural? Both.* Then do the same with butter. Ask *Can you count butter? No. Is it singular or plural? It's never plural – always singular.* Ss might want to argue that containers are countable items, e.g. *a packet of butter.* If so, tell them that containers are countable but they'll study this in the next lesson. With a *strong* or *mixed ability class*, you could check the examples and concept, then put *stronger* and *weaker Ss* together to discuss their answers.

Optional extra activity
Before Ss check their answers in Ex 3B, write the table on the board. Ss take it turns to add words to each column. They can dispute their classmates' answers but don't confirm the correct answers yet.

B Ss listen and check their answers. Recheck the rules: ask *Can you count it/them? Singular or plural?* and point out that uncountable nouns don't usually end with *-s*. Play the CD as many times as necessary to build Ss' confidence.

Answers:
countable singular nouns: an apple, a cucumber, a hot dog
countable plural nouns: carrots, sardines, grapes, leftovers
uncountable nouns: cola, chicken, butter, water, bread, wine, yoghurt, cheese, fruit juice
Leftovers: always plural.

⤷ LANGUAGEBANK 5.1 p136–7

Read and check the *first* section of 5.1 with Ss if necessary. *Stronger Ss* could read it at home. *Weaker classes* should do Ex A in class.

Answers: A 1 chicken 2 fruit 3 sardines 4 wine 5 meat 6 butter, margarine 7 sugar

PRACTICE

4A First, do an example to check understanding of task type. Ss then work alone and check in pairs before feedback.

Answers: 1 cheese 2 hot dogs 3 eggs 4 fruit 5 milk 6 vegetables

B Elicit Ss' answers for the first sentence. Give them 2 mins to write their sentences. Monitor closely and help with accuracy before Ss check in pairs. In feedback, invite Ss to tell the class about their answers, e.g. *Juan loves cheese but I don't.*

speakout TIP

Read the tip with Ss and ask them to write C or U next to the words in their table from Ex 1B. Ss can then add five more words to the table from the **Photo bank**.

LISTENING

5A You could first do a prediction activity. Write *Luis, Amy, Mike* on the board in three columns. Ss look at the photos. Ask, e.g. *Where are they from? Which is Luis/Amy/Mike's fridge? Why?* Encourage Ss to argue and justify their predictions. Write them on the board, e.g. *Luis – fridge B. He's a vegetarian.* Ss then listen and check their predictions. In feedback, elicit the correct answers. Find out how many Ss predicted the answers correctly. N.B. Prediction activities like this can be used with both listening and reading texts.

Answers: 1 C 2 A 3 B

B Ss need to understand specific parts of the audio script. You may need to play these sections (underlined in the audio script) more than once. In feedback, Ss could speculate about why these things are/aren't in the fridges.

Answers: 1 Carmen's birthday cake isn't in the fridge.
2 There's a hot dog in Amy's fridge but she's a vegetarian.
3 There's a banana in the fridge but Mike doesn't eat fruit.

Unit 5 Recording 2

1 Hi. My name's Luis, from Spain. Welcome to my fridge! What have we got here? Well, there's some chicken and some fish – some sardines. They're for the barbecue tonight. It's my wife Carmen's birthday. And we've got some fruit: grapes and an apple. And of course, the baby's milk. And we've got some wine and some fruit juice for the barbecue. And at the back there's a … oh no! Where is it? Carmen! Where's your birthday cake?

2 Hi, I'm Amy. I'm from Canada and I'm a vegetarian. And this is my fridge! On the top shelf I have some cheese, yeah, lots of cheese and a cucumber. And I've got some carrots. I love carrots! And on the next shelf, I've got some eggs and some yoghurt. Of course, I haven't got any meat. Hey, what's this? Look, a hotdog! Why is this here? And here I've got a bottle of water and lots of milk.

3 Hi, everyone. I'm Mike and I'm Australian. So, this is my fridge. Er … I've got some leftovers from … er from last week. And I've got lots of cola and … oh look, a banana – why's that in the fridge? I don't eat fruit. And there's some bread, it's quite old, and some butter, yup, that's very old. Well, that's me! I don't go shopping a lot. I usually eat at the university.

GRAMMAR nouns with *a/an, some, any*

6A Ss are familiar with the use of *a* and *an* and learnt that *any* is used in questions in Unit 4. They could therefore discuss the answers in pairs and then listen and check. In feedback, ask, e.g. *Why is it some cheese but any meat?* Because cheese is uncountable/the verb is negative.

Answers: some, a, some, any

B Do an example. Ss then complete the table alone and check in pairs. In feedback, elicit and check Ss' answers, e.g. *Why is it an apple?* Because it's countable/singular. (see the **Language bank** for help with this). It's also important to point out that *any* is used in negatives and questions. Tell Ss this will be practised in Ex 7C.

Answers: an, a; some, any; some, any

Optional extra activity
Ss read the audio script and underline examples of *a* and *an*, *some, any* used there.

⟹ LANGUAGEBANK 5.1 p136–7

If necessary read the *second* part of 5.1 with Ss to recap on the rules, including the fact that *any* is used with negatives and questions. The last point is important but you could leave it until p52–53, where Ss will learn how to use *some* in requests/offers.

Answers:
B B some chocolate C a banana D an orange
E a sandwich F some cheese G some biscuits
H some yoghurt I a cucumber J some fruit juice
K a chicken L some milk
C 1 any 2 Is, any 3 a 4 any 5 's 6 Is, any 7 some

PRACTICE

7A Read the title and give Ss 1 min to read the text first. Check/Teach *fresh (fish) grill, alcohol, lettuce, salad, raw (onions)*. Ss complete the text and compare answers. In feedback, check the rules for each answer.

Answers: 2 some 3 some 4 a 5 any 6 some 7 a
8 some 9 any 10 a

B Ss can choose any items from this page or the **Photo bank** on p157.

C Model and drill the example dialogue in open and closed pairs. Then give Ss 2–3 mins to talk. The student with the most correct answers wins. *Fast finishers* can choose more items to ask/answer.

SPEAKING

8A Elicit example answers for question 1. Monitor discreetly while Ss work and prompt them to self-correct if necessary.

B Do the example first. Monitor discreetly while Ss talk, making notes of any problems with new language to focus on later. In feedback, ask each group how similar their eating habits are.

Optional extra activity
Ss write sentences about their group's eating habits, e.g. *For breakfast, two people sometimes have cereal and we all drink coffee.*

Homework ideas
• Ss take a photo of their fridges and write a description of its contents. They can add the photo to their texts.
• Language bank 5.1 Ex A–C, p137
• Workbook Ex 1A–7, p28–29

A LIFETIME IN NUMBERS

Introduction

Ss learn quantifiers and practise them in a very informative and entertaining context. They then learn how to paragraph their own writing.

SUPPLEMENTARY MATERIALS

Resource bank p163

Ex 1B: realia: bring food and drink containers

Warm up

Revision of *a/some/any* in 5.1: memory game

Divide the class into half (or 4 groups). Give Ss the beginning of the sentence: *In my lunch bag there's some bread.* They then take it in turns to repeat the sentence and add another item, e.g. *In my lunch bag, there's some bread and an apple. In my lunch bag, there's some bread, an apple and some cheese*, etc. If Ss make a mistake, they're out of the game. The others continue until only the winner is left.

VOCABULARY containers

1A If you've brought some containers to class, use them to present the new language, e.g. *a bottle, a can*. Ss can then do Ex 1A and B afterwards. Otherwise use the pictures here. Elicit words Ss know, e.g. *water, biscuits* and teach new ones: *beans, jam, chocolate, toothpaste*.

Answers: A chocolate B coffee C biscuits D baked beans E toilet paper F milk G mineral water H tea I toothpaste J jam K rice

B Use the pictures to elicit words Ss know and teach/drill new ones. Then model the complete phrase, e.g. *a tin of beans, a bag of rice*. Highlight the linking between the final consonant of the container word and *of*, e.g. a bottle of = /əˈbɒtləv/. Drill the phrases chorally and individually to prepare Ss for the next exercise.

Answers: B mug C packet D can/tin E roll F carton G bottle H cup I tube J jar K bag

C Model and drill the example before Ss work in pairs. Monitor closely and prompt Ss to self-correct if they make mistakes. Give further feedback after the exercise if necessary.

Optional extra activity

Use the pictures of fridges on p48 and the **Photo bank** on p157. Give Ss 3 mins to find six new examples of containers or food/drink that comes in a container, e.g. *carton of fruit juice/yoghurt, bottle of cola/wine/oil, packet of crisps/pasta/cereal/sausages, bag of sugar.*

READING

2A If you have a *weaker class*, present the numbers on the board. Write *100* (one hundred) and *1,000* (one thousand), and model/drill them. Then drill *150* and *1,500*. Highlight the fact that *hundred* is followed by *and* (one hundred *and* fifty) but *thousand* isn't (one thousand, five hundred). Ss can then do the exercise in pairs. *Stronger classes* can do the exercise in pairs.

B Monitor closely to check how well Ss are doing. After they've listened and checked the answers, play the CD again. Ss listen and repeat the numbers.

Answers: 1 four and a half 2 twenty-one 3 sixty-one 4 eight hundred and forty-five 5 one thousand, two hundred 6 four thousand, three hundred 7 ten thousand 8 thirty-five thousand 9 sixty thousand 10 seventy-five thousand

3A If you have a *weaker* or *mixed ability class*, do a pre-task for the text. Ask Ss to look at the introduction to the text but cover the rest of it. Read out the questions and check *average* and *lifetime*. Put Ss in pairs/3s and give them 2–3 mins to look at the pictures in Ex 1A. They write their opinions using the numbers in Ex 2A, e.g. *chocolate: 10,000 bars*. Ss compare answers with another pair/group. In feedback, ask how similar their guesses were. Give Ss 2 mins to read the complete text and underline the food and drink words from the pictures in Ex 1A. In feedback, check their answers. Teach important words: *sheep, chickens* (countable), *cows, weight, cookies* (Am Eng for biscuits). Ss then complete the article with the numbers.

B After Ss have compared their answers, play the CD. Stop at each gap to give Ss time to write the correct answer if they got it wrong. Replay the CD if necessary. In feedback, ask who got the most correct answers. Discuss which answers were interesting/surprising/amusing.

Answers: 1) 21 2) 1,200 3) 4½ 4) 845 5) 35,000 6) 10,000 7) 60,000 8) 75,000 9) 61 10) 4,300

C Elicit some sample answers. Then give Ss 3–4 mins to discuss the questions in pairs. In feedback, ask what the most popular food and drink in your class are.

GRAMMAR *how much/many*; quantifiers

4A When Ss have completed the sentences, elicit the answers and write the two questions on the board.

Answers: 1 How much 2 How many

B Ss underline the correct answers and check in pairs. In feedback, point to the questions on the board and ask *Which noun is countable/uncountable?* Elicit the answers and draw a box around *cookies* and *food* on the board.

Answers: 1 uncountable 2 countable

Watch out!

Ss tend to overuse *many* rather than *a lot* and *lots of*, in positive statements mainly because of L1 interference. Check and correct this problem consistently to prevent early fossilisation.

C Do the first example with the class as they may not know *none* (= not one). Ss then work alone and check their answers in pairs. In feedback, ask *How many biscuits are there on each plate?* and elicit Ss' answers.

Teaching tip

To illustrate quantifiers with uncountable nouns, use bottles / glasses of water. Alternatively, draw four uncountable items on the board, e.g. 1) an empty bottle 2) a bottle with a little water 3) a bottle three quarters full 4) an almost full bottle Then ask *How much water is there in 1/2/3/4?* Elicit/Teach *none, not much, quite a lot, a lot/lots* and write the words under each bottle. Ask Ss *Which one is different?* Not much. *Why?* Because water is uncountable.

At this stage, it would be useful to draw the *Quantifiers* table from the **Language bank** (p136). Leave the right-hand column empty. Elicit the correct quantifiers and write them in the column. Ss copy the table down.

Answers: A none B not many C quite a lot D a lot/lots

➠ LANGUAGEBANK 5.2 p136–7

Check the notes and table if you haven't done so yet. *Stronger classes* could read the notes at home. *Weaker Ss* should do Ex A and B in class.

A Check *omelette* in question 4.

Answers: 1 How much 2 How many 3 How much 4 How many 5 How many 6 How many

B First, Ss look at the picture; check the use of *no* + noun versus *none*, e.g. *There are <u>no children</u> in the picture. There are <u>none</u>.*

Answers: 2 are no 3 is quite a lot of 4 are lots of/a lot of 5 is no 6 is lots of/a lot of

PRACTICE

5A First, teach *laugh, shampoo, make friends*, then do the example. Ss do the exercise alone and check in pairs. In feedback, check which answers are countable or uncountable, e.g. *How much milk* = uncountable. Also drill some of the questions if necessary, to prepare Ss for Ex 5C.

Answers: 2 much 3 much 4 many 5 many 6 many 7 much 8 many

B Check *about* and *over* on p161–162. Demonstrate the meaning with your hands/facial gestures. Monitor while Ss read the answers and give help where necessary.

C Check and drill the example first. The tone of the quiz is very light-hearted: reassure Ss that they're not expected to know the correct answers. In feedback, recheck the answers and discuss which facts surprised them.

Answers: 1 About 300 times. 2 7,500 litres. 3 200 bottles. 4 About 7,000. 5 About 15 times. 6 1,700. 7 Over 270 tubes. 8 About 2,000.

SPEAKING

6A First, check and drill the example. Ask Ss the same questions and elicit answers, making sure they use quantifiers and an extra piece of information. Ss then complete their own answers in the table. Monitor and help where necessary. Put Ss in small groups. Ss take it in turns to ask one student a question, and the group writes the answer in the table. Monitor discreetly and make notes of how well Ss are using quantifiers. Give feedback on this later.

B First, check *good diet* and *healthy lifestyle*. Then read the example and elicit Ss' opinions of their partners. Make sure they give reasons, using the information in their tables. Give Ss 4–5 mins for the activity. Again, make notes to add to those you made in Ex A. In feedback, invite *stronger Ss* to tell the class about their partners. Give feedback on their performance now or in the next lesson.

WRITING paragraphs

7A Tell Ss what the aim of this section is. Check *topic (the subject)* and *sweet food*. Ss then work alone and check their answers in pairs. In feedback, elicit reasons for each answer.

Answers: 1 b) 2 d) 3 c) 4 a)

B With *weaker classes*, you may have to do this exercise with the Ss. Otherwise, Ss work alone/in pairs before feedback.

Answers: sentences, one, paragraph

C Remind Ss to look for different topics as this will tell them where new paragraphs start. In feedback, check the answers. Elicit the topics of the four paragraphs: the introduction, exercise, diet, where to find more information.

Answers: 1st paragraph ends with … *some people do!* 2nd paragraph ends with … *2.5 litres of water a day!* 3rd paragraph ends with … *not so healthy as we think!*

D First, write two sentence prompts on the board: *I think X (a Ss name) has a good diet because …* *I don't think Y (a SS name) has a healthy lifestyle because …* Elicit some opinions from Ss, e.g. *I don't think Cedric has a very healthy lifestyle because he doesn't eat fruit or vegetables and he never does any exercise.* Put Ss together in the same group as in Ex 5A. They then work alone to write a draft report but should show/check each other's drafts. Monitor closely and prompt Ss to self-correct/rewrite a sentence if necessary.

Optional extra activity

If you have computer facilities in your school, find and check out a healthy living website. If you think it's appropriate for your Ss' age group/interests, they could use it to create/do a questionnaire about their diet and lifestyle.

Homework ideas

- Ss write the final draft of the report from Ex 6D, p51.
- Language bank 5.2 Ex A–B, p137
- Workbook Ex 1–6B, p30–31

ARE YOU READY TO ORDER?

Introduction

Ss learn and practise how to order food in a restaurant. They also learn about the way words are linked in spoken English, which helps them understand fast speech.

SUPPLEMENTARY MATERIALS

Resource bank p164

Ex 7: realia for role-play, e.g. simple menus

Warm up

Revision of food and drink: in the hot seat

Divide the class into two groups: A and B. Put a chair in front of the board. A student from group A sits there, facing the class. Write the name of an item of food/drink eaten or container used in restaurants, on the board behind the student, e.g. *bottle of wine, fish*. Student A can then asks his team ten *yes/no* questions to guess the word, e.g. *Can you eat/drink it? Is it countable/uncountable? Is it a vegetable/healthy?* Student 1 gets a point for the correct answer. Then group B has a turn. The team with the most points wins. N.B. This activity can be used with any lexical set.

VOCABULARY   restaurant words

1A First, look at the photos and ask e.g. *What can you see?* Teach/Check the difference between a 'good' restaurant, a fast food restaurant and a café. Ask *What kind of food can you eat in each one?* Elicit types of food that Ss know. Also use the photos to teach/check *waiter/waitress, customer, chef, to serve food/drinks*. This will be useful for Ex 2. Then give Ss 2 mins to discuss the questions. Monitor to see if they need more time.

B Reorganise Ss to compare their ideas. *Fast finishers* could recommend other places they know to the others.

2 With a *strong* or *mixed ability class*, Ss read the words on the left and cover the definitions. In pairs, they define words they know and then check. Otherwise, elicit words Ss know, e.g. *waiter/waitress, menu, chef*. Ss then match the others. In feedback, check/drill the answers. Write useful new phrases on the board, e.g. *ask for the menu, order food/drinks, a special dish, give a tip, pay the bill*. Tell Ss to write them in their vocabulary notebooks.

Answers: 1 d) 2 e) 3 c) 4 a) 5 f) 6 g) 7 b)

FUNCTION   ordering in a restaurant

3A First, elicit things people say in restaurants. Ss know simple requests so could say, e.g. *Can I see the menu/have the bill, please?* Check the example and new words in the exercise: *ready, eat in, takeaway, fries*, or do this later in feedback. Give Ss 3 mins to work alone and compare their answers. In feedback, elicit Ss' reasons for their answers, e.g. *it's polite/informal, fast food not restaurant food*, etc.

Answers: b) FF c) R d) R e) FF f) FF g) R h) FF i) FF j) R k) R/FF

B With *strong classes*, you could add: *What kind of restaurant is it?* Ss listen and check their answers in pairs. Play the CD again if necessary. In feedback, play the phrases again for Ss to repeat. (see answers in bold in the audio script)

Answers: a), d), g), j)

C Ss do this alone/in pairs before listening again. Alternatively, they can listen and read the audio script at the same time and underline the phrases.

Answers: 1 j) 2 a) 3 g) 4 d)

Unit 5 Recording 6

Wa=Waiter M=Man W=Woman

Wa: Good evening. A table for two?

M: Yes, please.

Wa: By the window?

M: That's fine.

Wa: Can I take your coats?

M/W: Thank you.

Wa: **Would you like something to drink?**

W: Er … yes, please. Could I have an orange juice?

M: And I'd like a cola, please. And can we have a bottle of mineral water?

Wa: Certainly. The menu …

M: Thank you.

Wa: **Tonight's special is** Chicken á la Chef de Saint Germaine de Paris Rive Gauche.

W: What's that?

Wa: It's grilled chicken with potatoes and green beans.

W: Is it French?

Wa: Not really …

W: But it has a French name.

Wa: Well, that's true … it's very good.

Wa: **Are you ready to order?**

M: Yes, I'd like some soup and the special.

W: The same for me, please.

Wa: Thank you.

4A *Stronger classes* could try to complete the phrases before they hear the CD and compare answers in pairs. In feedback, check *soup*. Explain that *Can/Could I …* have the same function (requests) though *could* is often seen to be more polite.

Answers: 1 I have, juice 2 we have, bottle, water 3 I'd, soup 4 same, me

B Ss listen and check their answers. In feedback, teach *grilled (chicken)*. If your Ss understand French, ask them why the name of the special dish is amusing.

Answers: soup and the special (grilled chicken with potatoes and green beans)

⇒ **LANGUAGEBANK** 5.3 p136–7

Check/Drill the requests and responses in open and closed pairs. *Weaker classes* can do Ex A now.

Answers: 1 Can/Could, please 2 'd like 3 would, like 4 Can/Could 5 Would, like 6 I'd

---

Optional extra activity

To help Ss prepare for Ex 5B, play the CD again. Ss listen and repeat the requests. Replay the CD until Ss can hear and reproduce the polite intonation.

5A Check the example and give a 2-min time limit. In feedback, model/drill each sentence, highlighting the stress and intonation.

> **Answers:** B: Yes, *can/could* we have two … B: *We'd* like the fish and … A: Would you like *any* vegetables? B: *Can/ Could* I have some carrots … C: The same *for* me, please.

B Give Ss time to work alone and rehearse the conversation. Monitor closely, helping with their pronunciation. *Fast finishers* can memorise the dialogue, and act it out to the class later.

6A Play the first two sentences and elicit the answers from the class. Ask Ss *What's the difference?* Elicit answers. N.B. In the first request, the voice is flat and sounds rude. In the second, the voice has a wider range and rises/falls on the stressed word *orange*, which makes it sound friendly and polite. In feedback, play the CD again to prepare Ss for Ex 6B. Ss listen and repeat the polite requests, and try making the impolite ones sound polite.

> **Answers:** 1 Could I have an orange juice? (impolite) 2 Could I have an orange juice? (polite) 3 Can we have a bottle of mineral water, please? (polite) 4 Can we have a bottle of mineral water, please? (impolite) 5 I'd like some soup, please. (polite) 6 I'd like some soup, please. (impolite) 7 The same for me. (impolite) 8 The same for me. (polite)

B Put Ss in pairs and check instructions: elicit a polite/ impolite request. While Ss work, monitor closely and notice Ss' stress and intonation. In feedback, help Ss to improve their voice range: tell them to stand up and sit down when they say the stressed word.

SPEAKING

7A If you've brought some simple menus to class, use them here if you have a *weaker class*. Either way, first, check any new vocabulary in the menus, e.g. *melon, roast lamb, seasonal.* Alternatively, Ss could use dictionaries if they have them.

> **Teaching tip**
> When you want to exploit the language in a text in more depth, split the class into groups, and number them 1, 2, 3 etc. Each student looks up new vocabulary in one part of the text(s) and then 'teaches' the others. For the menus here, Ss work in groups of 4. Each one looks up new words in one half of the two menus.

Then Ss work in pairs to answer the questions. They can use their imaginations about the special dishes! (They'll find out what they are in Ex B and C.) In feedback, have a brief discussion of Ss' answers.

B Ss now prepare for a restaurant role-play. Put them into A/B pairs and check the example dialogue so that the aim of the role-play is clear. Then Ss A look at menu A and decide what they will order while Ss B look at the information on p162, an explanation of the today's specials. Help Ss B with any vocabulary they need, e.g. *beef.* With *weaker classes*, Ss A could first work together in pairs to discuss their choices, while Ss B practise reading out the explanations of the specials in pairs. For the role-play itself, Ss B could stand up with a notebook, etc. as if in a restaurant. Tell Ss A to decide what to order after the explanations. Monitor discreetly while Ss talk, making notes of good and problematic language/ pronunciation for feedback later.

C Ss change roles. Follow the same suggestions as above. *Fast finishers* could do the role-play again with different partners. In feedback, invite pairs to act out their conversations to the class. Give feedback as required.

LEARN TO understand fast speech

8A First, look at the pictures and check the vocabulary: *hamburger, cola, fries, small, medium, large.* Ask *What's the name of hamburgers in local fast food restaurants?* e.g. *Big Mac, Giant Whopper.* Tell them the hamburger here is called a *Jackpot Special.* Ss listen and check their answers in pairs. In feedback, ask *How does the man speak?* Very fast!

> **Answer:** picture B

B Ss listen again and tick the phrases from Ex 3A. In pairs, they check their answers and could then order them.

> **Answers:** h), e), i), b), k)

Unit 5 Recording 9

A: Afternoon, what can I get you?
B: Uhhh … the Jackpot special, please.
A: Is that eat in or takeaway?
B: Take away.
A: Large fries with that?
B: No, medium …
A: Something to drink?
B: A cola.
A: Small, medium or large?
B: Small.
A: Anything else?
B: No thanks.
A: That'll be 9.95.
B: OK.

speakout TIP

Read the tip and write the example sentences on the board and draw the link between consonants/vowels. Model/Drill the phrases. You could also underline the stressed words: *evening* and *much*. Ss copy the phrases down.

C Check the example. It would be useful if Ss write the fast food phrases in their notebooks first, leaving space for the linking/underlining. Ss could work alone/in pairs.

D When Ss have listened and checked, invite them to write the phrases on the board. Other Ss suggest corrections if they disagree. Play the CD again if necessary. Ss then listen and repeat the phrases.

> **Answers:** Small, medium or large? Is that eat in or takeaway? Anything else? Thanks. Have a nice day!

E This is a light-hearted exercise to finish the class with. Ss should underline the stressed words and link consonants/ vowels first. Help them with this as needed. In feedback, Ss compete to see how fast they can say the same sentence.

> **Homework ideas**
> - Ss write a conversation based on the dialogue in Ex 5A and the role-play, Ex 7B–C.
> - Language bank 5.3 Ex A, p137
> - Workbook Ex 1–3C, p32

A CHEF IN GOA

Introduction

In this lesson, Ss meet the famous English chef, Rick Stein on the DVD. He presents a BBC TV food series and this programme takes place in Goa, India. Ss learn about the local food and how to cook fresh fish. Finally, they learn and practise how to describe and write a recipe of their choice.

SUPPLEMENTARY MATERIALS

Warm up: a map of India and/or Goa

Ex 4: authentic, simple recipes

Warm up

Create interest in the DVD programme and topic: spend about 10 mins on this lead in.

Culture notes

Goa is on the West coast of India and was formerly a Portuguese colony. Its tropical climate, beautiful beaches, charming colonial architecture and delicious food have made it an extremely popular tourist destination.

Rick Stein is a very successful English chef with a passion for seafood. He owns four restaurants in Cornwall which specialise in fish dishes from all over the world. Rick Stein has become a household name as a TV presenter, and has written and presented over a dozen cookery series for BBC TV, including *Seafood Odyssey*.

First, look at the photos on p54–55. Ask *Do you know this man? Where is he? Why do you think he's famous?* Elicit Ss' answers. Encourage them to speculate. Don't tell Ss the answers as they will cover this in Ex 1B. Show a map of India and ask, e.g. *What do you know about places in India?* Elicit/Show Ss where the places are on the map including Goa and look at the background photo. Ask *What do you think this area of India is like? Would you like to go there?* Discuss Ss' answers. Then move on to the topic of food. Ask *Do you like Indian food/curry? Why/Why not? Do you like any other foreign food?* Elicit and discuss Ss' answers. Write any useful new vocabulary on the board.

▶ DVD PREVIEW

1A Check the questions and elicit some initial answers before Ss discuss them in pairs. Monitor closely and provide any new words Ss need while they talk, e.g. *picnic, barbecue.* Discuss answers with the class. Again, teach/check words Ss want to use and write them on the board if they're useful. If *seafood* isn't mentioned, introduce/teach it here for the text in Ex 1B.

Teaching tip

It's a good idea to draw a column on the right-hand side of the board at the start of the lesson. Use it to write up new words/phrases that come up during the class and encourage Ss to copy it down in their vocabulary notebooks at the end of the lesson.

B Check the meaning of the title: *Seafood Odyssey.* Read out the questions and give Ss 1 min to read and answer. N.B. Ss have to find specific key information here. To encourage them not read every word, it's a good idea to give a very short time limit. Tell Ss not to worry about words they don't know. Ss check their answers in pairs, and reread the text if they don't agree. In feedback, elicit Ss' answers and check new vocabulary, e.g. *market.* With *stronger classes*, ask further comprehension questions about the text, e.g. *Where does Rick Stein travel? Why? Who does he talk to? What does he buy/cook in Goa?*

Answers: 1 an English chef 2 seafood 3 Goa

▶ DVD VIEW

2A With *weaker classes*, pre-teach *a washing-up bowl, a pan, spices, a boat* using the photos. *Stronger classes* read the word box but don't check new vocabulary yet: tell Ss they'll see seven of these items in the DVD. Ss watch the DVD and compare answers. Teach/Check new words here. Play the DVD again. Ss could shout *stop!* when they see/hear one of the answers. In feedback, invite any initial comments about the programme – the place, food, the people.

Answers: oil, the sea, a pan, spices, fish, a washing-up bowl

Alternative approach

Put Ss into A/B pairs. Ss A face the TV screen but Ss B sit with their backs to it, so they can hear but not see the DVD. Ss B must do the task. Play the DVD. Ss B then tell Ss A the answers they have. After that, Ss swap places. Play the DVD again. Ss now compare their answers. Monitor to check if they have identified the seven items. If not, play the DVD again with all the Ss watching.

B Give Ss time to read the words in the box and the gapped text. Teach *the best part of* = *almost/about.* Ask *Does he know Goa well?* Also check the words in the glossary. Play the first part of the DVD again up to *incredibly cheap.* Ss write their answers and check them in pairs. If necessary, repeat, stopping at each gap to elicit/check the answers. Ask *Does Rick Stein like the food here? Why?*

Answers: 1 eight 2 food 3 spices 4 vegetables 5 cheap

C With *weaker classes*, play the last part of the DVD (from after he's bought some fish and says *OK. OK.*) to give Ss more support for both Ex 2C and D. Otherwise, play it *after* Ss have done the exercise, stopping at each gap to elicit/check and drill answers (see words in bold in the DVD script). Also teach *flour, lime, salt* (for Ex D).

Answers: A drop B throw in D squeeze E turn over

D Ss should now know all the necessary vocabulary so give them 2 mins to order the instructions. They then compare answers. Don't check them yet – see below.

E Ss watch the last part of the DVD again (from after he's bought some fish and says OK. OK.) and compare their answers. Again, Ss could shout *stop!* at each answer. Round off this part of the class with a class discussion about the programme, what Ss noticed/liked, etc, or play the DVD again for them to watch for pleasure.

Answers: b) 7 c) 5 d) 3 e) 8 f) 4 g) 2 h) 6

DVD 5 Rick Stein's Seafood Odyssey

RS= Rick Stein W= Woman

RS: This is Goa – a place I've known and loved for the best part of eight years. To buy food here is a real joy. The variety of seafood, spices, vegetables is quite staggering and incredibly cheap. I want some of these, these ones. Nice, small fish. What are they?

W: Ah, nice.

RS: Nice, yeah. Fry 'em?

W: Yes.

RS: Yeah.

W: Ten rupees. Ten rupees.

RS: OK. OK.

RS: Have you ever thought what to do about cooking fish on a beach? Well, why don't you try deep frying them? You take a sort of washing-up bowl like this, just **throw** a bit of flour into it, then some salt, some cayenne pepper, some coriander, some cumin and some turmeric. **Throw in** some fish and then **drop** them **in** the pan. Not too many at a time because you don't want the oil to lose its heat but you do want to cook these really crisp. Stir them around in the oil. They're looking real good. **Turn** them **over**. I don't actually know what these fish are called but you could use whitebait. Just let them cook till they're … sort of … hard, till you could almost eat the bones. That'll take about three or four minutes. Take a couple of wedges of lime and you **squeeze** them over the fish. It's really good. There's just one small thing missing … that's an ice-cold beer.

speakout a special dish

3A First, check the instructions and list. Teach/Drill *ingredients, noodles, pepper, soy sauce*.

B Ss work in the same pairs/groups. Give them 4–5 mins to make notes about their dish and its name. Monitor closely and give help where necessary. They could also use the language in Ex 2D.

4A First, read and check the **key phrases** and teach/drill *delicious*. Ss then listen and tick the phrases they hear in order.

B Ss can check their answers in pairs (see answers in bold in audio script). Play the CD again if necessary. Ss can then listen again and read the audio script on p170. Teach the underlined new words, e.g. *heat, mix, celery sticks,* etc. They'll be useful in the following exercises.

Answers: ✓ The name of our dish is, It's very easy to make, you need some prawns, it's delicious, you'll love it!

Unit 5 Recording 11

M=Man W=Woman

W: **The name of our dish is** the Italian special. **It's very easy to make. You need some prawns,** a can of Italian tomatoes, a large onion, a red pepper and two celery sticks – the vegetables need to be cut into small pieces. You also need some pasta, olive oil, black pepper and lots of herbs.

M: You heat the oil in a frying pan and then put all the vegetables in together for about two minutes. Then you throw in the prawns, some black pepper and the tomatoes. Then add the herbs. You cook everything for a minute or two …

W: … and leave to cook slowly. Heat some water in a pan and add the pasta. Cook for three minutes then take the pasta out of the water. Mix with the sauce and then eat our dish with some salad.

M: **It's delicious. You'll love it!**

C Ss can use the audio script above as a model for this activity. Using their notes from Ex 3B, they think about where/how they can use the **key phrases** and the new vocabulary.

It would be useful for them to rehearse what they will say. Monitor and support Ss closely here.

D Ss can either sit or stand in front of the class, and use the board if necessary. Make notes of good language and any problems with the **key phrases**/vocabulary for feedback later.

writeback a recipe

5A Ask: *Do you use recipes? How often? What for?* Elicit and discuss Ss' answers briefly. Ss then read and answer the question in pairs. Check new language in feedback, e.g. *handful, olive oil, immediately.*

B Elicit/Check the meaning of *next* and *then*: they both mean the same but *next* is more commonly used in instructions. (We wouldn't usually say it in normal conversation, e.g. *I get up at 7 and have breakfast. Next I go to work.*) In feedback, elicit answers. Ask *Why can't Then/Next change places with and then?* Because *and then* comes in the middle of a sentence.

Answers: Next, Then

C Ss use their notes from Ex 3B and the text in Ex 4A as a model for the first draft of their description. Monitor and support Ss. Encourage them to show their drafts to other Ss to ask for advice and build confidence. Ss could add drawings/pictures to their text if they like.

Homework ideas
* Ss write a final draft of their special recipes, or another recipe for a typical dish from their country.
* Workbook Ex 4, p32

LOOKBACK

Introduction

Many of the **Lookback** exercises can be used to provide you with an informal assessment of your Ss' speaking skills. Fluency practice is usually given in the last exercise of each section. When assessing speaking skills, four things should be taken into account: accuracy of grammar, range of vocabulary used, fluency and pronunciation.

FOOD

1A *Strong Ss* should do this exercise alone. *Weaker Ss* can refer back to Ex 2A on p48 and the photobank on p157 for help.to find the answers. N.B. Allow this whenever Ss are having problems with a **Lookback** exercise.

Answers: 2 milk 3 cucumber 4 banana 5 ice cream 6 rice

B Check the example. *Weaker Ss* could write their sentences in pairs: this will enable you to provide more help and support if needed. *Fast finishers* can write two more sentences.

C Put *weaker* and *stronger Ss* in separate pairs. Monitor while Ss do this activity and make notes on their performance (accuracy of language, pronunciation and fluency) for feedback, or assessment if required.

NOUNS WITH *A/AN, SOME, ANY*

2A Alternatively, give Ss 2 mins to look at the fridges again and memorise the contents. They then do the exercise and check back afterwards.

Answers: 2 are some 3 aren't any 4 isn't any 5 's a 6 's some

B Ss write their sentences alone. They can refer to the fridges on p48 for reference.

C Monitor while Ss ask/answer the questions. Make notes on their performance for feedback/revision, or assessment if required.

CONTAINERS

3A Give Ss 1 min to do this. The winner is the first person to put up his hand and have all the correct answers. Alternatively, Ss do the exercise alone. *Fast finishers* can write another word snake with food words.

Answers: 1 cup 2 packet 3 bag 4 carton 5 bottle 6 jar 7 tube 8 mug 9 roll 10 can 11 bar 12 tin

B *Fast finishers* add more food and drink words to each container.

Optional extra activity

Ss work first work alone and draw a fridge with three shelves: they write/draw three items of food and drink on each shelf. Put Ss in pairs, facing each other. They then take it in turns to ask *yes/no* questions to find out what's in their partner's fridge, e.g. *Is there a carton of milk? Are there any vegetables?*

Alternatively, Ss draw the fridge/contents as above and describe it to their partner. He/She then draws it. They then compare the two drawings and check if they are the same.

HOW *MUCH/MANY*

4A Monitor closely to check the accuracy of Ss' sentences.

Answers: 2 How much chocolate do you eat every week? 3 How many brothers have you got? 4 How many people are there in your family? 5 How much sugar do you have in your coffee? 6 How much cola do you drink every week? 7 How many rooms are there in your flat/house? 8 How much salt do you like in your food?

B Ss work alone and write their answers down. Tell Ss not to show their answers to their partners at this stage.

C Check instructions carefully. Ss take it in turns to guess the correct question. If one gets it wrong, another has a turn.

IN A RESTAURANT

5A Check the vocabulary in the names of the dishes so that Ss are clear about what sort of dish they can invent. They can refer back to the menus on p53 for ideas.

Possible answers: 1 Roast beef with grilled vegetables and new potatoes. 2 Vegetable soup and pasta with tomato and onion sauce. 3 Cheese, tomato, mushroom and ham pizza with a side salad.

B Give Ss time to prepare for the role-play before putting them in groups. They can take it in turns to be the waiter. Monitor while Ss talk. Make notes on their performance for feedback/revision and assessment if required.

OVERVIEW

6.1 FAVOURITE THINGS
GRAMMAR | *was/were*
VOCABULARY | dates and time phrases
HOW TO | talk about the past

> **COMMON EUROPEAN FRAMEWORK**
> Ss can use simple descriptive language to make brief statements about possessions; can describe personal experiences in simple terms.

6.2 TIME TWINS
GRAMMAR | past simple
VOCABULARY | common verbs
HOW TO | talk about your life

> **COMMON EUROPEAN FRAMEWORK**
> Ss can ask and answer questions about past activities; can write very short, basic descriptions of events, past activities and personal experiences linked with simple connectors like *and*, *but* and *because*.

6.3 HOW WAS YOUR WEEKEND?
FUNCTION | making conversation
VOCABULARY | weekend activities
LEARN TO | keep a conversation going

> **COMMON EUROPEAN FRAMEWORK**
> Ss can give short, basic descriptions of events and activities, e.g. about last weekend; can participate in short conversations in routine contexts on topics of interest; can use simple techniques to start, maintain or end a short conversation.

6.4 CARLOS ACOSTA ⦿ **B B C** DVD
speakout | an interview
writeback | a profile

> **COMMON EUROPEAN FRAMEWORK**
> Ss can answer simple questions and respond to simple statements in an interview; can write short, simple biographies about people.

6.5 LOOKBACK
Communicative revision activities

B B C VIDEO PODCAST
Did you go out last night?

> This video podcast consolidates language around the topic of 'going out' in general and then focuses on what people did 'last night'. As well as plenty of authentic examples of the past simple in context, the material also recycles some useful time phrases. We recommend using the video podcast at the start of the unit to introduce Ss to the unit's topic or at the end of unit 6 as a round up.

FAVOURITE THINGS

Introduction

Ss learn/revise the past tense of *be*, dates and time phrases. They practise the new language in the context of talking about famous celebrities, special national and international days, and their own past.

> **SUPPLEMENTARY MATERIALS**
>
> Resource bank p165 and p166
> 6.1: photocopy the text from the Warm up
> Ex 1B: provide dictionaries/ask Ss to bring their own
> Ex 7: bring in notes/information on special dates around the world

Warm up

Introduce the topic of the lesson with a running dictation. Before class, make one copy of the text below for each Ss pair in your class, plus 3–4 copies to put round the classroom walls.

> Harrison Ford's got four children and three grandchildren. He's about seventy years old. He's a very good pilot and has got seven planes and a helicopter. What's he famous for? He's an American actor and he's famous for his role as Hans Solo in *Star Wars* and Dr Jones in the *Indiana Jones* films.

In class, put up the texts and organise Ss into A/B pairs. Ss A must run to read one of the texts on the walls, then run back and dictate a phrase/sentence to Ss B. Ss B may need to ask for repetition and/or spelling. Give a copy of the original text to each pair as they finish so they can check their texts: the others carry on. Check the text in feedback and discuss what else Ss know about Harrison Ford if time. This is a hectic, noisy activity but Ss usually enjoy it. N.B. A running dictation can be used with any short text, poem or song.

> **Culture Notes**
> **Harrison Ford**, born on 13th July, 1942, has made over 100 films for the cinema and TV. His first major role was Hans Solo in the first *Star Wars* trilogy (1977, 1980, 1982) and then as Indiana Jones, (1981, 1989, 1993, 2008). He may still make another one.

SPEAKING

1A Ss look at the photos. Ask *Who are these people? What are they famous for? Where are they from?* Tell Ss not to worry if they don't know them all. Elicit one or two answers and then check the example. Check *figure skater* using the photo, and *Olympic gold medallist.* At this point it would be useful to practise how to say the people's names. Give Ss 2–3 mins to talk. Monitor to see what Ss know and what to expect in feedback. Elicit answers in feedback and discuss them for 2–3 mins. (See audio script 6.1 for further information.)

Culture notes

Actor and comedian **Rowan Atkinson**, born 6th January 1955, is passionate about racing and owns several cars, including some Aston Martins.

Formula one racing driver **Lewis Hamilton**, born in England on 7th January 1985, was named after American athlete, Carl Lewis.

Rafael Nadal, born 3rd June 1986, became the World's number 1 tennis player in 2008 at the age of twenty-two.

Shizuki Arakawa, born 29th December 1981, in Tokyo Japan. One of her hobbies is gourmet cooking.

Shakira, born on 2nd February 1977, comes from a Middle Eastern background, which explains her belly dancing skills. She's also famous for her UNICEF work to provide education for poor children.

Actress **Cate Blanchett**, born 14th May 1969 in Australia, is also a theatre director in Sydney. Among her many films are two about Elizabeth I and *The Lord of the Rings* trilogy.

Charlie Chaplin, or Sir Charles Spencer Chaplin (1889–1977), was an English actor and film-maker. He started as a child performer in British music halls and then went to Hollywood where he made classic silent films such as *City Lights*, and later on, *The Great Dictator*.

B Check *childhood* in the rubric and then read question 1. If dictionaries are available, Ss check words they don't understand, e.g. *radio controlled*. If they're not available, teach the new words: *ballet, piano, poems*. Ask Ss what they remember about *John Cleese*, who was Basil Fawlty in the DVD in Unit 1 (see p30 for the **Culture notes**). Also check what they know about *Charlie Chaplin*. Ask Ss *Why is answer 1 Lewis Hamilton?* Because he's a racing driver and loves cars. Ss first think about the connections to the other celebrities and then discuss their opinions/guesses in pairs. In feedback, elicit Ss' answers/reasons, but don't confirm the names yet. N.B. Apart from being a prediction exercise for the listening task, this exercise should also activate use of the past simple. Throughout the exercise, listen closely and notice how well Ss are using it.

C Ss listen and check their answers. Play the CD again if necessary. In feedback, elicit other details that Ss remember. This will tell you more about Ss' knowledge of the past simple.

Answers: 2 B 3 E 4 D 5 A 6 F

Unit 6   Recording 1

1   Cars were important to Lewis Hamilton from an early age. He was a quiet boy, and one of his favourite activities was to play with radio-controlled cars. His other hobby was karate and he was a black belt at the age of twelve.

2   Shizuka Arakawa from Japan was the Olympic ice-skating champion in 2006, but skating wasn't her favourite sport when she was younger. She loved swimming and her other hobby was ballet.

3   Tennis player Rafael Nadal, or 'Rafa', is Spanish and was born in Manacor, Majorca. He was always a very good tennis player, but when he was young, his favourite sport was football. His favourite food was pasta and his favourite film was *Gladiator*.

4   When she was younger, Cate Blanchett's favourite film star was Harrison Ford. Her hobby was playing the piano and she was really good.

5   When she was very young, Colombian singer Shakira's favourite activities were writing poems and dancing. At the age of four, when she was at a restaurant with her father, she danced on the table to some Arabic music.

6   Rowan Atkinson is famous as Mr Bean. When he was young his favourite TV show was *Monty Python's Flying Circus* and his favourite actors were John Cleese and Charlie Chaplin.

GRAMMAR   *was/were*

2A   Write the sentences on the board to focus Ss' attention. Elicit the verbs *was* and *were* and underline them. Check the form: *was* is singular, *were* is plural. Ss copy the sentences down. *Stronger Ss* could do Ex 2A–D alone/in pairs and check their answers in **Language bank 6.1** on p138.

Answers: 1 was   2 were (both in the past tense)

B   Elicit/Check the tense. Ask *Which forms are the present/past simple of the verb 'be'?* Check *She was born in 1977.* Elicit personalised examples, e.g. *I was born in 1980, Anna was born in 1980.*

Answers: was, were

C   Again, write the negative sentence on the board and underline *wasn't*. Elicit the full form: *was + not* and write it on the board.

Answers: not

D   Elicit the question form and write it on the board. Highlight the inversion of the subject and verb. Also elicit the short answers: *Yes, he was./No, he wasn't.* Do the same for the plural form. Ask *Were Shakira's/your favourite activities writing poems and dancing?* Elicit *Yes, they were./No, they weren't.*

Answers: Was he a quiet boy?

Optional extra activity

Ss read the audio script on p171 and underline all forms of *was* and *were*.

⟹ LANGUAGEBANK 6.1 p138–9

Ss should check the tables for reference, in class or at home.

A   First, teach/check *yesterday, last night.*

Answers: 1 Were you a happy child?   2 How was your holiday?   3 Was Jack at the concert yesterday?   4 Were the windows open last night?   5 How many people were there at the party?

B

Answers: 1 was   2 was   3 wasn't   4 were   5 were

PRACTICE

3A   Play the first sentence. Ask *Is it past or present? P or N?* Ss then listen and write their answers, then check them in pairs. Play the CD again if they still have doubts.

Answers: 1 N   2 P   3 P   4 N   5 N   6 P   7 P   8 N

Unit 6 Recording 2

1 She's very kind.
2 She was very kind.
3 They were my favourite band.
4 They're my favourite band.
5 It isn't very funny.
6 It wasn't very funny.
7 We were very happy.
8 We're very happy.

B Play the first sentence and elicit the answer. Play and pause the CD after each sentence for Ss to write. Play it again for Ss to listen and underline the stress. In feedback, Ss listen and repeat the sentences with the correct stress. Model and highlight it if necessary.

Answers: 1 She was very <u>kind</u>. 2 They were my favourite <u>band</u>. 3 It <u>wasn't</u> very <u>funny</u>. 4 We were very <u>happy</u>.

C Write an example on the board: *She was /wəz/ very <u>kind</u>*. Model and drill the weak form, then play the first sentence again. Ss listen and repeat it. Play the other sentences. Ask *Which one doesn't have a weak form?* Number 3: *wasn't* is stressed.

D Elicit the two answers with *were /wə/*. Drill the sentences and play the CD again if Ss need more practice.

Answers: 1 was 2 were 4 were

4A First, check *afraid of the dark*. Then do the example and give Ss 2 mins to write the questions. Monitor and prompt Ss to self-correct any mistakes if necessary. In feedback, elicit and drill the questions. Check that Ss are using the weak form of *were /wə/*.

Answers: 2 Were you born in July? 3 Were you a very quiet child? 4 Were you afraid of the dark when you were a child? 5 Was you first English teacher a man? 6 Were your parents childhood friends? 7 Was your grandfather born in another country? 8 Was your grandmother a doctor or a nurse?

B Revise how to say years, e.g. *1995*. Monitor closely to make notes on accuracy. *Fast finishers* could ask more questions. Check Ss' answers in open pairs across the class and give feedback.

SPEAKING

5A Elicit some examples from the class. Then give Ss 2–3 mins to make notes of their favourite things.

B Ask Ss to note their partner's answers. After the pair work, Ss work in groups to exchange information and find out what they have in common. In feedback, Ss report back on their findings.

VOCABULARY dates and time phrases

6A Do an example first. Play the CD twice if necessary. Drill the answers in feedback in preparation for Ex 6B.

Answers: 1) 1990 2) 2010 3) 1987 4) 2002 5) 1951 6) 1872

B Monitor while Ss work and do any necessary pronunciation correction in feedback.

C Revise the months with an alphabet activity. Say the alphabet quickly. Ss say the month that starts with the letters as they come up, e.g. *April, December*.

> **Culture notes**
> On **World Health Day** (7th April) thousands of events focus on global health problems such as the child mortality rates, HIV/AIDS and malaria.

7A Read and check the special days. Ask *Which do you know? Which do you have in your country? What happens on these days?* Ss work alone/in pairs to match those they know, and guess those they don't.

B Play the CD. Ss check their answers in pairs. *Weaker classes* might have problems with the ordinal numbers. If so, move on to Ex 7D now or they could look at the dates in the audio script to check how they're written.

Answers: 1 F 2 D 3 H 4 C 5 E 6 G

C Check and drill Ss' answers.

Answers: The, of, the; the

D Put *weaker Ss* with *stronger ones* for this exercise. In feedback, elicit and drill the answers.

Answers: second, third, fourth, fifth, twelfth, twenty-first, twenty-second, thirtieth

8 Put Ss into A/B pairs. Check the instructions and drill the example on p160 and p165. Give Ss 1–2 mins to think about and write their important dates. They then take it in turns to ask/answer the questions. In feedback, nominate Ss A and B to ask/answer their questions in open pairs across the class. Give feedback as needed.

> **Optional extra activity**
> Ss work in groups and talk about a special day they have in their countries that isn't mentioned on the page, e.g. *friend's day, teacher's day, secretary's day*.

9A *Stronger Ss* can work with/help *weaker ones*. In feedback, check further. Ask a true question, e.g. *When was 3rd July?* Elicit the correct answer: *ten days ago, last week*.

Answers: 2 last 3 on 4 in 5 ago

B Monitor and check Ss' work. Encourage self-correction and help those who need it.

C Elicit some examples before Ss begin. Monitor discreetly, making notes of any problems with new language to focus on later. In feedback, write sentences with Ss' mistakes on the board. Ss correct them.

> **Homework ideas**
> • Write a paragraph about the special dates from Ex 8.
> • Language bank 6.1 Ex A–B, p139
> • Workbook Ex 1–6D, p33–34

TIME TWINS

Introduction

Ss learn and practise all forms of past simple regular and irregular verbs in the context of texts about two women, born on the same day but in very different circumstances. Ss then learn how to link sentences writing with *because* and *so* and write their life story.

SUPPLEMENTARY MATERIALS

Resource bank p167

Warm up: prepare *time phrases* as described below

Warm up

Revision of *was/were* and time phrases: pairs activity

Before class, write times phrases on separate pieces of paper, e.g. *yesterday afternoon, last Sunday, last August, two hours ago, on 31st December, a year ago, three days ago,* etc. In class, put them up around the classroom walls. Ss walk round the room in pairs and ask/answer questions, e.g. *Where were you three days ago? I was at work all day.*

READING

1A First, check the meaning of *twins*. Ss then cover the texts, look at the photos and discuss the questions. Elicit Ss' ideas in as much detail as possible. They can then look at the first paragraph of each text to check their answers.

Answers: Lia's from Yugoslavia and Carol's from the USA. They're time twins because they were born on the same day.

B Before reading, tell Ss not to worry about new words yet: they learn/revise the past simple in Ex 2. Give them 4–5 mins to order the texts and check in pairs.

C After Ss check their answers, tell them to cover the texts again. Elicit details Ss remember about the two women to check how well they use the past simple. It doesn't matter if they make mistakes – but don't correct them.

Answers:
Text 1 1A 2F 3E 4B 5C 6D
Text 2 1A 2C 3E 4D 5F 6B

D Ss work alone and make notes.

Unit 6 Recording 6

Lia was born in Yugoslavia on the 14th of July 1931. She <u>lived</u> in a small village and went to school when she was seven. In 1944, her family <u>moved</u> from Yugoslavia to Hungary because of the war. She <u>wanted</u> to go to university, but there was no money, so she <u>started</u> working in a sugar factory at seventeen. She **had** sugar for lunch and dinner every day for three years. She **got** married at twenty-five. She didn't have any children, but children always <u>liked</u> her. In 1969, she <u>moved</u> to Lake Balaton in Hungary and **made** a lot of money selling ice cream with her sister. She **bought** a house with the money, and now she rents rooms there.

Carol was born in the USA on the 14th of July 1931. She **went** to a school for child actors in New York and at eight years old she **had** her own radio programme. For a few years, she <u>stopped</u> going to school and <u>studied</u> at home with her mother. She **became** a well-known radio actress. Later, she <u>worked</u> in a bookshop in New York. She **met** her husband there in 1951. They **got** married and **had** five children. In the 1990s, she didn't see her children very much because they <u>lived</u> abroad. She and her husband sometimes <u>visited</u> them. In 2002, they **bought** a house by the sea and now their children come and visit them.

GRAMMAR past simple

2A Do the first verb as an example, (see all regular verbs underlined in the audio script above). Ss can then work alone and check their answers in pairs. In feedback, write the verbs on the board but don't check the pronunciation yet.

Answers:
Text 1: lived, moved, wanted, started, liked, moved
Text 2: stopped, worked, lived, visited

B Refer to the verbs on the board and elicit the rule. Underline the endings -*d* and -*ed*. Ask *When do you add 'd'?* With verbs ending in -e.

Answer: *d*, *ed*

Watch out!

The pronunciation of the -*ed* endings in regular verbs is a common problem for Ss. They over-generalise the rule for verbs like *wanted, decided* and pronounce all -*ed* endings in the same way: /ɪd/. It's very important to highlight and correct this mistake at all times to prevent fossilisation.

C First, play the CD for the example. Ask *Can you hear the last sound, /t/?* Play the CD, pausing for Ss to listen and write each verb in the correct place.

Revise/Teach the rules of pronunciation for -*ed* endings:

1 Verbs end in the /d/ sound after vowels and voiced consonants, except /d/, e.g. /b/, /v/, /z/, /g/, /m/, /n/, /l/

2 Verbs end in /t/ after unvoiced consonants except /t/, e.g. /p/, /f/, /s/, /k/

3 Verbs end in /ɪd/ after /d/ and /t/, e.g. *wanted, decided*.

In feedback, elicit Ss' answers. Point out that verbs ending in '*l*' like *travel*, double the consonant in the past tense. Play the CD again for Ss to repeat the verbs as many times as needed.

Answers: /t/ practised, /d/ loved, travelled, /ɪd/ hated, decided

D Ss now focus on irregular verbs. Tell them to find and underline the example *had* in the texts, (see irregular verbs in bold in the audio script). Then give them 1 min to underline the others. In feedback, elicit and write the verbs on the board.

Teaching tip

It's important for Ss to know that irregular verbs are vocabulary not grammar, and they have to learn them. Tell them to look at the **irregular verb list** on p127. Advise them to refer to it constantly and memorise new irregular verbs as they come up in the book.

It would be useful to read and check the **speakout tip** at this point. If Ss don't have dictionaries, they can look at the list on p127 to find the verbs.

Answers: 2 got 3 made 4 bought 5 went 6 met

E Write the gapped sentences on the board. Elicit the answers and point out that *did* is used in all persons, both singular and plural. Then drill the sentences using contractions.

Answers: 1 didn't have 2 didn't see Rule: didn't (did not)

▶ **LANGUAGEBANK** 6.2 p138–9

Check and elicit more examples of the spelling of verb endings, e.g. *try – tried* vs *play – played*. Ss should do Ex A and B in class: Ex A after Ex 3A, and Ex B after Ex 4C.

Answers:
A 1 studied 2 played 3 danced 4 worked 5 played
6 studied 7 loved 8 listened to
B 2 got up 3 didn't do 4 didn't drive 5 didn't have
6 met 7 told 8 didn't listen 9 didn't meet 10 ate
11 watched 12 didn't change 13 drank 14 went

PRACTICE

3A The sentences are about Lia and Carol. Give Ss 3 mins to complete the sentences and check their answers in pairs. In feedback, elicit and drill the verbs. For *try – tried*, tell Ss that verbs ending in *-y* change to *-ied*.

Answers: 1 walked 2 travelled 3 cooked 4 loved, listened 5 opened 6 enjoyed 7 stopped 8 tried

B Ss do this alone and then compare their answers, giving reasons. *Fast finishers* could try to fit each sentence in a suitable place in the texts. In feedback, ask Ss to justify their answers.

Answers: 2 L 3 C 4 L 5 L 6 C 7 L 8 L

4A Do question 1 with Ss and elicit the negative verb. Tell them to refer to p127 if necessary.

Answers: 1 didn't have 2 did 3 ate 4 went 5 bought 6 didn't speak 7 visited 8 started

B Here Ss do personalised practice, which should make the language more memorable. Elicit one or two examples, e.g. *Last year, I didn't have a car/did a lot of sport*. Ss then write their own sentences. Monitor and check the accuracy of their work, prompting them to self-correct.

C Ss take it in turns to read out a sentence. If their partner has the same answer, they tick it. In feedback, check which Ss had three answers the same.

VOCABULARY common verbs

5A Ss may disagree which verbs are used for telling a life story so tell them there are more than six possibilities. In feedback, elicit answers and write them on the board. Ask *Which are irregular?*

Possible answers: lived in, went to, moved to, wanted, started working, got married, bought (a house), stopped, became, worked in, met (her husband), had (five children),

B Make this a race: give Ss 1 min to find the answers. In feedback, elicit sentences about Ss' lives using these verbs, e.g. *I began school in 1994. I grew up in a city.* Also explain that both *learned* or *learnt* can be used but *learnt* is more common.

Answers: began, found, grew up, left, learnt, lost, won

6 Ss underline the differences. Tell Ss that the present simple uses two forms for the question: *do* and *does*, but the past simple only uses one, *did*. Ask follow up *Wh-* questions, e.g. *What sport did you like? When did you play it?* to check understanding.

Answers: *Do* is the auxiliary verb in the present simple, *did* is the auxiliary verb in the past simple.

Optional extra activity
Ss work in pairs/small teams to write five questions about the Lia and Carol texts. They then ask/answer the questions across the class, or in large groups.

▶ **LANGUAGEBANK** 6.2 p138–9

C Ss can refer to the last part of 6.2 when they do this exercise in class.

Answers: 2 Where did he live when he was young?
3 When did he begin film work? 4 What role did he have most fun playing? **The person:** Johnny Depp.

7A Here Ss prepare more personalised practice. In feedback, check the position of *last* in *When did you last see him?* Then model and drill the questions.

Answers: 1 did you meet 2 did you like 3 Did you do 4 did you speak 5 did you last see 6 did you do

B Elicit some questions/answers first. Monitor while Ss work and make notes of problems to address later.

SPEAKING

8A Ss work alone and make notes.

B Encourage Ss to extend the conversation by asking more questions, e.g. *Where did you meet her? How old were you? When did you get married?*

WRITING *because* and *so*

9A Check further in feedback. Write on the board, e.g. *I wanted to be an engineer. I went to university.* Ask Ss to join the sentences in two ways using *so* and *because*.

Optional extra activity
Ss write 4–6 sentences with *so* and *because* about Lia and Carol, e.g *Lia bought a house because she made a lot of money.*

Answers: 1 so 2 because

B Ss write their sentences on a piece of paper and give them to you. If appropriate, read them out to the class. They guess who it is.

C Elicit/Discuss the information needed to write a life story and write prompts on the board, e.g. *when/where born; school/university; work/job; married/children; where you live now.* Ss work alone to draft their life story using the prompts and the linking words. Encourage them to read each other's drafts. Monitor closely and prompt Ss to self-correct/rewrite if necessary.

Homework ideas
• Ss write a paragraph about the friend in Ex 7.
• Ss write the final draft of their life story in Ex 9.
• Language bank 6.2 Ex A–C, p139
• Workbook Ex 1A–5, p35–36

HOW WAS YOUR WEEKEND?

Introduction

Ss learn and practise the important social skill of how to make and maintain everyday social conversation. At the same time, they practise the past simple extensively.

SUPPLEMENTARY MATERIALS

Resource bank p168

Ex 6A: use video/audio recording facilities if possible

Ex 7: bring newspaper/online listings for weekend events in your town

Warm up

Revise language in 6.1 and 6.2: guessing game

Ss write down 4–6 dates/days that are important to them on a piece of paper, e.g. *20th April 1982, September 2008, last Saturday*. In pairs/small groups, they swap papers. They look at their partner's dates and ask *yes/no* questions to find out why they're important, e.g. *20th April 1988: Were you/your sister born then? Did your parents get married on that date?* In feedback, invite Ss to tell the class about interesting events in their partners' lives.

VOCABULARY weekend activities

1 Lead in. Look at the photos and ask *What do these people do at the weekend?* Teach/Check, e.g. *go to a football match, go for a walk*. Then ask Ss the questions in the rubric and elicit some sample answers. Check/Drill the examples. Ss then work in pairs and ask/answer the questions. Monitor and provide vocabulary they may need. In feedback, Ss tell the class about their partner's favourite days. Check new words and write them on the board.

2A Draw the example word web with *go* on the board and check the wrong phrase *swimming pool*. Ask *What verb does it go with?* Elicit *go to (the)*. Ss then copy down all the word webs from the book but leave out the incorrect phrases. Encourage Ss to compare their vocabulary records and check how Ss are organising their records of common collocations. Ss check their answers in pairs and correct any errors they agree on. *Fast finishers* can write down the correct verb for each incorrect phrase. In feedback, check answers and also elicit the verbs that go with the incorrect phrases. To follow up, elicit other phrases that go with each verb, e.g. *go running, watch a film*. Ss add them to their word webs.

Answers: watch: a newspaper play: the internet stay: to a hotel go for: for a restaurant

B Elicit one or two examples to check instructions.

Teaching tip

Checking instructions clearly and thoroughly is a crucial part of classroom management. Always do an example or demonstrate the activity to Ss so they are clear about what they have to do. This will make the activity run more smoothly.

Point to the word web on the board (from Ex 2A) and ask *Do you sometimes go to the gym at weekends?* Put a tick on the board for *Yes*, and a cross for *Never*. Ss then do the same on their own word webs.

C Ask *Do you often go clubbing at weekends?* and elicit answers. If nobody says *often*, ask a different question until they do. Write *often* in the word web on the board.

D Check the example and elicit/drill more questions using the verbs in the word webs.

FUNCTION making conversation

3A First, introduce the conversation. Ss look at the photo of Isabel and Marek. Ask them to speculate, e.g. *Where are they? What are they doing?* Check vocabulary, e.g. *win* and *won, lose* and *lost*, then play the CD. Ss listen and then check their answers in pairs. Play the CD again if necessary. In feedback, elicit answers and discuss Ss' speculations about Marek and Isabel. Ask *Was Marek happy to hear that Isabel had a boyfriend?* With *stronger classes*, you could also teach *guys* (informal word for 'men', though it can be used to refer to a group of people), *football match, score a goal* (underlined in the audio script).

Answers: 1 for a walk 2 her boyfriend 3 played 4 won

B You could remind Ss that they learnt how to show interest in Unit 3 on p32. Check the example and the phrases *Not bad = It was OK*, and *Nothing special = I didn't do anything special*. Ss then do the exercise alone or discuss it in pairs. Check the answers in feedback. Ss can practise saying the sentences in Ex 3C.

Answers: 2 Q 3 A 4 A 5 Q 6 A 7 I 8 Q 9 Q 10 I

C Check instructions and play the CD again. Ss listen and then compare answers in pairs. If there's a lot of disagreement, play the CD again. In feedback, play the CD again. Ss shout *stop!* each time they hear an answer. You can then replay each answer for Ss to listen and repeat, paying attention to stress and intonation.

Answers: 2, 3, 5, 6, 7, 8, 9, 10

Alternative activity

Tell Ss to listen and read the audio script on p171 at the same time, and underline the phrases, (see answers in bold in the audio script below).

Unit 6 Recording 8

I=Isabel M=Marek

I: Hi, Marek. **How was your weekend?**

M: OK. And yours? **What did you do?**

I: I went for a walk. **It was great!**

M: **Who did you go with?**

I: With my boyfriend, Diego. He's a football player.

M: **Oh. Where did you go?**

I: By the river. It was really beautiful.

M: **That sounds good.**

I: And you? What did you do?

M: Oh, I played football, cleaned the flat.

I: Who did you play football with?

M: With some <u>guys</u> from work. We play every weekend.

I: **Really?** Where did you play?

M: In the park. There's a <u>football pitch</u> there.

I: Did you win?

M: Of course. I <u>scored five goals</u>!

I: Ha! I don't believe you!

self-correct.

C Put Ss in groups of 2–4, depending on the size of your class. Saying their conversations in groups should be less intimidating than performing in front of the class. While each pair acts out their conversation, the others make a note of any differences to their own conversation. Monitor discreetly and make your own notes on Ss' performances. In feedback, find out who liked the party. Each group could also talk about the similarities/difference between their conversations.

▦→ **LANGUAGEBANK** 6.3 p138–9

Ss read the table. Recheck examples of sentences where *be* + adjective is used. With *weaker classes*, elicit answers to the questions that are true for them. Then tell them to do Ex A.

Answers: 1 was your 2 did you 3 That sounds
4 you go 5 did you 6 do at 7 That sounds 8 that's

Culture notes
St Patrick's Day celebrates the patron saint of Ireland. It's on 17th March and is Ireland's national holiday. Huge celebrations and parades take place all over the world, including in the Irish capital, **Dublin**.

4A Ask *What do you know about St Patrick's Day/Dublin?* Elicit what Ss know or tell them. Give Ss 3 mins to write the answers alone. Monitor closely, prompting them to self-correct accuracy errors. *Weaker classes* could use the audio script on p171 for support. In feedback, check and drill the answers. Ss could rehearse the conversation in pairs and act it out to the class. This would be useful preparation for Ex 4B.

Answers: What did you do? That sounds good. Who did you go with? So, why was it terrible? That's a shame.

B Give Ss time to prepare notes before they work in pairs. Tell them to show interest at least *twice* when they respond. Monitor discreetly and make notes on Ss' accuracy and pronunciation for feedback. Invite Ss to act out their conversation to the class. In feedback, write some examples of good/problematic language on the board. Ss correct the mistakes, alone or in pairs.

LEARN TO keep a conversation going

5A First, check the meaning of *keep a conversation going* = to encourage it to go on/continue. The exercise illustrates this. Do the first example with Ss and then they find the others alone. In feedback, elicit reasons from Ss (for the question *Why?*) and then refer them to the **speakout tip** below. This will clarify and highlight the aims of this section.

Answers: Seven. To have a good conversation and to keep it going.

B Elicit the extra pieces of information. Ask Ss to explain the link between the 1st and 2nd sentence, e.g. *the walk was great.*

Answers: It was great! Diego He's a football player. It was really beautiful.

6A Ss now do some less controlled practice where they have some choice about what to say. Give Ss 2–3 mins to complete the text alone. Monitor and provide support where needed.

B In pairs, Ss compare their answers. They then practise reading their conversations, taking it in turns to be Student A. Tell them to pay attention to stress, linking and intonation. Monitor and help Ss where needed. Encourage them to

Alternative activity
If you have video or audio recording facilities, record each pair saying/acting out their conversation. The whole class can then watch and compare them in feedback.

The recordings would also be very useful for oral assessment purposes. You could keep the recording and later grade Ss' performances according to accuracy, fluency and pronunciation.

SPEAKING

7A First, use the questions to elicit ideas about what would make a weekend perfect/terrible. N.B. If you've brought information about weekend events in your town, Ss could use them here as a source of ideas. Then give Ss 2–3 mins to make notes about what they want to say. Tell them they can be as imaginative/inventive as they like! *Weaker Ss* might prefer to work together or with *stronger ones*.

B First, illustrate what Ss have to do. Use the example and develop it, eliciting further responses, extra information, etc. Then put Ss in groups of 4–6. Monitor to check they're taking turns and participating fully. In feedback, invite Ss with the most original stories to act them out to the class.

Homework ideas
- Ss write about a special day/celebration in their countries.
- Ss write the dialogue about perfect/terrible weekend from Ex 7.
- **Language bank** 6.3 Ex A, p139
- **Workbook** Ex 1A–4B, p37

CARLOS ACOSTA

Introduction

Ss watch a DVD extract from the BBC series *The Culture Show* and learn about the life of Cuban dancer, Carlos Acosta. They then learn how to interview a person they admire and write their profile.

SUPPLEMENTARY MATERIALS

Warm up: a world map, Cuban/salsa music

Ex 3: photos of famous people your Ss admire/like

Warm up

Create interest in the DVD. Play some Cuban/salsa music if possible. Ask, e.g. *Do you like dancing? What kind of music do you dance to? Do you like ballet/salsa? Do you ever go to see dance/ballet? Why/Why not?*

Culture notes

Cuba is well known for its colourful history, politics, music and dance: from Fidel Castro and Che Guevara to salsa, samba, hip-hop and the Buena Vista Social Club.

The old part of its capital **Havana** has been restored and is once more a popular tourist destination.

The **Royal Opera House** in **Covent Garden** is the home of the Royal Ballet and the Royal Opera.

Carlos Acosta has danced there since 1998 and is one of the principal dancers.

Elicit and discuss Ss' answers. Write any useful new vocabulary on the board. Then move on to Ex 1.

DVD PREVIEW

1A If you have time, extend the exercise here with a prediction activity. Ss look at the photos and cover the text. Ask, e.g. *What do you know about Carlos Acosta? What does he do? Why is he famous? Where's he from?* Elicit answers from the class and write notes on the board. It doesn't matter if Ss don't know much about him: they'll find out later. (You can find information about him in the audio script but don't confirm Ss' answers now.) Give Ss 1 min to read the text to check if any of the information on the board is in the text. In feedback, check answers and teach/check *profile (v), travels the world.* Then lead in to the next exercise. Ask *Where was Carlos born? Where's Havana?* (Use the map from the **Warm up** to help.)

Answers: He's a dancer from Havana, Cuba.

B Ss look at the map and the photos. Ask: *What do you know about Havana? What's it like? Can you break-dance? Do you like watching it? Where's the Royal Opera House? What's it famous for?* Give Ss 3 mins to discuss how the photos are connected to Carlos's life. In feedback, draw two columns on the board, headed *Sure* and *Not sure*. Elicit Ss' predictions and ask *Are you sure/not sure?* Write the predictions in note form in the correct column. They'll check them in Ex 2A. N.B. You can use this approach with any factually-based reading or listening text.

▶ DVD VIEW

2A Ss watch the DVD, check their predictions and then compare answers. In feedback, check the facts on the board. Ask *Was this true/false? Was there any information?* Invite some initial impressions of the programme – Carlos, Havana, the people, atmosphere, colours, etc.

B Read and check new language in the statements, e.g. *champion, dance competition, miss school.* Ss watch the DVD and check their answers in pairs. If necessary, play it again.

Answers: b) 3 c) 7 d) 2 e) 8 f) 5 g) 6 h) 4

C Ss might not be sure about some key words in the text, e.g. *relatives, a foreigner* but tell them not to worry. They'll check these in Ex 2D.

D Play the DVD again so Ss can listen and check their answers. If necessary, play the DVD again, stopping at each answer for Ss to recheck. In feedback, ask *Do you know Cuba?* (or *Have you been to Cuba?*) *Would you like to go there? Why/Why not?* If there's time, play the DVD again for Ss to watch and enjoy. Discuss their opinions of Carlos Acosta. Ask *Have you seen him live? Would you like to?*

Answers: 1 heart 2 relatives 3 a foreigner 4 dance 5 speak 6 heat 7 sea 8 happiness

DVD 6 The Culture Show

VO=Voiceover C=Carlos Acosta

VO: Carlos Acosta is one of the greatest living ballet dancers. He was the first black principal dancer at Covent Garden in London. He is famous around the world and in his home country of Cuba he is a national hero. Carlos now travels the world but always sees Cuba as his home. All his family are still there. In Cuba he isn't a foreigner. He says that in Cuba a child learns to dance first and then to speak. He talks about the heat and the sea, about dance and music and happiness.

CA: Cuba is always going to be my home. In my heart, that's the only country, you know, and because that's where all my relatives are, my memories, you know, and this is the only place I'm never going to be a foreigner. You learn how to dance first, then you learn how to speak, you know, in Cuba. It's something that's been passed on through generation to generation. And it's also you know the heat, and the tropic, and the sea and … it's almost that's what, er, it's asking for, dance and music and happiness.

VO: Carlos was born in Havana, the youngest of eleven children in a poor family. He often missed school. He was a champion break-dancer in the streets but didn't want to be a professional dancer. When he was nine, his father sent him to ballet school. Carlos hated it. He told his father he wanted to do something else.

CA: So, I, I did tell him many times that I didn't want to be … and that I wanted to do something else – football, you know – but he didn't want to hear it. So, I went and I … but thank God he didn't want to hear it because thanks to that I'm here now.

VO: At ballet school, Carlos wasn't always a good student and didn't want to be a dancer. But, when he was thirteen, Carlos saw the Cuban National Ballet and he loved it so much that he changed his mind about ballet. He decided to work hard and three years later, at sixteen, he travelled to Europe for the first time. That year he won four major dance competitions and became famous all over the world. Now he is an international star and he dances in many countries, but he still goes home to Cuba several times a year to visit his family.

speakout an interview

3A Teach *hero* and *admire*. Show a picture/name a person who's done something most people think is good, e.g. Nelson Mandela. Ask *Did he do good things? Do people/you like/respect him? Is he a hero? Who else do you admire?* Elicit Ss' answers. They then discuss people they admire in pairs/groups. In feedback, elicit Ss' answers and write their names on the board. N.B. If Ss can't think of anybody they admire, give them a picture of a suitable famous person.

B Check the rubric and tell Ss to focus only the question while they listen. Play the CD. Ss write their answers and then compare them. Play the CD again if necessary. *Stronger Ss* might be able to guess the meaning of *orphan* and *orphanage*. Elicit Ss' answers and teach/drill these two words.

Answers: He works with poor children/orphans. He opened an orphanage in 1996.

Unit 6 Recording 9

I=Interviewer B=Baruti Kaleb

I: Thank you for coming on the show, Baruti. We are all very interested to know more about your work. But, first of all, let's start from the beginning … urm where were you born?

B: I was born in Johannesburg in 1962.

I: Can I ask you about your childhood?

B: Yes, of course. I was the fourth child in a very big family – there were eleven of us. My father was a teacher and my mother cleaned houses for rich people.

I: Did you go to school?

B: Yes, I did. Education was very important to my parents.

I: When did you decide to work with poor children?

B: When I was in school, one of my friends lost his parents. He had no family, no living grandparents, so he moved to a house for orphans. I visited him and when I saw his life there I decided to work with orphans.

I: When did you open your orphanage?

B: We opened it in 1996.

I: We?

B: Yes, my wife and I. We got married in 1990.

I: And who's your hero?

B: I'm glad you asked that – it's Mother Teresa. I often think about her words: 'I can do no great things, only small things with great love.'

I: That's very interesting. I have one more question: What's your favourite book?

B: Let me think about that. I like many books but *Long Walk to Freedom* is one of my favourites. It's the story of Nelson Mandela's life in his own words.

I: That sounds interesting, thank you. OK … now, it's time to ask the audience for questions. Are there any questions for Baruti … Yes, you at the back …

C Ss read the key phrases. Teach *interviewer* and *interviewee*. Play the CD. Ss tick the phrases they hear, and then check their answers in pairs (see answers in bold in audio script). Elicit Ss' answers. *Stronger classes* could read the audio script on p171 and check their answers. Elicit the complete sentences for each key phrase. Teach/Check any essential vocabulary, e.g. *orphan* and *orphanage*. In feedback, elicit other details that Ss remember, e.g. *He's from Johannesburg, South Africa.*

Answers: Can I ask you about your childhood? When did you decide to (work with poor children?) What's your favourite book? That's very interesting. Let me think about that. Are there any questions (for Baruti?)

Optional extra activity

Check Ss' comprehension further. Dictate/Write questions on the board and teach the words in bold, e.g. *Where's Baruti Kaleb from? What did his parents do? Why did he go to an orphanage? Why did he decide to work with orphans? When did he get married? When did they open an orphanage? Who's Baruti's hero? What's his favourite book?*

Ss listen to the CD again and write the answers. They then read the audio script on p171 and check. In feedback, Ss read Mother Teresa's quote and discuss what it means.

D Group Ss who admire the same person if possible. Give them 4 mins to discuss and write at least six questions. *Fast finishers* can write more. Remind Ss that they should only write questions they know the answers to! They can use the key phrases and audio script as a model. When they're ready, give them 5–6 mins to write the whole interview. Again, monitor and encourage Ss to self-correct errors in their writing.

E Regroup Ss so they are working with Ss who wrote interviews about different people. After each interview, the other Ss in the group ask their questions. While Ss talk, monitor discreetly and make notes on their performance. In feedback, invite Ss to tell the class about one of the special people.

writeback a profile

4A Elicit what Ss remember about Baruti from Ex 3C. Check *life-changing experience, early life* and the example. Give Ss 1 min to read the text quickly and match the paragraphs. Check answers in feedback. If you didn't do the *optional extra activity* in Ex 3C, ask some comprehension questions here.

Answers: a) 2 c) 4 d) 3

B Ss use their notes from Ex 3D and the text in Ex 4A as a model for the first draft of their profile. Monitor and support Ss. Encourage them to show their drafts to other Ss. N.B. If your Ss have a class blog, they can write their profile there.

Homework ideas
• Ss write a final draft of the profile in Ex 4B, adding photos if possible.

LOOKBACK

Introduction

There are many different ways of exploiting the **Lookback** exercises. As Ss have just finished the first half of the Student's book, you might want to prepare them for a more formal test. In this case, set aside a lesson for Ss to do all the exercises with no help from you or their books.

Monitor the speaking activities and make notes of Ss' performances (Ex 1C, 3B, 4B, 5B). At the end of the lesson, check answers in a more formal way and do any remedial teaching necessary. Ss should now have a clearer idea of what to work on for a formal test.

WAS/WERE

1A *Weaker Ss* could check their answers on p28–29 when they've finished the exercise. *Fast finishers* can prepare more jumbled sentences and write them on the board at the end. The first person in the class to write the new sentences correctly wins.

Answers: 1 I was at work yesterday afternoon.
2 Where were you at six o'clock? 3 I was at my friend's on Wednesday evening. 4 When were you at the shops?
5 Were you at home at half past twelve?

B Do an example first. Then give Ss 1 min to complete the tables. Monitor to help those who need it.

C First, put *weaker* and *stronger Ss* together to prepare the questions they need to ask, as in the example. Monitor while Ss work and prompt Ss to self-correct errors of accuracy. Put the Ss into different pairs to ask/answer the questions. Make notes on Ss' performance (accuracy of language and pronunciation) for feedback, or assessment if required.

DATES AND TIME PHRASES

2 Ss could do this exercise in teams. Give them a 3-min time limit to complete it. Don't give them any help or check the answers with the class. Feedback is a competition: each team takes it in turns to answer. If they get it wrong, they lose a point (–1). If they get it right, they win 2 points. The team with the most points wins.

Answers: 2 b) yesterday 3 c) in 4 d) last 5 e) last
6 f) on (the) 7 g) ago 8 h) in

3A *Weaker Ss* could look back in their books to find the answers. *Fast finishers* can write more examples for each verb.

B First, check the example and elicit more sample questions with the other verbs. Elicit answers and drill the questions/ answers in open and closed pairs. Monitor while Ss work and make notes on their accuracy and pronunciation for feedback, or assessment if required.

PAST SIMPLE

4A Do the first question as an example. Check *miss lunch* if necessary. Give Ss 1 min to complete the exercises alone.

B Do the example and give Ss time to note down another piece of information before they work in pairs. Monitor and assess your Ss' performance. In feedback, Ss tell the class one of their partner's answers with the extra piece of information.

PAST SIMPLE QUESTIONS

5A Ss work alone and write the questions. Monitor closely to check the accuracy of their sentences.

Answers: 3 Did you usually walk to school when you were ten? 4 Did you go abroad every summer when you were a child? 5 Did you play a lot of sports at school?
6 Did you like mathematics at school?

B Monitor and assess Ss' accuracy with question forms while they work. Give feedback as appropriate.

Alternative approach

Ss work in small groups and do a survey. They take it in turns to ask the questions and note down the number of people who answer *Yes* or *No*. In pairs, they then write a survey, e.g. *Three students were born in a hospital and three weren't.* They could then swap groups and read out/ compare their surveys. Alternatively, Ss make a poster with their information and display it on the wall. The class walk around and note similarities and differences. Discuss these in feedback.

Homework ideas
- Workbook Review and check 2, p38–39
- Workbook Test 2, p40

OVERVIEW

BBC VIDEO PODCAST

How was your last holiday?

In this video podcast, people talk about where they went on their last holiday and describe what it was like. The material consolidates Ss' general descriptive vocabulary and includes language associated with sightseeing, the weather and 'types' of holidays. The video podcast could work well as an introduction to the unit or at the end of lesson 7.1 or unit 7 to recap the key vocabulary and language learnt.

TRAVEL PARTNERS

Introduction

Ss learn comparative forms and adjectives to describe places in the context of talking about and comparing holidays.

> ### SUPPLEMENTARY MATERIALS
>
> Resource bank p169 and p170
>
> Ex 1D and 6A: photos of a variety of tourist places/scenes

Warm up

Talk about a holiday: discussion

Use this warm up to create interest in the topic and activate language connected to travel and places. Write on the board/dictate questions about holidays, e.g. *Where do you like to go on holiday? Why? Do you go on holiday often? Why/Why not? Do you go with your family/friends/on your own? Why?* etc. Ss work in pairs/groups to ask and answer the questions. Monitor to check what travel vocabulary they know. Then invite Ss tell the class about their partners' holidays but don't give feedback.

VOCABULARY travel

> **Culture notes**
>
> **Photo A:** shows two contrasting symbols: ancient **Mount Fuji**, the active volcano west of Tokyo, and the modern streamlined, high speed ('bullet') train which travels at up to 300 km/h (186mph).
>
> **Photo B:** an art gallery with modern abstract paintings.
>
> **Photo C:** the Blue Lagoon in Olu Deniz, the south coast of Turkey. It's one of the most beautiful beaches in Turkey and an extremely popular tourist destination.
>
> **Photo D:** The **Burj Al Arab Hotel in Dubai**, one of the world's first 7* hotels, was the tallest hotel in the world when it opened in 1999 (321m). It's said that the gold of the ceiling is gold leaf not paint.

1A First, Ss look at the photos. Ask Ss if they know what the places are and where they are. Then ask Ss to say what they can see. It doesn't matter if Ss don't know the locations. You can use the information in the **Culture notes**. Elicit places/things, e.g. *beach, mountain, high-speed train, art gallery, (modern) paintings, hotel foyer.* Teach/Check words they need for Ex B, e.g. *crowded (beach), empty (art gallery), interesting (paintings/architecture).* Then check the example adjectives. Drill *comfortable*: highlight the omission of the middle syllable or with your fingers: /ˈkʌmftəblə/. Then give Ss 2–3 mins to make their own lists. In feedback, tell Ss to check their words with the lists in Ex B below and tick words that are the same. Then elicit/check any remaining words on their lists and write relevant ones on the board.

B Do the example and give Ss 2 mins to match the words and check their answer in pairs. Ss can check their answers when they listen to the CD in Ex 1C below.

C Play the CD for Ss to check their answers from Ex 1A. Then play it again: Ss listen and underline the stressed syllables. Ss compare their answers. Play the CD again if necessary. In feedback, elicit the answers and write the underlined words on the board. Include any other words Ss used in Ex 1A. Check them further: Ss use the adjectives to describe something in the photos, e.g. *the beach is very crowded.* Drill any problematic words, highlighting the stress with your fingers.

Teaching tip

Humming/Using nonsense sounds to show word stress is usually very effective. Ss don't have to worry about the meaning of the word or the pronunciation of individual sounds. Model/Drill, e.g. *da DA da da for uncomfortable.*

Answers: <u>fast</u>, <u>slow</u>; <u>crowd</u>ed, <u>emp</u>ty; ex<u>pen</u>sive, <u>cheap</u>; <u>hot</u>, cold; com<u>for</u>table, un<u>com</u>fortable; <u>in</u>teresting, <u>bor</u>ing, <u>qui</u>et, <u>noi</u>sy

D Give Ss time to think about how they'll describe their photo. If you have other suitable pictures available, Ss can use them here. Monitor and make notes on problems with the target vocabulary and correct them in feedback.

SPEAKING

2A Introduce the quiz: read/check the introduction to it. Also check *self-catering apartment, go sightseeing, spring, summer.*

B Prepare Ss with the language they'll need to compare, e.g. for question 1, Student B answers *By plane.* Student A says *Me, too.* or *I don't. I like to travel by train.* Put Ss into pairs with a partner they don't know very well to make the quiz more 'authentic'. In feedback, pairs tell the class if they're good/bad travel partners and why.

LISTENING

3A Here Ss listen for gist so tell them to not to worry about language they don't understand: just listen for information about the two questions. Elicit Ss' answers in feedback. If necessary, play the last few lines again. With a *stronger class,* elicit other details they remember.

Answers: 1 Four 2 Yes

B Do the first answer together. Play the first part of the CD and stop at *by train.* Elicit the answers and play the rest of the CD. Ss write their answers and compare them. If necessary, play the CD again, stopping at the relevant points.

Answers: 1 a) M b) W 2 a) W b) M 3 a) M/W 4 a) M b) W 5 a) M/W 6 b) M/W 7 b) M/W

Unit 7 Recording 2

M=Man W=Woman

M: So, how do you usually travel? By plane or train?

W: Train. I think travelling by train's more comfortable than flying. And I don't like flying.

M: I put 'plane' because flying is faster than going by train.

W: Not always! OK, next question. Where do you like to stay: in a hotel or a self-catering apartment?

M: In an apartment. And you?

W: In a hotel.

M: Oh. But a hotel is more expensive than an apartment!

W: Yeah, but it's more comfortable. Hmm … next question. What do you prefer to do: go sightseeing or relax on a beach?

M: Oh, that's easy! I hate beach holidays! Boring!

W: OK – there's one we answered the same. So we agree about that.

M: Yeah, sightseeing's definitely more interesting!

W: Right. When do you like to go: in spring or summer?

M: In spring – I don't really like hot weather. Tourist places are more crowded in summer.

W: True. But the weather's better. Summer is hotter than spring. I love hot weather.

M: Well, we don't agree there. Anyway, next question. What do you like to eat: local dishes or the food you usually eat?

W: Local dishes, I think. You?

M: Definitely! That's two answers the same!

W: Mm, interesting. Next – what do you like to do in the evening? Go to a club or go to a restaurant?

M: Well, go to a restaurant.

W: Oh, good. Me, too. It's much quieter than a club.

M: Yes, I agree. Restaurants are quieter, more relaxing.

W: And the last question: how long is your perfect holiday?

M: Three months.

W: You can't have *three* months! The answer is either a week or a month.

M: OK, a month then.

W: Me, too!

W: So we've got four answers the same!

M: Maybe we *can* travel together.

C Ss look at their quiz answers again and compare them with the man and woman's answers. If they get four or more answers the same, they are good travel partners – though Ss may have different opinions!

GRAMMAR comparatives

Watch out!

Ss tend to find the rules of comparative forms and use of *than* quite confusing at first. Highlight form clearly and give Ss adequate spoken and written practice. Monitor and correct errors consistently to prevent fossilisation.

4A Write the gapped sentences on the board while Ss find the sentences in the audio script. Elicit/Complete the missing words. Check meaning: draw a plane and a train on the board (or show pictures of them) and write 1000 km/h under the plane and 300 km/h under the train. Ask *How fast does the plane/train go?* Elicit answers. Ask *Do they go at the same speed? No. Why?* Elicit/Say *Because the plane's faster than the train.* Do the same for the other two sentences. Then check form, using the sentences on the board. Elicit/Draw a box around the -er endings (*faster, hotter*) and more (*expensive*). Tell Ss/Elicit that in one-syllable adjectives ending in one consonant and preceded by a single vowel, we always double the final consonant, e.g. *big – bigger.*

Answers: 1 -er than 2 -ter, than 3 more, than

Alternative presentation

Present the comparative forms through pictures, using the same examples as here or your own, e.g. you can draw tall, short, old and young people on the board or use pictures. Don't write anything on the board until you've checked meaning, form and pronunciation. Then check **Language bank 7.1.**

B In *weaker classes*, play the CD first. Ss then underline the stressed words and listen again to check. Play the CD once more for Ss to repeat the sentences. Highlight the weak form and linking in *than̲ an* /ðənən/ in sentence 3.

> **Answers:** 1 <u>Fly</u>ing is <u>fast</u>er than going by <u>train</u>. 2 <u>Summer</u> is <u>hot</u>ter than <u>spring</u>. 3 A ho<u>tel</u> is more ex<u>pen</u>sive than an a<u>part</u>ment.

C *Stronger Ss* complete the table and look at **Language bank** 7.1 to check their answers. Otherwise, check Ss' answers here and elicit/check the rules of form before looking at the Language bank.

> **Answers:**
> short adjectives (adjective +) -er;
> long adjectives more (comfortable); more (+ adjective)

> **Optional extra activity**
> Ss read audio script 7.2 on p171–172 and underline all examples of comparative forms. They then practise saying them.

> ➡ **LANGUAGEBANK** 7.1 p140–1
> Read and check the table with *weaker classes*, who should then do 7.1, Ex A and B on p141.
>
> **Answers:**
> A 2 closer 3 bigger 4 more beautiful 5 easier
> 6 cheaper 7 more important 8 happier
> B 2 slower than 3 noisier than 4 hotter, than
> 5 cheaper than 6 worse, than

PRACTICE

5A Check the example with the class, pointing out that Ss should give their own opinions. They then work alone. Monitor and help where necessary.

> **Possible answers:** 2 Spring is more romantic than autumn. 3 Travelling by train is faster that travelling by car. 4 My language is easier than English. 5 Trainers are more comfortable than shoes. 6 Water's better for you than coffee. 7 A book is more interesting than a magazine. 8 A beach is more relaxing than a city.

B After Ss have compared their answers, they can work with other pairs to exchange information and find out what they all have in common. Monitor and prompt Ss to self-correct problems with the target language. In feedback, Ss report to the class about their findings.

> **Optional extra activity**
> Ss work in pairs/small groups and make comparisons between the photos in Ex 1, using the adjectives in Ex 1B.

6A First, brainstorm places Ss know/like in their own towns/countries, or abroad, and write some examples on the board.

> **Alternative activity**
> To make this a more extensive, in *monolingual classes*, give Ss two pictures each if you've brought them. In *multicultural classes*, Ss from the same country/region might like to work together. Ss then work alone/in pairs and write the sentences. *Fast finishers* can write more.

B Ss read their sentences to each other in pairs/groups and can agree/disagree if they know the places. They can also ask more questions about each place. Monitor while Ss talk, making notes of good language used/problems with the target language for feedback.

SPEAKING

7A Ss first look at the photos. Elicit the activities shown there: *surfing, sailing, horse riding, camping.* Then use them to elicit examples of good/bad things about holidays: *being in the sea/on the beach, being in the fresh air, taking a boat ride, relaxing, camping in cold weather with mountain goats!* Briefly elicit examples of good/bad holidays Ss have had. They then work alone and make notes in answer to the questions in the exercise. *Stronger Ss* can write more. Monitor closely to provide support/language where necessary.

B Ss ask and answer the questions, first Ss A and then Ss B. In feedback, Ss tell the class about their partner's experiences.

> **Homework ideas**
> * Ss write a paragraph comparing two places they know, with pictures/photos if possible.
> * Ss write three paragraphs about a good/bad holiday based on Ex 7.
> * Language bank 7.1 Ex A–B, p141
> * Workbook Ex 1A–4B, p41–42

THE LONGEST BUS RIDE

Introduction

Ss learn and practise the superlative forms in the context of reading about a bus journey which goes halfway round the world. Ss then plan their own journey and learn how to check and correct mistakes in their written work.

SUPPLEMENTARY MATERIALS

Resource bank p171

Warm up: prepare some prompts comparing countries/famous places, (see below)

Ex 1B and 6A: map(s) of the world

Ex 6A: optional project work

Warm up

Lead in to the topic of the lesson. Ask: *How do you prefer to travel when you go on holiday? Why?* Ss discuss the question in pairs. In feedback, elicit Ss' answers and find out what the most popular means of transport is. Ss then look at the photos in Ex 1. Ask: *Which places do you recognise? What do you know about them?* Elicit what Ss know. Then look at the map and photos in the text. Ask: *Which places does the bus go to?* Elicit details about the photos, using the **Culture notes** to help.

Culture notes

Photo A: the dunes of the Sahara desert.

Photo B: the peaks of Mt Everest: 29,035 feet (8,850m) high.

Photo C: A tiger reserve in the Himalayas.

Photo D: The **Taj Mahal**, in Agra, India: the mausoleum built by Emperor Shah Jahan in memory of his favourite wife, Mumtaz Mahal, and completed in 1653.

Photo E: The **Sydney Harbour Bridge** with the iconic **Opera House** in the background.

Photos in the text: 1) a view of the river Danube in Budapest 2) a street market in Lahore, Pakistan 3) the Petronas Towers in Kuala Lumpur, Malaysia. The tallest twin towers in the world (451.9m/1,482.6ft)

VOCABULARY places

1A Give Ss 2 mins to find the things from the box in the photos. In feedback, check/drill their answers and teach any words that are new to them, e.g. *tiger, lake*. Then elicit *river, market* from the photos in the text.

Answers: A a desert B a mountain C a jungle
D a famous building E a bridge/a city
Photos in text: 1) a river 2) a market 3) a city

B Do an example, e.g. *the Gobi desert*. In *multilingual classes*, group Ss from the same country/area together. In feedback, elicit Ss' answers. If you have a map of the world available, Ss can show the class where the places are. Write interesting places that might be useful for Ex 6A on the board.

Culture notes

Australia is often referred to as Oz, hence the name Ozbus. Australians are often called 'Ozzies'.

READING

2A Lead in to the text. Teach/Check *backpacker*. Ask *What do we call a person who travels round the world and stays in cheap places/hostels? They carry their things in a backpack.* Mime carrying a backpack. Then ask Ss *Are you a backpacker? Do you want to go backpacking? Why/Why not?* Discuss this briefly. Check the rubric and questions. Ss then read the first paragraph and compare their answers. In feedback, check/teach *journey:* when you travel from one place to another, e.g. *car/plane/bus journey*. Also teach *passengers* and *ultimate*.

Answers: The longest bus ride in the world. 2 Twenty

B Here Ss do a prediction activity, which will give them a reason to read. N.B. Native speakers rarely read a text unless they have a reason or purpose, e.g. information they want to find out. This is what motivates readers. Check the example. Ss should cover the text. Give them 2–3 mins to discuss and write their questions. Monitor closely to check the accuracy of their writing and support Ss who need it.

3A Give Ss 2–3 mins to read the text alone and find answers to their questions. It doesn't matter if they don't: the aim is to give Ss a reason to read the text. Ss then compare answers. In feedback, elicit answers they found/didn't find.

B First, check language in the statements: (*travel) through, tiger reserve.* Give a time limit of 2–3 mins. *Fast finishers* should prepare to explain why the false sentences are false. In feedback, elicit Ss' answers, giving reasons.

Answers: 1 F 2 F 3 T 4 F 5 F 6 T

C Write *Yes/No* on the board. Then check the question and elicit some answers with reasons, e.g. *Yes, because I really want to travel./No, I don't like travelling by bus.* Write the yes/no reasons on the board. Ss then work in small groups and discuss the question, making notes of the reasons. In feedback, nominate a student from each group to summarise the group's answers.

GRAMMAR superlatives

Watch out!

Ss tend to find the superlative forms easier once they've learnt the comparative. However, they often confuse the two forms when they speak, e.g. *the most long bus ride/it's more biggest than.* For this reason, highlight form clearly and give Ss spoken and written practice in full sentences.

4A *Stronger classes* could do Ex 4A and B alone and then check their answers in **Language bank** on p140. Otherwise, write the three gapped sentences on the board. Ss read and find the answers. In feedback, elicit the answers and complete the sentences. Elicit/Check the rules for short and longer adjectives and irregular superlatives. Underline *the longest, the most beautiful, the best* in the sentences. Ss then copy them.

Answers: 1 longest 2 most 3 best

B Ss underline the examples in the text. Elicit them and write the three sentences on the board. Ss then complete the box. Recheck the rules of form, including *the*.

Answers:
Text: most exciting, worst, greatest
Table: *the* + adjective + *est; the most exciting; the best, the worst*

C Write sentence 1 on the board, underline the three examples of *the*. Then ask *Is the pronunciation of the the same each time?* Play sentence 1 on the CD once or twice as needed. The first *the* is pronounced /ði:/ because it comes after a vowel, *the Ozbus*. The other two are pronounced /ðə/. Ss listen again and repeat the sentence. Then play the rest of the CD. Ss listen and repeat, chorally and individually.

Answers: 1 The Ozbus is **the** longest bus ride in **the** world. 2 People can see **the** most beautiful places in **the** world. 3 **The** best thing was **the** Taj Mahal.

⟫ LANGUAGEBANK 7.2 p140–1

Ss read the **Language bank** section 7.2 either in class or at home: point out that the spelling changes are the same as for the comparative. *Weaker/Mixed ability classes* should do Ex A in class. All Ss should do Ex B.

Answers:
A 2 the quietest 3 the most comfortable 4 the closest 5 the noisiest 6 the cheapest 7 the most interesting 8 the hottest 9 the fastest 10 the most crowded
B 2 The most popular 3 The deepest, the oldest 4 The biggest 5 The highest, The best 6 The busiest

PRACTICE

5A Check the example. Ss then write the questions alone. Monitor closely to check the accuracy of the target language. Elicit/Check and drill the questions in feedback.

Culture note
The Red Desert, so called because of its red earth, is in the outback of South Australia. It's famous for Uluru (Ayer's Rock).

B Ss do the exercise alone and then compare their answers. These will be checked in Ex 5C.

Answers: 2 What was the hottest place? 3 What was the friendliest place? 4 What was the longest you travelled in one day? 5 What was the most beautiful building you saw? 6 What was the most amazing experience of the journey?

C Ss listen to an interview with Jeff, from the text, and tick the questions/answers they've matched correctly. If necessary, play the CD, or parts of it, again. In feedback, elicit any details Ss remember about the places. They could then cover the answers and ask/answer the questions in pairs/open class.

Answers: 1 e) 2 a) 3 f) 4 d) 5 b) 6 c)

Unit 7 Recording 5

I=Interviewer   P=Passenger

I: So, Jeff. A few questions about the trip. <u>What was the coldest place you visited?</u>
P: The <u>coldest place was Mount Everest.</u> We stayed at Everest base camp and the temperature was minus thirty.
I: Really? <u>And what was the hottest place?</u>
P: Well, <u>it was hot in Pakistan but the Red Desert in Australia was hotter.</u>
I: Ah, was it? And <u>what was the friendliest place?</u>
P: <u>That's an impossible question.</u> I can't say. We met so many fantastic people. Everyone was wonderful.
I: OK. <u>What was the longest you travelled in one day?</u>

P: <u>One day we travelled about 400 kilometres in Pakistan.</u> That was a long day!
I: Very! So, <u>what was the most beautiful building you saw?</u>
P: There were some great ones in Nepal and Bali, but my favourite building <u>was the Taj Mahal in India. I think it's the most beautiful building in the world.</u>
I: Yes, it is. So, <u>what was the most amazing experience of the journey?</u>
P: <u>Seeing a tiger in the tiger reserve in the Himalayas.</u> A-ma-a-a-zing!

SPEAKING

6A For this exercise, refer back to the places Ss have read/talked about in this lesson. Ask *Would you like to make a long journey to any of these countries? What other places would you like to travel to?* Find out which parts of the world Ss would like to go to, e.g. *Asia, Africa, South America,* and group Ss accordingly.

B Monitor while Ss prepare their presentation: provide support and encourage them to self-correct.

C Ss in each group first decide which part of the journey each of them will talk about. During the presentation, the rest of the class listen and write additional questions to ask at the end. During the presentations, make notes on Ss' performances for feedback later.

D Each group discusses which journey was the most interesting, and why. They then present their conclusions to the class. Finally, have a class vote for the most interesting journey.

WRITING checking and correcting

7A Check the example. Ss then finish the exercise alone and check in pairs. In feedback, elicit the answers, including the type of mistake.

Answers: spelling: friendlier, stayed, comfortable; **past tense forms:** met, were, bought; **singular and plural:** people

B Give Ss 3–4 mins to write their sentences. Give them the opening prompt: *Last year/summer/August, I went to …* They then write four more sentences. Monitor but don't interrupt Ss during this exercise.

C Monitor while Ss check each other's work but don't interrupt. Collect in the corrections when they've finished, check them and give feedback in the next lesson.

Homework ideas
• Ss write a paragraph about why they'd like to go on the Ozbus.
• Ss write the plan of their journey in Ex 6 or a description of their last holiday, Ex 7.
• Language bank 7.2 Ex A–B, p141
• Workbook Ex 1A–5C, p43–44

CAN YOU TELL ME THE WAY?

Introduction

Ss learn and practise how to ask for and give directions, and equally importantly, how to check and correct them by using stress and intonation.

SUPPLEMENTARY MATERIALS

Resource bank p172

Ex 1: a map of England

Ex 4: maps of your town/area

Warm up

Ask Ss *What are the most interesting places to visit/go in your town/area? What places are not very interesting?* Give them 2 mins to think/write their lists. In *multilingual classes*, Ss can write about their home town or the town they're studying in. In pairs, Ss talk about the places on their lists and what's interesting, or not, about them. Monitor and check if/how well Ss use the vocabulary in Ex 2A. Elicit and discuss Ss' answers briefly in feedback.

VOCABULARY places

Culture notes

Brighton and **Hove** used to be two separate towns which have now grown into one.

The **Royal Pavilion** (or Brighton Pavilion) was built in the early 19th century for the son of King George III, and was the work of famous architect John Nash. Visitors can enjoy its lavish interiors which combine Chinese-style decorations with magnificent furniture and furnishings.

The **Brighton Pier** opened in May 1899 and is still a place of entertainment. There's a large amusement arcade and fairground rides, including roller coasters.

1A First look at the photos and ask *Do you know this town? Where is it?* Elicit Ss' answers and teach *pier,* using the photo. They then read the leaflet and discuss their answers to the questions in the rubric. In feedback, discuss Ss' answers and show them where Brighton and Hove is on a map if possible and tell them about the Royal Pavilion – see **Culture notes**.

B First, teach and drill the new vocabulary in the box. Use the map to convey/check meaning wherever possible. Ss find the places on the map and check with a partner if they're having problems. In feedback, elicit the answers and hold up your book to show Ss where the places are (or ask Ss to do this). Check/Drill the pronunciation of the places again. Ss then write down the words.

Answers: On the map, the bus station is on the right near the sea, the Theatre Royal is to the left of the park, car parks are marked P on blue background, the Tourist Information centre is next to the Town Hall, the Brighton Pier is on the right-hand side by the sea, a Museum and Art Gallery is in the park, the Clock Tower is by the *'You are here'* label, a park is where the Royal Pavilion and Dome is situated, Brighton Square is on the opposite side of North Street to the theatre and a library and swimming pool are in the top right-hand corner.

FUNCTION giving directions

2A First, check/teach and drill *directions,* then monitor while Ss look at the map to check how well they're doing. In feedback, elicit the three different routes but don't correct Ss at this point. They'll listen again in Ex C.

Possible answers:
Route 1: Down North Street into Castle Square to the sea.
Route 2: Down West Street, turn left, go along Grand Junction Road.
Route 3: Go down West Street, turn first left in to Duke Street, round to Prince Albert Street, Bartholomew East, turn left into Pool Valley, and left on Grand Junction Road.

B Before you play the CD, say *Listen to these directions. Is this route the same as yours?* Play the CD. Ss listen and compare their routes in pairs.

C Play the CD again. With *stronger classes*, you could play the CD again and pause the CD just before each gap for Ss to predict the missing word. Otherwise, play the CD once or twice for Ss to complete the words. Check answers and elicit the meaning of *go down, straight on, turn left* and *turn right,* then drill the phrases. In feedback, play the CD again for Ss to listen and repeat the dialogue. They then practise saying/reading it in pairs until they're confident and can do it from memory. Invite pairs to act out the dialogue, while the rest of the class check the route they drew on their maps.

Answers: 1 tell 2 Pier 3 go 4 end 5 on 6 left

3A Do the example with Ss. They then do the exercise alone and check in pairs. Don't do feedback yet – this is done in Ex B.

B Play the CD for Ss to compare their answers from Ex 3A. Elicit and check the answers before Ss listen again and repeat. Play the CD as many times as necessary until Ss are confident. Highlight and drill any specific words or phrases they have problems pronouncing. Pay close attention to sentence stress, word linking and intonation, e.g. *go straight_on, turn right_into.* Follow this up with a Ss–Ss 'test'. Ss take it in turns to point at a diagram: their partners give the correct directions.

Answers: 2 G 3 F 4 H 5 A 6 E 7 B 8 D

⇒ LANGUAGEBANK 7.3 p140–141

Check the table with the Ss and teach *go ahead. Weaker classes* could do Ex A, p141 in class.

Answers: Can you tell me *the* way to … Yes, you *turn* right at … Then go straight *on* for about … turn left *into* Menier Avenue … take *the* second street on *the* right.

4A Do an example with Ss. Elicit directions to the Royal Pavilion. Ss then work alone and choose three places. Tell them to check their directions with the examples in Ex 2B and 3A. While Ss write, monitor closely, prompting them to self-correct errors of accuracy. Try to check all Ss' work quickly before they do pairwork in Ex B.

Possible answers:
Royal Pavilion: Go down North Street and Castle Square and take the first left into the park.
Museum and Art Gallery: Go up Queens Road, turn right and go down Church Street until the end. It's in the park on the right.
The swimming pool: Go up Queens Road and take the first right into Church Street until the end. It's on the left before the park.
Church Street car park: Go up Queens Road, turn right into Church Street and take the second right.
Town Hall: Go down West Street and take the first left into Duke Street. Go down to Prince Albert Street and turn right into East Street. It's on the right.
Theatre Royal: Go down North Street and take the third left into Bond Street. It's on the right.

B Do an example of your own. Read your directions. The class follows them on their maps and tells you where they are. While Ss do the exercise in pairs, monitor discreetly and make notes on Ss' accuracy and pronunciation for feedback after Ex 4C. Invite Ss to read out their directions to the class, who follow them on their maps.

C Give Ss thinking time first. They then work with a different partner and take it in turns to give their directions. Monitor discreetly again. In feedback, write some examples of good and problematic language on the board. Ss correct the mistakes, alone or in pairs.

LEARN TO check and correct directions

5A Check the questions. Tell Ss to listen and follow the directions on the map of Brighton. With *weaker classes*, play the first two sentences on the CD so Ss can check where the speakers are on the map. Otherwise, play the whole conversation. Ss listen and follow the route. They compare their answers and listen again if necessary.

Answers: At the Royal Pavilion

B Check the rubric carefully. Ss then read and underline the phrases. In feedback, play the CD again. Pause at each phrase for Ss to listen and repeat with the correct intonation. Focus especially on the rise at the end of the phrase *The first right?* to prepare Ss for Ex 5C.

Answers: The first right? So third right, erm, left at the end of the road and then … On the left.

C First, Ss should all practise reading the conversation aloud. Monitor and help Ss with pronunciation. Do the example with Ss, making it clear that they each have to pause/check directions at the end of each sentence, not repeat the dialogue as it's written on the page. While Ss work in pairs, monitor to check Ss' intonation on the checking phrases. In feedback, Ss take it in turns to read a sentence/checking phrase each to the class. Correct and drill further if needed.

6A Do question 1 as an example. Play the CD and elicit the stressed word *third*. It would be useful for Ss to read the **speakout tip** here. They then repeat the two lines saying *third* higher, louder and longer. Play the three remaining dialogues. Ss underline the stressed words. Elicit/Check their answers.

Answers: 1 third 2 right 3 Pier 4 Road

B Play the CD again, pausing after each part B for Ss to repeat. They can then take it in turns to practise saying the dialogues in pairs. Monitor closely to check the stressed words and give feedback as required.

C First, do an example. Say the wrong name of a street, e.g. *The school's in Bath Road* (one word is wrong in the name of the street). Elicit the correction e.g. *No, it's in Bath Street.* Then set up the information gap activity carefully. First, divide the class into Ss A and Ss B and tell them which page to look at. Ss A work in pairs with other Ss A and Ss B do the same. They practise saying their set of sentences. Monitor and help Ss with pronunciation problems. Ss then work in pairs facing each other. Tell them not to show their page to their partners. Do the first example with the class to make sure Ss understand the activity. Monitor while they work, noticing any problems with stressed words. In feedback, invite pairs to read out a sentence. Drill/Correct stressed words if necessary.

SPEAKING

7 Elicit some well-known meeting places in your town and write them on the board. Make sure everybody knows where they are and the names of the streets/places nearby. If necessary, elicit/draw (or ask for a volunteer to do it) a rough map of your area on the board. Write the names of streets/places on it. N.B. If you've brought maps of your town/city, distribute one to each student. Make sure they're not too large/complex. A map of a small area of the town might be easier for Ss to use for this task. Demonstrate the activity. Ask for directions from one place to another. Interrupt and check the directions as much as you can. Then put Ss into pairs. They first decide on a starting point and then think about the places they want to visit. When they're both ready, they take it in turns to ask for/check directions. Monitor discreetly during this activity and make notes on Ss' performance for feedback later.

Homework ideas
- Ss write the directions for three places in the town/city from Ex 7 or draw/print out another map of a town they know well. Write directions from one place to three other places.
- Language bank 7.3 Ex A, p141
- Workbook Ex 1–4C, p45

BUENOS AIRES

Introduction

Ss watch a DVD extract from the BBC travel series *10 Best Holidays* and learn about life in Argentina and its capital Buenos Aires. They then learn and practice talking about a town/city and write a travel article.

SUPPLEMENTARY MATERIALS

Warm up: a world map, tango music

Ex 3A: pictures of famous towns/cities

Ex 3C: a map of Italy

Culture notes

Avenida 9th July is known as Avenida nueve de julio in Argentina/Spanish.

Diego Maradona, born on 30th October 1960, became the coach of the Argentinian football team in 2008.

The **Boca Juniors stadium** is known as La Bombanera (the Chocolate Box) because of its shape.

Warm up

Create interest in the DVD. Write *Sure. Not sure.* on the board. Ask Ss to close their books. Play some tango music, or show Argentina on a map. Ask *What type of music is this? Where does it come from?* (or *Where is this country? What's the capital city?*) *What do you know about Argentina/Buenos Aires? Which famous Argentinians do you know?* Elicit Ss' answers and ask *Are you sure? 100%? 50%?* If Ss are 100% sure, write the information in the *Sure* column; if not write it in the *Not sure* column. Then move on to Ex 1 where Ss can check their predictions.

▶ DVD PREVIEW

1A Ss look at the photos. Refer to the lists on the board and ask *Did you find any of this information in the photos?* Check and tick any information that's the same, e.g. *Maradona, famous footballer.* Put a question mark next to information that's not in the photos. Teach *polo* if necessary. Ss then answer the questions in Ex 1.

B Ss read the text alone and check their answers from Ex 1. In feedback, elicit answers and check new language, e.g. *(football) legend.* Ask *Name other football/tennis/sports legends.*

Answers: 1 play polo, watch football, eat beef, dance/watch tango, go to Avenue 9th July, visit La Boca 2 polo, football.

▶ DVD VIEW

2A Play the DVD. Tell Ss to watch the DVD and order the photos, and not worry about the language. Ss watch and check their answers in pairs. Play the DVD again if necessary. In feedback, check answers and invite any initial comments about what Ss have seen.

Answers: 1 Avenue 9th July 2 La Boca 3 football 4 tango 5 polo 6 beef

B Ss read the descriptions first. Check *poorest* and *widest.* Ss then do the exercise and check their answers in pairs.

Answers: 1 c) 2 a) 3 f) 4 d) 5 e) 6 b)

C Play the DVD again for Ss to check their answer from Ex B. In feedback, ask, e.g. *Can you dance the tango/play polo? Would you like to?*

D Ss first read the words and the extracts. Check *passion* and *emotion* but don't check new language in the extracts yet. Play the DVD again. With *weaker classes,* pause it after each gap to give time for Ss to write. In feedback, play the DVD again, stopping at each answer to elicit/check it. Here you could refer to the information with question marks on the board. Ask *Have you seen/heard anything about this?* Then ask further comprehension questions to check new language, e.g. *How many lanes does Avenue 9th July have? How does it cut through the city?*

Answers: 1 widest 2 south 3 football 4 career 5 famous 6 emotion 7 meat 8 vegetables

DVD 7   Holiday 10 Best

N=Nicki W=Woman M=Man J=Juan JF=Juan's father

N: And finally, the country that I'm in: Argentina.

The twenty-lane Avenue 9th of July is the widest street on the planet and if you need to know where you are in the city, it's an easy reference point as it cuts through the metropolis from north to south.

La Boca, the port where the first Spaniards landed, is one of the poorest regions in the city. The people of La Boca share one of Argentina's greatest passions: football. From its slums have come some of the greatest players and its most famous team. La Boca is where Diego Maradona, one of football's leading legends, began his career … So, why is football so important to Argentinians?

W: Because we are a very passionate country. We are Latins.

M: In every way we have passion: for football, for music.

We are also famous for the tango. People started dancing the tango in the 1800s.

N: It's a dance full of passion and emotion.

N: I've been riding on and off since I was eight or nine and I love horses and I've never played polo before and, apparently, Argentina is the place to learn.

N: Morning, Juan.

J: Morning.

N: Morning, Gada. First lesson: getting on the horse.

J: Come on, Nicki. You can do it!

N: I can do it. I've got to do it, haven't I? Here we go! Yay!

J: Hola, Nikki.

N: Yes! That was one! One out of a hundred!

The British originally came to Argentina for meat. Today, Argentina is still famous for its beef. It's considered the best beef in the world. Big meat-eaters over here, aren't you?

J: Yeah. I think the average of meat that a person in Argentina eats per year is, like, 80 kilos … in one year.

N: That's a lot!

J: The average. So that, that's a lot.

N: You can't be a vegetarian, can you, with all this fantastic meat?

JF: If you want, we have very good vegetables here!

N: Very social, isn't it?

JF: As you say, with family and friends, good table, good wine, you share wonderful moments. Never less than two, three hours.

N: That's it from Argentina and *Holiday 10 Best.* Join us next time. Goodbye!

3 Play the DVD again before Ss answer the questions. This time they watch for interest and to enjoy it. Give Ss 3–4 mins to discuss the questions in pairs/groups. In feedback, find out what Ss think are the two most interesting places.

speakout describe a town/city

4A Ask *What's your favourite town/city in your country?* Elicit and discuss reasons for Ss' answers. Group Ss who want to talk about the same place. In *multilingual classes*, group those who come from the same country/region. N.B. If there's only one student from each particular country/region, give them pictures of a famous city/town so that they can work in pairs. If you have internet facilities available, Ss could choose a place and search for the information they need. Ss then make a list of facts/information about their town/city. Monitor and support Ss who need help.

B Ss read the **key phrases**. Elicit sentences about the Ss' places and write one or two on the board as examples, e.g. *It's an old town in the south of France.* Ss then use their lists from Ex 4A to write sentences using the **key phrases**. Monitor closely and encourage Ss to self-correct. Don't give feedback at this point. Ss will be able to think about their notes again in Ex 4E.

> **Culture notes**
> The **Arch of Augustus** was built in honour of the Emperor Augustus in 27BC. It has a single gate 9.92m high and 8.45m wide.

C First, lead in to the topic. Ask *Where's Rimini? What do you know about it?* Elicit answers briefly. Show them a map of Italy if possible. Then check the rubric and tell Ss to look at the list of things in Ex 4A. Play the CD. Ss listen and then compare their answers in pairs. Play the CD again if needed. In feedback, elicit answers. If possible, elicit other details Ss remember about Rimini. Teach *cathedral* and *arch*.

> **Answers:** famous people

D Play the CD again. Ss tick the **key phrases** and check their answers in pairs (see answers in bold in the audio script). In feedback, elicit/drill the complete sentence for each **key phrase**. *Stronger* classes could read the audio script on p172 and check their answers.

> **Answers:** We want to talk about, (it's) an old city, It's got a, One of the most important place in … is, a typical food from … is, is a … place, You can …

Unit 7 Recording 10

M=Man   W=Woman

M: **We want to talk about** Rimini, **an old city** on the Adriatic coast in Italy. **It's got** a beautiful beach and you can swim in the sea in the summer. **One of the most important places in** Rimini **is** the cathedral, and also the Arch of Augustus.

W: Ah, but for me the most important place is the beach.

M: Yes, for me, too. And at night, the bars on the beach. You can go dancing – it's really good fun.

W: And what about the food? Well, **a typical food from** Rimini **is** 'puntarelle' or pasta with fresh vegetables, but the fish is really amazing. The city is by the sea so the fish is very fresh.

M: So, we think Rimini **is** a beautiful, relaxing **place**. **You can** sit on the beach all day, eat great food and dance all night.

E First, give Ss (the pairs who worked together in Ex 4A–B) time to add information to their notes if necessary. They also need to decide what each of them will talk about, and rehearse what they're going to say. Monitor to support and encourage Ss to self-correct. *Weaker classes/Ss* could use the audio script as a model for their own presentation. Ss then work in groups with another pair (or pairs). They take it in turns to talk about their town/city and decide which places they'd like to visit. In feedback, invite Ss from each group to tell the class where they'd like to go, and why. Give feedback on Ss' performance now or in the next lesson.

writeback a travel article

5A Lead in to the text. Give Ss 1 min to read it quickly and underline the information about Rimini they already know. Elicit Ss' answers. They then read the article again to find out at least *four* things they didn't know. Elicit and discuss Ss' answers. Ask *Do you like Fellini films? What's your favourite?* etc. Some Ss may know Rimini so could tell the class about it. Check the four topics with Ss. They work alone to divide the text into four paragraphs. In feedback, ask *Why are paragraphs important?* Because they make the text easier to organise and write; and they help the reader to understand more easily.

> **Answers:**
> Paragraph 1: ends with *have fun*
> Paragraph 2: with *childhood in Rimini*
> Paragraph 3: with *good place to eat fish*

B Ss use their notes from Ex 4 and the text in Ex 5A as a model for the first draft of their article. Remind them to divide it into 3–4 topics/paragraphs. Monitor and support Ss. Encourage them to show their drafts to other Ss and ask their advice. N.B. If they have a class blog, Ss can put their article there.

> **Homework ideas**
> * Ss write two paragraphs about their answers to the questions in Ex 3.
> * Ss write a final draft of the article about a town/city, with photos if possible.

LOOKBACK

Introduction

Lookback exercises can be used to provide extra practice or to prepare Ss for the next exercise in the Student's book, e.g. a role-play. They can also be extended to provide a freer practice and to develop Ss' confidence in their use of English.

SUPPLEMENTARY MATERIALS

Ex 5B: bring the same maps as used in Ex 7, p73

COMPARATIVES

1A Check the rubric, information and example. Then give Ss 5 mins to write the sentences alone. *Weaker Ss* could check their answers on p69 and/or p140. *Fast finishers* can try to write more than eight sentences. Monitor Ss' work and check the answers in feedback. N.B. There are more than eight possible/correct sentences.

Possible answers: The plane is more expensive/faster than the train. The train is cheaper/slower than the plane. The train/plane is more boring/interesting than the plane/train. The train is more uncomfortable/exciting/relaxing than the plane.

B Elicit an example opinion. Then give Ss 2 mins to think and make notes of their answers. Monitor and prompt *weaker Ss* to self-correct if necessary. Ss then discuss their opinions in pairs and try to convince their partners that they are right. Monitor while Ss talk and make notes on their accuracy and pronunciation for feedback, or assessment if required.

Possible answers: The train is better because its cheaper and more interesting/exciting because you can visit/see a lot of places. It's more relaxing because you can eat and sleep on the train. The **plane** is better because it's faster: it only takes 7 hours. It's more relaxing because you can eat and watch movies. The train is more crowded/uncomfortable.

Optional extra activity

If you have internet facilities available, Ss could research possible journeys from Moscow to Beijing with five places to visit on the way and download timetables, photos, etc.

This exercise could also become a more extended project. Ss plan/do research either at home or at school, collect information, write the texts, find pictures, etc. Ss choose tasks they are best suited to, e.g. writing, drawing, research.

They bring all the information to the next class and prepare their presentation of their journey to the class. It can be paper-based (e.g. an informative poster to display in the class) or computer-based (e.g. as part of the class blog, or via PowerPoint).

VOCABULARY: PLACES

2 Make this into a race. Give Ss 1 min to complete it on a piece of paper. Stop Ss after 1 min. Ss exchange papers. Elicit/Check answers and write them on the board (or Ss write). The pair with the most correctly spelt answers wins.

Answers: 1 a lake, a river 2 a jungle 3 a village, a city 4 a market 5 a desert 6 a mountain

SUPERLATIVES

3A Ss complete the quiz with the correct superlatives. Check Ss' answers before they go on to Ex 3B.

Answers: 2 biggest 3 The best 4 The safest 5 The most beautiful 6 The most popular 7 The fastest-growing 8 The busiest

B Ss do the quiz and check their answers in the key. Monitor to make sure they don't look at it until they've finished! Also make notes on their accuracy and pronunciation for feedback, or assessment if required.

CHECKING AND CORRECTING

4A Do the first question as an example, e.g. Ss write *I spell my name Jon (instead of John)*. Give Ss 2 mins to complete the exercises alone. Monitor and provide advice if needed.

B Demonstrate the activity with a *strong student*, highlighting the stressed word in the correction *France*. Monitor and assess your Ss' pronunciation. Do any necessary remedial work in feedback.

GIVING DIRECTIONS

5A Ss work alone and write the directions. Monitor closely to check the accuracy of their sentences and the pronunciation of *the*.

Answers: 1 Go down Grand Avenue and take the first left. 2 Turn right at the bank and go straight on. 3 Take the third right and then turn right into Park Lane. / Take the third right into Park Lane and then turn right. 4 It's on the left. 5 Go straight on until the end of the road and then turn right. 6 Can you tell me the way to the supermarket?

B If possible, use the same maps as in Ex 7, p 73. Monitor while Ss talk and make notes on their accuracy and pronunciation for feedback, or assessment if required.

OVERVIEW

BBC VIDEO PODCAST
What was the last film you saw?

In this video podcast, people talk about how often they go to the cinema and what kinds of films they most enjoy. They also talk about the last film they saw and their favourite actors. The video podcast would work well alongside lesson 8.3 to extend the lesson, or at the start of the unit to test Ss' existing knowledge or at the end of unit 8 to check what Ss have learnt.

IN THE PICTURE

Introduction

Ss learn/revise and practise the present continuous in the context of website blogs. They also practise everyday verb + preposition phrases and learn how pronouns can make a text more concise.

SUPPLEMENTARY MATERIALS

Resource bank p173 and p174

Ex 2: pictures of holiday/free time activities for present continuous

Warm up

Revision of comparatives and free time activities: a quiz

Before class, write numbers 1–12 on small pieces of paper (or Ss can do it) and put them in a bag/hat or similar. In class, draw a grid on the board as below but *without* the adjectives. Group Ss into teams/pairs. In turn, each pair takes a number out of the bag, e.g. 8. Tell them the adjective for number 8, e.g. *interesting*. For example:

SAMPLE KEY

1 easy	2 romantic	3 relaxing
4 noisy	5 cheap	6 good
7 comfortable	8 interesting	9 bad
10 expensive	11 bad	12 boring

Ask them to make a correct comparative sentence with free time activities, e.g. *Reading is more interesting than watching TV.* If necessary, provide prompts, e.g. *listen to (music/radio), play (piano/tennis), go/go to (shopping/cinema), have (party/dinner).* Ss get a point for a correct sentence. The team/pair with the most points wins.

SPEAKING

1A Create interest and lead in to the topic. Ask *How often do you use the internet? What are your favourite websites? Do you belong to social networking sites, e.g. Facebook? Do you share photos on them? Why/Why not?* Elicit/Discuss Ss' answers briefly. Then check vocabulary in the sentences in Ex 1: *take photos, special occasions, nature.* Ss do the exercise alone.

B Monitor while Ss compare their answers. To follow up, they could talk to another pair and make a summary of their similarities/differences, e.g. *We don't take photos on special occasions. We have different favourite subjects.* In feedback, invite/nominate Ss from each group to present the summary to the class.

Teaching tip

It's a good idea to nominate – say the name of the student you want to answer. It allows you to involve all the Ss and prevent any one student from dominating the class.

GRAMMAR present continuous

2A Ss look at the photos. Ask: *Where are the people? What do you know about these places?* Elicit and discuss Ss' answers. Use the **Culture notes** to confirm answers and/or tell Ss about the places, e.g. *Cannes is famous for its film festival.*

Culture notes

Cannes is a beach resort in the south of France. It's famous for its annual **Film Festival** which takes places in May. The **Palme d'Or** is the prestigious award given to the best film.

The **Hermitage** museum in **St Petersburg** has one of the largest and most important art collections in the world.

Caracas is the capital of **Venezuela**. The song *My Way* was made famous by Frank Sinatra in 1969. It became a signature song for him in the latter part of his career.

Karaoke originated in **Tokyo** in the 1970s and is now extremely popular all over the world. The word karaoke means 'empty orchestra' in Japanese.

With *stronger classes*, ask *What are the people in the photos doing?* Elicit answers to assess how well Ss can use the present continuous. Otherwise, Ss go straight to the matching activity. Check language in the sentences *live (jazz), clean up, lie, karaoke.* In feedback, ask *What tense is used in the sentences?* Elicit/Tell Ss what it is and go to Ex 2B.

Answers: 1 D 2 A 3 C 4 E 5 B

Watch out!

Ss are familiar with the verb *be* but they often leave it out when using the present continuous. This is because the auxiliary verb is not usually stressed so Ss don't hear it and therefore don't produce it. Highlight form clearly and monitor carefully for Ss' errors to avoid bad habits developing.

B Ss underline the verbs in the sentences. With *weaker classes*, check answers before they complete the table. *Stronger classes* could do Ex 2B–D alone/in pairs and check their answers in **Language bank** on p142. While they complete the table, write the gapped sentences on the board. In feedback, elicit answers and write them in the gaps. Underline and check the form of the present continuous: *be + verb + -ing.*

Answers: 'm; 're, -ing; 's, -ing

C Elicit and check the concept, e.g. *I'm talking to you now. You're listening to me at the moment. Is it now or every day?*

Answer: at this moment

D Again, write the gapped questions on the board and elicit/ write the answers. Ss copy them down.

Answers: 1 are 2 's (is)

E Play the CD (of the questions in Ex D). Ss check their answers from Ex D. Play it again for Ss to repeat. Drill the questions individually to check Ss' stress and intonation.

Optional extra activity

Before moving to the **Language bank**, do further controlled oral practice with 'activity' pictures. Show your pictures to the class and elicit sentences, e.g. *What are they doing? They're playing football. Is she sending a text? No, she isn't. She's talking on the phone*, etc. Then do substitution drills in open pairs using the pictures before handing them out to Ss and do a 'chain' drill. For this activity, Ss stand in a circle/ sit in a group. Give them one picture each. They ask the person on their left a question about it, using the present continuous. He/She answers it and then asks the question to the next person on their left, and so on.

⟱ LANGUAGEBANK 8.1 p142–3

Read and drill sentences in the first two tables with *weaker classes*. Also check the spelling rules. They should do Ex A, p143 now and Ex B after Ex 3A, p78.

A Ss can check their answers with the spelling rules.

Answers: 1 living 2 going 3 coming 4 putting 5 feeling 6 making 7 getting 8 standing 9 driving 10 meeting

B Pre-teach/Check *play cards, take a break, speaker phone, boss, joke.*

Answers: G: I'm reading. B: What are you reading? G: I'm reading some reports. What are you doing? B: Karl and I are playing cards and listening to music. G: Hey, why aren't you working? B: I'm taking a break. G: I'm talking on the speaker phone. The boss is listening. B: Are you joking? Boss: No, he's not joking!

PRACTICE

3A Briefly check the verbs in the box and give Ss 3 mins to write the answers. Tell them to check the spelling of the *verb + -ing* forms in the **Language bank** on p142. In feedback, elicit answers and check the form and spelling. Model/Drill any verbs Ss have problems with.

Answers: 1 're chatting, enjoying. 2 are taking 3 'm reading, 're swimming 4 's listening, 're having 5 'm feeling, 's making

B Ss discuss answers in pairs, giving reasons. Elicit these in feedback.

Answers: 1 D 2 C 3 B 4 E 5 A

C Give Ss time to think about the questions. Then check the example. Monitor closely to help *weaker Ss*. In feedback, Ss ask/answer questions across the class. Prompt Ss to correct their own and others' mistakes as necessary.

D Elicit some examples from Ss, e.g. *I think my boyfriend's playing computer games at the moment or maybe he's listening to music.* Give Ss time to write their sentences. Monitor while they talk and make a note of errors to focus on in feedback.

speakout TIP

Read and check the tip with Ss. Elicit more examples of what they're doing now, e.g. *I'm speaking English.*

VOCABULARY verbs + prepositions

4A Do an example with Ss. Suggest that they find examples of verbs and prepositions in the previous exercises if they're not sure.

Teaching tip
As prepositions are always difficult for learners of English, stress the importance of learning 'words that go together'. Remind Ss to underline collocations such as verbs and their prepositions in texts, and record them in their vocabulary books.

Answers: 1 to 2 of 3 for 4 about 5 on 6 to 7 on 8 at 9 about 10 about

B Ss listen and check their answers from Ex 4A. Then play the first phrase again and highlight the weak form and linking of *to the* /təðə/. Ss listen again and repeat the phrase until they're confident. Play the remaining phrases, pausing the CD for Ss to repeat each one.

C Check the example and elicit other nouns that go with *listen to*. Draw a word web on the board for *listen to* and add the nouns to it. Ss then do the activity, noting down the nouns they thought of. In feedback, draw word webs for each verb on the board and elicit/add the nouns to them. Ss copy them down.

Alternative extension activity
Ss work in pairs/small groups and make posters of two or three of the word webs. If possible, display them on the classroom walls.

SPEAKING

5 Set up this information gap activity carefully. First, divide the class: half As and half Bs. Check the example for both pictures. Then Ss A look at their picture and answer the questions in pairs. Ss B do the same. Monitor and help Ss with vocabulary if necessary. Then put Ss into A/B pairs, facing each other and not showing their pictures. Give Ss 4–5 mins for the activity. They take it in turns to ask/answer questions until they find the eight differences. Monitor and make notes on Ss' performance for feedback later. In feedback, nominate Ss to list the differences to the class.

Answers: In Student A's picture Keiko's wearing sunglasses; Kimoko's talking not texting on her mobile, and she's wearing a green top not a blue one; Mike's holding a sandwich, not eating an apple; Andrea's looking at his mobile, not at the Coldplay/concert poster; Angie's looking at her watch; Jim's holding a newspaper, not reading it; Viktor's running but he isn't carrying a bottle of water.

READING

6 Ss should be familiar with most of the language in the texts. Give them 2 mins to read the blogs quickly and find the missing sentences. They check their answers and must give reasons. Check answers in feedback and teach any words/phrases Ss need, e.g. *just a bit older, non-stop music, take a look.*

Answers: 3, 5

Optional extra activity
In pairs, Ss write two/three false statements about each blog and give them to another pair to correct, e.g. *Jules is staying with his parents.* (Jules is staying with his *two best friends from college.*)

WRITING pronouns

7A Read and check the example. Ask *Why is it important to use pronouns in this way?* It makes a text more concise/less repetitive.

B Monitor while Ss work and check where they draw their arrows. Nominate different Ss to answer in feedback.

Answers: *They*: my two best friends from college; *it*: our first film (x2); *she*: Angelina Jolie; *they*: all our friends; *it*: (my new) digital camera

C Check the example first. Ss should first work alone, though *weaker Ss* might prefer to work in pairs. In feedback, nominate Ss to read out one sentence at a time. Invite them to write the sentences on the board if it would be useful for them.

Answers: *He* has got a new CD and *he* played the songs from *it*; I just chatted to *them*…; I put one of *them* on … *It* is my favourite website.

D First, elicit specific events Ss have been to and write them on the board. Tell them they can write about a real event or invent one. Give them 5 mins to make notes for a first draft. They could also work in pairs if they need mutual support. Monitor and encourage Ss to show their notes to each other. Finally, remind them to use pronouns and include the names of two classmates. Ss write the final draft in class or at home.

Homework ideas
- Ss take/find some photos of friends/family and describe what they're doing.
- Ss write the final draft of their blogs in Ex 7D, or a different one.
- Language bank 8.1 Ex A–B, p143
- Workbook Ex 1–6B, p46–47

LOOKING GOOD

Introduction

Ss learn how to describe people's looks and clothes in the context of talking about famous film stars. They also revise and practise the present continuous and present simple.

SUPPLEMENTARY MATERIALS

Resource bank p175

Photo bank p158

Warm up: mobile phones/strips of paper

Ex 3E: pictures of pop/film stars

Warm up

Revision of present continuous and clothing vocabulary

Ss write their mobile phone number on a piece of paper and give them to you. Hand them out to different Ss. Tell them to send this text to the number they have: *What are you wearing?* Ss reply to the message saying, e.g. *I'm wearing a red T-shirt and jeans.* Ss then identify the person who sent the text and say hello. N.B. If Ss can't use mobile phones, tell them to write the answer to the question on a piece of paper. Collect/Redistribute the papers to different Ss who then identify the person who sent the message.

Culture notes

Actress **Michelle Yeoh**, born 1962 in Malaysia, is best known for *Crouching Tiger* and *Hidden Dragon*.

Scarlett Johansson, born 1984, is an American actress and singer. Her films include *Vicky Cristina Barcelona* and *Iron Man II*.

Will Smith, born 1968, is an American actor and rapper. His films include *Men in Black* and *The Pursuit of Happyness*.

Sean Connery, born 1930, is best known for his seven James Bond films.

Gael Garcia Bernal, born 1978, is a Mexican actor/director. His films include *The Motorcycle Diaries* and *Blindness*.

British theatre/film actress, Dame **Judy Dench**, born 1934, has played *M* in recent James Bond films.

SPEAKING

1A Elicit/Drill the names of the people in the photos and check the example. Then give Ss 2 mins to do the exercise.

B Check *good-looking*. Ss then discuss the question in pairs. Tell them to give reasons, e.g. *appearance, hair, eyes, smile* to activate the descriptive language they know. Use the information in the **Culture notes** as prompts if necessary. Elicit/Discuss answers in feedback.

VOCABULARY appearance

2A Check new vocabulary using the photos, e.g. *dark, curly, beard, late 70s, early 80s, make-up.* Ss match the photos and compare answers before feedback. Check Ss' answers and drill the pronunciation. Check the difference between the use of *have got* and *be* with descriptive language: *have got* + adj + noun; *be* + adj. Elicit more examples of the language using the photos/your Ss, e.g. *Mia is in her teens/She's got long dark hair.*

Answers:
1 a) C and F b) B c) D d) C and D e) A, C and D
2 a) D b) C and F c) B and E d) A, B and F e) A and B

B Ss listen and write the answers. In feedback, elicit/check the descriptions. N.B. Michelle Yeoh looks younger than she is.

Answers: 1 Michelle Yeoh 2 Will Smith

C Play the CD, pausing after each question for Ss to write. In feedback, check the meaning of question 2. Ask *Does the questions ask about character/appearance?* Contrast this with *What's she like?* which can be about both character and appearance.

Answers: 1 Is it a man or a woman? 2 What does she look like?

D First, drill the questions in open pairs across the class. Ss answer with information about one of their classmates. They then work in pairs, taking it in turns to ask/answer the questions using the film stars. Monitor and prompt Ss to self-correct.

▶ PHOTOBANK p158

APPEARANCE AND CLOTHES

1A–B Check the use of *fat* and *thin* versus *overweight* and *slim*. After they've labelled the photos, Ss write sentences about each picture, e.g. *He's short and overweight and is wearing a blue shirt and trousers.* Ss should do these exercises in class to help with the listening.

Answers: B: 1 N 2 I 3 D 4 H 5 J 6 C 7 B 8 E 9 F 10 G 11 M 12 A 13 L 14 K

2 This is a very useful exercise to check in class if time allows. Ss write sentences describing each person's clothes, e.g. *She's wearing a black coat and trousers and a black jacket.*

Answers: adj: tall, short, slim, overweight, bald, straight, curly, long, short U: hair, jeans, trousers, shorts
C sing: suit, jacket, shirt, tie, top, skirt, sweater, dress, T-shirt, coat C pl: socks

LISTENING

3A Check the words *fashion* and *beauty*. Play the CD and elicit Ss' answers. Check *masculine* and *feminine*.

Answer: ideas of beauty

B Give Ss time to read the text before listening. Play the CD and Ss then compare answers. Play it again if necessary. Ask Ss to put their hands up if they agree with the stereotypes. They'll have a chance to discuss this later.

Answers: 1 blonde 2 blue 3 dark 4 masculine

C Before playing the CD, reassure Ss that they only need listen for the names of the stars.

Answers: Sean Connery, Gael Garcia Bernal, Will Smith, Judy Dench, Scarlett Johansson

D First, check the rubrics. Tell Ss to only write words/short phrases in the table/their notebooks.

Answers:
W1: tall, good-looking
W2: black hair, dark brown eyes, feminine face, good-looking
W3: red hair, good-looking
M1: grey eyes, lovely, kind, intelligent
M2: slim, blonde hair, blue eyes

E First, elicit some opinions to illustrate what Ss have to talk about. While they talk in groups, monitor and make notes of their performance. Focus on examples of good language/ errors with the target language in feedback.

Unit 8 Recording 5

I=Interviewer   W1=1st woman   W2=2nd woman
W3=3rd woman   M1=1st man   M2=2nd Man

I: Excuse me, ladies. Do you have a moment?

W1:   Yes?

I: Just a quick question. Research says that these days women prefer men with feminine faces.

W1:   Really?

I: Yes. It's true, honestly!

W1:   I don't agree at all. I like masculine faces.

I: Can I show you some photos?

W1:   Sure.

I: So which of these guys do you like best?

W1:   Sean Connery. He's definitely the best looking man here. And he's tall, isn't he? Yeah, I like tall men. And I like a man with a beard.

I: Uh-huh. What about you?

W2:   I'm not sure. I like this one, what's his name?

I: It's Gael Garcia Bernal. He's a Mexican film star.

W2:   Yeah? Well, he's got quite a feminine face and he's very good-looking. I like his eyes – he's got dark brown eyes and I like men with dark eyes and black hair. But I think it's more in the personality, in the smile, so I like this one best. Will Smith. He's got a really nice smile.

I: Thank you. And here's another lady. Excuse me. Have you got a moment?

W3:   Well …

I: I'm doing a survey about the changing face of beauty. Can I ask you some questions?

W3:   Yes, OK. Yes.

I: I've got some photos here. Can you tell me which of these people you like? Do you think any of them are good-looking?

W3:   Well, I don't really like any of them …

I: No? So what sort of man *do* you like?

W3:   What sort of man do I like? Well, my husband's over there. I think he's good-looking. I like his hair. I love guys with red hair.

I: Which one? The one looking in the shop window?

W3:   No, he's over there. He's wearing a white T-shirt and he's talking to – that blonde woman. Excuse me.

I: And then I talked to some men to find out if they really prefer blondes – just like they did fifty years ago. Do you think it's true that men prefer blondes, sir?

M1:   What? No, not at all! Beauty comes in all shapes and sizes and ages. Look at this photo of Judy Dench. She's lovely. She isn't young, but she's got beautiful grey eyes and she always wears beautiful clothes. She looks kind and intelligent.

M2:   Yeah, she does. But I still prefer blondes, you know , like Scarlett Johansson. She's lovely, slim, blonde hair, blue eyes – that's the sort of woman I like.

M1:   Scarlett Johansson, *slim*?

M2:   Well, OK, but she's not *fat*.

M1:   No, that's true.

I: OK, guys. Thanks for talking to us.

GRAMMAR   present simple/continuous

4A Write the two sentences on the board and elicit, underline and check the answers. *Stronger classes* can do Ex 4A–C alone and check their answers in **Language bank** on p142.

> **Answers:** 1 wears, present simple 2 's wearing, present continuous

Watch out!

Ss tend to confuse both the form and meaning of the present simple and continuous, mainly due to L1 interference and/or confusion with the *do* and *be* auxiliary verbs. It's important to contrast/provide practice where both tenses are used. In Ex 4–6, raise Ss' awareness by prompting self-correction while monitoring in feedback.

B Elicit and check the answers using the two sentences on the board. Also check the concept of the present simple to talk about things which are always true, e.g. *She works in Paris.*

> **Answers:** 1 present simple 2 present continuous

C Ss can check their answers in the **Language bank** on p142.

> **Answers:** do, wear; are, wearing; wear, am wearing

➡ LANGUAGEBANK 8.2 p142–3

Weaker/Mixed ability classes should do the exercises in class and write answers for the Ex B questions.

> **Answers:**
> A 2 watch, am watching 3 have, are having 4 am writing, phone 5 listen to, are listening to 6 stays, is staying
> B 2 Are, studying 3 Does, work 4 Is, working
> 5 Is, wearing 6 Does, wear 7 Do, do 8 Are, doing
> 9 Do, listen 10 Are, listening

PRACTICE

5A First, check *businessman* and *walker* in the cartoons.
N.B. Some languages use the verb phrase *wear a bag* so ask Ss *What's the man/woman carrying?* and elicit answers. Check Ss' answers after their discussion of the problems.

B Ss do the exercise alone and then compare their answers. In feedback, recheck the concept of the two tenses.

> **Answers:** 1 wear 2 's wearing 3 isn't wearing
> 4 's wearing 5 don't wear

C First, check *high-heeled shoes*. This time Ss have to provide the verbs themselves so recheck the use of *wear* and *carry* in feedback. Ask Ss to justify their use of tenses here.

> **Answers:** 1 don't 2 wear 3 wear 4 's wearing
> 5 's wearing 6 's not carrying 7 's carrying

6 Give Ss 1 min to look around at the clothes other Ss are wearing. Then pair them with Ss from a different part of the classroom to make this exercise more challenging.

SPEAKING

7A Give Ss 3 mins to think/make notes. Elicit some example answers before Ss work in pairs. Monitor and make notes on their accuracy. Give feedback on this to help them with Ex B.

B Take notes on examples of good language and problems for later. Invite Ss to tell the class about their partners in feedback.

Homework ideas

- Ss write a paragraph describing their favourite celebrity with a photo, after Ex 3.
- Ss write a description of their favourite kinds of clothes and when they wear them, after Ex 7.
- Language bank 8.2 Ex A–B, p143
- Workbook Ex 1A–5C, p49

WHAT DO YOU RECOMMEND?

Introduction

Ss learn and practise how to talk about and recommend films. They also practise how to link word to help them be better listeners and make their pronunciation sound more natural.

SUPPLEMENTARY MATERIALS

Resource bank p176

Ex 7–8: download/copy current film listings

Warm up

Revise descriptions: pair/group activity

Tell Ss to look at the people in the film posters and to pick out one person. Give them 2–3 mins to note down a brief description. Then demonstrate the activity. Ask: *Is it a man/ woman? Is he tall or short? Is he slim or overweight? Is he bald? Has he got a beard?* Elicit some example answers. Ss then work in pairs. Give them 2 min each to ask/answer their partner's questions. Nominate Ss to describe the person to the class.

SPEAKING

1A Activate Ss' interest in the topic. Ask *Do you like watching films? How often? Once/twice a month? Every week?* Elicit Ss' answers and have a brief discussion. Check the rubric and elicit some answers to the first question. Ss then work alone and write their answers to the questionnaire.

B Ss compare and make notes of their partner's answers. In feedback, nominate Ss to tell the class about their partner. Prompt them to self-correct if/when necessary.

VOCABULARY types of film

Culture notes

The Notebook (2004) is a love story centred around an old man (James Garner) who reads from a faded notebook to a older, invalid woman (Gena Rowlands) and together they relive the unforgettable love they shared.

Computer-animated adventure film **Ice-age 3** (2009) is set in prehistoric times and was directed by Oscar®-nominated Carlos Saldanha.

Drama **Glory Road** (2006) was inspired by a true story of Texas Western's Coach Don Haskins (Josh Lucas), who led the first all-black starting line-up team to the 1966 NCAA national basketball championship.

Night at the Museum 2 is a 2009 American comedy and the film's line-up included Ben Stiller, Amy Adams, Owen Wilson, Steve Coogan, Ricky Gervais and Robin Williams.

Award-winning Swedish romantic vampire (horror) film **Let the Right One In** was remade in English and released in 2010.

Sci-fi action adventure **Star Trek: The Future Begins** (2009) is a chronicle of the early days of Kirk and his *USS Enterprise* crew members and was directed by J.J. Abrams.

Romantic musical comedy **Mamma Mia!** (2008), based on music by Abba, starred Meryl Streep and Pierce Brosnan.

Crime action thriller **The Taking of Pelham 123** (2009) pitted Denzel Washington and John Turtorro against a group of hijackers, lead by John Travolta, who take over a subway train in order to rake in a hefty ransom.

2A Ss look at the posters. Ask *Have you seen any of these films? Who was in them? Did you enjoy them? Why/Why not?* Ss answer in pairs or in open class. Check/Teach and elicit the pronunciation of the words in the word box, using the film posters and/or Ss' knowledge of the films. Point out that we often describe films with an adj + noun, e.g. *a romantic comedy, an action thriller.* (*romantic, horror, animated, action* and *sci-fi* cannot be used as nouns so need to be followed by *film.*) Ss then do the exercise alone and check in pairs. *Stronger Ss* could use adj + nouns. In feedback, elicit Ss' answers and/or use the **Culture notes.** To check further, elicit examples of other films of the same genre, e.g. *Aliens* for sci-fi film.

Answers: B comedy C musical D action film E animated film F horror film G drama H sci-fi film

B Don't check new words in the exercise before Ss do it but monitor to see what they know/don't know. In feedback, check answers and teach new vocabulary, e.g. *UFO* (Unidentified Flying Object), *alien, space, scary.*

Answers: 2 musical 3 comedy 4 sci-fi film 5 horror film 6 action film 7 drama 8 animated film

C Check the example. Ss answer the questions in pairs. Monitor and note down any problems with the pronunciation/ meaning of the new vocabulary for feedback.

FUNCTION recommending

3A Introduce the context of the conversations: *two friends are choosing a DVD to rent.* Also reassure Ss that they only need to listen for the *types of films* mentioned: they'll listen to the CD again later. Ss listen and compare answers (in bold in the audio script). Do feedback. Briefly elicit other information about the films *Speed, French Kiss, Chocolat.*

Answers: romantic comedy, comedies, action films, romantic films, dramas

B Tell Ss to focus on the questions. *Stronger Ss* could also note down words they don't understand. After Ss have compared answers, play the CD again if they still have doubts.

Answers: 1 They decide to rent *French Kiss* because John likes Meg Ryan and comedies. 2 The woman says she'd like to see *Chocolat* because she likes Johnny Depp.

Unit 8 Recording 6

Conversation 1

M=Man W=Woman

W: OK, what do you feel like watching?

M: Hmm. I don't know really. <u>What do you recommend?</u>

W: Erm, … Well, <u>how about *French Kiss*</u>? Do you know it?

M: No, I don't think so. What's it about?

W: Well, it's a **romantic comedy**. It's about an American woman. She goes to France and meets a French guy and … they fall in love. It's quite old, but it's really funny.

M: Sounds OK, I suppose. Who's in it?

W: Meg Ryan and Kevin Kline.

M: Oh, I like Meg Ryan. Mmm. <u>Do you think I'd like it?</u>

W: Yeah, I think so. You like **comedies**, don't you? And it's very funny.

M: Yeah, OK. Why don't we get it then?

W: Great. Excuse me. Can we have this one, please?

Conversation 2

M=Man W=Woman

W: What was the last DVD you saw?

M: Let me think. Oh – I know, it was *Speed*.

W: *Speed*? Is it new? What's it about?

M: No, a bit old actually. It's an **action film**. It's about a bus and it can't stop. It has to go at top speed or … or it explodes. It's great!

W: Right. Who's in it?

M: Sandra Bullock and the guy is, the actor is, er, … Keanu Reeves.

W: <u>Do you think *I'd* like it?</u>

M: Well, do you like **action films**?

W: Not really. I prefer **romantic films** and **dramas**.

M: Oh, then I *don't* think you'd like it. Well. Oh, I know. <u>I think you'd like that **French film**</u>, you know, with the actress Juliette Binoche. What's it called? Oh, yeah: *Chocolat*.

W: *Chocolat*? Do I know it? Oh, with Johnny Depp? Mmm! Now that *is* a good recommendation. Have you got the DVD?

4A Ss now focus on recommendation language in the recording. Check the example. Ss then write the answers alone and check in pairs.

B Ss listen to an extract from recording 8.6 and check their answers from Ex 4A. Elicit and check their answers and then play the CD again. Pause after each sentence for Ss to repeat. Drill further if necessary: highlight/elicit the stress and intonation to prepare for Ex 5.

> **Answers:** 2 How about *French Kiss*? 3 Do you think I'd like it? 4 I don't think you'd like it. 5 I think you'd like that French film.

> ⟱ **LANGUAGEBANK** 8.3 p142–3
>
> Ss read the table on p142 and can refer to it when they do Ex A p143. *Weaker Ss* could do it in class.
>
> **A** Check *borrow*.
>
> > **Answers:** What *do you* recommend? What films *do you* like? *There's* a good film called *Rush Hour*. Who's in it? What's *it* about? Do you think I'd like *it*?

---

5 Give Ss 1 min to decide on the film they'd recommend. Then check/drill the example dialogue before Ss work in pairs. Monitor discreetly while Ss talk. Make notes of how well they use the target language for feedback later.

LEARN TO link words to speak faster

6A The table here contains another extract from audio script 8.6. Ss complete the questions and compare them with a partner. Answers are checked in Ex B.

> **Answers:** 1 do you recommend 2 's it about 3 's in it? 4 'd like it 5 don't we get it then

speakout TIP

Read the tip and drill the example. Ss will practise word linking in Ex C.

B Play the CD: Ss check their answers from Ex 6A. They should write them in their notebooks to prepare for Ex C.

C Play the CD again. Ss listen for the word linking in each question and draw the word links. Invite Ss to write the sentences with word links on the board. Then elicit/drill them. Reinforce this with extra listening/repeating if needed.

> **Answers:**
> 3 Who's‿in‿it?
> 4 Do you think‿I'd like‿it?
> 5 Why don't we get‿it then?

D Ss might need to practise the conversation several times until they can say the questions confidently. Monitor closely to help them with word linking. In feedback, invite Ss to act out the dialogue to the class.

7A Elicit films that Ss know well, or hand out film listings to Ss if you've brought them. They discuss/decide which eight to choose. Help them with the English titles if necessary.

B Give Ss time to think/make notes on the film and provide support to those who need it. Ss then work in pairs and take turns to be A/B. Monitor closely and encourage Ss to self-correct any problems with the target language in preparation for Ex 8.

SPEAKING

8 Elicit some current films that are on in your town/country (or use the film listings from Ex 7 again). Give Ss time to prepare and provide help with vocabulary if necessary. Monitor discreetly and make notes on Ss' performance. In feedback, elicit/discuss the films Ss chose and their recommendations for the class. Give feedback as required.

> **Homework ideas**
> - Ss write a paragraph about the films they like and why from Ex 2.
> - Ss write a dialogue recommending a film they saw recently or write a description of their favourite films from Ex 8.
> - Language bank 8.3 Ex A, p143
> - Workbook Ex 1A–3C, p50

FESTIVAL HIGHLIGHTS

Introduction

Ss watch an extract from a BBC current affairs programme which is about *Bestival*, a summer music festival. Ss then learn and practise talking about an event and writing a review.

SUPPLEMENTARY MATERIALS

Ex 2: a map of England with Isle of Wight on it

Ex 6A: use internet facilities if you have them

Ex 6/7: download/copy information about events taking place in your area/country

Warm up

Lead in and create interest. Ask *What type of events are there in your area/region? Do they happen regularly?* e.g. festivals, concerts, sports events, exhibitions, theatre/shows. Ss discuss the questions in pairs/small groups. If you have a *multilingual class*, Ss from the same country/region could work together. In feedback, elicit Ss' answers and encourage the class to ask further questions about the events.

▌ DVD PREVIEW

1 Ss look at the photos first and elicit information about them. Ask, e.g. *What are the people doing/wearing? Where are they? Do you go to events like these?* Teach/Check *music festival* and elicit music festivals Ss know of/like. Check the words in the box for question 3. Give Ss 3–4 mins to discuss the questions in Ex 1A in pairs. In feedback, invite Ss to report their answers back to the class.

Culture notes

The Isle of Wight is a small island off the south coast of England between Bournemouth and Portsmouth.

Bestival is a three-day music festival and is much smaller than many of the more famous ones like Glastonbury. It's well known for its 'fancy dress' days and for piloting innovative ideas, including an inflatable church where people can get married. The local **Women's Institute (WI)** also gets involved, providing cheap food and drink for the festival-goers.

2 Ss read the text alone and answer the questions in pairs. In feedback, elicit answers and check *surprising, well-known, take place*. Find out if Ss know about the Isle of Wight, and Bestival. If not, show them a map of England and use the Culture notes.

Answers: A music festival on the Isle of Wight every September.

▶ DVD VIEW

3A Ss first read the sentences. Check/Teach new language *put up a tent, a beach hut, a tea tent* and do an example. Ss underline their answers and compare them.

B Tell Ss to watch the DVD and look out for the information in Ex 3A. Then play it again for them to check and compare their answers. In feedback, elicit answers and invite initial comments about Bestival.

Answers: 1 singing 2 boots 3 sofa 4 beach hut 5 orange 6 tent 7 at night 8 eating and drinking

4 Check the rubric and statements carefully (underlined in the DVD script). Teach *playground, grownups, mix together*. Ss watch the DVD again, note down their answers and compare them. In feedback, Ss shout *stop!* when a true answer comes up. Elicit and correct false answers in feedback.

Answers: 2 T 3 F 4 T 5 F 6 T

5 Ss first read the extracts (in italics in the DVD script) but don't check new language yet. Play the DVD again. With *weaker classes*, pause it after each extract to give time for Ss to write. In feedback, check the answers (in bold in the DVD script). Also discuss the opinions with Ss and check any new language you think is useful.

Answers: 1 garden 2 wife 3 holiday 4 free 5 jobs 6 young 7 people 8 cakes

Optional extra activity

If time, play the DVD again for Ss to watch and enjoy. Then ask *What do you think about Bestival? Would you like to go? Why/Why not?* Ss discuss their opinions in groups or in open class.

DVD 8 Inside Out

VO=Voiceover M1=1st Man M2=2nd Man M3=3rd Man
W1=1st Woman W2=2nd Woman W3=3rd Woman

VO: All over the world, festivals bring people together. But why do people go? For the music? The food? The fun and games? We went to Bestival in the Isle of Wight, England to find out. But the first question is – where do we sleep?

M1: Um, I've got a beach hut up here to stay in. I've got the key.

VO: One man said it was like sleeping in the back garden.

M2: *It's like opening your back door, going down to the end of your garden, getting in your shed with your baby and wife, and then calling it a holiday.*

VO: You can stay in a hut, but most people here sleep in tents. There are a lot of different people here – families, young people, older people. We asked: Why do so many different people come to festivals?

W1: *Well, I suppose it gives everybody a chance just to be themselves, and just ... be free ... and be away from their normal jobs.*

W2: People will respect each other and have, um, sort of some of those old-fashioned traditional values, but actually values that everyone really likes.

M3: The thing I always think about festivals is they're just playgrounds for grownups.

VO: And, of course, there's one reason everyone's here: the music. This really is a festival for all the community, young and old mixing together. In the tea tent these women are having a good time. Why do they go to festivals?

W3: *The community getting together and the young mixing with the older people. We make cakes, we do pop festivals, we'll go anywhere, do anything.*

VO: So, if there's one answer to the question, 'Why are you here?', one thing that everyone talks about is this: being together.

speakout describe an event

6A Ask *What was the best event you went to recently?* Elicit and discuss Ss' answers briefly. Tell them they're now going to talk about this event. Read/Check the rubric and questions and teach *recommend*. Put Ss who want to talk about the same even in pairs. In *multilingual classes*, group those who've travelled from the same country/region recently. Give them 4–5 mins to make notes. Monitor and help Ss with vocabulary they need. N.B. If Ss haven't been to an event recently (or even if they have) and you have access to internet facilities, they could search for information about a local event that's already taken place.

B Check the rubric and play the CD. Ss listen and compare answers. Play the CD once or twice, depending on the doubts Ss have when they compare their answers. In feedback, elicit Ss' answers and check/teach useful words *stage, picnic*.

Answers: A Double-X concert, in City Park. Yes.

Alternative approach
Before Ss listen to the CD, they look at the first four questions in Ex 6A again. Tell them to make notes of the answers to these questions as they listen.

Unit 8 Recording 9

Recently **I went to** a concert in the park with my boyfriend and some other friends. **It was in** City Park. **We went because** we all like the band, Double-X, and we listen to their music all the time. The concert only lasted two hours, but we took a picnic with us and went out early in the afternoon – **it was a free concert,** you see, so there were already a lot of people sitting out in the park in front of the stage. We got a really good place, close to the stage. We chatted and lay in the sun all afternoon – and then in the evening more and more people came and it got quite crowded. Then the concert started and well, it was – fantastic! Double-X is an amazing band, and better *live*! **I really liked the concert because** everyone was dancing and singing – we had a great time.

C Ss read the **key phrases**. Elicit example sentences about Ss' events from Ex 6A as examples, e.g. *Last week I went to the film festival in Cannes.* Play the CD again. Ss tick the **key phrases** and check their answers in pairs (see answers in bold in the audio script). In feedback, elicit/drill the complete sentence for each keyphrase. *Stronger classes* could read the audio script on p173 and check their answers.

D First, give Ss time to rewrite/fine tune their notes with the **key phrases**. Monitor closely and encourage Ss to self-correct inaccuracies in their writing. Ss then work in groups, taking it in turns to talk about their event, using their notes. Other Ss in the group ask their two questions at the end. The group then decides which events they like to go to. Monitor discreetly and take notes on Ss' accuracy, fluency and pronunciation. In feedback, invite Ss from each group to tell the class about the events they recommend. Give feedback on Ss' performance now or in the next lesson.

writeback a review

7A Give Ss 1 min to read the text quickly and decide what type of event it is. Elicit their answers after they've discussed them in pairs. Check Ss have understood *comedian*.

Answers: a comedy show

B Check the rubric and topics. Ss then do the exercise alone. In feedback, check the answers and ask *Do you like comedy shows? Do you go to any? Why/Why not?*

Answers: a) 4 b) 2 c) 3 d) 1

C Ss use their notes from Ex 6A and the text in Ex 7A as a model for the first draft of their review. Monitor and support them. Encourage them to show their drafts to other Ss and ask for advice. Also remind them to write only 80–100 words. If they have a class blog, Ss can put their review there.

Homework ideas
• Ss write a final draft of the review in Ex 7C.

LOOKBACK

Introduction

The **Lookback** exercises are very flexible and can be exploited in a variety of ways, e.g. as fillers if there's time at the end of the lesson or to provide a change of pace and interaction between other activities.

ACTIVITIES

1A Ss could do this as a race in pairs. The first to finish with the correct answers wins. *Weaker Ss* could look back in the unit to find/check their answers on p79.

> **Answers:** 2 lie on the beach 3 listen to jazz 4 have a great time 5 look at art 6 have a coffee 7 read a book
> *Hidden message:* feel good

B Check the rubric and put Ss into groups. Give them 4 mins to discuss their answers and see what they have in common: *who prefers to do things alone/with other people/outside?* Monitor while Ss talk and make notes on their accuracy and pronunciation for feedback, or assessment if required.

PRESENT CONTINUOUS

2A Do question 1 as an example. Ss then work alone and write the answers. Check answers and spelling in feedback.

> **Answers:** 1 's raining 2 's flying 3 's sitting 4 are talking 5 's working 6 are driving 7 are playing 8 's making

B Tell Ss to be quiet, listen carefully for noises that match the sentences in Ex 2A and tick them. If necessary/appropriate, Ss then look through the window or go outside for a few minutes to check the other sentences.

DESCRIBING APPEARANCE

3A Check the examples. Then give Ss 2–3 mins to write the other questions. *Fast finishers* can write more questions. Check and drill the answers before they do Ex B. N.B. Ss could also do this with pictures of famous people if you have them.

> **Answers:** 3 Has he/she got long hair? 4 Is he/she tall? 5 Is he/she wearing a black sweater? 6 Is he/she in his/her twenties? 7 Has he/she got brown shoes? 8 Has he/she got blue eyes?

B Demonstrate the activity with an example of your own first. Monitor discreetly while Ss talk and make notes on their performance for feedback, or assessment if required.

CLOTHES

4A Make this into a race. Ss work in pairs. Give them 1 min to complete the words on a piece of paper. Stop them after 1 min and get Ss to swap papers. Elicit/Check the answers and invite Ss to write them on the board. The pair with the most correctly spelt answers wins.

> **Answers:** 2 shoes 3 socks 4 jeans 5 trousers 6 skirt 7 T-shirt 8 jacket 9 top

B Do this as a competition in pairs/teams. Number the teams. Team A starts by saying a clothes word. Team B have 5–10 seconds to look round the classroom and find someone who's wearing the item. Then Team B says a word for Team D, and so on. Teams get a point for each correct answer.

> **Optional extra activity**
> Ss look at p158 and write six of their own jumbled clothes (and describing appearance) words from there. They then swap papers with other Ss, who have to write the words correctly.

PRESENT SIMPLE AND PRESENT CONTINUOUS

5A Ss could write other questions if any of the ones here don't apply to Ss in your class. Monitor closely to check the accuracy of their questions.

> **Sample answers:** 2 Does X usually use an electronic dictionary? Is she/he using an electronic dictionary now? 3 Does X often chew gum? Is he/she chewing gum at the moment? 4 Does X always speak English in class? Is X speaking English now? 5 Does X often wear black? Is X wearing black today?

B When Ss have answered the questions, do feedback in open pairs across the class. Encourage Ss to self-correct or correct each other.

RECOMMENDING

6A Monitor while Ss write and encourage them to check each other's work. They then practise reading the dialogue aloud in pairs.

> **Answers:** A: I want to read a good book. What do you recommend? B: What kind of books do you like? A: Travel books and good stories. B: I've got *Life of Pi* by Yann Martel. It's very good. A: What's it about? B: It's about a boy and a tiger on a boat. A: Do you think I'd like it? B: Yes, I do. A: OK. Can I borrow it? B: Sure.

B Ss could walk around the room for this activity or work in three different pairs. Monitor while Ss talk and make notes on their accuracy and pronunciation for feedback, or assessment if required.

OVERVIEW

BBC VIDEO PODCAST

How do you get to work?

In this video podcast, people talk about how they travel to work and what they like and don't like about their journeys to and from work. They also discuss what they like to do on their journey to work. The material consolidates Ss' transport vocabulary and contextualises common phrases associated with travelling around a city. We recommend using the video podcast at the start to introduce the unit's topic or end of unit 9 as a round up.

TRAVEL IN STYLE

Introduction

Ss learn and practise the use of articles and verb + noun collocations in the context of transport. They listen to and talk about imaginative ideas for transport, both real and imagined.

SUPPLEMENTARY MATERIALS

Resources bank p177 and p178

Photo bank p159

Ex 6B: ask Ss to bring dictionaries, or provide them

Warm up

Lead in to the lesson topic: mingling activity

Before class, write the names of different types of transport from the box in Ex 1A on stickers, one for each student (or ask Ss to do this). Put one sticker on the back of each person. Ss then walk round the class and ask and answer yes/no questions to find out the type of transport without using any other transport words, e.g. Does it go on the road? Is it big? Is it for lots of people? Stop the activity when most Ss have found out their type of transport.

VOCABULARY | transport collocations

1A Before Ss open their books, ask: Have you got a car? What type of car is it? How often do you use it? Do you have a bike? Why/Why not? Discuss Ss' answers briefly. Ss look at the pictures and the word box. Elicit the words in the photos and check/teach the other words. Ask: What do you think of the types of transport in the photos?

Answers: A train B plane, car C helicopter

B Write the example word web on the board and check instructions. Check/Mime the verbs in the word webs, e.g. get on/off. Tell Ss to write the correct versions of word webs in their notebooks as they do the exercise. In feedback, nominate Ss to write their word webs on the board. The class decide if they are correct and suggest other words which collocate with each verb. Check go on foot.

Answers: take a plane; get on a ~~car~~ bus/train/bike/horse; get off a ~~taxi~~ plane/bike/horse/motorbike; go by ~~foot~~ bus/plane/train/taxi/car; ride a ~~plane~~ motorbike

---

 **PHOTOBANK** p159

1 Ss do the exercise and tick the words they already know. Check answers and pronunciation. Ss then copy the words and underline the stressed syllable.

Answers: 1 E 2 N 3 L 4 O 5 P 6 C 7 M 8 J 9 H 10 B 11 G 12 A 13 K 14 D 15 F 16 I

2 In feedback, elicit Ss' answers and recheck the pronunciation.

Answers: land: taxi, scooter, tram, bike, underground/subway train, van, motorbike, train, bus, lorry/truck, car; sea: ship, boat, ferry; air: helicopter, plane

C Ss could point to the photos in the **Photo bank** for this exercise. In feedback, check answers and add new words to the word webs on the board.

D Do an example with Ss and encourage them to show interest in response to their partner's answers, e.g. A: *I usually go by bus.* B: *That's a good idea. How long does it take?* Ss work in pairs/groups and should make notes of their partner's(s') answers before reporting back to the class in feedback.

LISTENING

Culture notes
The term **World Fair** has become known as a Universal Exposition or **Expo,** which takes place every five years. It's is a very large international exhibition where participating countries show the best of their culture and industry, and where trade is promoted. The last Expo was in 2010 and was held in Shanghai, China.

2A Ss read the sentences and look at/match the pictures. Check Ss' answers and elicit more detail about each type of transport. Check/Teach *garage.* Ask *Do these types of transport exist? Are they a good idea?* Use the **Culture notes** to talk about what a World Fair is if necessary.

Answers: 1 A   2 C   3 B

B Tell Ss the museum guide is in a transport museum. Check Ss understand the type of museum by asking questions like *What can you see in museums like this?* Tell Ss to listen and focus only on answering the two questions. Check answers in feedback and elicit any other details Ss heard.

Answers: 1 All of them.   2 On foot/By bike.

C Tell Ss to listen carefully and take brief notes if possible. Play the CD twice if Ss still have doubts after the first listening. Play the relevant extracts from the CD (underlined in the audio script) in feedback, stopping after each one to elicit and check Ss' answers. Teach *keep in good condition, strong.* N.B. *No way* was originally an American English phrase. It means *I don't believe it/It's not possible* and is widely used colloquially in the UK nowadays.

Answers: 1 Monorails are difficult to build and expensive to keep in good condition.   2 The car was too heavy and small planes weren't strong enough to carry them.
3 Helicopters are very difficult to fly so they would cause traffic problems in the sky, and they're too noisy.

Unit 9 Recording 1

G=Guide   V1=1st visitor   V2=2nd visitor   V3=3rd visitor
G: So, ladies and gentlemen … Let's move into the transport section now. Could you all come over this way? Let's look at these photos. As you can see, these early methods of transport have two things in common – they're all great ideas, great ways to travel through the air rather than on the ground … but they weren't successful! **There was a big problem with each one.**
V1: But the monorail – that was successful.
Guide: Well, yes and no. *Look at this photo on the left. It's from the World Fair in Seattle. That was in 1962. Monorails were a very popular idea in America at that time. People wanted to leave their cars at home and go to work by public transport.* <u>But they weren't successful – monorails are difficult to build and expensive to keep in good condition. So you're right.</u> There are some monorails in the world, but not very many.
V2: Hey, look at this photo. Is that a car under a plane?

G: Oh, yes this was a very interesting idea. **People wanted to fly from Los Angeles to New York** – and then drive straight into the city centre from the airport.
V2: No way! How?
G: Well, the idea was that the car came off the bottom of the plane and then – you got in and drove away. This was in the 1940s. Ah, yes. Look, here's the date: 1948. It was a nice idea – no airports or waiting around – but it wasn't successful.
V2: Why not?
G: **There was an engineering problem** – <u>the car was too heavy and small planes weren't strong enough to carry them.</u>
V3: What's this? A helicopter in the garage?
G: Yes, indeed. **We laugh at this now, but people were very serious about it at the time. People wanted to leave home in the morning, say goodbye to the family and go to work by private helicopter.** The idea was very popular, but of course, it was impossible. <u>Helicopters are very difficult to fly – and can you imagine the traffic problems in the sky? So noisy!</u>
V2: Yes. Very noisy. There's far too much traffic these days in my opinion.
G: I agree. People should go to work by bike, or on foot. By far the best way to travel.

D Give Ss 3 mins to discuss their ideas in pairs/groups. In *mixed ability classes*, put *strong* and *weak Ss* together. After 3 mins, move Ss to talk to a different group and exchange ideas. Monitor discreetly and make notes on their performance. In feedback, invite Ss to answer the questions and talk about the most popular ideas in each group.

Answers: Monorails. See the **Culture notes** below.

Culture notes
From 1950–1980 major **monorails** were installed in California, Seattle and Japan as well as in amusement parks like Disneyland. More recently, with the rise of traffic congestion and urbanisation, **monorails** are being used more widely, e.g. in Japan and Malaysia.

GRAMMAR   articles: *a/an*, *the*, no article

3A Ss first read the extract (see italics in audio script for Ex 2B) and then listen and complete it. Play the CD again if necessary. Check answers in feedback. With *stronger classes*, elicit reasons for each answer to check if they can see any patterns in the use of articles.

Answers: 1 the   2 the   3 –   4 –   5 a   6 –   7 –   8 –   9 –   10 –

Watch out!
Articles cause confusion for learners because either they're used in a different way in their L1, or they're not used at all. However, there are patterns in the use of articles which help, e.g. *no article before plural nouns.* Patterns like these are taught in this lesson. It's essential for Ss to learn, record and revise them as fixed/semi-fixed phrases.

B Check the instructions. Ss then work alone/in pairs and match the rules. Check answers and elicit more examples for each rule. In *weaker classes*, do the exercise with Ss, checking as you go along.

Answers: b) 4, 7   c) 3, 6   d) 8, 9, 10   e) 2   f) 1

➠ LANGUAGEBANK 9.1 p144–5

Ss read the tables and notes. Ask *Which rules weren't in Ex 3B above?* Ss would benefit from doing Ex A–C on p145 in class, referring to the notes on p144 for help.

A Check *colleagues, countryside*.

> **Answers:** 2 a 3 – 4 a 5 the 6 – 7 – 8 – 9 – 10 the 11 the 12 –

B Pre-teach/Check *airline, sick*.

> **Answers:** 2 a 3 the 4 a 5 – 6 the

C

> **Answers:** P: Where can I buy *a* dictionary? MT: There's a bookshop … I think they *sell dictionaries*. P: I need *an* English–Spanish dictionary … The only problem is *that books* … MT: Does your school have *a* library?

C Model and drill the two words. Ss then listen and write the sentences. Check them and then play the CD again. Highlight the sentence stress and weak forms in each sentence. Ss listen again and repeat.

> **Answers:** 1 There was <u>a</u> problem. 2 It was <u>a</u> good idea. 3 <u>The</u> photo on the left. 4 In <u>the</u> city centre.

PRACTICE

4A Ss complete the sentences from audio script 9.1. (see sentences in bold) They then compare answers and note which rule applies to each answer.

B After Ss have checked their answers, elicit the rule for each one. *Strong classes* could underline other examples of *a/an, the, no article* in the audio script.

> **Answers:** 2 the 3 a, the 4 –, – 5 an 6 –, – 7 –, the, –, – 8 –

5A Elicit other possible answers to the example question, e.g. *on foot, by bus*. Ss then work alone, choose an ending and write their answers. Monitor and support them if needed.

B Monitor and encourage Ss to self-correct while they do this activity. In feedback, Ss read out their answers to the class. Nominate other Ss to guess the question. Give feedback as required.

speakout TIP

Read and check the tip. Ask *Do you record nouns like this? Why is it a good idea?* Review the way Ss are recording their vocabulary.

SPEAKING

6A Check the rubric and the example. Teach *inventions* and *invent*. Ss then work in pairs to discuss the problems. Monitor and help them with vocabulary they need.

Possible answers:
The Horseless Sulky: it's only big enough for two people; it's very slow.
The Lightning Bug: it's very small, it's difficult to get in/out.

B Set up this information gap activity carefully. First, divide the class into As and Bs. Ss A look at their information and check new words in their dictionaries. Ss B do the same. Help them with vocabulary as needed.

Teaching tip

Ss at lower levels usually feel more comfortable with bilingual/electronic dictionaries. These are useful of course, but if possible, encourage Ss to use an English–English one (e.g. the *Longman Wordwise Dictionary*) for elementary learners. They usually contain useful ideas for teaching Ss how to use them efficiently.

Put Ss into A/B pairs, facing each other. Tell them to exchange the information first, take notes and then decide why their invention is better. Make notes on Ss' performance. In feedback, nominate both Ss A and Ss B to tell the class why their invention is better. The class then vote for the best one.

Homework ideas
- Ss describe their inventions from Ex 6B and say why it's better than the other one.
- Language bank 9.1 Ex A–C, p145
- Workbook Ex 1A–5, p51–52

CITYBIKES

Introduction

Ss learn and practise language to talk about permission and obligation in the context of city transport systems. They read about the free bikes people in Paris can use to reduce air/traffic pollution.

SUPPLEMENTARY MATERIALS

Resource bank p179

Speakout TIP (after Ex 2): Ss need monolingual dictionaries for the pronunciation activity

Warm up

Revision of articles: dictogloss

Use the following text (based on recording 9.1) for the dictogloss.

In the 1950s people wanted to travel to work quickly and easily so they thought of new methods of transport.

One idea was a private helicopter! People wanted to go to their garage, get in their helicopter and go to work. The idea was very popular … but of course, it was impossible. Helicopters are very difficult to fly … and you can imagine the traffic problems in the sky ... very busy and very noisy!

Did the ideas work? Is traffic better now?

First, dictate it at normal speed while Ss listen. Dictate it again, pausing for a few seconds after each sentence for Ss to take notes. Tell them *not* to write every word. Then read it again at normal speed while Ss add to their notes. They then work in pairs and rewrite the text from the notes. It doesn't matter if they leave out information but the text must be grammatically accurate with correct spelling. Then hand out copies of the text so Ss can check their writing, paying particular attention to the use of articles. Monitor and nominate Ss to read out good examples of the text in feedback. Use the last question in the text to lead in to Ex 1.

SPEAKING

1 Read the questions and elicit a few responses. Give Ss 2 mins to discuss their answers in pairs. Nominate Ss to report back to the class. Find out what the most popular means of transport is and whether Ss worry about pollution in towns/cities. If possible, elicit/teach *convenient, polluting, green.* Otherwise, do it in Ex 2A.

VOCABULARY adjectives

2A Give Ss 2 mins to decide which three adjectives express their opinion about cycling and why, e.g. *I think cycling is dangerous because cars and lorries go too fast on the roads.* They then compare answers to see if they agree or not. In feedback, each pair reports their opinions back to the class.

B Give Ss 2 mins to write down the opposites.

C Ss listen and tick their correct answers. In feedback, elicit sentences about different types of transport using each pair of words, e.g. *Travelling by plane is very unhealthy.*

Answers: <u>sa</u>fe / <u>dan</u>gerous, <u>ea</u>sy / <u>di</u>fficult, <u>heal</u>thy / un<u>heal</u>thy, <u>green</u> / po<u>llu</u>ting, con<u>ven</u>ient / in<u>con</u>venient, <u>com</u>fortable / un<u>com</u>fortable

D After Ss have listened and compared answers, play the CD again for them to listen, repeat and recheck the underlined syllables. In feedback, elicit and drill the words further if necessary. Pay particular attention to *comfortable* (●●●)

Answers: see answers for Ex 2C

speakout TIP

Read the tip with Ss and look up *dangerous.* They then choose three words they're not sure how to pronounce and look them up in their dictionaries.

3 Check the example and give Ss time to prepare. Monitor and make a note of problems. In feedback, nominate Ss in turn to give their opinions and/or to respond in open class.

READING

4A Tell Ss look at the photos. Ask *What do think the article is about?* and elicit answers. Then read the rubric and check the example. Ss then write two more questions they want to know. N.B. This activity activates Ss' knowledge of the world and gives them a reason to read the article. It doesn't matter if they don't find the answers.

Sample answers: 2 How many bikes are there? 3 Who are they for? / Where can you find them?

B Give Ss 3 mins to read and find the answers to their questions. Tell them not to worry about new language in the text yet. In feedback, nominate Ss to tell the class which answers they found. Check *pick-up stations, metro (underground), uphill/downhill.*

C Ss read the sentences first. Then give them 3–4 mins to check and write the correct answers. They then compare them with a partner. Elict/Check the answers.

Answers: 1 F You can leave it in any station in the city. 2 T 3 F They can use the bikes. 4 F They can't. People have to be over 14 to use the bikes. 5 T 6 F They don't ride them – they take the metro home.

D Ss work in pairs/small groups and make a list of advantages/disadvantages of a Citybike system in their town, using the adjectives from Ex 2A. *Multilingual classes* will need more time to talk about and compare different towns/cities. In feedback, nominate one person from each group to tell the class what they decided and why.

GRAMMAR *can/can't, have to/don't have to*

5A Ss use the article to help them do the exercise and check answers. Go straight on to Ex B to check the concept/use.

Answers: 1 can 2 can't 3 have to 4 don't have to

Watch out!

Ss often add *to* after modal verbs, e.g. *I can't/must to go.* Highlight the form clearly for Ss and give thorough controlled practice. Correct the problem at appropriate stages of the lesson to prevent fossilisation.

B Do the first example with Ss. They do the others alone and check in pairs. In feedback, check concept further, e.g. for question 1, ask *Is it necessary to take the bike back to the same pick-up station? No. Why? Because it's OK to leave it at any station.* Contrast/Check the use of *can't/don't have to* further, e.g. *You can't/don't have to speak your own language in class.*

Answers: 1 c) 2 d) 3 a) 4 b)

C Ss complete the table using information from the article in Ex 4B. *Strong classes* could check their answers in the **Language bank** on p144. Recheck the concept for each sentence in feedback.

Answers: can't, use, to, don't, pay

D Ss now focus on the pronunciation of the target language. Write the words from the exercise on the board and drill the pronunciation of each one. Ss copy the words down. Then do question 1 as an example. Play the CD, elicit the correct answer and underline it on the board. Then play the other sentences. Ss compare answers. In feedback, play the CD again, pausing after each sentence for Ss to answer.

Answers: 1 /kən/ 2 /kɑːnt/ 3 /hæftə/ 4 /dəʊnhæftə/

E Ss listen again and repeat. Check Ss' pronunciation individually and prompt self/peer correction if necessary.

⟱ LANGUAGEBANK 9.2 p144–5

If there's time, it would be a good idea for Ss to do the exercise in class. They can refer to section 9.2 while they're working.

A Check the signs first.

Answers: 1 can't go, have to 2 can, don't have to
3 have to, can't 4 can, don't have to 5 can't, have to
6 can, can't

B Check *formal, light (jacket).*

Answers: 2 can wear 3 don't have to come
4 can't come 5 have to get 6 don't have to get

Optional extra activity
Ss write a list of ten things they *can, can't, have to* and *don't have to* do in class/the school. If appropriate they could also include what the teacher *can/can't,* etc do. They can make a poster to put on the wall. Alternatively, get Ss to design letters explaining the rules of the class/school to new Ss and post them on the class blog online.

PRACTICE

6A Check the example. Ss then do the exercise and check their answers in pairs. In feedback, check concept, form and pronunciation again.

Answers: 2 have to 3 can't 4 have to 5 can't 6 have to
7 don't have to 8 can, have to

B Do question 1 as an example. If a sentence is not true for their town/city, Ss should rewrite it so that it is true, e.g. *You can't drive on the left in my town. You have to drive on the right.* In feedback, check/correct Ss' answers.

SPEAKING

7A Check the rubric and the information in the table. Divide Ss into groups of As, Bs and Cs and tell them to look at the relevant pages. Ask *What are the cards for? They provide discounts on things to do in the cities.* Then give them 2 mins to complete their columns. Monitor to help Ss with vocabulary and check they're doing the exercise correctly. Before moving on, check/teach *fun fair, zoo, aquarium.*

B First, elicit the questions Ss need, e.g. *How much is the card? What type of transport can you use? Do you have to pay to go into the museums? Is there any other information?* Make sure Ss are facing each other and not showing each other their books. Give them 4–5 mins to ask/answer and write the information. Stop the activity when most Ss have finished. Then check what they have to do next: discuss/decide which city has got the best system. While they talk, take notes on language problems for later. In feedback, invite Ss to tell the class about their decisions.

Answers:
Amsterdam: €53 for 3 days/72 hours, all public transport, free entry to over 25 museums and a free coffee.
Madrid: €58 for 72 hours, no public transport but free bus tour, entry to over 50 museums and Madrid Fun Fair, Zoo and Aquarium.
Prague: 790 crowns/€32 for 4 days, free entry to over 50 museums and sights and unlimited travel on public transport for an extra 330 crowns/€13.

C Check the example and elicit other questions Ss could ask, e.g. *How much is a bus ticket? Do you have to buy the tickets before you get on the bus? Where can you buy them? Do you have daily/weekly/monthly travelcards?* Drill and write the questions on the board for *weaker Ss.* Ss talk about two/three places they know and make notes about their partner's towns/cities. *Fast finishers* can do more or join another pair to exchange information. Monitor and make notes as usual. In feedback, Ss tell the class about differences between the places they talked about.

Homework ideas
• Ss write a description of the transport system in their town/city and how it could be better, using information from Ex 7C.
• Language bank 9.2 Ex A–B, p145
• Workbook Ex 1A–5C, p53–54

SORRY I'M LATE

Introduction

Ss learn and practise how to make excuses, apologise and tell a long story using linking words.

SUPPLEMENTARY MATERIALS

Resource bank p180

Warm up

Revision of *can/can't, have to/don't have to*

Ss write four sentences about what they *can, can't, have to, don't have to* do at work/college or at the start of their work/college day, e.g. *I have to get to work by 9 o'clock in the morning. I can drive to work and leave my car in the cark park. I don't have to wear a suit to work but I can't wear jeans.* In pairs/groups, Ss read out their sentences and find out what they have in common. In feedback, they report any similarities back to the class.

VOCABULARY excuses

1 Ss work in pairs and discuss the question for 1 min. Elicit Ss' answers and have a brief discussion. Then ask *When was the last time you were late for something? Why? Was it a problem?* Ss discuss for 2 mins. Monitor to check if Ss use any of the language from Ex 2 below. In feedback, invite Ss to tell the class about any unusual reasons for their partner's lateness.

Watch out!

When using the language of excuses/apologies, Ss often have problems with the verbs *lose/miss* and *leave/forget*, e.g. *I lost the train. I forgot my keys at home.* instead of *I missed the train. I forgot (to bring) my homework. I left it at home.* This is mainly due to L1 interference. Teach/Check the differences between the verbs with clear examples and give sufficient practice.

2A Ss match the excuses and compare their answers. In feedback, elicit other examples for each verb, e.g. *I lost my homework/mobile.*

Answers: 2 c) 3 a) 4 e) 5 b)

B Ss can write new sentences alone/in pairs. Monitor to check the accuracy of their writing and prompt self-correction.

FUNCTION apologising

3A Ss look at the cartoon and the questions. Elicit ideas of who the people are and what the cartoon is about.

Possible answers: The woman is the boss. The man is her employee. The man was late and is all sweaty because he's been running. He's apologising to his boss who obviously doesn't believe his excuses.

B Ss read the text to check their answers. In feedback, check *commuter line, hit, accident, seriously* if necessary.

Answers: He's late because the train hit a cow on the line and the train was delayed.

4A Check the answer to question 1 as an example. Then encourage Ss underline the other answers alone.

B Play the CD for Ss to listen and check their answers. In feedback, check the difference between *terribly* (adv) and *terrible* (n). *I'm afraid* means *I'm sorry to say* (often used for explanations/apologies/excuses). When Ss listen again and repeat, encourage them to show (with their intonation) that they really mean what they're saying! Elicit/Drill more apologies using examples from Ex 2A.

Answers: 1 really 2 terribly 3 terrible 4 afraid

C Ss discuss the answers in pairs. Drill the responses with the appropriate intonation to show anger/understanding. Then drill the excuses from Ex 4A and responses in open pairs across the class.

Answers: 1 ✗ 2 ✗ 3 ✓ 4 ✓ 5 ✗

▶ **LANGUAGEBANK** 9.3 p144–5

Check the table and notes on p144. Drill new language in sentences, e.g. *I'm so sorry ... I feel terrible about the mess.* Ss can refer to the table/notes when they do Ex A on p144.

Answers: S: Oh, *I'm* really sorry. I'm afraid *I* left it at home. T: Don't worry *about* it. S: Sorry, *but* I don't remember. *I'm* afraid I forgot to do it. T: Don't *let* it happen again!

5A Elicit possible answers for the first part of the conversation. Give Ss 2 mins to prepare the rest of it before they practise saying it. Monitor/Provide support at both stages. In feedback, nominate Ss to read out their conversations to the class and prompt correction.

B Ss can work with the same/a different partner. Ask *Would you apologise in the same way to a boss and a friend?* Elicit/Give examples. Again, monitor closely but this time, make notes on problem areas for feedback in Ex 5C.

C Ss act out their conversations in groups/to the class. In feedback, write examples of incorrect functional language and intonation on the board. Ss then correct them in pairs.

LEARN TO tell a long story

6A Check *online diary extracts* in the rubric. You could also check the meaning of *Service: 0 points* (N.B. You can say *zero,* or *no*), *Originality: 10 points* in extract 3. It refers to the train services and their excuses. Give Ss 2 mins to find the reasons why the man was late, and 1 min to compare their answers. Tell them not to worry about new words in the extracts. Do feedback and check words Ss might need for Ex 6B, e.g. *middle of nowhere, signal problem, air-conditioning, sweaty.*

Answers: 1 The train didn't go very fast. 2 He woke up late, missed the train, the next one stopped for 20 minutes. 3 The train stopped twice, once for no reason and then because there was a cow on the line.

B Tell Ss to focus on the questions. Then nominate Ss to give the answers.

Answers: Days 1 and 2

C Ss read the diary and listen at the same time, underlining information that's different (see the phrases in bold in audio script)

> **Answers:** 1 The recording says the man was two hours late for work but the text says one hour. 2 The recording says the train stopped for 40 minutes but the text says 20 minutes.

> **Optional extra activity**
> Ss write 5–6 questions about the audio script on p173 (or the text in Ex 6A) to ask each other in pairs/groups. *Fast finishers* could write more.

Unit 9 Recording 7

L=Liam   K=Kamal

K: Hey, Liam. Did you stay in bed too long this morning?

L: Ha-ha! It's these trains – they're terrible!

K: Why? What happened *this* time?

L: Well, first of all, the train was late leaving the station, but only about a quarter of an hour or so. After that, it just went at walking speed – all the way to London. Really! There was a guy on a bike on the road next to us. I think he got to London before we did!

K: Well, **you're two hours late** – and the boss wants to see you …

K: Hey, Liam. The boss wants to see you. Whoa! What happened to you? You're all wet!

L: Believe me, it's a *long* story. First of all, I got up late because I didn't hear my alarm, so I only woke up at 8.30. I ran to the train station – usually I walk – but I missed the train by two minutes! Then I waited for the next train, the 9.15, and everything was fine until we just stopped – just *stopped* – in the middle of nowhere. The guard said that there was a signal problem. After that, the air-conditioning stopped working, so it was like an oven – at least a thousand degrees! Finally, **after forty minutes, we started moving** – very, very slowly. What could I do? Uh-oh, there's the boss.

K: Yeah. She's not happy. Two and a half hours late, Liam. Good luck!

7A Ss now focus on linkers in an extract from recording 9.7. Do the first one as an example and check *oven, degrees* if necessary. Ss then circle the other linkers and compare answers. Nominate Ss to answer in feedback.

> **Answers:** *because* I didn't hear … *so* I only woke up … *but* I missed the train … *Then* I waited … *and* everything was fine … *After that*, the air-conditioning stopped … *Finally*, after 40 minutes …

B Check Ss' answers after they've discussed them. Then read/check the **speakout tip**. With *stronger classes*, you could raise awareness further by eliciting the purpose of each linker, e.g. *then* and *after that* to show the sequence of events; *so* to introduce a consequence.

> **Answers:** 1 First of all, Finally 2 Then, After that

> **Optional extra activity**
> Ss underline the linkers in the online diary in Ex 6A. Tell Ss to make notes about the punctuation before and after each linker. Ss compare notes at the end before reporting back to the class.

SPEAKING

8A First, look at the photos and ask *What's happening in each photo?* Elicit/Teach *It's raining heavily/pouring with rain. There's a flood/The road is flooded. There's a traffic jam on the motorway. A tree is blocking the road/The wind blew a tree on the road.* Write the new language on the board for Ss to copy. Then check the questions in Ex 8A and elicit some answers, using the photos, e.g. *I'm really sorry I'm late. There was a tree on the road.* Then give Ss 4–5 mins to think about the event they are late for and make notes. Monitor and support Ss where needed.

B First, check the rubric and examples. Elicit and drill more examples of phrases that show interest, e.g. *No! Really? What happened next?* While Ss work in pairs, make notes of their performance. They could then work with another partner and try to improve on their first story. In feedback, invite Ss to act out their stories/conversations to the class,

9 Elicit the start of the story, e.g. *I had a terrible journey this morning.* Tell them to use linkers from Ex 7A wherever possible, e.g. *First of all, I … Then …* Monitor and encourage Ss to work together, compare their first drafts, etc. Ss who finish their story can read it out to the class.

> **Homework ideas**
> * Ss write the final draft of the story in Ex 9.
> * Ss write a dialogue about an occasion when they were late.
> * Language bank 9.3 Ex A, p145
> * Workbook Ex 1–3, p55

AIRPORT

Introduction

Ss watch an extract from the BBC series *Airport* which shows the everyday experiences of people who work in and use airports. Ss then learn and practise talking about a problem and write an email about it.

SUPPLEMENTARY MATERIALS

Ex 5D: use audio/recording facilities if available, or Ss record themselves on their mobiles

Warm up

Lead in and create interest in the topic. Tell Ss to write one question about flying/airports, e.g. *Do you like flying /airports/ planes? Why/Why not? Do you often fly? Where? Do you travel first class? What's the best/worst flight you had?* Organise Ss into two circles, one inside the other. (If this is not possible, Ss work in groups, sitting opposite each other in two rows.) Ss in the outside circle face those in the inside circle and ask the student facing them their question. They then move round and ask the same question to each person in the circle. In feedback, elicit any unusual answers. If possible, elicit/teach airport vocabulary for Ex 2, e.g. *check in*.

DVD PREVIEW

1 Check the rubric and elicit some sample answers. Ss then discuss their answers. In feedback, Ss tell the class about their partners. If the opportunity arises, teach airport language from Ex 2 (see examples in the answer key below)

Possible answers:
good things: flying's exciting, flying is faster, flying can be cheaper, airports have tax-free shopping
bad things: airports are usually crowded, boring queues (at check-in/security/passport control), planes are often late, food/drink is expensive (in the departure lounge), flights are expensive/uncomfortable/frightening (take off)

2A If you taught airport vocabulary in Ex 1, Ss do the exercise now. If not, teach *departure* and then see if they can work out the order. With **weaker classes**, teach the vocabulary and elicit the order but don't confirm it – Ss check in Ex 2B.

B Ss listen and check their answers. Play the CD for them to listen and repeat the phrases. Remember to encourage Ss to link words ending in consonants to words starting with vowels, e.g. *check in, wait in, get on, takes off*.

Answers: b) 8 c) 2 d) 4 e) 7 f) 6 g) 5 h) 3

C Do the example with Ss. They then continue the exercise in pairs. In feedback, ask *Which of these actions do/don't you like?* Elicit answers and discuss them briefly.

3 Ask *What do you know about Heathrow airport?* Elicit/ Prompt answers, e.g. *It's in London. It's very big. There are five terminals.* If any Ss know Heathrow, ask *What's it like?* Then check the questions. Give Ss 1 min to read the information and discuss their answers in pairs. In feedback, write some of their ideas for question 2 on the board. Teach *day-to-day, control tower, delayed*. Finally, ask for Ss' opinions: *What type of day-to-day events are on the* Airport *programme?* Discuss the question briefly.

Answers: 1 Because there's a computer problem in the control tower. 2 Ss' own answers.

DVD VIEW

4A Ss first read the sentences and check if any of their answers on the board (from Ex 3 question 2) are the same. Give them 3 mins to check new words in their dictionaries, if they have them. If not, teach/check *queue, play chess, argue, skateboarding*.

B Play the DVD. Ss watch and tick the correct sentences. In feedback, elicit answers and invite initial comments about the programme.

Alternative approach
Play the DVD without the sound. After Ss compare answers, play it again if they have a lot of doubts, but with the sound turned up.

Answers: ✓ 1, 2, 3, 5, 7, 8

C Ss read the sentences in the table. Check *Zen* (calm and meditative as in the practice of Zen Buddhism). Ss watch the DVD again and match the sentences. After they've compared answers, play the DVD again if necessary. In feedback, check answers (see sentences in bold in the DVD script). Then ask *Have you ever had a problem at an airport/on a plane?* If so, Ss tell the class about it. If not, ask *What type of problems do people have?* Discuss Ss' answers and write any vocabulary that's useful for Ex 5A on the board.

Answers:
Woman 1: can't find a place in a hotel.
Man 1: wants to go to Berlin.
Woman 2: is there with her son and daughter. She's trying to get to Amsterdam.
Man 2: thinks everything is very calm, very 'Zen'.

DVD 8 Airport

VO=Voiceover M1=Man 1 M2=Man 2
W1=Woman 1 W2=Woman 2

VO: Heathrow Airport is having a bad day. Hundreds of passengers can't fly because of a computer problem in air traffic control. In Terminal 1, more and more passengers are arriving. Some aeroplanes are leaving, but many flights are cancelled. Everyone is hoping to find a flight. Some of the waiting passengers are having a snack while others are spending their time outside. It's a hot summer day. Back inside the terminal, it's getting hotter and hotter. Some people came here five hours ago.

W1: I'm here with my grandmother and my parents and it, it's terrible for us to wait here for such a long time. You know, we have to sleep at the airport **because no hotel is available**. So, it's just terrible.

M1: Have a look at this. Improvisation at its best. I'm glad they're sleeping now. **I was hoping to get to Berlin soon.**

VO: People are still trying to find a flight.

W2: I've had my son go on the internet, my daughter be in one queue, me be in the other queue and on the mobile, all at the same time, **trying to get to Amsterdam for 9.30 tomorrow morning**.

M2: After five hours queuing, **you really become really Zen, you know ... and here it's pretty calm.**

VO: The airport managers find an interesting solution to one of the problems ... garden chairs. With the chairs to relax in, some passengers are finding new ways to pass the time.
Inside Terminal 1, it's late at night, after midnight ... and many passengers are still here, waiting for their flight.
Around 300 flights left Heathrow that day, but 319 flights were cancelled, and over 500 people spent the night in the terminal.

speakout deal with a problem

5A Read/Check the rubric with Ss. Give them 2 mins to read the problems carefully. Check *baggage/luggage, heavy, long-distance flight, screaming (child), pick up, come out.* Ss then discuss/decide on the three worst problems, giving reasons. In feedback, elicit/discuss Ss' decisions and reasons.

B Check the rubric and play the CD. In feedback, elicit the answer and ask *Do you think he was right to complain?*

> **Answer:** problem 5

Unit 9 Recording 9

A=Attendant P=Passenger

A: Your meal, sir.

P: Thank you. Excuse me.

A: Yes, can I help you?

P: Hope so! **I'm sorry, but there's a small problem here.** I ordered a vegetarian meal – but this is meat.

A: Oh, just a moment. I checked and we don't have a record of your order.

P: What?! But I *always* order vegetarian. I'm a frequent flyer.

A: I understand, sir, **but** we don't have any more vegetarian meals.

P: I don't believe it! You always have extra meals in business class.

A: Yes, but this is economy class.

P: **You don't understand. Let me explain one more time.** I don't eat meat. I ordered vegetarian. I can't fly to Tokyo without dinner. **It's your job to** bring me a meal. A business class vegetarian meal is fine.

A: Just a moment. Here you are, sir. A vegetarian meal.

P: Thank you – but this is already open. And it's cold. **Can I speak to the person in charge,** please?

C Ss read the **key phrases**. Check *person in charge* and play the CD again. Ss tick the **key phrases** and compare their answers (see answers in bold in the audio script). In feedback, play the CD again. Stop at each **key phrase** on the CD and elicit/drill the complete sentence. Tell Ss that *I see, but …* means the same as *I understand but …*

> **Answers:** Tick all sentences except *I see, but …* and *It's your job to find a hotel.*

D Give Ss time to choose the problem and decide which role they are going to play. They then think about their roles and make notes about what they want to say, using the **key phrases**. They could also look at the audio script on p173–174 for help. Monitor and provide support where needed. Ss then do the role-play. Monitor discreetly and take notes on their performance. In feedback, invite pairs to act out their role-play to the class.

> **Teaching tip**
>
> If you have video/audio recording facilities, Ss could record their role-play. The class/You watch it and give feedback. Ss could also record the role-play on their mobile phones. They listen and re-record the role-play until they are satisfied. They then play it for the class or in groups, and get feedback from you/other Ss.

writeback an email

6A Ss look at the email quickly and decide what it's about. Check *What a nightmare!* They then work alone/with a partner to complete the email. Monitor and encourage Ss to self-correct inaccurate language. Ss can then pass round their completed emails for other Ss to read, or email them to you/other Ss.

> **Sample answers:** 1 Jane 2 Rio de Janeiro 3 was terrible 4 7p.m. 5 the plane was late 6 waited in the departure lounge 7 ten 8 I was hungry 9 had a sandwich 10 bought a book 11 read for an hour 12 had a coffee 13 took off 14 12.30 15 the flight attendant dropped a coffee over me 16 complained 17 love Paul

B Ss use the model in Ex 6A for their own email. They could use the problem they talked about in their role-play, or one from their own experience. Encourage them to show their drafts to other Ss and ask for help/advice.

> **Optional extra activity**
>
> Ss could email you/other Ss to simulate a real-life situation. Encourage Ss to write replies/brainstorm how they would solve the issues.

> **Homework ideas**
>
> • Ss write a final draft of the email in Ex 6B and send it.
> • Workbook Ex 4, p55

LOOKBACK

Introduction

The activities here are designed to provide revision and communicative practice in a motivating way. Ss practise the grammar, vocabulary and functions from the unit via speaking activities. This not only helps the Ss but gives you the opportunity to assess their ability to *use* the language they've learnt in the unit. Assessment is usually done through monitoring and doing any remedial work needed. However, it is also useful to focus on *individual* Ss while they do the activities and compare their performance with their results in more formal tests.

TRANSPORT

1A Ss could do this as a race in pairs. The first pair to finish with the correct answers and spelling wins.

Answers: 1 ch<u>ea</u>p, expensive 2 un<u>hea</u>lthy, healthy 3 p<u>o</u>lluting, green 4 d<u>a</u>ngerous, safe 5 diffi<u>cu</u>lt, easy 6 sl<u>ow</u>, fast

B Do the example and tell Ss they must ask a maximum of 10 *yes/no* questions to find the answers. This exercise could also be done as a competition in teams.

2 Give Ss 3 mins to do the exercise in groups. The group with the most correct examples wins. *Weaker Ss* can look back to p88, 92 and 94.

Suggested answers: 1 motorbike, horse 2 a car, bus, van, train 3 a bus, plane, motorbike, horse 4 check in, go through security/passport control, do some tax-free shopping, wait in the departure lounge, go to the departure gate, get on the plane 5 Ss' own answers.

ARTICLES

3A Ss should do this exercise alone. Monitor to assess their problems before checking/correcting answers.

Answers: 1 an, the 2 – 3 a 4 –,– 5 a 6 a 7 –,–

B Give Ss 3 mins to write the questions. Check/Correct them before they ask other Ss. They then ask/answer the questions in small groups and make a note of the *yes/no* answers to each question. To follow up, each group writes sentences summarising their answers, as in Ex 3A.

Answers: 2 Did you have breakfast this morning? 3 Do you live in a town/city centre? 4 Do you think bikes are better than cars for travelling in the town/city centre? 5 Have you got a motorbike? 6 Did you take a taxi home last weekend? 7 Do you go home by train?

CAN/CAN'T, HAVE TO/DON'T HAVE TO

4A Give Ss 2 mins to underline the correct answers and compare them. Then check their answers and elicit other examples for each place.

Answers: 1 can't 2 don't have to 3 have to 4 can't 5 can 6 don't have to

B Give Ss 5 mins to write the sentences. In *mixed-ability classes*, *weaker Ss* work in pairs/3s. Help and encourage them to self-correct or correct each other. *Fast finishers* can write questions about other places.

C Monitor while Ss read out their sentences. Note down problems with accuracy and pronunciation for feedback, or assessment if required.

TELL A LONG STORY

5A First, check the meaning of *knock on the door*. Check the instructions and do an example. Then put Ss in pairs and tell them to take turns to complete their stories. Monitor to check if they need help/advice. This is a light-hearted activity and the results could be quite amusing.

B While Ss read their stories, monitor and make notes on their performance for feedback, or assessment if required. Invite Ss to read out the funniest stories to the class.

Optional extra activity

Copy the situations below. Ss work in pairs, taking it in turns to apologise/make an excuse.

1 A classmate/work colleague wants you to go to her birthday party on Saturday. It's your daughter's birthday on the same day.

2 Your mother wants you to go shopping for a birthday present for your sister. You want to go to the cinema.

3 A friend wants you to help him with his homework but you have to play football tonight.

4 You have an important meeting/test tomorrow morning. Your friends want you to go out with them tonight.

Homework ideas
• Workbook Review and check 3, p56–57
• Workbook Test 3, p58

OVERVIEW

10.1 LIFE'S A LOTTERY
GRAMMAR | *be going to; would like to*
VOCABULARY | plans
HOW TO | talk about future plans/wishes

COMMON EUROPEAN FRAMEWORK
Ss can describe future plans; can ask and answer questions and exchange ideas and information on familiar topics in predictable everyday situations, e.g. discussing future plans.

10.2 SURVIVE!
GRAMMAR | *will, might, won't*
VOCABULARY | phrases with *get*
HOW TO | make predictions

COMMON EUROPEAN FRAMEWORK
Ss can identify specific information in simpler written material he/she encounters such as short articles describing events; can interact with reasonable ease in structured situations, e.g. predicting future events with prompts.

10.3 LET'S DO SOMETHING
FUNCTION | making suggestions
VOCABULARY | adjectives
LEARN TO | respond to suggestions

COMMON EUROPEAN FRAMEWORK
Ss can make and respond to invitations and suggestions; can describe arrangements in simple terms.

10.4 WILD WEATHER ⊙ BBC DVD
speakout | the weather
writeback | reply on a message board

COMMON EUROPEAN FRAMEWORK
Ss can exchange limited information on familiar matters, e.g. the weather; can understand and produce short, simple messages relating to matters in areas of immediate need.

10.5 LOOKBACK
Communicative revision activities

BBC VIDEO PODCAST
What are your plans for the future?

In this video podcast, people talk about their plans for the future. The material includes a wide range of personal, professional and academic aspirations and utilizes key verb phrases from the unit. The video podcast would work well after lesson 10.1 to extend the lesson, or at the start of the unit to test Ss' existing knowledge or at the end of unit 10 to check what Ss have learnt.

LIFE'S A LOTTERY

Introduction
Ss learn and practise how to talk about future plans and wishes using *be going to/would like to* and read about the plans of a young couple who've won the lottery.

SUPPLEMENTARY MATERIALS
Resource bank p181 and p182
Warm up: prepare/copy the *find someone who* activity given in the Warm up
Ex 5: use recording facilities/Ss' mobiles

Warm up
Lead into the lesson topic with this *find someone who* activity. Prepare/Copy the activity using the example below.

Find someone who …	
	Name
does the lottery every week	
likes playing bingo	
plays cards	
likes pub quizzes	
buys scratch cards	
plays board games	
enters competitions online/in newspapers and magazines	
buys draw tickets	

In class, give Ss one copy each and check new words, e.g. *scratch cards/draw tickets*. Elicit/Drill the first question: *Do you do the lottery every week?* Ss walk around the class/work in small groups and ask one of the questions until they find someone who answers *Yes*. They then write their name down and move on to ask another student a question. Ss can write down the same name only once. In feedback, check how many Ss do each activity.

LISTENING

1A Ss cover the text and look at the photo. Ask *What/Who can you see? Why do they look so happy? Where do they work?* Ss then read the article to check their answers. In feedback, check new language, e.g. *win the lottery, enjoyable*.

Answers: Elaine and Aled won £1.3 million in the lottery but they're going to stay in their jobs.

B Elicit one or two predictions and write them on the board, e.g. *go on holiday, travel round the world*. Then give Ss 2 mins to make notes of six other things. In feedback, write Ss' ideas on the board.

C Check the rubric. Ss read the plans and write S (same) for those which are the same as their ideas on the board. Play the CD twice if Ss still have doubts after the first listening. Check and discuss Ss' answers from the board/their books (see phrases in bold in audio script). Elicit other details Ss heard in the interview. Ask *Which of your ideas weren't mentioned?* Play the CD again while Ss listen and read the audio script on p174.

Teaching tip
Giving Ss an opportunity to listen and read the script at the same time usually gives Ss a sense of satisfaction and helps them to understand spoken English better. It will also prepare them for Ex 2B.

Don't check the use of *be going to* and *would like* yet but teach any other words/phrases Ss want to know, e.g. *Mercedes, Ferrari, the Canary islands*.

Answers: move house, get married, have a holiday, buy some clothes

D Ask *Would you do the same things as Elaine and Aled? Do they want the same things?* Elicit some opinions briefly. Ss then discuss their own ideas for 2–3 mins. In feedback, elicit opinions and then ask *Who likes/doesn't like their plans?*

Unit 10 Recording 1

I=Interviewer E=Elaine A=Aled

I: Elaine and Aled, the luckiest couple in Britain today – welcome to the programme!

E/A: Thank you.

I: So Elaine, tell us about that moment when you found out.

E: I saw the winning numbers on television and I phoned Aled straight away!

A: I didn't believe her at first. I thought 'You're lying!'

E: I didn't believe myself! I was in shock!

I: And is it true that you're *not going to stop* working?

A: That's right. We enjoy our jobs and we've got lots of friends here. I don't like doing nothing. I think hard work's good for you.

E: Definitely. People think working in a fast food restaurant is boring, but it's not. We have a lot of fun. It's an important part of our life.

I: So *what are you going to do* with the money?

E: Well, first of all, we're going to **get married** this summer. We already had plans to get married before we won the lottery, maybe in two years, but now we can do it this summer.

I: Congratulations!

A: Or next summer.

I: Ah.

E: This summer.

A: And *we'd like to move*. At the moment I'm living with my parents and Elaine's living with hers. So *we're going to look for a house* to buy.

E: By the sea.

A: Yes, maybe by the sea, or …

I: Are you going to take a break? Travel around the world maybe?

A: No, I don't think so, but we're going to **have a holiday**. We're going to the Canary Islands.

I: Fabulous. And have you got any other plans? Maybe a new car – or clothes?

E: Yeah, *I'm going to buy some new clothes.* I'm going shopping with my mum and sister this weekend. Cars? Well, Aled doesn't drive so no, *he isn't going to buy a car.*

A: Right, not now, but *I'd like to learn to drive* and then maybe in the future …

I: *What would you like to* drive?

A: I'd like a Mercedes … or maybe, or maybe a Ferrari.

El But we haven't got plans to buy a car now.

I: OK – great! Thanks very much for talking to us today. Oh, just one last question. How did you celebrate when you first heard the news?

E: Well, we went out and had a burger!

GRAMMAR *be going to; would like to*

2A Ss read the sentences from the interview and match them. With *weaker classes*, you might want to read the rules with them. In feedback, check the concept further: e.g. *Aled wants a Mercedes or a Ferrari. Is it a definite plan or not?* (No, he'd like a Mercedes/Ferrari but he doesn't know when.) Tell Ss that *want* and *would like to* has the same meaning but *would like to* is more polite.

Answers: 1 have 2 don't have

B Ss read the table of forms and then look for the sentences in the audio script. (see phrases in italics in the audio script above) Give Ss 2–3 mins to underline the sentences and complete the table.

C Play the extracts from the interview for Ss to check/correct their answers from Ex 2B. In feedback, write some sentences/questions on the board and highlight the form *be + going to + verb* and *would to + verb*. Also point out that when the main verb is *go*, you don't have to use *going to go* as it's repetitive, e.g. *I'm going to the cinema.*

Answers: 'm, 're, isn't; (going) to; 'd, 'd; (like) to; are, (going) to; would, to

Optional extra activity
Ss underline other examples of the target language in the audio script. Give them time to compare their answers in pairs/3s.

D Ss circle the correct sounds. Play the first sentence as an example and elicit the answer. Then play the rest. Elicit the correct pronunciation of *would*. Ss then listen and repeat the sentences chorally and individually to check they're using the weak forms. N.B. You could also focus on other examples of the weak form of *to* in the sentences – see examples in the answer key.

Answers: 1 /tə/ 2 /wud/

➠ LANGUAGEBANK 10.1 p146–7

Ss can refer to the tables and notes when they do Exs A-C. *Weaker Ss* should do them in class.

A Elicit where *Rome* is.

Answers: 1 'm going to 2 're going to look at 3 Are you going to be 4 're not going to wait 5 're going to buy 6 's Steve going to

B

Answers: 1 'd like to 2 'm going to 3 'd like to 4 'm going to

C

Answers: 1 like 2 would 3 like 4 'd 5 would 6 don't 7 want 8 'd

PRACTICE

3A First, check *start my own business, keep all the money.* Monitor while Ss write to see how accurate their sentences are. Elicit answers in feedback. Prompt Ss to self-correct/correct each other's errors of meaning, form and pronunciation.

> **Answers:** 2 I'd like to drive a sports car. 3 I'm going to have a holiday in the Caribbean. 4 I'm not going to buy any presents for my family and friends. 5 I'd like to move to another country. 6 I'd like to buy a boat. 7 I'd like to start my own business. 8 I'm not going to keep all the money for myself.

B Check the instructions and do an example. Monitor and help Ss with accuracy.

C Demonstrate what Ss have to do. Elicit an answer, e.g. *I'd like to move to Monte Carlo.* Respond with *I wouldn't. I'd like to move to Paris* or *Me too.* Give Ss 3–4 mins to talk while you monitor discreetly. Ss then report similarities/differences to the class. Give feedback as necessary.

VOCABULARY plans

4A Ss complete the gaps and compare answers. In feedback, elicit Ss' plans using some of the collocations.

> **Answers:** 2 get 3 do 4 go 5 stay 6 learn 7 go for 8 start 9 move 10 buy

B Ss take turns to be Ss B but should cover the exercise when they answer. In feedback, read the **speakout tip** and ask Ss to write the lists now/at home.

C Make this into a race. Give Ss 2 mins to write at least one example for each verb. The person with the most correct answers wins. Ss add the words to their lists in Ex 4B.

> **Possible answers:** 1 a picnic/bath/lunch 2 tired, new clothes, home, up 3 do (your) homework, the washing-up 4 swimming, dancing 5 at home, in bed 6 (to speak) English, to play chess 7 a drive, a swim 8 an online business, a French course, a yoga class 9 to Greece, into a room 10 some food for dinner, a DVD

SPEAKING

5A Check the rubric and the examples. Teach/Check *this weekend, next week.* Give Ss 1 min to complete the 'You' column. Monitor and help with vocabulary they need.

B Check/Drill the example and also one with *I'd like to …* Ss work in groups of 3–4 and complete the answers for two students. Make notes on their performance, particularly with the target language.

C Give Ss time to prepare what they'll say before they report back to the class. Encourage them to ask for your help with this. Make notes again while Ss talk and give them feedback on examples of good language/problems.

> **Teaching tip**
>
> To give a different perspective on a speaking activity use video/audio recording facilities, or Ss can use their mobile phones, to record the reporting back. Ss can then watch/listen to themselves and give their own feedback.

Homework ideas
- Ss write a paragraph about their plans/wishes from Ex 3B.
- Ss write about one of their friend's plans, Ex 5.
- Language bank 10.1 Ex A–C, p147
- Workbook Ex 1A–4B, p59–60

SURVIVE!

Introduction

Ss learn and practise *will*, *won't*, *might* for prediction in the context of how to survive at sea and in the desert/jungle.

SUPPLEMENTARY MATERIALS

Resource bank p183

Ex 5A: Ss bring bi-lingual or monolingual dictionaries, or provide them if possible

Warm up

Lead in to the topic with a ranking activity. Write these phrases on the board: *A sailing round the world alone B climbing Mount Everest C crossing the desert in a 4x4 (truck/jeep) D exploring the Amazon jungle.* Ask *Which activity is the most dangerous? Why?* Elicit a few answers. Then tell Ss to work alone and order the activities 1–4, where 1 is the most dangerous. Ss then work in pairs to discuss, argue and agree on the order together. Then put two pairs together to do the same thing. If there's time, Ss could decide on the order as a class. Otherwise, elicit each group's first choice and reasons for it.

VOCABULARY phrases with *get*

1A Check the meaning of the lesson title *Survive!* Then Ss look at the photos and read the questions. Give them 2 mins to discuss their answers in pairs. Nominate Ss to give their answers to the class and discuss which situation is the most dangerous.

Answers: 1 Photos: Top left: at sea Bottom left: in a jungle Top right: On a mountain (In the mountains) Bottom right: in the desert 2 Ss' own answers

B Check/Teach *thirsty, shark, snake, insect, raft, sweat* and elicit Ss' answers.

Answers: 2 S 3 D 4 S 5 S/D

C Check *sunburnt* and any other words in the box that Ss are not sure of. They then write their answers and compare them. In feedback, check answers and then read the **speakout tip** with Ss. Ask *How many meanings does 'get' have in this exercise?* Only one: *become.* Elicit more examples of *get* for other meanings, e.g. *get to work/school/the airport, get a ticket, get some new clothes, get out/in/on/off.*

Answers: 2 thirsty 3 tired 4 wet 5 hungry 6 lost
7 sunburnt 8 bored

READING

2A Ss read the text and tips. Check *bottom, rubbish, ground, take off.* Give them 1–2 mins to predict/guess the answers.

B Ss compare their answers, giving reasons for their choices.

C Divide the class into A/Bs. Give them 4 mins to read the texts alone and check their answers to Ex 2A. Tell them to ask you/a partner (reading the same text) if they have any problems with the language. Put Ss into A/B pairs. Bs tell As their answers to Ex 2A. As confirm/correct them and say why this tip is important. Then As tell Bs their answers and Bs do the same. Do feedback and check all the answers. Discuss which facts in the texts surprised Ss.

Answers: 2 Do 3 Don't 4 Don't 5 Don't 6 Don't
7 Don't 8 Don't 9 Do 10 Do

GRAMMAR *will, might, won't*

Watch out!

As mentioned in Unit 9, Ss often add *to* after modal verbs, e.g. *I won't/might to go.* They've just learnt and practise *be going to* so it's likely they'll make mistakes here. Highlight the form clearly for Ss and give thorough controlled practice. Correct the problem while monitoring and in feedback to prevent fossilisation of this error.

3A Ss read the sentences (from the texts on p162/165) and complete the rules. To check the language concepts further, Ss look at the texts again and underline examples of *will*, *might*, *won't*. In feedback, nominate Ss to read out the sentences. After each one, ask *Is it possible/certain/certain not to happen?*

Answers: 1 a) 1 b) 3 c) 2 2 will, will not

B Ss need to focus on the pronunciation of *'ll* so highlight this when they repeat sentence 1.

C First, check new words in the sentences. Then ask *Which sentences are in the present simple/predictions?* Ss then listen and underline the sentences they hear. Monitor while they compare their answers and play the CD again, twice if necessary, if they're not sure. Check Ss' answers. They could then listen again and repeat them. Isolate/Drill *I'll* and contrast it with the word '*I*'. Show Ss that their tongues should lightly touch the hard ridge behind their top teeth when they say *I'll*. Use the diagram on the board to make it clearer for Ss.

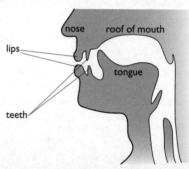

Answers: 1 You'll get too hot. 2 We'll fall into the water.
3 They'll sweat too much. 4 I get hungry.

LANGUAGEBANK 10.2 on p146–7

Ss can refer to the tables and notes in 10.2 on p146 when they do the exercises.

A Check the meaning of *run away, come back.*

Answers: 1 'll 2 will 3 might 4 'll 5 won't 6 'll

B Question 3 refers to watching a DVD/video.

Answers: 2 might, 'll 3 might not, won't 4 might not, won't 5 might, 'll 6 might, 'll

PRACTICE

4A The sentences here are from the texts on p162 and 165. Check the first example with Ss. They then complete the exercise alone and check in pairs.

> **Answers:** 2 'll 3 might 4 might 5 'll 6 won't 7 won't 8 might

B Give Ss 2–3 min to check their answers in the texts. Ask *How many correct answers did you get?*

> **Optional extra activity**
> Divide Ss into two, Ss A and Ss B. Ss A write a list of six *Do/Don't* tips for survival in the mountains, and Ss B do the same for the jungle, e.g. *Do/Don't wear warm clothes/boots.* Ss A then swap lists with Ss B. They underline *Do* or *Don't* in the lists and then check their answers with their partner.

SPEAKING

5A Look at the cartoon and teach *plane crash*. Ss then discuss their answers in pairs. Monitor closely to provide Ss with vocabulary they might need, especially for question 3. Alternatively, tell Ss to use their dictionaries. In feedback, elicit Ss' answers and write the problems from question 3 on the board, e.g. *might get hungry.*

> **Possible answers:** 1 The plane crashed. The engine broke down. 2 Nervous. Frightened. 3 They might need medicine/bandages for people who are hurt/injured. The radio might not work so they can't report the crash. They might not have a map so don't know which way to go. They might not have much food/drink so they'll get hungry/thirsty. It'll be difficult to get out of the jungle/for people (rescuers) to find them.

B Read the words in the box and teach *a box of matches*. Check the example and then refer to the problems on the board. Elicit one or two other objects which would be useful for the people on the plane. Ss then work alone and choose three objects.

C With *weaker classes*, elicit other objects that might be useful and write them on the board if necessary. Ss then decide which three to choose. Otherwise, Ss think of three objects themselves, using dictionaries to find words they need.

> **Sample answers:** a compass, a map, a GPS phone, water, insect repellent, bandages, antiseptic cream, clothes/boots

D Tell Ss to discuss, argue and agree on five objects, as they did in the warm up. Monitor and make notes of problems with the target language for feedback. Ss could then work with another pair/group to choose five objects. Alternatively, have a class discussion/vote to decide on the most important object of all.

WRITING *too, also, as well*

6A Ss read the sentences from the survival texts. Check *catch fish* if you haven't done so before. Ask *Would you drink water from fish eyes?!* Then elicit the position of the words.

> **Answers:** 1 At the end of the sentence. 2 After *be* but before a main verb. 3 At the end of the sentence.

B Read the story with Ss and check *a rest, smell*. Ss then work alone/in pairs to decide.

> **Possible answers:** We (*also*) stopped for a rest in the afternoon (*too/as well*). Sam taught us … and *also* how to cook it (*too/as well*). I ate some and Sam *also* ate some (*too/as well*)

C Ask *Where are the two people? Who are they? Are they lost/on a camping holiday?* Elicit/Discuss possible ways in which the story could continue and end, e.g. *go to bed, get up, have breakfast, go home.* Elicit what problems they might have, what they'll need and what else might happen, e.g. *do they have to find water to drink/food to eat?* Ss have to decide on the context of the story and how to continue it: they could do this in pairs/small groups. They make notes and start the first draft, asking for help if they need it.

> **Homework ideas**
> • Ss write a final draft of the story, Ex 6C.
> • Language bank 10.2 Ex A–B, p147
> • Workbook Ex 1A–8, p61–62

LET'S DO SOMETHING

Introduction

Ss learn and practise how to make and respond to suggestions in the context of an article about twelve ways to have fun.

SUPPLEMENTARY MATERIALS

Resource bank p184

Ex 1: Ss need monolingual dictionaries, e.g. The *Longman WordWise Dictionary*

Ex 8B–C: if feasible, Ss bring/use their mobile phones (otherwise use paper.)

Warm up

Revision of outdoor/indoor free time activities

To lead in to the topic of the lesson, ask Ss write down 2–3 activities they'd like to try/learn but never have, e.g. *go sailing, go to art classes, act in a play.* Monitor/Help Ss with vocabulary if necessary. Elicit/Drill the question, e.g. *Would you like to go sailing/go to art classes?* Ss then work in small groups, and compare their answers. In feedback, Ss from each group tell the class which activities they have in common, e.g. *We all want to go to art classes. Hiroshi wants to learn to sail but Andrei and I don't.*

VOCABULARY adjectives

1A Ss look at the word box and underline words they don't know/are not sure of. Read the **speakout tip** with them here. If you have a copy of the *Longman WordWise Dictionary*, show it to them now. Advise them to use a dictionary like this if they haven't got one yet. Ss then check the words in the box using dictionaries. Check the answer to the question.

Answers: Very good

B Check the example, using finger highlighting or saying *DA-da-da.* Ss then do the exercise alone and compare answers.

C Ss listen and check their answers, then listen and repeat. If they're having problems with the word stress, they can try saying, e.g. *da-DA-da* to help.

Answers:
O great, cool
Oo awesome, lovely
Ooo brilliant, wonderful, excellent
oOo amazing, fantastic

READING

2A This exercise leads in to the topic of the text. Check *indoors* and *outdoors* in the questions. Ss then complete and discuss each sentence in pairs. In feedback, nominate Ss to tell the class what they have in common.

B First, look at the article together and read the introduction. Ask *What's the article about?* Check/Teach language in the list: *movie marathon, snacks, card game, fitness DVD, aerobics.* Ss then tick five good ideas, working alone.

C Ss compare their answers and explain why they chose these five ideas. Elicit/Discuss their answers in feedback. They could also suggest other interesting things to do.

FUNCTION making suggestions

3 Tell Ss to look at the ideas in the article again and check the rubric. If necessary, tell Ss not to worry about understanding every word. They should focus only on noting down the number of the activities on the web page. Play the CD and then Ss compare answers.

Answers: 1 Ten 2 Six

Watch out!

Ss often make errors with the use of the *verb + -ing* in suggestions. They tend to say things like *How about to go/What about to going …* Check the form of the verbs used with each suggestion clearly and give Ss sufficient controlled practice. Prompt Ss to self-correct when they make a mistake.

Unit 10 Recording 6

Conversation 1

M=Man W=Woman

W: Hi, Sergio. <u>Let's do something different tomorrow.</u> It's Saturday.

M: OK. **How about going to an art gallery?** There's a new exhibition on at the Tate.

W: Ur, I don't really feel like doing that. I'd like to stay in. **What about having a 'movie marathon'?** You know, we could just sit at home all day and watch films, eat junk food.

M: <u>Mmm. Do we have to?</u> I saw a film last night. I don't want to sit around all day anyway. I know! **Let's cook something.** Or *I* can.

W: *Sounds lovely.* **Why don't we invite Augusto and Carla** for lunch?

M: *Brilliant!* I'll try a new recipe and we can have a food tasting.

Conversation 2

M=Man W=Woman

W: Hey, Tom. Are you busy this weekend?

M: Er, No, I don't think so.

W: Great. Let's do something!

M: OK. What do you want to do?

W: Well, **how about going for a bike ride** and having a picnic?

M: A bike ride? That sounds a bit tiring. <u>Why don't we play computer games?</u>

W: <u>You're joking!</u>

M: No, really. Why not?

W: Well, because, I sit in front of my computer all week – I'm not going to turn it on tomorrow! Look, <u>let's go to the theatre.</u> Actually, there's a Shakespeare play on in the park: Romeo and Juliet.

M: <u>Hmm. I can never understand Shakespeare plays.</u>

W: OK, well, <u>why don't we read it together first?</u>

M: <u>Oh, but</u> can we get tickets?

W: Yes. It's free.

M: Ah, fantastic! Come on then.

4A Check the example. Ss then do the others alone and compare. Elicit their answers in feedback (see answers in bold in audio script) and write the sentences on the board. Elicit/ Underline the verb form used (*going, having, cook, invite*). Point out that *we* in question 3 could also be *I* in suggestions. Ss then copy the sentences down.

Answers: 2 What about 3 Let's 4 Why don't we

B Ss complete the suggestions using Ex 4A as a model. They then listen and check their answers. In feedback, check the form of the verbs carefully.

Answers: 1 about going 2 about doing 3 don't we do 4 Let's go

C Play the CD again and elicit answers to question 1. Play it again if necessary. Ss then discuss the answers in pairs. In feedback, play the CD again and elicit their answers.

> **Answers:** Yes. It starts high

D Ss now listen and repeat. If they have problems with the high start and high rise-fall at the end, demonstrate when they should stand up (for the high parts) and sit down (for the falling parts). Play the CD again. Ss stand up/sit down to the rhythm several times – until the novelty wears off!

5A Elicit answers for question 1. Ss then work alone and complete questions 2–4. In feedback, check the verb forms again carefully.

> **Answers:** 1 going 2 trying 3 have 4 go

B Demonstrate the question *How about going swimming?* with both positive (high start/high rise-fall at the end) and negative (low start/low rise-fall at end) intonation. Ss respond with *OK* or *No, thanks* appropriately. Then drill the suggestions (with positive/negative intonation) and responses in open pairs across the class. Ss then practise the other suggestions in pairs. Do feedback in open pairs across the class. Prompt self-correction.

LEARN TO respond to suggestions

6A Check the rubric. Ss then read the suggestions and responses. Check *don't really feel like, tiring.* Play the CD. Play it again if Ss still have doubts after comparing answers. Elicit and drill answers in feedback. *Strong Ss* could check their answers in the audio script. They could also underline other examples of suggestions/responses there (see sentences in italics in audio script) and read them out in feedback.

> **Answers:** 1 b) 2 c) 3 e) 4 d) 5 a)

B Elicit Ss' answers. In feedback, emphasise that it's always important to know the appropriate responses to make in any conversation/social interaction.

> **Answer:** a) + b) – c) + d) – e) +

> ⇒ **LANGUAGEBANK** 10.3 p146–7
>
> Ss should refer to the table/notes when they do Ex A on p147.
>
> **Answers:** J: I don't feel *like* stopping S: Let's *have a* coffee J: Why *don't* you make … S: That's a good *idea*. *How* about a … S: That might be a *problem*.

7 Check the rubric and the examples. Then give Ss time to choose the activities and prepare their suggestions. Monitor and help Ss if they need it. While Ss work in pairs, make notes of problems with accuracy and pronunciation. In feedback, nominate pairs to act out their suggestions to the class. Give feedback and correct drill problems with the target language.

SPEAKING

8A Ss can use ideas from the article here, the **warm up** at the beginning of the lesson or something else. Give them 3 mins to decide and complete column 1. Be available for Ss to ask you for vocabulary if they need to. Also check that Ss are completing the column correctly.

B Check the rubric and the instructions in the flowchart. Elicit examples of language for each box, e.g. *Hi, Tom. It's Sam here.* Ss then work in pairs and take turns to go first. To make the role-play more authentic, pairs should sit back-to-back and pretend they're on the phone. They could use their mobiles as realia. If appropriate, Ss could use their mobiles to call each other. They then add information about the arrangements they've made in the first student's column of the table in Ex 8A. N.B. If you notice Ss were making a lot of mistakes with their suggestions and responses, give feedback on this before they move on to the next role-play.

C Put Ss with different partners. Give them 3–4 mins to do the same role-play but with different suggestions. Tell them to check the table when they make arrangements so that they don't have two at the same time! Also remind them to note down the new arrangements in the second student's column. After 3–4 mins, move Ss again to repeat the role-play with a third partner and write their arrangements in the last column. During this series of role-plays, monitor discreetly, making notes of Ss' performance for feedback later.

D Ss should now have a completed table of arrangements. Give instructions and elicit some example sentences, e.g. *I'm going to the zoo with Alana at 4 o'clock on Sunday.* Put Ss in small groups. While one student talks, the others should listen and make notes of the arrangements, e.g. a) if any activities are the same as theirs or b) are at the same time. In feedback, invite Ss to tell the class about similar arrangements they have to other Ss in their group.

> **Homework ideas**
> * Ss write a dialogue with different suggestions using the model in Ex 8B.
> * Language bank 10.3 Ex A, p147
> * Workbook Ex 1–3C, p63

WILD WEATHER

Introduction

Ss watch an extract from the BBC series *Wild Weather*. The programme focuses on Bergen, the wettest place in western Europe, and the second largest city in Norway. They then learn and practise how to talk about the weather, and write about it in a reply to a message board.

SUPPLEMENTARY MATERIALS

Ex 2: optional extra activity: copies of an international/country weather forecast, or use internet facilities if you have them

Ex 3A: a map of the world

Warm up

Lead in and create interest in the topic of the lesson. Write *spring, summer, autumn* and *winter* on the board. Ask *Which season do you like best? Why?* In **multilingual classes**, you could first ask *What's the weather like in your country in the different seasons – hot, cold, wet, dry?* Ss discuss their answers in pairs/small groups and report their answers back to the class.

▶ DVD PREVIEW

1A First, look at the photos and ask *What's the weather like in the photos?* Elicit language Ss know. Ss then read the phrases and match them with the photos. In feedback, check answers and elicit more descriptions of the photos if possible, e.g. *a calm, peaceful day, the wind is blowing, thunder and lightning*.

Answers: 1 D 2 B 3 F 4 A 5 C 6 E

B Check the rubric and drill the example in open and closed pairs. Pay particular attention to the answers: Ss might want to say, e.g. *It's ~~like~~ sunny*. While Ss practise, monitor to check they're saying the questions/answers correctly. Give feedback on this if necessary.

2A Check the words in the box, especially the difference between *cold* and *cool, warm* and *hot*. Ss read the weather forecast first. Check *temperature, degrees, Celsius* and *make sure*. Give Ss 3–4 mins to complete the text alone and compare answers.

B Ss listen and check their answers. In feedback, ask *Do you watch the weather forecast? Is it usually right?*

Answers: 2 warm 3 wet 4 cool 5 dry 6 cold

Optional extra activity

Ss look at the weather forecast online/in newspapers and choose a city to give a forecast for to the class/in groups.

▶ DVD VIEW

3A Check the title and elicit examples of *wild weather* that Ss know/have in their country: *storms, floods, hurricanes*. Ask the question in the rubric. Tell Ss to read the text and then discuss their answers in pairs. They could use places in their own country for examples if possible. It might be useful to have a map of the world in the class. Elicit Ss' answers in feedback. If Ss don't say Norway is a wet place, suggest it.

Possible answers: Hot: tropical countries Wet: the Amazon, Norway Wind: coasts, tropical countries Cold: the Arctic/Antarctic, Canada, Russia

B Check the rubric and reassure Ss that they only have to watch out for three things: the two people and the topic of the programme. Play the DVD. Ss watch and make notes and then compare their answers. Play it again if Ss aren't sure of the answers.

Teaching tip

To help Ss learn paralinguistic features and other visual clues, Ss could watch the DVD first with the sound turned off. They compare answers and then watch it again with the sound.

In feedback, elicit Ss' answers and invite initial comments about the programme.

Answers: 1 *Wet.* 2 In an umbrella shop. For Bergen's local TV station.

C Here, Ss need to listen for specific information at certain points in the programme but are supported by the multiple choice answers. Ss read the sentences first. Check *tons*. Ss then watch the DVD again, underline the answers and then compare them. If necessary, play the DVD again, and pause at/rewind the sentences containing the answers (in bold in the DVD script). N.B. Listening for single words in a text is very useful for the development of Ss' listening skills. After checking the answers, broaden the discussion by asking *Would you like to live in Bergen? Why/Why not?*

Answers: 1 two 2 three 3 cans 4 two hundred and twenty-five 5 1990 6 83

Optional extra activity

Ss might enjoy watching the DVD again just for pleasure – to see/understand/ask you about details they didn't notice before. Or they might prefer to watch it and read the audio script at the same time. Have a vote to see what the class wants to do, then play the DVD again.

DVD 10 Wild Weather

DM=Donal MacIntyre SK=Shopkeeper B= Benedikte

DM: I'm Donal MacIntyre. I'm about to follow water's journey around the planet. This is *Wild Weather*. I'm going to start my journey with water in the wettest place in Western Europe: Bergen, city of rain on Norway's western coast. **It rains here two out of every three days.** So, what's the one thing you need in a city like this? Umbrellas – lots of them.

SK: We have **some special umbrella for little rain, lot of rain and storm.**

DM: For every occasion?

SK: Yes.

DM: This city is so proud of its rain that **they can it and sell it to tourists** because they've got lots of it.
And crashing down on the roof of the average family house every month is a staggering 18 tonnes of rain. **That's 225 tonnes a year.** This place is seriously wet.
This is TV2, Bergen's local TV station. Benedikte Rasmussen has the unenviable job of presenting the weather.

B: **The longest period of rain was in 1990.** And I know this because I've checked it now, but it turns out that it was raining from the 3rd of January to the 26th of March that year and **that's about eighty-three days,** and I can't remember, but I, I think I was quite fed up of rain after those days.

speakout the weather

4A First, look at the photos. Elicit which season is illustrated in each photo, and why. If you have *multilingual class*, the seasons might be different, depending on which hemisphere Ss come from. Then read/check the rubric with Ss. Give them 4–5 mins to write the sentences. Check the questions in feedback: Ss will answer them in Ex 5A.

> **Answers:** 1 What's your favourite kind of weather? Why?
> 2 What kind of weather do you hate? Why? 3 What was the weather like on your last holiday? 4 What's your favourite season? Why? 5 What do you like doing in spring, etc?
> 6 What's the best season to visit your country/city? Why?

B Check instructions and play the CD. With *weaker classes*, play the first part and elicit the question it answers. After listening, Ss compare answers. Play the CD again if they're still not sure. Check the answers in feedback. Then ask *Do you feel the same as these people? Who? Why?* Discuss Ss' answers.

> **Answers:** 1 five 2 four 3 two 4 one 5 three 6 six

C Ss read and check they understand the **key phrases**. Then play the CD again. They tick the **key phrases** they hear and compare their answers (in bold in the audio script). In feedback, play the CD again. Pause at each **key phrase** and elicit the complete sentence. Ss tell you any other details they remember about each **key phrase**.

> **Answers:** Tick all sentences.

Unit 10 Recording 10

1 Oh, I think spring is the best. **I love it when** the flowers come out and the birds start singing – **that's when** everything is so fresh. **It's the perfect time to** take a walk along the Danube.

2 **It rained every day, but we had a great time.** We went to museums, sat in cafés and played cards.

3 In winter **I love skiing** – getting up early to spend the whole day on the mountain skiing – fantastic! I love having a hot chocolate in a local café at the end of the afternoon – it's the perfect time to do that.

4 **I really don't like it when** it's very hot, especially in the city. There are so many tourists about – I get so hot and tired, it's awful!

5 Oh, **I really like it when it's hot** and then there's a big summer storm, with lots and lots of rain … I love the way the air cools down and it feels fresher.

6 Well, definitely not in the rainy season! I think **the best time to visit** Malaysia **is** May to September **because** after that it gets really wet – it feels like it never stops raining!

5A First, give time for Ss to check the questions in Ex 4A again and practise saying them quietly to themselves. They then need time to think about the answers they're going to give using the **key phrases**. Tell them to make notes if it helps them. They can also look at the audio script on p174 for help. Monitor and provide support where needed. Ss should then be ready to interview each other. Remind them to make notes of their partner's answers. Monitor discreetly and make sure Ss are writing notes. Also note down any strengths and weaknesses in the language they use.

B Regroup Ss so that they don't work with the same partner. Ss take turns to talk about their partners. The others listen and make notes. The group then compares the information it has to find similarities and differences.

C Check the example and elicit answers to one or two of the options, e.g. *most people like summer best because …* Ss then write sentences about the people they talked about. Invite Ss to report back to the class, who must listen carefully and compare their own answers with those of the person talking. In feedback, ask the questions from Ex 4A again and elicit the majority answers, e.g. *Most people like sunny weather best.*

writeback reply on a message board

6A Ss complete the message board. Then ask Ss *What time of the year are you going to recommend?* They can talk about this in pairs/groups or as a class. It's a particularly interesting question for *multilingual classes*. In feedback, elicit answers from as many Ss as possible.

B Read through the reply, eliciting possible answers for each gap. Ss then complete the reply alone and show it to a partner. In feedback, nominate Ss to read out their replies. The class listens and checks if they have similar ones. They then vote on the best/most interesting reply.

> **Homework ideas**
> - Ss write two paragraphs about their most/least favourite season and say why, Ex 5.
> - Ss write a different reply to the message in Ex 6A (and put it on the class blog/send it to a classmate).
> - Workbook Ex 4, p63

LOOKBACK

Introduction

When assessing your Ss speaking skills, you need to consider four things: accuracy of grammar and spelling, range of vocabulary used, fluency and pronunciation. It's a good idea to give Ss marks out of five for each area, making a total of twenty marks.

VERB PHRASES

1A Give Ss 1–2 mins to do this exercise as a race. The first to finish with the all correct answers wins.

Answers: 1 go, stay 2 go, go for, stay, do, have, go 3 get, move

B Do the first sentence as an example. Elicit the question *On your next holiday do you want to stay home or go abroad?* Elicit answers with *(not) going to/would like to*, e.g. *I'd like to go to Thailand. I'm not going abroad. I'm going to stay at home.* While Ss talk in pairs, note down problems for feedback, or assessment if required.

GOING TO; WOULD LIKE TO

2A Check *Weekend wish list* – the things the person wishes they could do but might not be able to. Then do the examples and check what Ss know about *Gone with the Wind*. Ss do the exercise alone and compare answers. Monitor and make notes for feedback.

Answers: 3 I'd like to go to the U2 concert but there aren't any tickets. 4 I'm going to meet Andy for a drink. He said he'd like to. 5 I'm going to watch *Gone with the Wind*. I borrowed it from Cindy. 6 I'd like to sleep a lot but I haven't got time.

B Elicit examples for Ss' wish list, e.g. *go dancing (broke my leg last week), go clothes shopping (just got paid)*. Write them on the board and elicit sentences using *going to/would like to*. Give Ss 3 mins to write their lists. Monitor all Ss and check their lists if possible, before Ex B.

C Give Ss time to think and prepare their sentences before they work in pairs. In feedback, Ss report back to the class about their partner's plans. Give feedback and assess Ss' speaking skills as needed.

PREDICTIONS

3A First, elicit information about the cartoon, e.g. *the hotel is high in the mountains in the middle of nowhere. There are only goats and birds there.* Ss then read the information.

B Check *get hurt, peaceful*. Elicit the answer to question 2. Tell Ss they should give their own answers/opinions, e.g. *We'll/we won't/we might get bored. Weaker Ss* could work in pairs. Monitor and help if necessary.

C Ss compare their answers. To extend the practice, they could then work with another pair to compare further. Monitor and make notes for feedback.

D Ss decide in their pairs/groups if they'd like this kind of weekend, giving reasons. Nominate/Invite Ss from each group to tell the class what they think.

MAKING SUGGESTIONS

4A Ss correct the sentences alone/in pairs. *Weaker Ss* could look back at p102–103 for help.

Answers: 1 Why don't we have … 2 Let's have … 3 What about starting at … 4 That's a great idea! 5 Sounds good. 6 That might be a problem.

B Read the rubric and elicit examples of party food, drink, etc. Also discuss other ideas, e.g. *type of party (fancy dress, themed, 80s, Halloween)*. Put Ss into small groups They make suggestions and respond appropriately to each other. Make notes on how well they use this language.

Optional extra activity
Each group designs and draws an invitation to their party. (use computer facilities if available, or take materials/coloured pens to class). They each take a copy with them to show to the next group in Ex 4C.

C First, Ss make a list of what they agreed on in Ex 4B: place, food, etc. They must all write it down so that they can pass the information on to the other groups.

Teaching tip
An easy way of reorganising the groups is: 1) name each group A, B, C, etc, and 2) number Ss 1, 2, 3, etc. 3) Tell all the number 1s to sit together, all the number 2s to sit together, etc.

In their new groups, Ss take turns to describe their party. Each one then decides which party to go to. In feedback, invite Ss to tell the class about the party they chose. Give feedback and assess Ss' speaking skills.

THE WEATHER

5A Check the example and give Ss 3–4 mins to complete the sentences. *Fast finishers* write more sentences with jumbled weather words on the board. In feedback, check Ss' answers.

Answers: 2 rains 3 cloudy 4 snows 5 windy 6 stormy

B Give Ss 4 mins to write their sentences. *Weaker Ss* can work together. Monitor and check all Ss' writing if possible. Otherwise they could hand them in for you/other Ss to check later/at home.

C Monitor and assess how well Ss use weather language and adjectives. They report back to the class about their partners in feedback.

OVERVIEW

B B C VIDEO PODCAST

Do you have a healthy lifestyle?

In this video podcast, people talk about health and fitness and how they maintain a healthy lifestyle. They also talk about what they do when they feel ill and how to aid recovery. The video podcast could be used at the end of lessons 11.1 or 11.2 to further show the target language in context, at the start of the lesson as an introduction or the end of unit 11 as a round up.

MY HEAD HURTS

Introduction

Ss learn and practise how to give advice using should/shouldn't in the context of common cures for colds and flu.

SUPPLEMENTARY MATERIALS

Resource bank p185 and p186

Photo bank p158

Ex 6 optional extra activity: Ss research the topic of flu online if you have internet facilities

Warm up

Lead in to the lesson topic with revision of body parts. Point to an arm/leg and elicit/say the words arm/leg. In pairs, Ss then point to parts of their partner's body and name those they know, e.g. eye, mouth. In feedback, check the words Ss know but don't teach/drill new ones yet. This will be done in the **Photo bank** in Ex 1.

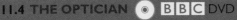 **VOCABULARY** the body

1A Ss look at the photos. Ask What's wrong with the people? Elicit/Teach They're ill. They're in pain. His leg hurts. Ss will learn the names of specific ailments/problems in the exercises below but check/elicit what Ss already know, e.g. He/She's got a cold/headache. Ss then work in pairs. Give them 1 min to name the parts of the body they know in the photos. Ss then do the **Photo bank** exercises.

> ▥▶ **PHOTOBANK** p158
>
> **Body parts**
>
> **1** In mixed-ability classes, stronger and weaker Ss can work together. In feedback, check/drill the answers.
>
> **Answers:** 1 R 2 Q 3 E 4 B 5 G 6 N 7 L 8 I 9 A 10 J 11 P 12 M 13 F 14 C 15 H 16 D 17 O 18 K
>
> **2** Ss do this in pairs.
>
> **Answers:**
> one: back, mouth, neck
> two: arms, ears, eyes, feet (foot), hands, knees, legs, elbows, shoulders, lips, thumbs
> eight: fingers
> ten: toes

B Check the meaning of throat, stomach. Elicit the pronunciation of all the words but don't correct it. Play the CD for Ss to check, then listen and repeat. Highlight the fact that ch in stomach is pronounced /k/. Play the CD as many times as needed for Ss to be confident with their pronunciation

C Ss work in pairs and take turns pointing to parts of the body in the picture. Monitor to check their pronunciation, and give feedback as needed.

LISTENING

2A Check *cold*, *medicine* and *rest* in the questions. Ss then work in pairs to discuss them. Nominate Ss to report their partner's answers to the class.

B Ss know the words *leg, nose, throat, head, arm* so should be able to work out what the phrases mean from the photos. Give them 2 mins to check the photos and compare answers. With *weaker classes*, check/teach the health problems, using the photos. In feedback, elicit Ss' answers and model/drill the pronunciation if necessary. Use mime to check the meaning of *cough* /kɒf/. With *stronger classes*, teach other details if appropriate, e.g. *he's blowing his nose, his throat hurts, he's got a scarf round his neck, she's got a thermometer in her mouth.*

Answers: A a runny nose, a sore throat B a temperature C a headache D stomach ache E his leg hurts

C Elicit an example. Ss then do the exercise in pairs. In feedback, elicit and write their answers on the board in three columns (C/F/Both). Ss should copy the table down for Ex 2C.

D Play the CD. Ss listen and tick the problems from Ex 2C that they guessed correctly. If more than half of the Ss still have doubts after comparing their answers, play the CD again to help build their confidence with listening skills. Check and discuss Ss' answers (see phrases in bold in audio script). Briefly elicit other details Ss heard in relation to the symptoms.

Answers:
cold: runny nose
flu: a headache, your arms and legs hurt, a high temperature
both: sore throat, cough

E Check *suddenly* and *slowly* in the sentences. *Stronger Ss* should be able to answer the questions without listening again but *weaker ones* might need to. The best solution is for Ss to listen and read the audio script at the same time – this will be useful for all of them. Check answers (in bold italics in the audio script) in feedback and answer any questions Ss have about language in the script.

Answers: 1 suddenly, can't 2 slowly, can

Unit 11 Recording 2

P=Presenter   D=Doctor

P: And this week in *Health Matters*, we're talking about colds and flu. What's the difference, and more importantly, how to cure them? With me in the studio is Dr Elizabeth Harper. Dr Harper, how is flu different from a common cold?

D: Well, *flu starts very suddenly.* One minute you're fine, the next minute you feel terrible. You've got **a headache** – often a very bad headache – and **a cough.** You've got **a sore throat** and **your arms and legs hurt.** You're very hot. Usually you've got a **temperature of over thirty-eight degrees** centigrade and you're too ill to do anything. *You can't work.* You just want to go home and *go to bed.* Sometimes *you have to stay in bed for a week or more.*

P: Awful. I see, yes. And what about a typical cold?

D: *A cold starts slowly.* Maybe it takes two or three days to start. It's a cold when you've got **a sore throat, or a cough and a runny nose** and you don't feel very well. But – and here's the big difference – *if you can get up and go to work, then you've probably got a cold, not flu.* After a week you feel better. *After flu, you often feel very tired for* a very long time, maybe two or three weeks!

P: Mmm. OK, so the next question.

speakout TIP

Read the tip with Ss and elicit other words containing the /f/ or /k/ sounds with a different spelling, e.g. with /f/ – cou*gh*, lau*gh*, *ph*oto, geogra*ph*y; with /k/ *ch*emist/*ch*emistry, *Ch*ristmas, stoma*ch* a*ch*e. In the case of *thumb*, there's a silent letter: *b*. Other examples of this: clim*b*, com*b*, cu*p*board, coul*d*, tem*pe*rature.

3A This exercise practises verbs used to talk about health problems: *have got, hurt* and *feel.* Check the example and mime the meaning of *earache, backache.* Ss then do the exercise and compare their answers. Check/Drill the answers in feedback.

Answers: 2 cough 3 runny nose 4 temperature

B Invite Ss to mime one or two problems first. Monitor to check how well they've grasped the new language. In feedback, nominate Ss to mime problems to the class, who guess what it is.

READING

4A Check the title of the article and teach *cure* (n + v). Then, elicit/check the vocabulary in the illustrations, e.g. *water, stay in bed, medicine, oranges, soup, lemon, herbal tea, honey.* The other dish is *kimchi* soup – Ss will learn what it is in the text. Give Ss 2 mins to read and underline ideas that relate to the pictures. *Fast finishers* can circle other 'cures' mentioned. Ss then compare their answers. Give them more time if they need it. Check answers in feedback. Elicit where the cures are from, and any other ideas in the article. Check *antibiotics, cold virus* if necessary.

Answers: drink lots of water and get lots of sleep, don't have medicine, eat lots of fruit like oranges, eat (Doug's grandmother's) chicken soup, drink herbal tea with honey and lemon, eat *kimchi* – a soup made from cabbage and spices.

B Refer to Jean's idea and ask *Do you agree with him? Do you do this in your country?* Nominate/Discuss Ss' answers briefly. Then give them 3 mins to read and note down their answers to the questions.

C Ss compare their ideas and should give reasons if possible, e.g. *You have to drink lots of water.* Check Ss' answers, with reasons, and then have a class vote on the most common/ effective treatment for a cold.

GRAMMAR *should/shouldn't*

5A *Strong classes* do Ex 5A and B and check their answers in the **Language bank** on p148. In *mixed ability classes*, put *strong* and *weak Ss* together: the *strong ones* help/explain to the *weak ones*. Otherwise, Ss do the exercise alone. Check the answer and concept of advice/recommendation by asking *Do you have to drink lots of water? No, but it's a good idea. Do you have to stay at home? No, but it's not a good idea to go to work/school. You'll feel awful.*

Answers: 1 a good idea 2 a bad idea

B Ss read the table of forms and find the sentences in the article to complete it. While they read, write the sentences from the table on the board (with gaps) for Ex 5C.

Answers: drink, eat, shouldn't

C Play the extracts from the interview for Ss to check/ correct their answers. In feedback, check and write them in the gaps. Then elicit/underline the form: *should* + verb and *should* + *not* + verb. N.B. *Should* can also be used to ask for advice. Ask *Should I get lots of sleep (when I have a cold?)? Should I go to work?* Elicit Ss' answers *Yes, you should./No, you shouldn't.* Drill the questions/answers in open pairs across the class, giving other prompts, e.g. *go dancing/go the gym, eat fruit.* Ss then underline other examples of *should/shouldn't* in the audio script. Elicit and check them. Play the CD again for Ss to listen and repeat. Highlight the pronunciation of the weak form *should* /ʃəd/ and the strong form *shouldn't* /ʃʊdnt/. Point out that the '*l*' in *should* is silent.

Optional extra activity

Ss discuss cures for *flu* in the same way as the article did for colds. This should work well in *multilingual classes* but can also be done with *monolingual classes*: Ss might know of some interesting local/family cures. To expand the activity further, Ss could also search for more unusual information online if facilities are available.

⏩ LANGUAGEBANK 11.1 p148–9

Ss can refer to the tables and notes when they do Ex A–B. *Weaker Ss* should do them in class.

A Check *mess*.

Answers: 2 Should he, c) 3 Should I, a)
4 Should they, b) 5 Should she, e) 6 Should we, f)

B Check *delicious*.

Answers: 2 should try 3 should change 4 shouldn't wear 5 shouldn't go 6 should have 7 shouldn't stay

PRACTICE

6A Ss first read the problems and advice. Check the example and monitor while Ss write to check the accuracy of their sentences. Elicit answers in feedback. Prompt Ss to self-correct or correct each other's errors of meaning, form and pronunciation.

Answers: 2 b), h) You should eat something/shouldn't miss breakfast. 3 g), e) You should take an umbrella/ shouldn't go out now. 4 d), a) You should go home now/ shouldn't be here in the lesson.

B While Ss work in pairs, monitor and help with accuracy.

SPEAKING

7A Check the example and elicit one or two more. Give Ss 5–6 min to discuss their ideas and write their list. Monitor to help with vocabulary they need and prompt them to self-correct if necessary.

B Regroup Ss and check instructions. Give them 3 mins to read out/justify their lists. Then stop them, and give another 3 mins for them to write a revised list of five tips. While Ss work, make notes on their performance, particularly with the target language. In feedback, discuss Ss' answers and have a class vote for the number one tip for good health.

Homework ideas

- Ss write their five top tips for good health, Ex 8.
- Language bank 11.1 Ex A–B, p149
- Workbook Ex 1A–5D, p64–65

NEVER FELT BETTER

Introduction

Ss learn and practise adverbs of manner and common verbs in the context of health and how to describe the way things are done, e.g. I walk slowly.

SUPPLEMENTARY MATERIALS

Resource bank p187

Ex 4 optional extra activity: download/copy a cartoon strip for Ss to write a story, e.g. Peanuts

Warm up

Lead in to the topic of the lesson by asking When was the last time you forgot to do something important? What did you forget? Why? What advice can you give to help you remember in the future? Ss answer the questions in small groups. Monitor to provide vocabulary they may need. Nominate/Invite Ss to tell a partner's story to the class in feedback.

VOCABULARY common verbs

Culture note

In Ancient Rome, the poet Juvenal first wrote the proverb 'mens sana in corpore sano' meaning 'a healthy mind in a healthy body'. We still use it today to mean that if the body is healthy, the mind will be too.

1A First, check the title (Ss may have the same one in their language) and discuss what the quiz is about. Teach keep and be fit. After reading the word box, Ss complete the quiz alone and compare answers. Tell them not to worry about new words yet. Monitor and check how well they're doing the quiz. Check Ss' answers. Don't ask them the questions in the quiz but teach new language there: without stopping, four sets of, PIN number, password.

Answers: 2 run 3 climb 4 read 5 hear, understand 6 concentrate 7 remember 8 forget

B Demonstrate by doing the example and eliciting Ss' answers to the question. N.B. Ss will come across adverbs in the quiz answers. Encourage Ss to use their knowledge of the adjectives to understand the meaning of the adverbs. They will study adverbs in detail in Ex 2. Give Ss 4–5 mins to ask/answer the questions and check the results in the key. In feedback, ask Ss if they agree with their scores, and why/why not.

C Check the instructions and examples. While Ss do the activity, they could make word webs with other possible nouns that collocate with these verbs. In feedback, invite Ss to write the word webs on the board. The class can suggest other nouns to add.

GRAMMAR adverbs of manner

Watch out!

It's important to clarify both the form/spelling of adverbs and their position in a sentence. Highlight these points clearly and give Ss thorough controlled practice.

2A Ss read the sentences from the quiz and underline the correct forms. Elicit answers and write slow and slowly on the board. Ask How do we make adverbs? Add -ly to the adjective. Underline it: slowly. Then elicit the spelling change for easy – easily – y changes to i. Then ask How do we use adverbs? To say how/when we do something. Elicit/Check with other examples, e.g. I remember perfectly what I ate yesterday (how) and I go to bed very early/late. (when). Ask Are late and early regular or irregular adverbs? Irregular. Ss write them down.

Answers: 1 slowly 2 easily; how

B Check the example before Ss do the exercise. Monitor while they work to see if they know the irregular adverbs: fast, well. Check/Drill the adverbs in feedback and elicit sentences using them.

Answers: slowly, clearly, fast (irreg), loudly, perfectly, well (irreg), healthily

---

▶ LANGUAGEBANK 11.2 p148–9

Read and check the tables and notes in 11.2 on p148 with Ss, especially the position of adverbs in sentences. They should refer to the table when they do the exercises.

A

Answers: 1 angry, angrily 2 beautifully, beautiful 3 easily, easy 4 quiet, quietly 5 good, well 6 terribly, terrible

B To follow up, Ss could write questions using how and when, e.g. When did he wake up? How did he make breakfast?

Answers: 2 angrily 3 quickly 4 easily 5 slowly 6 late

PRACTICE

3A Check the first example with Ss. Teach/Elicit that hard is both an adjective and an adverb. Ss then complete the exercise with their own answers. Monitor to help/advise and check accuracy.

B Give Ss 2–3 mins to compare their answers. In feedback, nominate Ss to tell the class their partner's answers for each sentence. Also recheck the difference between the way adjectives and adverbs are used: adj + noun, be/feel + adj, verb + adv.

Answers: 2 quickly/slowly 3 well/badly 4 good/bad 5 fast/slowly 6 healthily/unhealthily 7 quiet/noisy 8 lazy/energetic

WRITING adverbs in stories

4A Ss cover the text. Elicit details about the pictures. This can be done in the present tense, e.g. *he's riding his bike/ listening to music, his arm's in a sling/plaster*, etc. Ss then order the pictures and compare. Elicit their answers and move on to Ex 4B.

> **Answers:** D, A, C, B

B Check the example sentence and elicit the end of it. Also check *broken (arm)*. Ss then use the prompts to write the rest of the story in the past simple. *Weaker Ss* can work together. Check/Help them with the accuracy of their writing if needed. *Fast finishers* can add more details to their story. Ss could then swap their stories with other Ss/pairs and compare them with their own. Monitor closely to check the accuracy of Ss' writing and prompt correction if necessary. In feedback, choose a good example of the story to read out to the class. They compare it with their own and make any changes needed.

> **Possible answer:** … got on his bike. He rode down the road and didn't look ahead. A cat ran in front of him. He fell off his bike and broke his arm. That evening, he sat at home with a broken arm.

C Ss first write the adverbs. Check form and meaning before they add them to their stories. Ss then compare their adapted stories in pairs/groups. Nominate Ss to read their story to the class, and check if the adverbs are in the appropriate place.

> **Answers:** quickly, carefully, carelessly, dangerously, early, fast, late, sadly, slowly **Sample story:** On day, Ken got up, had breakfast *quickly* and got on his bike. He rode down the road *dangerously* and didn't look ahead. A cat ran in front of him. He fell off his bike and broke his arm *badly*. That evening, he sat *sadly* at home with a broken arm.

D Elicit ideas for the next part of the story. Ss then write it alone/in pairs. Monitor closely to help/correct if necessary.

E Ss swap stories and compare them with their own. Ss can also give positive feedback to each other, and make helpful suggestions for improving the story. Monitor to make sure Ss are doing this sensibly. In feedback, invite Ss to read their story endings to the class, who then vote for the most original idea. Alternatively, Ss pass the stories round the class so that everyone can read them, or display them on the walls. Ss read and make comments/suggestions to whoever wrote them.

> **Optional extra activity**
>
> Ask *Did you ever do anything silly/funny like Ken – recently or when you were a child?* N.B. *Silly* is used in the question because it would be more appropriate for Ss to talk about fairly light-hearted events, not serious accidents. *When did it happen?* e.g. *I went fishing but I when I tried to get the fish out of the water, I fell in.* Elicit some answers briefly and then give Ss time to prepare notes/ideas. Give prompts to help them: *When? Where? Why? What? How? What next? Finally …* Ss work in small groups and take turns to tell their stories. The others can ask for more detail if they want to. In feedback, Ss tell the class the silliest/funniest story they heard.

SPEAKING

5A Check the rubric. Tell Ss to read the diary and tick (✓) the healthy things Julie did and put a cross (✗) next to the unhealthy things. Discuss the first thing in her diary as an example. Ss compare their answers and check if they have the same opinion of what's healthy or not. They should give reasons for this. Check their opinions in feedback and come to a consensus if possible.

> **Answers:**
> **Saturday** wasn't a very healthy day. Although she slept well and relaxed with her friends, Julie ate too many carbohydrates (popcorn, coke, pizza, cake) and didn't have any exercise.
> **Sunday** was a healthier day. She drank too much coffee but she had healthy food – fruit, cereal, a big salad, a healthy dinner – and did healthy things: she had lunch with her brother, went swimming and went to bed early.

B Check the list here against what Julie wrote in her diary so that Ss are clear about what to do, e.g. *relaxing = going out with friends*. Encourage them to use at least four adverbs in the diary if possible. Also encourage them to be honest – though this in not mandatory! They could write the one they wish they'd had. Give Ss 4–5 mins to make notes. Monitor closely to provide help/vocabulary, etc.

C Ss take turns to tell the other Ss about their health diary, using their notes. They then discuss and decide who had the healthiest weekend. Do feedback here. Ss tell the class about the healthiest person in their group. They then talk about what they can/will do differently next weekend. Monitor and make notes of good language/problems at all stages of this activity. In feedback, elicit some of their good intentions. Tell them to write them down and check them after next weekend. Then give feedback as needed – or do a 'grammar auction' in the next class.

> **Homework ideas**
> - Ss write their stories about a silly mistake from Ex 4. They could write about a silly story in a cartoon strip.
> - Ss write the answers to the questions in two paragraphs from Ex 5C: 1 Did you have a healthy week last week? What did you do/eat? 2 What are you going to do differently next week?
> - **Language bank** 11.2 Ex A–B, p149
> - **Workbook** Ex 1A–6B, p66–67

HELP!

Introduction

Ss learn and practise how to offer and thank people for their help. They do this in the context of an article about how willing, or not, people are to help others nowadays.

SUPPLEMENTARY MATERIALS

Resource bank p188

Ex 1B: Ss can use dictionaries to check the meaning of the words in bold

Ex 4B Optional extra activity: prepare prompt cards as described in the activity

Ex 6B: use recording facilities/Ss mobile phones

Warm up

Lead in to the lesson topic by demonstrating/miming a situation where you need help, e.g. trying to move a table/lift a heavy pile of books/reach up to a high shelf. Say *Can you help me, please?* Then ask Ss *When did you last help a person? When did you last ask for help?* Elicit answers or Ss can discuss them in pairs first.

VOCABULARY problems

1A First, Ss look at the photos. Ask: *What's happening in each picture? What can you say to offer to help?* Elicit answers, e.g. *The old woman's carrying a heavy suitcase. Can I carry your suitcase?* Ss then work in pairs and discuss the questions for the other three photos. Monitor and provide vocabulary they need. However, Ss will learn other ways of offering to help later in the lesson so don't teach them any new language now. Check their answers in feedback.

Possible answers:

The woman is phoning someone because her car broke down: *Can I help you?*
An old woman is carrying a heavy suitcase: *Can I carry your suitcase?*
A man fell off his bike: *Can I help you up?*
A woman is standing on a crowded bus with a sleeping baby: *Would you like to sit here?*

B Here Ss learn language they'll need for later in the lesson. First, read/check the meaning of the words in bold by miming the actions, e.g. *lift, drop* or by using the photos, e.g. *stand*. *Stronger Ss* might be able to work out the meaning of the words from the context. Alternatively, they can check them in their dictionaries. Ss then discuss their answers in pairs for 2–3 mins. Elicit Ss' answers/opinions and recheck the meaning of the verbs. Ask Ss what *they* usually do in these situations.

READING

2A Ss read the introductory paragraph of the article but cover the rest of it. Ask *Who are Michael and Kitty? What did they want to do? Why?* Give Ss time to think and discuss their answers. Teach *in trouble, situation, reporter, walk on by.* Then give Ss 1 min to read the article and number the pictures. In feedback, ask Ss *Which words in the article helped you?*

Answers: A 2 B 1 C 3

B Teach/Check new words before Ss read, or in feedback, e.g. *sign, pull, drunk, dead.*

Teaching tip

It's a good idea to develop the skill of deducing the meaning of new words from their context. However, if you have **weaker Ss** or **slow readers**, they might benefit from more support, such as knowing new words before reading them. Ss can of course use their dictionaries to check new words: this is also an important skill, which encourages independence.

Give Ss 3–4 mins to read and answer the question. In feedback, check answers. Then ask *Do you agree with the article? Are people afraid of helping others these days? Why/Why not?* Elicit and discuss Ss' answers.

Answer: The first situation – the dropped papers.

FUNCTION offering to help

3A Check the rubric and play the CD. Ss listen and then compare answers. In feedback, check answers and ask Ss to tell you the words that helped them to decide which picture it was.

Answers: 1 B 2 C 3 A

B Ss read the sentences first. Check *ambulance.* Then play the CD again. Ss write the answers and then compare them. Play the CD again if necessary as they might have problems hearing the *'ll* sound. *Stronger Ss* could try to complete the gaps first, then listen and check. Check Ss' answers (in bold in audio script) and teach *mess* and *That's all right.* Then move to Ex 3C where they'll practise the pronunciation.

Answers: 1 Let 2 Shall 3 'll

Unit 11 Recording 4

Situation 1

W1 = 1st Woman   M1 = 1st Man

W1: Oh, no. My papers!
M1: <u>Here,</u> let me help. What a mess!
W1: Thank *you very much.*
M1: No *problem.*

Situation 2

W2 = 2nd Woman   M2 = 2nd Man

W2: Er, <u>Excuse me – sir?</u>
M2: Uhhh.
W2: <u>Are you all right?</u> **Shall** I call an ambulance?
M2: No, Yes, Uh, Thanks *so much.*
W: That's *OK.*

Situation 3

W3 = 3rd Woman   M3 = 3rd Man

W3: Hmm, Uh, Mmm.
M3: <u>Oh, look.</u> I'll do that for you. Where do you want it?
W3: Just over here, in front of the window … Thanks *a lot.* That's *kind of you.*
M3: You're *welcome.*

C Tell Ss to listen carefully to the pronunciation of *Shall* and *I'll.* Check what they heard and if they can say it. If Ss didn't hear the *'ll* sound, play the CD until they can. Show them how to say the *'ll* sound if necessary, with the tip of the tongue touching the hard ridge behind their top teeth. Play the CD again for Ss to listen again and repeat the sentences, both chorally and individually. Beat the stress and highlight the intonation with your hands as they repeat.

4A Check the example and teach/mime *reach* in question 3 and *stuck* in e). Ss then do the matching activity and check their answer in pairs. Model and drill the offers first. Then drill both problems and offers in open pairs. Follow this up with a substitution drill to help Ss with Ex 4B. Give prompts, e.g. *I can't open the door. I can't reach the top shelf/window, I can't lift this suitcase/rucksack/these books.* Ss repeat the sentences with the prompts. (Also see optional activity below) In feedback, elicit the language used to make offers (*I'll, Let me, Shall I, Can I*). Ss then copy the offers down and underline the functional language.

Answers: 2 c) 3 a) 4 b) 5 d)

B Give Ss 2–3 mins to practise using examples from Ex 4A. *Stronger Ss* can add their own. Monitor to check accuracy and pronunciation and give feedback as needed.

Optional extra activity
To provide more variety and support for *weaker Ss*, use prompt cards with examples like those suggested for the substitution drill in Ex 4A above, e.g. *dropped purse, fall down, cut finger.* Write/Copy a set of prompts, cut them up and hand out a set to each pair.

speakout TIP

Read the tip with Ss and then illustrate it. Play the CD for Ex 3A again, pausing after each introductory comment and checking what was said (see underlined examples in the audio script). Prompt Ss to give you more examples, e.g. mime carrying a pile a heavy books. Ss could say, *Those books are heavy – let me help you.*

LEARN TO thank someone

5A Play the CD, pausing after each conversation for Ss to write. Play it again if they still have doubts after comparing their answers. Check and then drill the answers (see answers in bold italics in audio script).

Answers: 1 you very much 2 problem 3 so much 4 OK 5 a lot 6 kind of you 7 welcome

B Elicit Ss' answers and practise the pronunciation using the CD. Highlight the stress/intonation.

Answers:
Thanking someone: Thank you very much. Thanks so much. Thanks a lot. That's kind of you.
Respond to thanks: No problem. That's OK. You're welcome.

▶ **LANGUAGEBANK** 11.3 p148–9

A Ss should refer to the table/notes when they do Ex A, p149. Check *top* and *tight* in conversation 5.

Answers: 1 'll check 2 Let, have 3 Shall/Can, carry 4 Shall, turn 5 Let, open

6A Check the rubric and flowchart, and elicit/drill the first answer. Give Ss 1 min to order the conversation and practice saying it in pairs. Monitor to check their pronunciation. Nominate *strong Ss* to act out the conversation to the class. Then give feedback so that Ss are well prepared for Ex 6B.

Answers: 4, 5, 3, 2, 1

B Ss work in A/B pairs facing each other and not showing their books to their partners. They read the relevant exercises and ask you for help with vocabulary if needed. Remind them to use the flowchart in Ex 6A. Ss then take it in turns to start with *Are you OK?* Monitor discreetly while they work, and note problems with the functional language. *Fast finishers* can create more dialogues, or rehearse the ones they've done and act them out to the class in feedback. N.B. If you have recording facilities, you/Ss can record their dialogues. Or Ss can use the recording function on their mobile phones. They can listen again and repeat the dialogues until they're satisfied with them. Give feedback on Ss' performance as necessary.

SPEAKING

7A Check the rubric and play the CD. Ss listen to the sound effects for different situations and note down what's happening. Play the CD again, pausing after each situation for them to complete their notes and compare answers. Check answers and teach vocabulary they need, e.g. *supermarket checkout*.

Answers: 1 A woman dropped and broke a lot of glasses. 2 A man is at the supermarket checkout but can't find his wallet. He forgot to bring it so he can't pay the bill. 3 A man cut his finger when he was chopping/cutting vegetables. 4 A man fell off their bike. 5 A man is coughing badly. 6 A woman is feeling very cold.

B Give Ss time to think of how they'll offer to help. Then play the CD again, pausing after each situation to elicit some responses. Ss then work in pairs, taking it in turns to respond to each situation. In feedback, play the CD once more and elicit different ways of offering to help.

Homework ideas
• Ss write three dialogues using the flowchart and ideas from Ex 6–7.
• Language bank 10.3 Ex A, p149
• Workbook Ex 1–4B, p68

THE OPTICIAN

Introduction

Ss watch an extract from the legendary BBC series *The Two Ronnies*. They also learn and practise how to ask for advice at a pharmacy and write a response to a medical problem in a website message.

SUPPLEMENTARY MATERIALS

Ex 4A: Ss may need dictionaries – if they're available. Use monolingual dictionaries such as the *Longman WordWise Dictionary*

Warm up

Favourite TV programmes: Group/Pair discussion

Put Ss in groups of 2–3. *Ask What's your favourite TV comedy show of all time? Why?* and tell Ss they have to give three reasons. Ss discuss the questions in pairs/groups for 3–4 mins. N.B. If there are Ss who don't like comedy shows, they can talk about their favourite TV programmes together. In feedback, nominate Ss to tell the class about their partner's favourite show.

DVD PREVIEW

1A First, look at the photos. Check the example and the meaning of *optician*. Ss work in pairs and talk about photos B–F. Monitor and teach any words they need. In feedback, check answers. Ss who needed new words should explain them to the class. If possible, elicit more detail from the photos, e.g. *The optician's using a machine to check the woman's eyes.*

Answers: 2 B He's a dentist. He checks someone's teeth. C She is a doctor. She checks people's health. D He's a fitness instructor. He teaches people how to do the gym exercises correctly. E He is a hairdresser. He cuts people's hair. F He's an accountant. He checks people's money/accounts.

B Check the rubric and advice. Elicit Ss' answers. Encourage *stronger Ss* to be funny in their answers. The intention is for Ss to find this activity amusing, and prepare them for the DVD comedy sketch. Ss discuss their ideas further in pairs, and then as a class.

Possible answers: Yes, because he understands what it's like to wear glasses – the problems, solutions, etc. / No, because he might not see very well and give you the wrong kind of glasses.

C Check the example and ask *Is this good advice? Why/Why not?* Elicit answers briefly. Ss then discuss and write their advice. Monitor to help with the accuracy of their sentences before they do Ex 1D.

Possible answers: 2 smokes 3 is overweight 4 has bad teeth 5 can't do maths

D Ss compare their answers. Invite groups to tell the class about their best advice.

▶ DVD VIEW

Culture notes

The Two Ronnies was one of the most successful TV family comedy shows. It ran from 1971 to 1987 and appealed to people of all ages. Repeats of the shows on TV are still very popular.

2A Check the rubric and give Ss 1 min to read the information and compare their answers. In feedback, ask *Which one is Ronnie Barker? The tall one.* You could also teach *simple, complicated* and *sketch.*

Answers: Because both stars are called Ronnie.

B Ss read the questions first. Check *greengrocer's* and *baker's* if necessary. The questions are very simple and allow Ss to enjoy watching the sketch. However, if Ss like watching the DVD without sound first, then you could do that here instead. Check Ss' answers in feedback and ask *Which parts of the DVD were the funniest?* Discuss Ss' answers to se if they agree.

Answers: 1 At the optician's. 2 a) 3 b) 4 a) 5 b)

3 Ss should first read and check the sentences. Teach/Elicit the meaning of words they need. *Stronger Ss* may be able to order the sentences before they watch. If so, they can watch the DVD again with the rest of the class, and check. Play the DVD again. Ss order the sentences and compare answers. Play it again if there's a lot of disagreement or doubt. In feedback, check the order (see answers in bold in the audio script). For question d) *What do you see with?* check that Ss understand that *see* and *C* and *eye* and *I* have the same sound. Play this part of the DVD again if necessary. For question e), ask *Why does he say this? Because Ronnie Corbett thinks the hat stand is the letter I, and the shelves are the letter H.*

Answers: b) 6 c) 2 d) 3 e) 5 f) 7 g) 4

DVD 11 The Two Ronnies

RC=Ronnie Corbett RB=Ronnie Barker

RC: Hello. **Anybody there?** Ah, good morning. I'm sorry, I meant … oh sorry! Sorry, sorry. I meant to, er, I've, I've meant to, er I meant to, er, I, I …

RB: Good morning, Miss Prendergast. You're early.

RC: Ah, good morning.

RB: Oh I, oh I'm sorry. Good morning, sir.

RC: Good morning. Erm … **Could I have,** erm … **two pounds of potatoes, please?**

RB: No, no, no, sir. This is, this is an optician's, sir.

RC: What?

RB: Optician's. Look, it says so over the door.

RC: Oh, sorry. So it does, yes. Well, it doesn't matter because I was coming in here anyway, 'cause I've got it down on my list: greengrocer's and optician's. You see?

RB: Oh, I see, yes.

RC: Yes. It was, it was the wife's idea actually.

RB: Oh yes. Do sit down, will you?

RC: Thank you very much. Erm, you're, er, you're a … Sorry. I …

RB: That's it. Don't worry. We've got plenty more. Try the one at the back. There.

RC: A?

RB: I said: Try the one on the back.

RC: No … A.

RB: A? No, no, not A, no.

RC: B?

RB: No. Keep going.

RC: C?

RB: Keep going.

RC: D?

RB: No.

RC: E? E!

RB: Yes, very good, yes, E! Try the next line, will you?

RC: Erm … no, sorry.

RB: Don't worry. I'll give you a clue. Erm … Oh! **What do you see with?**

RC: Your eye.

RB: I. And, er, what do you do with your eye?

RC: See.

RB: C, very good indeed. Very good. Now then, now then, **try the next line on your own.**

RC: Erm, I'm sorry … Is there, is there a next line? I can't …

RB: No, probably not, probably not. Now, then. What about that?

RC: A.

RB: A! And I didn't help you at all with that one, did I?

RC: No, no. No, I got that … I?

RB: Ah no, that's the hat stand there.

RC: Oh, sorry. H?

RB: H. **No, you're reading all the furniture!**

RB: There we are. Now tell me, is that, **is that better or worse?**

RC: That is worse.

RB: Oh. Ah, well, let's see. Now what, what about, what about that? How's that?

RC: That's, um … that's fractionally better. Actually, it is …

RB: Now, what about if I, if I do this?

RC: Oh, no. That's worse! No, no.

RB: Try this nice red pair on. There we are. Let me have those. Thank you. Try those. Have a look at those. There you are – look in the hand mirror. See what you think.

RC: I think this makes me look a little old. What do you think?

RB: Oh, yes, it does, doesn't it? Oh. Wait a minute, this is not a mirror. This is a photograph of an old lady! They're no good to you at all.

RC: No, no. Have you any others at all?

RB: Ah. Well, erm … There's, ah, there's these.

RC: What about these? These are … Oh! Wonderful! I can see everything as clearly as …

RB: No, no. **They're mine! They're mine!**

RC: No, no, these are yours, there.

RB: Are you sure?

RC: Yes, you …

RB: Good gracious. I can see … I mean the whole thing's become clear. How wonderful!

RC: Isn't that lovely? Erm, I trust you'll just send me on the bill.

RB: Certainly not, I wouldn't dream of such a thing! No, no, no. I mean, you've … you've, ah … You've helped me just as much as I've helped you.

speakout at a pharmacy

4A Check instructions by eliciting Ss' answers to the first situation. They may have different opinions but must be able to justify them. Give them 3–4 mins to discuss and give reasons for their answers. Monitor closely and provide any words Ss need, or tell them to use their dictionaries. They could then compare their answers with another pair if time. Otherwise, nominate Ss to give their opinions and teach/ check new words they use. Ss will need *ear drops* for Ex 4B.

> **Answers:** a) a doctor's/pharmacy b) a hospital c) a doctor's/pharmacy d) a pharmacy e) a dentist's f) a pharmacy

B Check the rubric and play the CD. After listening, Ss compare their answers. Play the CD again if necessary. Check their answers in feedback (see answers in bold in audio script). Also check *mild* and *strong*.

> **Answers:** The woman has got an earache. The pharmacist gives her some ear drops to use three times a day. If it doesn't get better, she should see a doctor.

Unit 11 Recording 7

P=Pharmacist C=Customer

P: Hello, can I help you?

C: Yes, **have you got anything for an earache?**

P: An earache? Hmm … **When did it start?**

C: Yesterday afternoon. I took some paracetomol, but it didn't help.

P: And do you have any other pain?

C: No, just my ear.

P: Do you often have earaches?

C: No, it's the first time, but it hurts a lot.

P: OK. I'm going to give you some ear drops. They're very mild.

C: Sorry, I don't understand. Mild?

P: They're not very strong. **Put these drops in your ear,** three times daily.

C: Three times a day?

P: That's right. When you get up, at lunch and just before you go to bed. If it doesn't get better, **you should see a doctor.**

C: Thank you. How much is that?

C Ss read and check they understand the **key phrases.** Play the CD again. Ss listen and tick the ones they hear and compare their answers. In feedback, play the CD again. Pause at each **key phrase** and elicit the complete sentence. Also elicit other details Ss remember about the conversation.

> **Answers:** Have you got anything for an earache? When did it start? Put these drops in your ear … You should see a doctor.

writeback a website message

5 Ss read the questions on the message boards. Check the meaning of *stressed*. To engage Ss in the activity, ask *Do you know anyone with similar problems? What should they do?* Elicit answers and write any useful/new vocabulary on the board. Give Ss 2–3 mins to discuss which question they want to reply to. Monitor and provide support to *weaker Ss*. Then give them another 3–4 mins to complete Message 3. Monitor and prompt them to self-correct when needed. When they've finished, they swap messages with another pair, while you help *slower Ss* if necessary. In feedback, nominate pairs to read out their replies. The class listens and checks to see if they have similar ones. They then discuss the advice and vote on the best message.

> **Sample answers:** Great Amigo, me, do a lot of exercise, shouldn't drink coffee, try nicotine chewing gum, get anxious, find it to difficult

> #### Homework ideas
> - Ss write two paragraphs about their favourite TV comedy shows or programmes, saying why, after Ex 3.
> - Ss write advice to the other message in Ex 5 (and put it on the class blog/send it to a classmate).

LOOKBACK

Introduction

If you have a *strong class*, it's a good idea to ask Ss to write their own versions of some of the discrete-item test types, as used in most of the Ex A–B test types in the **Lookback** section. Ss can write their tests in pairs/groups and then give them to another pair/group to answer. Ss usually find this kind of activity quite rewarding as it is not only competitive but shows them how much language they know.

HEALTH PROBLEMS

1A Ss do this exercise as a race. The first to finish with the all correct answers wins.

Answers: A: wrong B: cough, nose, sore throat A: arms, legs, flu B: temperature A: headache B: fingers A: eyes, tired B: backache

B Elicit what makes this text a poem, e.g. the words *cough* and *off* rhyme. Ss then practise reading it in pairs and perform it to the class.

Optional extra activity
If your Ss enjoy this kind of activity, encourage them to write their own poems, alone or in pairs/groups. They can use the same language as in this poem as a topic, or choose another area such as *adverbs* or *should/shouldn't*.

ADVERBS

2A Ss do the exercise alone and compare answers before feedback.

Answers: 2 quietly 3 fast 4 well 5 carefully

B Elicit Ss' answers to question 1. Then give them 3 mins to complete the sentences using their own opinions. Monitor Ss and check the accuracy of their sentences if possible, before Ex 2C.

C Monitor and make notes on how well Ss use adverbs. Check their answers in open pairs across the class. Give feedback and assess Ss' speaking skills.

COMMON VERBS

3 Ss work alone and then compare answers. To extend the practice, they could write different endings for each phrase 1–6, e.g. *Can you read that sign over there?* Monitor while Ss work and give feedback.

Answers: 2 d) 3 f) 4 a) 5 e) 6 b)

SHOULD/SHOULDN'T

4A Ss could discuss their answers in pairs. Elicit their advice in feedback.

Possible answers: A You should rest. You shouldn't use the computer. B You should take an aspirin. You shouldn't carry heavy bags. C You should go to the doctor. You shouldn't go to the interview tomorrow. D You should put your feet up. You shouldn't go dancing tomorrow.

B Give Ss time and support to prepare and rehearse their role-plays. *Weaker* Ss could refer back to p113 and p115 for help. Monitor and make notes on Ss' performance for feedback and assessment. In feedback, invite Ss to act out one of the role-plays. Do remedial work as needed.

OFFERING TO HELP

5 Check the example and give Ss 3–4 mins to write advice. *Fast finishers* rehearse saying the advice. If you want to assess Ss' writing skills, collect in their work.

Possible answers: 1 Don't worry. I'll clean it up. 2 Are you hurt? Shall I call an ambulance? 3 Can I help you? Shall I get the guard? 4 Oh, no! Are you OK? Let me get a cloth. 5 Are you hurt? Let me put a plaster on it. 6 That's OK. I'll buy you one.

6A Give Ss 2 mins to add the missing words. *Weaker Ss* can work together. Check answers in feedback.

Answers: B: Thank *you*. A: Let's look on the computer. B: And can *you* get me a taxi A: *Shall* I phone for one now? A: Thanks *a* lot. B: You're welcome.

B Ss can rehearse the dialogue, saying it to themselves before they read it in pairs. Monitor and assess Ss' pronunciation. In feedback, invite pairs to act out the dialogue to the class. Give feedback as needed.

Optional extra activity
Ss choose another problem and role-play asking for advice in a pharmacy, using the **key phrases**.

OVERVIEW

12.1 UNFORGETTABLE
GRAMMAR | present perfect
VOCABULARY | outdoor activities
HOW TO | talk about experiences

COMMON EUROPEAN FRAMEWORK
Ss can understand and describe past activities and personal experiences; can understand and write short, simple messages on postcards relaying news.

12.2 AFRAID OF NOTHING
GRAMMAR | present perfect and past simple
VOCABULARY | prepositions
HOW TO | talk about past experiences

COMMON EUROPEAN FRAMEWORK
Ss can understand short, simple texts a sentence at a time, picking up familiar names, words and basic phrases and rereading as required; can discuss and express how he/she feels about personal experiences.

12.3 I'VE GOT A PROBLEM
FUNCTION | telephoning
VOCABULARY | telephoning expressions
LEARN TO | say telephone numbers

COMMON EUROPEAN FRAMEWORK
Ss can interact with reasonable ease in structured situations and short conversations over the phone; can ask people for things and tell people things over the phone.

12.4 SHARK THERAPY ◉ BBC DVD
speakout | a frightening experience
writeback | a story

COMMON EUROPEAN FRAMEWORK
Ss can tell a story about a personal experience in a simple list of points; can write very short, basic descriptions of past events in a simple narrative form.

12.5 LOOKBACK
Communicative revision activities

BBC VIDEO PODCAST
What's the most exciting thing you've done?

In this video podcast, people talk about whether or not they like London and give reasons. They also describe the most exciting thing they have done in London, using the present perfect (and some superlative adjectives). We recommend using the video podcast at the start of the lesson to introduce Ss to the unit's topic, at the end of lesson 12.1 or unit 12 to recap the key vocabulary and language learnt.

UNFORGETTABLE

Introduction
Ss learn and practise using the present perfect simple to talk about unforgettable experiences.

SUPPLEMENTARY MATERIALS
Resource bank p190

Ex 1A: a world map

Ex 5A: download/bring pictures of interesting experiences/activities Ss might have had/done

Ex 6A: bring any picture postcards you have from different countries

Warm up
Review outdoor activities: *alphabet game*

Ask Ss *How many outdoor activities do you know?* Give them 2 mins to think of/write as many as they can in pairs. Then say each letter of the alphabet, eliciting activities Ss know, e.g. *A: athletics, B: basketball,* etc. When there's a letter with no activity, quickly move on to the next one. Sample activities include: *athletics, baseball, bungee jumping, canoeing, climbing, flying, football, go-karting, golf, hang gliding, horse riding, jogging, kite surfing, paragliding, photography, quad biking, rafting, rugby, sailing, scuba diving, tennis, windsurfing, water skiing.* In feedback, teach activities on the list that Ss didn't mention.

Culture notes
Wildlife safaris by elephant are very popular in **Nepal** as they are a great way to spot rhinos, deer, monkeys and occasionally tigers in the south's lowland jungle.

The **Nile** is a major north-flowing river in Africa, generally regarded as the longest river in the world. It is very popular to sail down the Nile in boats called feluccas, stopping off at famous, ancient sites on the way.

There are thirty-three volcanoes in **Guatemala**, some of which are highly active. A very active and unpredictable volcano, Pacaya is still the most popular one to climb!

Hot-spring water is one of **Iceland's** main sources of energy. Icelanders take thermal baths regularly because of their medicinal benefits, which bring longevity and good health.

Jordan is popular with tourists who visit the ancient red-rose city of Petra and the Dead Sea.

VOCABULARY outdoor activities

1A Ss look at the photos. Ask *What activities can you see?* Elicit Ss' answers. Teach/Check *ride, sail, trek,* and the name of the river Nile. Ask Ss to suggest where the activities are taking place. Use information from the **Culture notes** to check information about the places/activities. Ss then complete the phrases and compare answers. Check/Drill the phrases in feedback. Ss could also suggest other activities to add to each set of phrases.

Answers: 1 ride 2 climb 3 sail 4 go 5 swim 6 watch

B Check the questions and elicit one or two sample answers. Give Ss 3–4 mins to discuss their own answers in pairs. Monitor to check how well Ss are justifying their answers, and what vocabulary they're using or need. In feedback, nominate Ss to answer and teach/check adjectives they need to justify their answers, e.g. *It's too dangerous.*

> **Answers:** 1 A ride an elephant B sail down the Nile in a small boat C climb a volcano D swim in a thermal spa E go camel trekking 2–3 Ss' own answers.

LISTENING

2A Introduce the listening about people's experiences of a lifetime. Check the meaning of *survey*. Write 1, 2, 3 4 on the board: clarify that Ss listen for four activities as one won't be mentioned. Ss listen and compare answers. Play the CD again if necessary and check their answers. Or Ss could recheck them when they listen again in Ex 2B.

> **Answers:** C, A, B, D. They didn't mention E.

B Ss read the table and listen to the CD again. Do feedback after they've compared answers. Check comprehension further, e.g. ask *Where did she climb a volcano? When did he go to Egypt? What did she think about thermal spas?*

> **Answers:** 1 climbed a volcano 2 sailed down the Nile 3 none

Unit 12 Recording 1

I=Interviewer S1=1st speaker
S2=2nd speaker S3=3rd speaker

Interview 1

I: Excuse me. Do you have a second? We're asking people about experiences of a lifetime – for a survey.
S1: Oh. Er, yes, if it's quick.
I: Great! Could you look at this list? *Have you done* any of these things?
S1: Hmm, Yes, yes, I have actually. Well, one of them! I've been to Guatemala and I've climbed that volcano, I think.
I: Anything else?
S1: No, no, I don't think so. Sorry, I have to run.

Interview 2

I: Excuse me.
S2: What?
I: *Have you ever ridden an elephant?*
S2: What? Why? Uh, no. *No, I haven't.*
I: We're doing a survey on experiences of a lifetime. Can I show you this list? Have you done any of these activities?
S2: Oh, OK. OK. Let's see. Er … No, no, no, no, no. Oh, I've sailed down the Nile, so that's one thing. In fact I went to Egypt last year, with the wife – our wedding anniversary.

Interview 3

I: Excuse me. We're doing a survey – about experiences of a lifetime.
S3: Right.
I: Two minutes. Could you just look at this list? Have you done any of these things?
S3: OK. Well, I don't travel that much, so – I haven't been to Iceland, but it looks nice – swimming in a thermal spa looks fun.
I: And the other things?
S3: Hmm, no, well, I've seen some of them on TV. Is that OK? Does that count?

GRAMMAR   present perfect

3A Ss read the sentence. Ask *Who said this? Stronger classes* can read/underline the rules alone but *weaker ones* might need more support. In *mixed-ability classes*, *strong Ss* could work with *weaker ones*. N.B. If it's done sensitively, this is a useful strategy for most classes: the need to help/explain language challenges *stronger Ss* and increases their language awareness. In feedback, check the concept further: ask, e.g. *Has the woman been to Guatemala? Yes. Do we know exactly when? No. Is it important? No.*

> **Answers:** 1 don't know when 2 what

B Ss read the table and listen to complete the gaps.

C Play the CD again and elicit/write the completed sentences on the board. Check and underline the positive, negative and question forms of the present perfect and teach *past participle: have + (not) past participle,* etc. Ss will practise irregular past participles in Ex 4 but tell Ss they are the same as the past simple in regular verbs. Check further using 3rd person forms with examples from the listening. Ask, e.g. *She's (has) been to Guatemala. They haven't been to Jordan. Have you ever been to Jordan?* Check *ever* here: in your life. (cf. *never*) Ss now listen to the CD again to practise their pronunciation. Highlight/Drill the sentence stress as indicated in the answers below.

> **Answers:** I've sailed down the Nile. I haven't been to Iceland. Have you ever ridden an elephant? No, I haven't.

> **Optional extra activity**
> Ss underline all examples of the present perfect in the audio script.

> ➡ **LANGUAGEBANK** 12.1 p150–1
>
> Ss can refer to the tables and notes when they do Ex A–C. *Weaker Ss* should do **Ex A** after the past participle practice exercises in Ex 4A–C, and Ex B after Ex 5B.
>
> **Answers:**
> A 1 Have you ever eaten Japanese food? 2 I've eaten Japanese food two or three times. 3 We've never slept in a hotel before. 4 They've driven across the Europe many times. 5 Has he ever been to England? 6 She's had three husbands. 7 I've spent too much money. 8 She's learnt Arabic, Spanish and Chinese. 9 Have you ever climbed a mountain? 10 My parents have never used an iPod.
> B *Have you* ever been to Australia? No, I *haven't.* Yes I *have.* And have you *been* to China, too? No, but I've been to Korea. You've *travelled* in many countries … Yes I *have.* I've *met* a lot of people and I've *tried* a lot … But you haven't *learnt* to speak English …

PRACTICE

4A Check the example and give Ss 2 mins to complete the verbs in pairs. They should be able to guess the infinitives from the past participle forms. They then check their answers in the **irregular verb list** on p127. In feedback, check the verbs and drill the past participles.

> **Answers:** 2 fly 3 have 4 meet 5 be, go 6 see 7 sleep 8 swim

B Check the example and some true/false statements. Encourage Ss to use past participles from Ex 4A. Give them 3–4 mins to write their own sentences while you monitor to help *weaker* Ss.

C Give two examples of your own for Ss to guess, e.g. *I've been a teacher for five years.* They then do the same thing in pairs. In feedback, nominate/invite Ss to read out their statements to the class: they guess if the sentences are true or false.

speakout TIP

This tip will appeal to Ss who like rhymes and patterns. Read and check the tip with Ss. They copy the verb lists and add more to each group. They can check their answers on p127.

Answers:
kept, sleep – slept
broken, take – taken, wake – woken, forget – forgotten
known, fly – flown, blow – blown
given, ride – ridden, bite – bitten
drunk, ring – rung, do – done, begin – begun

SPEAKING

5A If you've brought pictures showing a range of activities, use them here to provide support/stimulus, especially for *weaker Ss*. Elicit examples for question 1 using the pictures, then stick them on the board/round the walls. Give Ss 3–4 mins to write their questions. Monitor to check the accuracy of their sentences and provide vocabulary needed to prepare them well for Ex 5B.

B Check/Drill the examples. Ss then work in small groups and take turns to ask and answer the questions. Make notes on their performance, particularly with the present perfect. Do feedback in open pairs across the class: nominate one student to ask a question and another one to answer. Recheck the concept of the present perfect when you give feedback on problems they had.

WRITING postcard phrases

6A If you've brought some postcards, use them here as realia. If not, use the one in the book. In either case, ask Ss, e.g. *Have you ever sent/received a postcard? Where from? Do you like sending/getting them?* Then check instructions and give Ss 1 min to answer the question. In feedback, ask *What helped you to find the answer?* Before moving on to the conventions of postcard writing, do further comprehension of the text, e.g. *What's the weather like there? Where do they sleep?*

Answer: Egypt

B Check the example. Ss then do the exercise alone/in pairs. In feedback, draw a postcard outline on the board and elicit answers to complete it.

Answers: 1 address 2 place, date 3 Hi

C Read and check the example. Check how subject pronouns, *be* and auxiliary verbs can be left out in postcard writing. Ss complete the gaps and compare answers. In feedback, check the meaning of *I wish* but not the grammar!

Answers: 1 *We must go now!* 2 *We'll see you soon.*
3 *We wish you were here!*

D Ss now practise writing postcard phrases. Elicit the changes from the class.

Answers: 2 ~~I~~ have to stop now. 3 ~~I'll~~ speak to you soon.
4 ~~I~~ hope you're all OK.

7 If you have postcards, stick them up on the board or pass them round to give Ss inspiration about places they could write about. Ss can use a piece of paper in the shape of a postcard to write their final draft. Check the rubric carefully. Ss then work in pairs/alone. Monitor and prompt Ss to self-correct/help each other. If they finish the postcards in class, they can exchange them. Otherwise, they can do this at the start of the next lesson.

Homework ideas
- Ss write the final draft of their postcards and send it to a friend/give it to a classmate.
- Language bank 12.1 Ex A–B, p151
- Workbook Ex 1A–6B, p69–70

AFRAID OF NOTHING

Introduction

Ss contrast and practise the present perfect and the past simple. They also review/learn more prepositions of movement and talk about exciting but scary situations.

SUPPLEMENTARY MATERIALS

Resource bank p189 and p191

Ex 3B: the same/similar pictures as for Ex 5A in lesson 12.1

Warm up

Review past participles: board pelmanism

Before class, write six irregular verbs and their six past participles from the **irregular verb list** on p127 on twelve separate A4 sheets. On the other side of each sheet, write numbers 1–12, mixing up the verbs/participles. In class, stick the papers face down on the board. Do an example: elicit any two numbers, turn over the papers and show Ss. If the verb–participle matches, it's a pair. If not, put them back face down in the same places. The idea is that Ss remember where they are when they need them. Ss work in pairs/teams and take it in turns to choose two numbers. The winners are the team with the most matching pairs.

READING

Culture notes

Vic Armstrong's resemblance to and friendship with Harrison Ford, established on the film *Raiders of the Lost Ark*, merited Vic the opportunity to double as Ford and to become the Stunt Coordinator on the Indiana Jones film series. The **Indiana Jones** film mentioned in the text is *The Last Crusade*, where Indiana (played by Harrison Ford) and his father (Sean Connery) search for the Holy Grail. Although he had a double standing by, Ford insisted on doing many of his own stunts to help his character portrayal. Ford only agreed to let Armstrong do the stunt of jumping from a horse onto a tank because Armstrong thought that he'd lose his job otherwise.

Gangs of New York starred Daniel Day Lewis, Leonardo DiCaprio and Cameron Diaz. The director was Martin Scorsese.

1A Ss read the definition and look at the film stills (photos of scenes from a film). Ask *What's the man doing in the photos?* Stunts. *Have you seen any of the films mentioned here? Do you remember these stunts? Can you describe any other famous stunts?* Then elicit Ss' answers to check the meaning of *stunt*.

B Give Ss 2–3 mins to read the text and to find the stunt vocabulary. Nominate Ss to read it out to the class. Then ask *Would you like to be a stuntman? Why/Why not?* Discuss their answers in open class.

Answers: fallen out of windows, jumped off bridges, ridden a motorcycle through fire, climbed up the outside of a skyscraper, driven into a wall and jumped from a horse onto a German tank

C Ss read the article again carefully and correct the sentences if they are false. Give Ss time to compare answers before checking with the class.

Answers: 1 F He played Indiana Jones in stunts. 2 T 3 F It's Martin Scorsese 4 T 5 T 6 F He thinks it's the best job in the world. 7 T

D Ss work in pairs/alone. *Weaker Ss* can refer to the **irregular verb list** on p127 if necessary. In feedback, nominate three Ss to answer – one saying the verb, the next the past simple and the last the past participle. Encourage peer-correction from the other Ss.

Answers: jump, jumped, jumped; ride, rode, ridden; climb, climbed, climbed; drive, drove, driven

GRAMMAR   present perfect and past simple

Watch out!

Ss often have difficulty understanding the difference between these two tenses initially. It takes quite a lot of exposure to English for them to acquire it. This is usually because their L1 uses the same forms but in different ways. It's therefore useful for Ss to compare how the tenses are used in both languages. Even in *multilingual classes,* Ss should be able to notice the similarities/differences by themselves.

2A Ss underline the correct tense in the sentences from the article. Ask them to check their answers using the article. In feedback, check answers and ask *What's the difference?* Ss' answers will tell you what they know/don't know.

Answers: 1 present perfect 2 past simple

B Ss underline the answers. In feedback, check the two concepts further. Ask *Has Vic Armstrong worked on many James Bond films? Yes, he has. Do we know exactly when? No. Is it important? No.* Then ask *Did he work on Gangs of New York? Yes, he did. Do we know exactly when? Yes – in 2002.*

Answers: 1 don't say 2 say

Optional extra activity

Ss underline all forms of the past simple and present perfect in the article.

⇒ LANGUAGEBANK 12.2 p150–1

It would be useful to read and check the notes with Ss. They could refer to them when they do the exercises in class.

Answers:
A 1 've been 2 went 3 was 4 loved 5 've also visited 6 were 7 've never travelled 8 has driven
B 2 Have you met, met 3 Has Lea been, went 4 Has Paolo ever had, had 5 Have you read, read 6 Have your children finished, finished

PRACTICE

3A Check the example and the meaning of *make something to wear*. Ss then write the questions alone. Try to check all the verbs in Ss' questions so that they'll be prepared for Ex 3B.

Answers: 2 Have you ever broken your arm? 3 Have you ever eaten anything unusual? 4 Have you ever watched a live football match? 5 Have you ever made something to wear? 6 Have you ever been to a really hot or cold country?

B Check instructions carefully and drill the example. Emphasise the importance of asking follow-up questions in the past simple if their partner answers *yes*.

Optional extra activity
For further practice, Ss could do Ex 5A on p119 again, but this time asking follow up questions in the past simple. If you have the same/similar pictures that you used there, Ss could use those again, too.

4A First, Ss write the past participles for each verb: they can refer to p127 if necessary. They then practise saying them to each other in pairs and deciding which sound column it belongs in. Monitor and help *weaker Ss* if necessary. *Fast finishers* could add other past participles with the same sounds.

Answers:
/e/ slept, met, read
/ʌ/ sung, won, done
/əʊ/ spoken, flown, chosen
/ɪ/ driven, written, given
/ɔː/ bought, thought, brought

B Play the CD for Ss to check their answers. Ss then listen and repeat the words. Elicit other words with the same sounds. N.B. This sort of activity helps raise Ss' awareness of the usefulness of phonemic symbols. Encourage them to use symbols when they record vocabulary/check words in dictionaries.

VOCABULARY prepositions

5A Ss look at the pictures and discuss the question in pairs. They don't need to be too specific at this stage. Check Ss' answers and teach *ring of fire* if Ss want to know it.

Answers: 1 He's riding a motorbike/doing stunts.

B Ss should know some of the prepositions from previous units but check/mime *towards* and *away from*, and any other words Ss aren't sure of. Ss do the matching exercise and then compare answers. *Stronger Ss* could put the prepositions in sentences, e.g. *He's jumping over a wall. He's riding through a ring of fire.* In feedback, nominate Ss to give their answers, in sentences if possible. Check answers and drill the words.

Answers: A over B through C out of D away from
E under F down G towards H up I across J into

Optional extra activity
In pairs/groups, Ss tell each other to do things, using imperatives and the prepositions above, e.g. *Stand up. Walk towards the door.*

C Ss write the opposites and compare their answers.

Answers: down – up; over – under;
away from – towards; out of – into

6 Check the example in question 1 with the class. Ss then complete the others alone/in pairs, before checking with another partner/pair. In feedback, elicit answers and write them on the board, or invite Ss to write them.

Answers: 2 towards/away from 3 under/over, over/under 4 through/into/out of/across 5 up/down 6 through/towards/away from 7 through/into/out of 8 into/out of

SPEAKING

7A Ss read the phrases and tell you which are positive/negative. Ask an example question, e.g. *How do you feel about doing homework?* Elicit Ss' answers and ask them to give a reason, e.g. *I love it. It really helps me to remember what I learnt in class!* Ss then write relevant phrases from the box next to the situations in Ex 6. Don't check their answers yet.

B Check the example dialogue. Highlight the use of *verb + -ing* after the preposition *about*. Remind/Tell Ss that verbs after prepositions are always in the *-ing* form. Drill the same question with other examples from Ex 6. Ss then ask/answer questions in pairs. Remind them to give reasons for their answers. Monitor and do feedback in open pairs across the class. Find out how many Ss have positive/negative feeling about these situations.

Optional extra activity
Extend the practise using the pictures you brought to class for Ex 5A, p119, or Ss' own ideas. They work in pairs/groups and ask/answer the same questions as in Ex 7B, e.g. *How do you feel about going to zoos/clubbing? I'm afraid of them. I love it.*

Homework ideas
- Ss write their answers to the questions in Ex 3A, p120 and Ex 5A, p119. Ss add extra details if their answers are *yes*.
- Ss write about the situations which you *love/don't like/are afraid of/are not keen on* from Ex 7B.
- Language bank 12.2 Ex A–B, p151
- Workbook Ex 1A–4, p71–72

I'VE GOT A PROBLEM

Introduction

Ss learn and practise expressions for making phone calls about both personal and business problems. They also learn how say phone numbers.

SUPPLEMENTARY MATERIALS

Resource bank p192

Ex 8: pictures of exciting/frightening situations and mobile/imitation phones (or ask Ss to bring their own mobile phones)

Warm up

Lead in to the lesson topic with a live listening

Teaching tip

In a live listening, you tell the Ss a story/anecdote/ narrative which relates to and provides a model of a speaking activity that Ss will do in the lesson. You can ask comprehension questions about it, use target language that Ss will focus on later, or Ss just listen – and practise hearing authentic English.

Tell Ss a short story about one of the experiences in Ex 1: it can be a true story, or an invented one. Elicit comments from Ss and/or ask comprehension questions. Then move to Ex 1, where they will practise talking about their own experiences.

SPEAKING

1 First, Ss look at the photo and describe it in pairs. After 1 min, ask, e.g. *Where are the people? What are they doing? How do they look/feel? Why? What's the woman doing? Why?* Elicit Ss' answers, e.g. *They're waiting for a train – it's late.* Then ask *Has this ever happened to you? When? What did you do?* Elicit Ss' answers briefly. Ss then read the questions in Ex 1. Check *lock yourself out, meeting* and *appointment.* Give Ss 3–4 mins to discuss answers. Monitor to provide vocabulary and assess what feedback you'll need to give. Stop the activity when all Ss have answered most of the questions. Nominate Ss to tell their stories and prompt them to self-correct or correct each other.

VOCABULARY telephoning expressions

2A Check the phrases in the box and do the example. Also check *answerphone.* Ss do the exercise alone.

Answers: 2 leave a message 3 ring, back 4 call 5 answer

B Ss compare their answers. In feedback, check Ss' answers and drill the phrases.

FUNCTION telephoning

3A Check the rubric and tell Ss they'll listen to three phone calls. Give them time to reread the situations in Ex 1A if necessary. It would also be useful to pre-teach *customer services.* Ask *Who do you phone when you lose your credit card? Which department?* Remind Ss not to worry about understanding every word. They should focus only on matching the situations. Play the CD. Ss then compare answers. If they have doubts, play the relevant conversations again. Check Ss' answers. Ask *What did they lose?* Also check the difference between *mobile* phone (GB) and *cell* phone (USA), and ask Ss where Central Park is (in New York).

Answers: 1 two 2 one 3 one

B One aim of this exercise is to highlight informal and formal language used when talking to friends/people you don't know/customer services, e.g. *Just tell him to call me.* versus *Could you ring back …* Check the rubric and play the CD again. In feedback, check answers and do more comprehension. Elicit other information Ss remember, e.g. *When did Kevin go out? Who lost their credit card? Where did the man leave his phone?*

Answers: In conversation 1

Unit 12 Recording 4

Extract 1

A=Sean   B=Debbie

A: Hello.

B: Hi, Sean. It's Debbie.

A: Hi, Debbie. What's up?

B: Is Kevin there?

A: No, he's not. He went out about ten minutes ago.

B: Oh.

A: What's up?

B: Well, I locked the keys in the car. Kevin has the spare key.

A: Oh, what a drag!

B: Could I leave a message for him?

A: Of course.

B: Just ask him to call me.

A: On your mobile?

B: No, that's in the car. I'll give you a number.

A: Hold on – OK, go ahead.

B: OK, let's see. It's 3-double 2, 6-3, 2-8.

A: Got it. I'll tell him.

B: Thanks, bye.

A: Bye.

Extract 2

A=1st assistant   B=Customer   C=2nd assistant

A: Berkley Bank.

B: Hello. Could I speak to customer services, please?

A: Just a moment.

C: Customer services.

B: Hello, I've got a problem. I think I've lost my credit card.

C: I see. I'm sorry, this line is very bad. Where are you calling from?

B: I'm in Madrid, actually. In fact I'm calling from a public phone and I've only got one minute on this card. Could you ring me back?

C: Of course. Could you give me the number there?

B: Just a moment … It's 34 for Spain, 91 for Madrid, then 308 5238.

C: Let me check that. 34 91 308 5238.

B: That's right.

C: Fine. Put the phone down – I'll call you back straight away.

Customer: Thank you.

Extract 3

A=Woman B=Man

A: Hello?

B: Oh, thank goodness. Hello, uh … Who's this?

A: My name's Marianne.

B: Thanks for picking up.

A: Well, the phone rang so I picked it up.

B: Yes, well, that's my cell phone. And you found it.

A: Oh, OK. It's yours. Do you want to get it back?

B: Yes, thanks. Where are you?

A: Central Park, by the fountain. It was here in the grass.

B: Ah, yes, I thought it might be.

A: So where are you?

B: Not far away. I can be there in ten minutes.

A: OK, I'll wait here.

B: Great. Thanks a lot!

4A Ss now listen in more detail to the telephone phrases in the three conversations. Check the example and the word box. Ss do the exercise alone and compare their answers. Play the CD for them to check their answers. If necessary, play it again, and then do feedback. Pronunciation will be focused in the next two exercises.

> **Answers:** 2 there 3 leave, message 4 ask, call 5 speak 6 moment 7 ring 8 number 9 check 10 back

B Check the example and give Ss 1 min to match the descriptions. In feedback, ask Ss *Was the language in conversation extracts 1 and 2 the same as in 3 and 4?* (No.) *Why?* (The language in 3 and 4 is more formal/polite.) Direct Ss to the examples in **Language bank** on p150 if necessary. Elicit examples of formal and informal phrases in the conversation extracts.

> **Answers:** b) 3 and 4 c) 1 d) 2

C Ss now focus on pronunciation. Play the first sentence and elicit the stressed word. Ss underline *Debbie*. Remind Ss that the main sentence stress usually falls on nouns/verbs, which carry the main information. Give Ss 3 min to underline the stress in the other sentences. They work alone or in pairs, depending on how confident they are. Encourage them to say the sentences out loud and if they're not sure, to try putting the stress in different places to see which sounds more natural. Monitor closely to help those who need it.

D Play the CD for Ss to check the stress and compare answers. In feedback, play the CD again and elicit their answers. Drill/Beat the stress with your hands to help them if necessary. Ss then listen and repeat the sentences until they're confident.

> **Answers:** 1 It's <u>Debbie</u>. 2 Is <u>Kevin</u> there? 3 Could I leave a <u>message</u> for him? 4 Just <u>ask</u> him to <u>call</u> me. 5 Could I <u>speak</u> to customer <u>services</u>, please? 6 <u>Just</u> a <u>moment</u>. 7 Could you <u>ring</u> me <u>back</u>? 8 Could you give me the <u>number</u> there? 9 <u>Let</u> me <u>check</u> that. 10 <u>Put</u> the <u>phone</u> down – I'll <u>call</u> you back <u>straight</u> away.

> ⇒ **LANGUAGEBANK** 12.3 p150–1
>
> Check the language tables and notes, which explain common problems for Ss. They can refer to the information when they do Ex A on p151.
>
> > **Answers:** 1 It's, b) 2 there, c) 3 message, f) 4 e) 5 ring/call, d) 6 a)

5A Ss first read the flowchart to familiarise themselves with it. Check the example and answer any queries. For the phone number 3114020, teach Ss to say, e.g. *double one* not *one one* and *oh* for the number *0. They* will practise this more in Ex 6. Ss then work alone and complete the flowchart using the extracts in Ex 4A and the **Language bank** to help them. In feedback, elicit and check/correct Ss' answers.

> **Answers:** Hi, Jill. How are you? OK, thanks. Is Gerry there? No. He's not here. Could I leave a message for him? Can you ask him to call me? What's your number? Let me check that. No. It's 3114020.

B Ss take it in turns to be Sam and Jill. They can use imitation phones if you have them, or their mobiles. Monitor closely and help Ss with sentence stress and intonation. Make notes of persistent mistakes with the target language. Ss may be having problems with phone numbers but will practise this next. Do feedback in open pairs across the class. Prompt self-correction and give feedback as needed.

LEARN TO say telephone numbers

6A Recheck the use of double one (*11*) and oh (*0*). Play the CD for Ss to check and repeat.

> **Answers:** double, oh, oh

B Write the number on the board and play the CD again. Elicit the break and draw a line in the correct place. Then elicit/underline the main stress: *3*11–*40*20. Ss repeat the number again. Read and check the **speakout tip** with Ss. They can then practise saying their own phone numbers in pairs/to the class.

> **Answers:** 311, 4020

7A Elicit/Drill the first number. Ss then take turns to say the others in pairs. Nominate Ss to answer and check/drill the rhythm of saying numbers.

> **Answers:** 1 seven double nine, six oh seven two 2 double nine five, four two seven oh 3 eight oh one, three double oh five 4 five eight oh, double seven one three

B Put Ss in A/B pairs, facing each other. Remind them not to show each other their books. Check the pronunciation of the names on the list and drill the question. Ss then take turns to ask/answer the questions and write the phone numbers. They can then check their lists together. In feedback, elicit the questions/answers in open pairs across the class. Give Ss feedback on errors/pronunciation.

SPEAKING

8A Give Ss 5–6 mins to choose a situation and write the key words, using the model in Ex 5A to help. Also tell them to write the prompts clearly as another pair will be using them in Ex 8B. Monitor to check if Ss need help.

B Put Ss into groups of 4. They exchange flowcharts and read them. Give each pair 2 mins to practise reading the dialogue before they act it out. Each pair should sit back-to-back and pretend to use their mobiles if they have them. Monitor and note problems with telephone language. In feedback, nominate pairs to act out their dialogues to the class. Give feedback and correct drill problems with the target language.

> **Homework ideas**
> - Ss write a dialogue for another situation in Ex 1, using the model in Ex 5A.
> - Language bank 12.3 Ex A, p151
> - Workbook Ex1–4B, p73

SHARK THERAPY

Introduction

Ss watch an extract from the BBC series *Wild*, in which a famous diver faces her worst fear and swims underwater with sharks. Ss learn and practise how to talk and write about exciting/frightening experiences.

SUPPLEMENTARY MATERIALS

Warm up: pictures of wild/scary animals as prompts

Ex 4 optional extra activity: copy and reorder the DVD script

Ex 5B: a map of Australia showing the Red Desert/Ayers Rock

Warm up

Lead in and create interest in the topic of the lesson. If you've brought pictures of wild animals, use them as prompts here. Ask: *Do you like animals/have any pets? Which animals do you like best/least?* Elicit/Discuss Ss' answers briefly. They then write two lists of their five *most/least* favourite animals. They compare their lists and discuss what they have in common. Discuss Ss' answers in open class.

▶ DVD PREVIEW

1 Check the names of the animals in the photos and drill the pronunciation: *shark, rat, tiger, spider, bear, snake.* Ss then read questions 1–3 and ask for clarification if necessary. Give them 3 mins to discuss and answer the questions. Ss report back to the class about interesting/unusual experiences their partners had.

2A Ss should be familiar with these adjectives so could complete the sentences and then compare answers. In *mixed-ability classes*, *stronger Ss* could work with *weaker ones* and help if necessary. In feedback, check the adjectives, especially the meaning/use of *nervous*. N.B. Many Ss will have the same word in their L1 but with a different meaning (false friend). Use other examples of nervous to contrast with *excited/upset/worried*, e.g. *I always feel nervous before an exam. I was excited about seeing my favourite band. I was upset when they didn't phone me.*

Answers: 1 afraid 2 excited 3 proud 4 nervous
6 embarrassed

B This exercise checks Ss' understanding of the adjectives above while giving Ss personalised practice. Check instructions by eliciting Ss' answers to question 1. e.g. *I'm afraid of spiders/snakes.* Ss work alone to complete the sentences. Monitor to check accuracy and answer Ss' queries where necessary.

C Give Ss 4 mins to compare their answers and note down similarities and differences. In feedback, ask *What do you have in common?* Ss report back their answers to the class.

Culture notes

Tanya Streeter, born 1973, is a world champion free-diver. She can hold her breath under water for up to 6 minutes and has dived to depths of 160 metres (525 feet). It was crucial for her to overcome her fear of sharks as it interfered with her ability to free-dive.

The **Tiger Shark** gets its name from the stripes on its side and grows to a length of 3–4 metres. They are commonly found in the shallow waters of the Bahamas.

The **Bahamas**, capital Nassau, is made up of a large group of islands in the Atlantic, off the Southeast coast of the USA and close to the Caribbean.

▶ DVD VIEW

3A First, Ss look at the photo of the woman and the question in the rubric. Elicit/Check where the Bahamas are on a map if possible. Ask *What's her job? Where is she?* Then check the meaning of the title of the lesson: *Shark Therapy.* Ask *What do you think the DVD is about? What's the woman going to do? Why?* Ss then read the programme information and check the answers to their questions. In feedback, elicit Ss' answers and check *overcome her fear, face to face, tiger shark.* Ask *Do you think this 'therapy' is a good idea?* Discuss Ss' answers briefly.

Answers: To overcome her fear of sharks; she needs help or 'therapy'.

B Ss read the questions. Check the meaning of *swimsuit, knife, protect herself, stick, bite.* Play the DVD. Ss watch and make notes and then compare their answers. Play it again if Ss aren't sure. In feedback, elicit answers and invite some initial comments about the programme.

Answers: 1 black 2 stick 3 Two

C Ss read the sentences first: elicit/check the meaning of *mask.* Play the DVD again. Ss note down the correct words and compare answers. N.B. At this stage, Ss need to listen for specific words at certain points in the programme so be prepared to pause and replay these parts if necessary, and pause/rewind the sentences containing the answers (in bold in the DVD script). You could also check the American usage of *to do great* as in *Tanya did great* (she did very well).

Answers: 2 ~~friendly~~ big 3 ~~mask~~ suit 4 ~~meat~~ fish heads
5 ~~right~~ left 6 ~~frightening~~ wonderful 7 ~~feeling~~ fear

D Give Ss 2–3 mins to answers the questions. Check and discuss their opinions in feedback. If possible, make a link with Ex 5A, where Ss talk about their own exciting/frightening experiences.

Answers: 1 proud 2 Ss' own answers

Optional extra activity

Ss talk about the things they said they're afraid of in Ex 2B, and answer the question *Would you like to overcome these fears? How? What could you do?*

DVD 12 Wild

VO=Voiceover T=Tanya J=Jim

VO: Tanya Streeter is a world famous diver but she's afraid of sharks. So she decides to go for … shark therapy.
At first, it isn't easy. The sharks arrive. Tanya feels nervous as she watches the sharks from the boat.

T: I didn't think that there were going to be this many of them. And **I didn't think that they were going to be … quite so …** erm, big.

VO: Tanya prepares to dive. She's feeling very frightened.

T: This isn't good. I've got to get more brave.

VO: Tanya dives into the water, and the sharks swim towards her … the shiny suit attracts them. When she swims back to the boat, one shark follows her!

T: OK.

VO: Not a good start for Tanya's shark therapy … so she asks the shark expert … Jim Abernathy to help.

T: And how about my suit because I have noticed that the Caribbean reef sharks in particular seem to be quite interested in my rather shiny suit.

J: Er, I noticed the suit and I think we should change the suit completely … and I think we should go with all black.

T: All black? OK.

VO: And it's time for the big dive – with the tiger sharks. **Jim throws fish-heads into the water to attract the sharks.**
And as Tanya dives, the sharks come to her straightaway. Jim gives Tanya a stick to protect herself.

T: Oh, my gosh! Thank you.

J: Tanya, there's another one behind you. Keep the stick vertical.

T: That's a big shark.

J: Tanya, it just turned back towards you. Tanya, Tanya … Tanya! **Tanya, look behind you over on your left.** Use the stick first.

VO: After some time, Tanya starts to feel more comfortable with the sharks.

T: It's just beautiful.

VO: Her fear has gone. The shark therapy has been successful.

J: **That was wonderful! Tanya did great.**

T: It's a real relief to have done this today. I do feel like I've accomplished something. **I've started to overcome my very real fear.**

Optional extra activity

Photocopy and enlarge the DVD script above. Change the order of 4–6 sections of the script and make enough copies for each Ss in your class. Play the DVD again. Ss put the sections into the correct order as they watch/listen again.

speakout a frightening experience

4A Ss now move on to planning to talk about their own experiences. Check the rubric and questions. Then give them time to think before they make notes. While they do this, monitor and provide help if necessary. N.B. Ss are only making notes at this stage, Ss will talk about and compare their experiences in Ex 4D.

Culture notes

Ayers Rock is a world famous landmark in Central Australia, about 450km from **Alice Springs**. It's a World Heritage site and also known by its aboriginal name, Uluru.

'The outback' is an Australian term for dry, remote areas of the country, while 'the bush' describes less remote wooded areas, usually with eucalyptus trees.

B   First, write *Ayers Rock* on the board, or elicit it using pictures and/or a map. Ask *Do you know this place?* Discuss Ss' answers, using the culture notes if appropriate. Then check the rubric and play the CD. Ss listen and compare answers. The answer to the second question could be very detailed, but Ss should answer to the best of their ability. Play the CD again if more than half the class has doubts. Elicit as much detail as possible in feedback. Also check/teach *bark* and *bite* from the audio script. Finally, discuss the experience with Ss.

Answers: It was frightening. The man was in Australia and one day he went for a walk in the outback, near Ayers Rock and got lost. Then some wild dogs came and started jumping and barking around him. He was really frightened but because he didn't move or look at the dogs, only one dog bit his arm and after twenty minutes they went away.

Unit 12 Recording 8

This happened in Australia, when I was about twenty-five. I spent a few days at a hotel in Alice Springs and went to Ayers Rock and, well, anyway, **one day**, I went out for a walk, in the outback.

It was a lovely day so I walked and walked, **and then** I realised I didn't really know where I was. I was a bit stupid, really – because I decided to go further. I guess I thought I'd find the way back. Urm, anyway, **after that** I heard some dogs.

First I heard them barking, and **then** I saw them – there was a group – maybe five or six dogs, wild dogs, coming towards me. **I felt really frightened**, but I remembered some advice I, I read in my guide book: Don't move, and don't look at the dogs. So I froze, like a statue – I didn't move, and I looked at a tree, not at the dogs, and didn't move my eyes. The dogs were all around me, jumping and barking. I thought they were going to bite me. **Then** one dog *did* bite my arm, just a little, but still I didn't move.

In the end, after about twenty minutes, the dogs went away. I stayed there for a few more minutes and **then** luckily found my way back to the hotel. **It was the most frightening experience I've ever had!**

C   Ss read and check the **key phrases**. Then play the CD again for Ss to tick them. In feedback, play the CD again and pause at each **key phrase** (in bold in the audio script). Elicit the complete sentence.

Answers: Tick all sentences.

D   Give time for Ss to check their notes from Ex 5A and rewrite/revise them using the **key phrases**. They can also use the audio script on p175 to help. Provide support to Ss who need it, or ask *stronger Ss* to help. Ss then take turns to talk about their experiences in groups. Remind them to ask two questions after each turn. Monitor discreetly and note down the strengths and weaknesses of the language Ss use. In feedback, Ss tell the class about their own/a partner's experience. Ss then decide which was the most exciting and/or frightening experience. Give feedback now or later.

writeback a story

5A Ss now prepare to write about their experience from their notes. First, they work alone and order David's notes. Monitor to check *weaker Ss'* progress.

B   In *mixed-ability classes*, *stronger* and *weaker Ss* can compare their answers. In feedback, elicit the answers in the correct order. Then ask Ss to use the keyphrases to reconstruct the man's story. Give them time to practise doing this in pairs if necessary, and then check them as a class.

Answers: 2 realised I didn't know where I was 3 heard some dogs 4 dogs ran towards me 5 remembered advice 6 didn't move, didn't look at the dogs 7 dogs jumped and barked 8 one dog bit my arm

C   Ss write the first draft of the story. Provide support where needed, and encourage them to ask each other for advice. They could put their final drafts on posters with pictures/illustrations or on the class blog.

Homework ideas

- Ss write a final draft of the experiences described in Ex 6C.
- Workbook Ex 5, p73

LOOKBACK

Introduction

You could exploit the last **Lookback** section in a slightly different way if you want to give your Ss more autonomy. Put them into pairs/small groups and ask *Which areas of language here do you feel most/least confident about? Which would you like to do first?* Give Ss 15 mins to do the sections they choose. Monitor and provide support as needed, while you also assess Ss' performance.

> **Optional extension**
> To provide further leaner autonomy, write/copy the answers for Exs 1A, 2A, 3A, 4A, 5A and 6A onto separate pieces of paper/card and place them in a box on the teacher's desk or around the classroom for Ss to access and correct their work when they finish each exercise.

In feedback, check Ss' answers to the discrete-item exercises. Ask e.g. *Why did you choose these sections? How well did you do them? What did you learn?* Discuss Ss' answers. Then give feedback on the speaking activities as required.

OUTDOOR ACTIVITIES

1A Ss have done vowel completion exercises before so this exercise shouldn't need extra explanation. However with *weaker Ss* do the first one as an example with them.

> **Answers:** 1 go trekking 2 ride an elephant 3 swim in a river 4 climb a mountain 5 go scuba diving 6 take a boat down the Nile 7 watch a play outdoors 8 go fishing 9 swim in a thermal spa 10 climb a volcano 11 watch birds 12 ride a horse

B While Ss talk in pairs, note down problems for feedback, or assessment if required.

PRESENT PERFECT

2A Write the first sentence as a model on the board if necessary.

> **Answers:** 1 I've never eaten fish eyes. 2 I've never been to an art gallery. 3 I've never seen a sunrise. 4 I've never driven a Mercedes. 5 I've never drunk tea with milk for breakfast. 6 I've never played golf. 7 I've never cooked dinner for my parents. 8 I've never spoken English on the phone. 9 I never been to an outdoor festival. 10 I've never heard Oasis live.

B Monitor while Ss do this stage and give help where necessary.

C While Ss talk in pairs, note down problems for feedback, or assessment if required.

PRESENT PERFECT AND PAST SIMPLE

3A Tell Ss to use the first sentence as a model and to check their answers using the **irregular verb list** on p127 if necessary.

> **Answers:** 2 taken 3 flown 4 swum 5 cycled 6 slept 7 climbed

B While Ss talk in pairs, note down problems for feedback, or assessment if required.

> **Optional extra activity: A grid quiz**
> Draw the grid below on the board with the numbers but no verbs (this is the key for you). Ss work in teams: A, B, C, etc. Then demonstrate what to do. Ss choose a number from the grid and you tell them the verb, e.g. *swim*. Ask e.g. *Have you ever swum in the sea?* Elicit *Yes, I have./No, I haven't.* If the answer is *Yes*, ask *When/Where did you swim in the sea?* Elicit, e.g. *Last summer/In Spain.* Ss then take it in turns to choose a number and select two Ss from their team to perform the dialogue. They get a point for each correct verb and another for the correct response. The team with the most points wins.
>
> Grid Key:
>
> | 1 swim | 2 win | 3 go |
> | --- | --- | --- |
> | 4 write | 5 buy | 6 drive |
> | 7 sing | 8 meet | 9 fly |
> | 10 read | 11 give | 12 see |

PREPOSITIONS

4A Go through the first word web with the Ss if necessary. Elicit example sentences using the prepositions to demonstrate how they work in context.

> **Answers:**
> **through:** a forest, a building, a station, the city, the room
> **down:** a road, some stairs, a mountain, a river **over:** a road, a bridge, a mountain
> **into:** a forest, a swimming pool, a building, the station, a city, a room
> **across:** a road, bridge, a river, the city, a room

B While Ss talk in pairs, note down problems for feedback, or assessment if required.

ADJECTIVES

5A Ss have completed unjumbling exercises before so this exercise shouldn't need extra explanation. However with *weaker Ss* do the first one as an example with them.

> **Answers:** 1 proud 2 excited 3 afraid 4 nervous 5 embarrassed 6 frightened

B Monitor while Ss do this stage and give help where necessary.

C While Ss talk in pairs, note down problems for feedback, or assessment if required.

TELEPHONING

6A Write the first two exchanges between A and B as a model on the board if necessary.

> **Answers:** 1 It's 2 Can I speak to 3 I'll 4 Can you call back 5 Can I leave 6 ask her to call 7 give me your 8 I'll ask

B While Ss talk in pairs, note down problems for feedback, or assessment if required.

> **Homework ideas**
> • Workbook Review and check 4, p74–75
> • Workbook Test 4, p76

PAGE	UNIT	PHOTOCOPIABLE	LANGUAGE POINT	TIME
145	1	What do you need?	**Vocabulary: objects** • review the names of everyday objects • practise speaking skills in discussing which objects to take in different situations	25–35
146	1	Meet and greet	**present simple: *be*** • practise the verb '*be*' in affirmatives, negatives and interrogatives • review countries and nationalities	30–40
147	1	Whose are these?	**Grammar: *this/that, these/those*, possessive '*s*** • use possessives to decide who various objects belong to • review the names of everyday objects	20–30
148	1	Can I have one ...?	**Functional language: making requests** • make requests in various tourist locations • review the names of objects in tourist places	25–35
149	2	A good job?	**Vocabulary: jobs** • talk about jobs, and the qualities involved • practise speaking skills by answering a questionnaire	25–35
150	2	Are you typical?	**Grammar: present simple: *I/you/we/they*** • practise the present simple to talk about national stereotypes	30–40
151	2	Working 9 to 5?	**Grammar: present simple: *he/she/it*** • practise the present simple to talk about jobs • review vocabulary for daily routines	30–40
152	2	Tour operators	**Functional language: asking for information** • practise functional language for asking for information about tours • review ways of telling the time	25–35
153	3	I'm Friendly Fred!	**Vocabulary: adjectives of personality** • review adjectives of personality and adverbs of frequency • practise speaking skills by describing people's personalities	20–30
154	3	Late again!	**Grammar: frequency adverbs** • practise frequency adverbs to talk about daily lives • review some adjectives of personality	30–45
155	3	Have you got it?	**Grammar: *have/has got*** • use *have/has got* to talk about possessions and family members • practise speaking skills: asking questions and elaborating	25–35
156	3	What's good for you?	**Functional language: making arrangements** • make arrangements and plan an evening's free-time activities • review telling the time	25–35
157	4	You've hit my television!	**Vocabulary: rooms & furniture** • practise vocabulary of rooms and furniture • practise speaking skills in the context of a guessing game	25–35
158	4	The ideal home	**Grammar: *there is/are*** • use *there is/are* to describe an 'ideal home' • review vocabulary of rooms, furniture and prepositions of place	30–40
159	4	Do's and don'ts	**Grammar: *can* for possibility** • use *can* for possibility in the context of places in a town • practise speaking in the form of a quiz	25–35
160	4	Can I help you?	**Functional language: shopping** • practise functional language for shopping and saying '*no*' politely	20–30
161	5	Well, I like it!	**Vocabulary: food/drink** • practise food and drink vocabulary through personalisation • practise speaking skills – agreeing and disagreeing	20–30
162	5	What's in your dish?	**Grammar: nouns with *a/an/some/any*** • use nouns with *a/an/some/any* to describe ingredients • review vocabulary of food	30–40
163	5	How many calories?!	**Grammar: *how much/many* and quantifiers** • use *how much/many* + quantifiers to talk about food nutrition • review vocabulary of food/drink containers	25–35
164	5	Tea for two	**Functional Language: ordering in a restaurant** • practise functional language for ordering in a restaurant	30–40
165	6	When was the party?	**Vocabulary: dates and time phrases** • practise dates and time phrases • practise speaking skills – sharing information	20–30
166	6	Before they were famous	**Grammar: past simple: *was/were*** • use the past simple to talk about celebrities • review some vocabulary of jobs	15–25
167	6	Snapped!	**Grammar: past simple** • use common verbs in the past simple to talk about personalized situations • review some common verbs	25–35

RESOURCE BANK

Index of photocopiables

PAGE	UNIT	PHOTOCOPIABLE	LANGUAGE POINT	TIME
168	6	The weekend started here	**Functional language: making conversation** • make conversation about last weekend • review vocabulary of weekend activities	20–30
169	7	Lost	**Vocabulary: places** • practise vocabulary to describe places and geographical features • practise speaking skills – sharing information	30–40
170	7	My car's better!	**Grammar: comparatives** • use comparatives to discuss alternative types of transport • review some travel vocabulary	25–35
171	7	The longest journey	**Grammar: superlatives** • practise superlatives in the context of world records • review some travel vocabulary	25–35
172	7	An Englishman in New York	**Functional language: giving directions** • practise functional language for giving, checking and correcting directions	30–40
173	8	What do they look like?	**Vocabulary: appearance** • review and practise vocabulary to describe appearance • practise speaking skills – describing appearance	25–35
174	8	I'm on the phone!	**Grammar: present continuous** • practise the present continuous in the context of activities in different places • review some verbs and prepositions	20–30
175	8	What do you usually do?	**Grammar: present simple/continuous** • use the present simple and present continuous to describe things happening now and every day	20–30
176	8	It's recommended	**Functional language: recommending** • practise functional language for recommending films	30–40
177	9	Fast planes	**Vocabulary: transport and adjectives** • use vocabulary of types of transport and adjectives to describe transport • practise speaking skills – giving opinions, agreeing and disagreeing	20–30
178	9	The trains in Spain …	**Grammar: articles** • practise the use of articles in the context of transport • review some collocations related to travel	30–40
179	9	Laws around the world	**Grammar: *can/can't, have to/don't have to*** • use *can/can't, have to/don't have to* to talk about strange transport laws • practise speaking skills – discussion	20–30
180	9	What happened was …	**Functional language: apologising** • practise functional language for apologizing and making excuses	25–35
181	10	The best plans	**Vocabulary: plans** • practise collocations to talk about plans. • practise speaking skills – sharing information	20–30
182	10	Planning ahead	**Grammar: *be going to; would like to*** • use *be going to* and *would like to* in the context of future plans • review some collocations related to plans	25–35
183	10	The future is ours to see	**Grammar: *will, might, won't*** • use *will, might* and *won't* to talk about predictions • practise speaking skills – sharing personal information	25–35
184	10	What shall we do?	**Functional language: making suggestions** • practise functional language for making suggestions, in a variety of contexts	30–40
185	11	Name that illness!	**Vocabulary: health problems** • practise vocabulary to describe health problems • practise speaking skills – guessing words from mimes	20–30
186	11	Speed counselling	**Grammar: *should/shouldn't*** • use *should/shouldn't* to give advice	25–35
187	11	The mime game	**Grammar: adverbs of manner** • practise forming adverbs of manner in different contexts • review some common verbs	15–25
188	11	Let me help you!	**Functional language: offering to help** • practise functional language for offering to help	15–25
189	12	Get me out of here!	**Vocabulary: prepositions** • practise prepositions of movement in the context of a map • practise speaking skills – sharing information	25–35
190	12	Been there, done that.	**Grammar: present perfect** • practise the present perfect in the context of experiences • practise speaking skills – asking for and sharing information	20–30
191	12	I've done it!	**Grammar: present perfect and past simple** • practise the present perfect and past simple to talk about experiences	30–40
192	12	Can he call me?	**Functional language: telephoning** • practise functional for telephoning	25–35

Worksheet A

Work in pairs. Label the things in the suitcase with the words in the box.

| mobile phone | sweater | file | camera |
| chewing gum | umbrella | | |

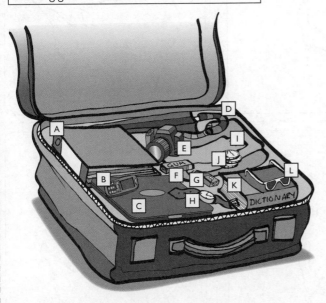

What five things do you need in the following situations? Decide with your partner.

Worksheet B

Work in pairs. Label the things in the suitcase with the words in the box.

| laptop | batteries | dictionary | watch |
| sunglasses | coins | | |

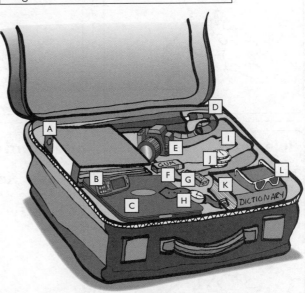

What five things do you need in the following situations? Decide with your partner.

Role card 1

Name: Jack

Country: Britain

Role card 5

Name: Hiro

Country: Japan

Role card 9

Name: Mike

Country: the USA

Role card 2

Name: Harriet

Country: Britain

Role card 6

Name: Keiko

Country: Japan

Role card 10

Name: Trisha

Country: the USA

Role card 3

Name: Dimitri

Country: Russia

Role card 7

Name: Giseppe

Country: Italy

Role card 11

Name: Marek

Country: Poland

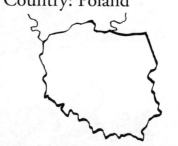

Role card 4

Name: Tatiyana

Country: Russia

Role card 8

Name: Andrea

Country: Italy

Role card 12

Name: Angelika

Country: Poland

Grammar: *this/that*, *these/those*, possessive *'s*

Manisha and Ben are at the airport, coming back from their honeymoon. Study the picture for one minute. Try to remember which object belongs to which person.

Worksheet A

1

They're *Manisha's / Ben's*
_____

4

It's *Manisha's / Ben's*
_____

2

It's *Manisha's / Ben's*
_____

5

It's *Manisha's / Ben's*
_____

3

It's *Manisha's / Ben's*
_____

6

They're *Manisha's / Ben's*
_____

Worksheet B

1

They're *Manisha's / Ben's*
_____

4

It's *Manisha's / Ben's*
_____

2

They're *Manisha's / Ben's*
_____

5

They're *Manisha's / Ben's*
_____

3

It's *Manisha's / Ben's*
_____

6

It's *Manisha's / Ben's*
_____

Role card 1

Super Souvenirs

You have:

Postcards   £1.00

AA batteries   £3.50

Souvenirs   £9.50

Role card 2

Big Bite Sandwiches

You have:

Cola   £1.25

Coffee   £2.00

Sandwich   £3.00

Bottle of water   £1.00

Role card 3

EXCHANGE DIRECT

You can change Euros:

	You buy	You sell
GB pounds	1.2	1.3
Dollars	1.6	1.7

Role card 4

Train station ticket office

	Single Ticket	Return Ticket
Paris	£80	£115
Manchester	£35	£50
Brighton	£20	£30

Role card 5

You want:

* some AAA batteries for your MP3 player.
* a cola.

Role card 7

You want:

* a coffee.
* to change 1,000 Euros to GB pounds.

Role card 6

You want:

* to change 125 dollars to Euros. (You have 115 dollars in notes and 10 dollars in coins.)
* a return ticket to Paris.

Role card 8

You want:

* a single ticket to Manchester.
* two postcards.

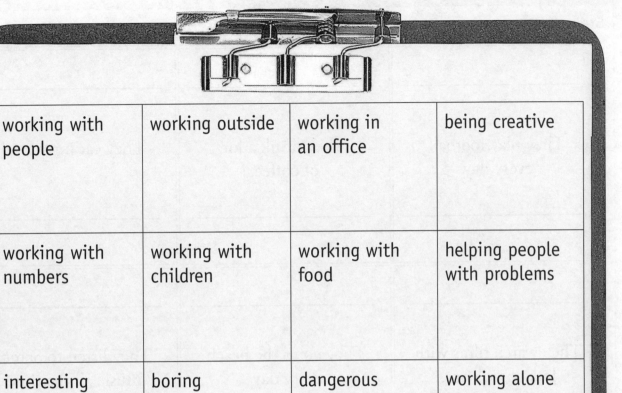

working with people	working outside	working in an office	being creative
working with numbers	working with children	working with food	helping people with problems
interesting	boring	dangerous	working alone

police officer	doctor	nurse	shop assistant
lawyer	chef	accountant	receptionist
businessman/ businesswoman	engineer	politician	hairdresser
actor/actress	sportsman/ sportswoman	teacher	personal assistant (PA)

Stereotypes

1 _____	2 _____	3 _____
They play football every day. _____	They drink a lot of coffee. _____	They eat junk food. _____
4 _____	5 _____	6 _____
They watch films with lots of violence. _____	They go to the beach every day. _____	They listen to Samba music all the time. _____

Responses

a) We like watching DVDs and going to the cinema. We like all films, not only films with violence.

b) It's true that Samba music is popular in my country, but we also listen to other types – Hip-Hop, Electronica, Jazz ... I like Rock!

c) This is not true! We often eat healthy food. Sushi is very popular at the moment.

d) We drink coffee every day, yes, but we also drink fruit juice.

e) Haha! Yes, this is very popular, but we don't play it every day! We do other sports, too. I start work at half past nine, so I get up at seven o'clock and go running on the beach every day. We love football and our national team is brilliant!

f) This is not true. When it's hot in the summer I go to the beach at the weekend, but from Monday to Friday I work all day!

Student A

1 He _____ at 9.00, then has a healthy breakfast.

2 He _____ work at 10.00 and trains for four hours.

3 He _____ lunch, then _____ home at 3.30.

4 In the evening, he _____ a salad for dinner.

5 He _____ (not) to bed late.

HE IS A(N) _____.

Student C

1 She _____ at 6.00, but she _____ (not) breakfast.

2 She _____ work at 7.30.

3 She has meetings in the morning, then _____ lunch at 12.30.

4 She _____ work again at 13.00 and works very hard.

5 She _____ home at 10.00 and _____ to bed at 12.00.

SHE IS A(N) _____.

Student B

1 He _____ at 5.30 every day.

2 He _____ breakfast, then _____ to work at 6.30.

3 He _____ work at 7.00. In the morning, he answers the telephone and meets visitors.

4 He _____ lunch at 12.00.

5 He _____ work at 5.30. He _____ (not) out in the evening.

HE IS A(N) _____.

Student D

1 She _____ at 6.00p.m. but she _____ (not) breakfast.

2 She _____ work at 9.00p.m.

3 She checks the patients in the evening, then _____ 'lunch' at 1.00a.m.

4 She _____ work again at 2.00a.m. and helps the doctors.

5 She _____ home at 6.00a.m. and _____ to bed at 11.00a.m.

SHE IS A(N) _____.

The _____ Tour

Slogan: _____

This is a tour of: _____

The tour starts at: _____

The tour leaves from: _____

You will see: _____

_____

You will visit: _____

_____

The tour finishes at: _____

It costs: _____

We *accept / don't accept* credit cards.

Role card 1

Intelligent Ian

I am Ian.

I always …

I usually …

I hardly ever …

Role card 2

Stupid Stan

I am Stan.

I always …

I usually …

I hardly ever …

Role card 3

Funny Felix

I am Felix.

I always …

I usually …

I hardly ever …

Role card 4

Serious Sabrina

I am Sabrina.

I always …

I usually …

I hardly ever …

Role card 5

Talkative Trisha

I am Trisha.

I always …

I usually …

I hardly ever …

Role card 6

Kind Kate

I am Kate.

I always …

I usually …

I hardly ever …

Role card 7

Unfriendly Uma

I am Uma.

I always …

I usually …

I hardly ever …

Role card 8

Quiet Quentin

I am Quentin.

I always …

I usually …

I hardly ever …

My parents always … ☆	I go swimming in the sea.	I study in the evening.	*I never …* ☆	My best friend is talkative.	**FINISH**
My parents call me at the weekend.	I get home late.	*I hardly ever …* ☆	I do my homework.	My teacher gives me homework.	People from my country are friendly.
My teacher is friendly.	*I usually …* ☆	People in my country play football.	I go out with my friends.	I go to the cinema.	*My friend usually …* ☆
I sometimes … ☆	I have a big breakfast.	I get up early on Sunday.	*My teacher often …* ☆	My friend has dinner with me.	I am serious.
START	I am late for class.	My family spends holidays together.	*I always …* ☆	My brother or sister sings in the shower.	I have lunch at a restaurant.

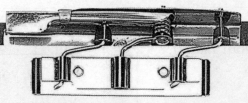

Have you got …?	You	Names
… lots of brothers and sisters.		
… a really talkative friend.		
… a son or daughter.		
… a car.		
… a pet.		
… an interesting job.		
… a best friend.		
… a favourite football team.		
… _____.		
… _____.		

Role card A

1 Hi, it's _____ (use your name).

2 fine. / free / tonight?

3 How about / go / 'The Strings' concert?

4 on / 'Q club' / 10.00. What about / meet / 8.00?

5 OK, see / then.

Role card B

1 Hi, _____ (Student A's name), how are you?

2 Yes, / am. What / want / do?

3 / good. Where / on?

4 Sorry, / busy at 8.00. How about / meet / 9.30?

5 Bye!

Role card 1

What/Where/When:

Rosy Cinema, 'In the middle of winter',

Film 20.30

Suggest meet: *19.00*

Meet: *20.15*

Role card 3

What/Where/When:

New café,

'Le Greasy Spoon',

Breakfast

Suggest meet: *7.00*

Meet: *9.30*

Role card 2

What/Where/When:

New club,

'Jumpin' Joe's'

Dancing

Suggest meet: *8.00*

Meet: *11.30*

Role card 4

What/Where/When:

Rock bar

Band: 'Bass line'

Doors open 18.00, Show 19.30

Suggest meet: *17.30*

Meet: *18.30*

Student A

Put these words somewhere (across ⇨, diagonally ⬈ ⬉ or down ⬇) in the grid:

kitchen   armchair   lamp   sofa

	1	2	3	4	5	6	7	8
A								
B								
C								
D								
E								
F								
G								
H								

Miss!

Hit 'a'!

You've hit my (sofa)!

Student B

Put these words somewhere (across ⇨, diagonally ⬈ ⬉ or down ⬇) in the grid:

wardrobe   balcony   desk   hall

	1	2	3	4	5	6	7	8
A								
B								
C								
D								
E								
F								
G								
H								

Miss!

Hit 'a'!

You've hit my (desk)!

Design your ideal home

Where is it? In a city? In the country? On water? _____

Is it a house or a flat? _____

How many rooms are there? _____

Is there a balcony? _____

Draw a simple floor plan of the rooms below:

What furniture is in each room? Add some furniture to your floor plan.

What is the name of your ideal home? _____

Choose *can* or *can't* to make true sentences.

1 In Australia, you *can/can't* buy kangaroo meat in a supermarket.

2 In Vanuatu, an island in the South Pacific Ocean, you *can/can't* visit a post office under the sea.

3 In Singapore, you *can/can't* buy chewing gum at a newsagent.

4 In Dubai, you *can/can't* ski inside a sports centre.

5 You *can/can't* have a hamburger at McDonald's in India.

6 In Brazil, you *can/can't* go to a restaurant where you pay for your food by the kilo.

7 In Sweden, you *can/can't* stay in a hotel made of ice.

8 In England, you *can/can't* leave your bags unattended in a bus or train station.

9 In France, you *can/can't* kiss on a train.

10 You *can/can't* throw tomatoes at each other in the street during *La Tomatina*, in Spain.

Student A

You are a shop assistant in a sports shop.
You have got:

> ### 'Michael Air' Trainers
> Sizes: 36 – 40 – 42 – 44 – 46
> You haven't got any size 38
>
> ### Scotland football shirts
> Sizes: S – M – L
> You haven't got any size XL.
>
> ### England football shirts
> Sizes: S – M – L - XL

If you haven't got what your partner wants,
try to sell them something else.

You are a customer in a newsagent.
You want to buy:

- The book *'To the end and back'* in paperback only.

- A drink, but not cola or anything with orange in it.

Student B

You are a customer in a sports shop.
You want to buy:

- 'Michael Air' trainers, size 39.

- 'A Scotland football shirt as a present for your brother. He's very large so he needs a size XL. He also likes England.

You are a shop assistant in a newsagent.
You have got:

> ### The book *'To the end and back'*
> Hardback only, no paperback.
>
> ### Drinks
> Cola
> 'Fizztang' orange
> 'Swype' lemonade
> Orange Juice

If you haven't got what your partner wants, try
to sell them something else.

Worksheet A

Worksheet B

Healthy food/drink:

1 _____
2 _____
3 _____
4 _____
5 _____

Unhealthy food/drink:

1 _____
2 _____
3 _____
4 _____
5 _____

Food/Drink I don't like:

1 _____
2 _____
3 _____

Food/Drink I like:

1 _____
2 _____
3 _____

Food/Drink popular in my country:

1 _____
2 _____
3 _____

Food/Drink not popular in my country:

1 _____
2 _____
3 _____

Sweet food/drink:

1 _____
2 _____
3 _____

Savoury food/drink:

1 _____
2 _____
3 _____

For breakfast in my country, we usually eat/drink:

1 _____
2 _____
3 _____

For breakfast in my country, we don't usually eat/drink:

1 _____
2 _____
3 _____

Spaghetti Bolognese

Ingredients

an _____   some _____

some _____   some _____

some _____   some _____

      some _____

Greek Salad

Ingredients

a _____   some _____

some _____   some _____

some _____

a _____

Chicken Curry

Ingredients

an _____   some _____

some _____   some _____

and _____   some _____

      some _____

Prawn Paella

Ingredients

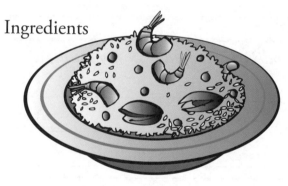

an _____   some _____

some _____   some _____

some _____   some _____

some _____   some _____

and _____

onion(s)	tomato(es)	herbs	spices	oil	garlic
beef	pasta (Spaghetti)	potato(es)	chicken	rice	cucumber
olives	cheese (Feta)	stock	a lettuce	coconut milk	prawns

a jar of jam	an avocado	a bag of rice	a packet of crisps
Calories: quite a lot	**Calories:** quite a lot	**Calories:** not many	**Calories:** a lot
Salt: not much	**Salt:** none	**Salt:** none	**Salt:** none
Carbohydrates: a lot	**Carbohydrates:** not many	**Carbohydrates:** a lot	**Carbohydrates:** quite a lot
Saturated fat: not much	**Saturated fat:** a lot	**Saturated fat:** not much	**Saturated fat:** quite a lot
Sugar: quite a lot	**Sugar:** none	**Sugar:** none	**Sugar:** not much

a mug of black coffee (no sugar)	a bar of chocolate	a can of baked beans	a carton of orange juice
Calories: not many	**Calories:** lots	**Calories:** not many	**Calories:** not many
Salt: none	**Salt:** not much	**Salt:** not much	**Salt:** none
Carbohydrates: not many	**Carbohydrates:** a lot	**Carbohydrates:** not many	**Carbohydrates:** not many
Saturated fat: none	**Saturated fat:** quite a lot	**Saturated fat:** none	**Saturated fat:** none
Sugar: none	**Sugar:** a lot	**Sugar:** not much	**Sugar:** quite a lot

	a jar of jam	an avocado	a bag of rice	a packet of crisps	a mug of coffee (no sugar)	a bar of chocolate	a can of baked beans	a carton of orange juice
Calories								
Salt								
Carbohydrates								
Saturated fat								
Sugar								

RESTAURANT

Starter
Price

1 _____ _____

Description: _____

2 _____ _____

Description: _____

Main Course

1 _____ _____

Description: _____

2 _____ _____

Description: _____

3 _____ _____

Description: _____

Dessert

1 _____ _____

Description: _____

2 _____ _____

Description: _____

Drinks

1 _____ _____

2 _____ _____

3 _____ _____

Student A

	Monday	Tuesday	Wednesday	Thursday	Friday	Saturday	Sunday
December 2010	20	21 My birthday	22	23	24	25 Football match	26
January 2011	27	28	29	30 End of Year Party	31	1	2 Fishing trip
	3	4 Cultural day	5	6	7	8 Trip to Scotland	9
	10 Class picnic	11	12 Trip to the museum	13	14	15	16 Today, 5 p.m.

Ask your partner when the following things were (*When was/were …?*):

1 'The Greentones' concert.
2 The first day of his/her English course.
3 The last day of his/her English course.
4 His/Her test.

5 The class party.
6 His/Her birthday.
7 The family party.
8 Baby 'Jo' born.

Student B

	Monday	Tuesday	Wednesday	Thursday	Friday	Saturday	Sunday
December 2010	20	21	22 Class party	23	24 family party	25	26
January 2011	27 Baby 'Jo' born	28	29	30	31	1 'The Greentones' concert	2
	3 first day of my English course	4	5	6	7	8	9
	10	11	12	13 My birthday	14	15 Last day of my English course	16 9 a.m. - Test Today, 5 p.m.

Ask your partner when the following things were (*When was/were …?*):

1 His/Her birthday.
2 End of year party.
3 The trip to Scotland.
4 The trip to the museum.

5 The class picnic.
6 The football match.
7 The fishing trip.
8 Cultural day.

Grammar: past simple: *was/were*

Student A

What were they before they were famous? Match the famous people to the jobs in the box.

| a cleaner   a sportsman (a footballer)   a teacher   TV presenters |
| a toy shop assistant   performers in a music video |

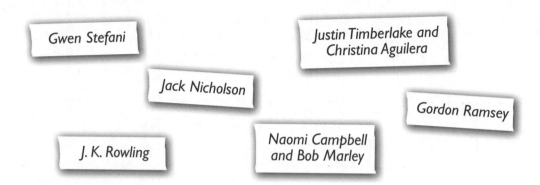

Listen to your partner's sentences and check your answers.

Jennifer Anniston was a waitress.	Mick Jagger and Tina Turner were hospital workers, but not at the same hospital.	Sting and Whoopi Goldberg were builders (a construction worker and a bricklayer), but not in the same place.
Cameron Diaz was a model.	Sean Connery was a body builder. In 1953 he was 3rd in the Mr Universe competition.	Britney Spears was a sportswoman (a gymnast). She was also a TV presenter on *The Mickey Mouse Club*.

Student B

What were they before they were famous? Match the famous people to the jobs in the box.

| a waitress   hospital workers   a body builder   a model |
| builders   a sportswoman (a gymnast) |

Jennifer Anniston

Cameron Diaz

Britney Spears

Sting and
Whoopi Goldberg

Sean Connery

Mick Jagger and
Tina Turner

Listen to your partner's sentences and check your answers.

Gwen Stefani was a cleaner.	Gordon Ramsey was a sportsman (a footballer).	Naomi Campbell and Bob Marley were performers in a music video.
J. K. Rowling was a teacher.	Jack Nicholson was a toy shop assistant.	Justin Timberlake and Christina Aguilera were TV presenters on *The Mickey Mouse Club*.

1 I started school when I was seven.	**4** I had two pets.	**7** I often saw my grandparents.	**10** I met lots of new friends.
2 I liked fish.	**5** I had a mobile phone.	**8** I studied English every day.	**11** I enjoyed playing sport.
3 I made cakes.	**6** I went to Disneyland.	**9** I often moved house.	**12** I hated weddings.

go shopping	stay in bed
go clubbing	watch a football match
play golf	watch a film at the cinema
play a new computer game	go out for a meal
stay with some friends	go for a long walk
go to an art gallery	learn to salsa dance
go to a show/concert	sing in a karaoke club
cook dinner for some friends	have a party

Label the compass below with the words in the box.

| North-West | South | South-West | South-East | East | West | North-East | North |

Choose six of the features below and draw them somewhere on your island above.

| a mountain | a market | a famous building | a river | a bridge | a lake | a city | a jungle | a village | a desert |

Becak

A Good for the environment:
B Comfortable:
C Fast:
D Cheap:

Humvee

A Good for the environment:
B Comfortable:
C Fast:
D Cheap:

Hot-Air Balloon

A Good for the environment:
B Comfortable:
C Fast:
D Cheap:

Gondola

A Good for the environment:
B Comfortable:
C Fast:
D Cheap:

Tuk-Tuk

A Good for the environment:
B Comfortable:
C Fast:
D Cheap:

Microlite

A Good for the environment:
B Comfortable:
C Fast:
D Cheap:

Tram

A Good for the environment:
B Comfortable:
C Fast:
D Cheap:

Ski-doo

A Good for the environment:
B Comfortable:
C Fast:
D Cheap:

Junk

A Good for the environment:
B Comfortable:
C Fast:
D Cheap:

Hovercraft

A Good for the environment:
B Comfortable:
C Fast:
D Cheap:

Canal Barge

A Good for the environment:
B Comfortable:
C Fast:
D Cheap:

Sky Train

A Good for the environment:
B Comfortable:
C Fast:
D Cheap:

Worksheet A

1 Answer the questions.

1 The fastest VW Van went at
  a) 102.84 mph.
  b) 95.67 mph.
  c) 223.32 mph.

2 The longest tram line has
  a) 100 stops.
  b) 72 stops.
  c) 70 stops.

3 The oldest working train began in
  a) 1855.
  b) 1902.
  c) 1871.

4 The highest helicopter flight was
  a) lower than Mt Everest.
  b) the same height as Mt Everest.
  c) higher than Mt Everest.

5 The smallest plane was
  a) 5.7 metres long.
  b) 3.7 metres long.
  c) 0.5 metres long.

2 Ask Student B to find out the answers.

3 Listen to Student B's questions and tell them the answers.

The record for the longest Quad bike journey is held by Josh and Anna Hogan, from the USA. They drove 27,141 km (16,865 miles) and went through 17 countries.

Gregory Dunham rode the world's tallest motorbike in California, USA in 2005. It was 6.187 metres tall.

The most expensive cruise ship was built in 2009. 'Project Genesis' includes a 'park' the size of a football field. It cost $1.24 billion to make and has space for over 5,000 passengers.

On the 13th of November, 1998, Gary Duval drove the world's highest limousine (3.33 metres) in California, USA.

The fastest furniture in the world was created in the UK on 11th May, 2007. Two men drove a motorized sofa at 92 mph (148 kmph).

Worksheet B

1 Answer the questions.

1 The longest Quad bike journey went through
  a) 7 countries.
  b) 17 countries.
  c) 70 countries.

2 The most expensive cruise ship cost
  a) $6.8 million.
  b) $9.5 billion.
  c) $1.24 billion.

3 The tallest motorbike was made in
  a) Delhi, India.
  b) London, UK.
  c) California, USA.

4 The fastest furniture was
  a) a sofa.
  b) a bed.
  c) a table.

5 The highest limousine was
  a) 8.42 metres high.
  b) 7.3 metres high.
  c) 3.33 metres high.

2 Ask Student A to find out the answers.

3 Listen to student A's questions and tell them the answers.

The longest tram line in the world is on the coast of Belgium. There are 70 stops and trams go along the 68 km route every ten minutes.

The smallest plane was made in Puerto Rico, USA in 2004. It weighs 162 kg and is just 3.7 metres long!

The world's oldest working train is called 'Fairy Queen' and carries passengers in Delhi, India. It was first used from 1855–1908, but began service again in 1997. It has a maximum speed of 40 kmph.

On 21st June, 1972, Jean Boulet flew a helicopter to 12,442 metres, making this the highest helicopter flight. The helicopter went higher than Mt Everest!

The fastest VW Van was driven to 102.84 mph (165.5 kmph) by a German team in Northampton, UK, in June 2009.

Worksheet A

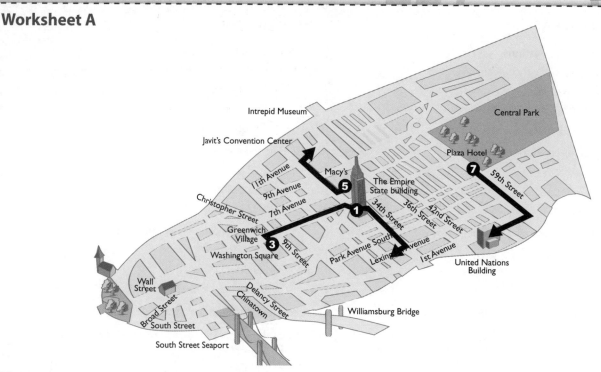

Directions

2 Start from South Street Seaport. Go down South Street and take the second right. Go down Broad Street and it's at the end.

4 Start from Greenwich Village. Go straight on, then turn right into 9th Street. Take the second left, then the first right.

6 Start from Javit's Convention Center. Turn left and go down 111th Avenue. Turn left into 42nd Street, then turn right. It's on the right.

8 Start from Williamsburg Bridge. Go down Delancy Street, then take the first left. It's on the right.

Worksheet B

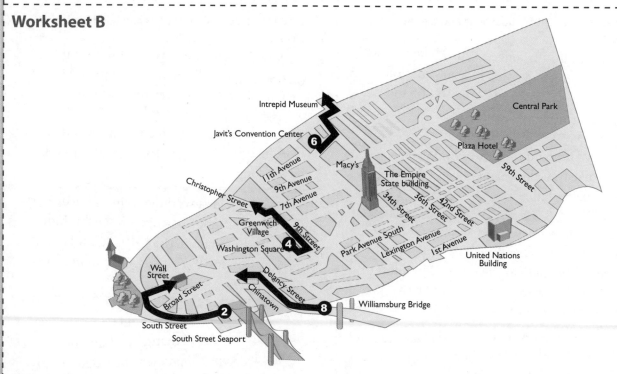

Directions

1 Start from the Empire State Building. Turn right and go down 34th Street, and take the second right. It's on the right.

3 Start from Greenwich Village. Turn right and go down 9th Avenue. Take the fifth right. It's on the left.

5 Start from Macy's. Turn left and go down 36th Street. Take the 3rd right, and it's on the left.

7 Start from The Plaza Hotel. Turn right and go down 59th Street. Take the fifth right and go down Lexington Avenue. It's on your left.

Find twelve ways of describing people's appearance in the word search.

1 Another way of saying someone is fat. _ _ _ _ _ _ _ _ _ _.
2 When a man is more than 6 foot/1.83 metres, he is _ _ _ _.
3 Another way of saying someone is thin. _ _ _ _.
4 When a woman is less than 5 foot 3 inches/1.62 metres, she is _ _ _ _ _.
5 When a man has no hair, he is _ _ _ _.
6 when someone has lots of curls, they have _ _ _ _ _ _ _ _ _ _.
7 the hair that grows on a man's chin: a _ _ _ _ _.
8 the hair that grows on a man's upper lip: a _ _ _ _ _ _ _ _ _.
9 women put _ _ _ _ _-_ _ on when they use lipstick.
10 A man aged between 30 and 39 is _ _ _ _ _ _ _ _ _ _ _ _ _.
11 A very smiley person has a _ _ _ _ _ _ _ _ _.
12 A person has two large ones, a nose and a mouth on their face. They have two _ _ _ _ _ _ _.

Find the words across ⇨ **and down** ⇩.

I	N	H	I	N	F	W	F	H	J	E	E	T	I	E
D	I	N	H	I	S	T	H	I	R	T	I	E	S	S
S	I	D	T	C	E	Y	C	M	I	L	E	S	L	B
R	O	T	E	E	R	F	K	P	A	R	E	H	I	B
S	V	A	E	S	H	O	R	T	T	Q	E	R	M	I
W	E	R	T	M	J	R	S	D	S	E	G	H	W	G
S	R	E	O	I	K	M	E	F	S	E	H	J	F	E
E	W	S	I	L	L	A	E	G	D	R	H	M	W	Y
R	E	B	I	E	L	K	W	J	U	F	S	E	M	E
V	I	M	D	E	D	E	R	T	S	T	E	B	H	S
G	G	W	E	M	O	U	S	T	A	C	H	E	H	E
H	H	R	R	E	G	P	S	E	H	J	S	A	E	G
J	T	A	L	L	T	A	L	K	I	E	S	R	W	T
K	H	A	R	R	I	E	F	R	B	A	L	D	D	D
E	C	U	R	L	Y	H	A	I	R	B	A	L	L	S

Take turns to describe the following people:

you   your best friend   your mother or father   your partner   a teacher

Situation 1

At a party

1 We ＿＿ (dance) to the music.

2 I ＿＿ (chat) to my friends.

3 We're …

4 I'm …

Situation 2

On holiday

1 Some of us ＿＿ (swim) in the sea.

2 I ＿＿ (read) a book on the beach.

3 We're …

4 I'm …

Situation 3

In an English class

1 I ＿＿ (ask) about pronunciation.

2 We ＿＿ (listen) to each other.

3 Some of us are …

4 We're …

Situation 4

At a football match

1 We ＿＿ (enjoy) the game.

2 I ＿＿ (feel) nervous.

3 We ＿＿ …

4 The other team …

Situation 5

At home

1 We ＿＿ (watch) TV.

2 I ＿＿ (lie) on the sofa.

3 My partner / flat mate is …

4 We're …

Situation 6

At a concert

1 We ＿＿ (listen) to loud music.

2 I ＿＿ (take) photos of the band.

3 The band is …

4 We're …

Situation 7

In the park

1 I ＿＿ (have) a picnic.

2 I ＿＿ (play) football.

3 We're …

4 Some people are …

Situation 8

At a restaurant

1 I ＿＿ (look) at the menu.

2 We ＿＿ (talk) to each other.

3 We're …

4 Some people are …

Situation 1	Situation 5
I'm singing karaoke.	My friend is having lunch.
I'm feeling excited.	I'm feeling hungry.

Situation 2	Situation 6
The teacher is wearing shorts.	We're shopping for clothes.
The sun is shining.	We're trying on some T-shirts.

Situation 3	Situation 7
I'm studying English.	I'm chatting to my friend on my mobile.
I'm using a website to help me.	I'm talking about last weekend.

Situation 4	Situation 8
I'm reading a newspaper.	I'm feeling really tired.
I'm laughing at a story.	I'm drinking a black coffee.

Interview other students to find out what they are doing and when they do it.

Name	What are they doing?	When do they usually do this?

Think of a film title for each of the types of film below.

My recommendations

A horror film
Ingredients: scary people, blood

Title: _____

A comedy
Ingredients: funny people, jokes

Title: _____

A musical
Ingredients: music, songs

Title: _____

An action film
Ingredients: explosions, danger

Title: _____

A romantic film
Ingredients: people in love, a happy ending

Title: _____

A sci-fi film
Ingredients: robots, spaceships

Title: _____

A drama film
Ingredients: realistic characters, emotion

Title: _____

An animation film
Ingredients: talking animals, computer graphics

Title: _____

Talk to your partner and find out what kind of films they like. Then choose two of your titles from above and recommend them to your partner.

Worksheet A

Choose two types of transport for each category below. You can use each type more than once.

1 Fast
  a) _____
  b) _____

2 Convenient
  a) _____
  b) _____

3 Safe
  a) _____
  b) _____

4 Polluting
  a) _____
  b) _____

5 Healthy
  a) _____
  b) _____

6 Comfortable
  a) _____
  b) _____

7 Romantic
  a) _____
  b) _____

8 Exciting
  a) _____
  b) _____

Worksheet B

Choose two types of transport for each category below. You can use each type more than once.

1 Dangerous
  a) _____
  b) _____

2 Green
  a) _____
  b) _____

3 Uncomfortable
  a) _____
  b) _____

4 Slow
  a) _____
  b) _____

5 Boring
  a) _____
  b) _____

6 Unromantic
  a) _____
  b) _____

7 Unhealthy
  a) _____
  b) _____

8 Inconvenient
  a) _____
  b) _____

	16 Are *a* / *an* / *the* / – roads good in your city?	**I always travel by ... if I can.**	**15** Is it popular to ride *a* / *an* / *the* / – bike in your city?	**14** Do you like driving *a* / *an* / *the* / – car? Why (not)?	**13** Are *a* / *an* / *the* / – taxis cheap in your country?
FINISH					
9 How often do you ride *a* / *an* / *the* / – bike?	**I hate travelling by ...**	**10** What types of *a* / *an* / *the* / – transport are common in the city where you live?	**11** Are *a* / *an* / *the* / – trains popular in your country?	**12** On the bus, do *a* / *an* / *the* / – young people offer their seats to *a* / *an* / *the* / – old people in your country?	**Travelling by ... is slow.**
Travelling by ... is romantic	**8** Is it popular to ride *a* / *an* / *the* / – horses in your country?	**7** In your country, do *a* / *an* / *the* / – people pay when they get on or get off *a* / *an* / *the* / – bus?	**I like travelling by ...**	**6** Do you ever go anywhere by *a* / *an* / *the* / – helicopter?	**5** What's *a* / *an* / *the* / – capital city of your country? Do you live there?
START	**1** How often do you take *a* / *an* / *the* / – taxi?	**2** When you go to the supermarket, do you go on *a* / *an* / *the* / – foot, by *a* / *an* / *the* / – car or use another type of transport?	**I never travel by ...**	**3** Is there *a* / *an* / *the* / – monorail in your city?	**4** In your country, do people drive on *a* / *an* / *the* / – right or on *a* / *an* / *the* / – left (on the road)?

Card 1

Illinois, USA, / have to / drive / using / steering wheel.

Card 5

Thailand / have to / wear / shirt / driving.

Card 9

Ontario, Canada / can't / take friend / airport / your car. / only / to work.

Card 2

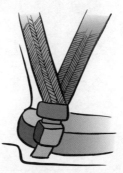

New York, USA / don't have to / seatbelt / drive.

Card 6

Alaska, USA / can't look at / moose / from / plane.

Card 10

Finland / break / law / your car / have to / pay percentage / your salary.

Card 3

San Francisco, USA / can / drive / eight years old.

Card 7

Alabama, USA / can't drive / without shoes.

Card 11

The Philippines / your license plate ends with a 1 or 2 / can't / drive / Monday.

Card 4

Brewton, USA / can drive anybody's car. / don't have to / permission.

Card 8

France / can't kiss / railway.

Card 12

Memphis, Tennessee, / woman / can't drive / without / man walking in front.

You shouted at an advertisement in the street.

You took off your clothes on a plane.

Your teacher was found at your house, in a wardrobe.

You pushed your teacher down the street in a shopping trolley.

You borrowed your friend's car without asking.

In a fish shop, you picked up a big fish, kissed it and said; 'marry me'.

At a rock concert, you gave someone a glass of water and said; 'I have to do this'.

You sat on the roof of the school and cried.

You stood in the middle of the street and shouted; 'Turn left! Turn left!'.

In the middle of class you stood up and ran out.

You drove your car through the park.

You wrote; 'I am happy' on your T-shirt and sat on the bus all day.

Crossword A

Prepare clues for the answers about life plans you have.

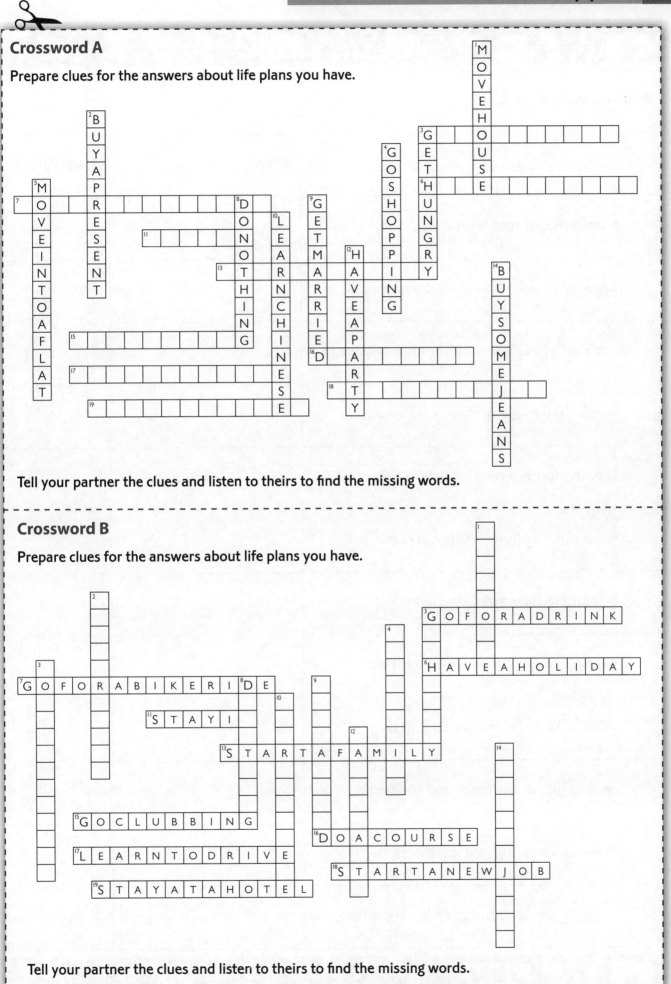

Tell your partner the clues and listen to theirs to find the missing words.

Crossword B

Prepare clues for the answers about life plans you have.

Tell your partner the clues and listen to theirs to find the missing words.

Who do you think ...	Name	True/False?
1 ... would like to start a business.		
2 ... is going to do nothing next weekend.		
3 ... is going to buy some clothes next weekend.		
4 ... would like to get married on a beach.		
5 ... is going to get a new job next year.		
6 ... would like to move to another country.		
7 ... is going to have a holiday soon.		
8 ... would like to go for a drink with me.		
9 ... would like to learn another language.		
10 ... would like to travel around the world.		
11 ... is going to go jogging next week.		
12 ... is going to buy a present for a friend.		

Worksheet A

Use *will* (*'ll*), *might* or *won't* to complete the predictions.

1 My country _____ win the next world cup.

2 It _____ be sunny next weekend.

3 I _____ get a great present for my next birthday.

4 Our teacher _____ give us homework today.

5 There _____ be an interesting programme on TV tonight.

6 Someone _____ cook for me next week.

7 My mother _____ call me today.

8 I _____ sleep well tonight.

9 My partner _____ have a good time next weekend.

10 I _____ live in another country in my life.

Compare your predictions with the other students. Are any true?

Worksheet B

Use *will* (*'ll*), *might* or *won't* to complete the predictions.

1 My country _____ have a hot summer next year.

2 The President of my country _____ win the next election.

3 I _____ meet a very interesting person this year.

4 I _____ get hungry today.

5 There _____ be lots of traffic on my way home today.

6 The situation in my country _____ get better in the next 10 years.

7 My English _____ improve a lot this year.

8 I _____ receive some good news this week.

9 Our teacher _____ make us study grammar tomorrow.

10 My partner _____ have something interesting for dinner tonight.

Compare your predictions with the other students. Are any true?

Role card 1A

You and your partner are organizing a class party, for the end of the course. Make the following suggestions:

- Hire a DJ
- Cook some food yourselves
- Invite everybody in the school for free

Listen and respond to your partner's suggestions, then agree on three things.

Role card 1B

You and your partner are organizing a class party, for the end of the course. Make the following suggestions:

- Hire a band
- Buy some food
- Sell tickets

Listen and respond to your partner's suggestions, then agree on three things.

Role card 2A

You and your partner are planning a short holiday. Make the following suggestions:

- Go camping
- Stay in the mountains
- Do lots of activities e.g. walking, climbing.

Listen and respond to your partner's suggestions, then agree on three things.

Role card 2B

You and your partner are planning a short holiday. Make the following suggestions:

- Stay at a hotel
- Stay near the beach
- Do nothing – just relax!

Listen and respond to your partner's suggestions, then agree on three things.

Role card 3A

You and your partner are planning to raise some money for charity, to help victims of a natural disaster. Make the following suggestions:

- Hold a 'mini-lotto' to raise money
- Create posters to ask people for money
- Start an email campaign to ask politicians to help

Listen and respond to your partner's suggestions, then agree on three things.

Role card 3B

You and your partner are planning to raise some money for charity, to help victims of a natural disaster. Make the following suggestions:

- Do a parachute jump
- Do a sponsored walk
- Hold a sale – sell all your old things

Listen and respond to your partner's suggestions, then agree on three things.

Role card 4A

It is your friend's birthday soon. You and your partner are deciding what to buy him/her as a present. Make the following suggestion, and think of two more ideas to suggest:

- Take him/her to a restaurant
- _____ (your idea)
- _____ (your idea)

Listen and respond to your partner's suggestions, then agree on the best idea.

Role card 4B

It is your friend's birthday soon. You and your partner are deciding what to buy him/her as a present. Make the following suggestion, and think of two more ideas to suggest:

- Buy him/her a shopping voucher
- _____ (your idea)
- _____ (your idea)

Listen and respond to your partner's suggestions, then agree on the best idea.

I haven't got any money.	My friend gave me a birthday present but I don't like it.
I always get a cold in winter.	I've got lots of work and not enough time.
I can't sleep at night, and I feel tired in the day.	I want to get a boyfriend/girlfriend.
I want to stop eating chocolate.	My friend has cooked dinner and I don't like the food.
I want to learn English quickly.	I have a boring job.
I want to be more fashionable.	I want to make friends.
I can't concentrate in class.	I am a teacher and my students never do their homework.
I've got a job interview next week.	I want to do something interesting at the weekend.

Speed counselling

My problem: _____

_____

	Useful? ✓/✗
Advice 1	
Advice 2	
Advice 3	
Advice 4	
Advice 5	
Advice 6	

Speed counselling

My problem: _____

_____

	Useful? ✓/✗
Advice 1	
Advice 2	
Advice 3	
Advice 4	
Advice 5	
Advice 6	

Verb phrase cards

swim in the sea	run across the room	read a book	climb a mountain
speak your language	say the numbers 1–10	type an email	wash a car
play a computer game	play the guitar	eat some spaghetti	watch TV

Adjective cards

fast	slow	clear	happy
loud	angry	good	bad
quiet	dangerous	careful	sad

Role card 1

You try to ask for something in a shop but don't speak the language.

Role card 2

You try to pay for your meal in a restaurant and don't have enough money.

Role card 3

You can't start your car.

Role card 4

You are alone in the street late at night and can't find a taxi.

Role card 5

You are in a bookshop but you don't know which book to buy to help you learn more English.

Role card 6

You are afraid of flying.

Role card 7

You have lots of work to do in the next four hours.

Role card 8

You are carrying lots of heavy bags and feel very tired.

Role card 9

You can't find your mobile phone.

Role card 10

You are in a café, trying to carry lots of glasses to the table.

Role card 11

Your computer won't work!

Role card 12

You are lost in a city.

Map A

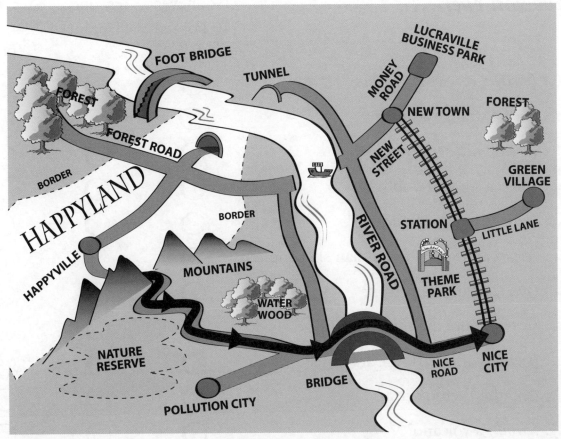

Map B

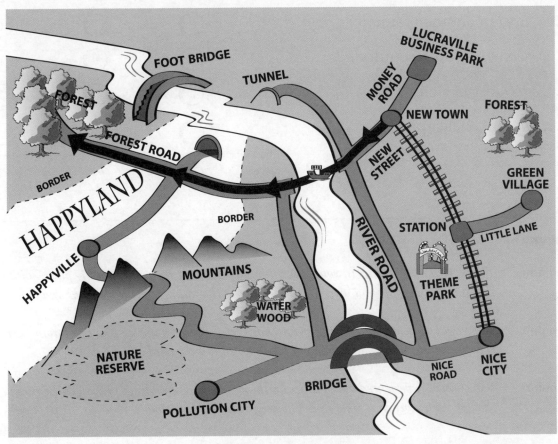

Have you ever ...	No, never. (0 points)	Yes, once. (1 point)	Yes, more than once. (2 points)
1 ... *(visit)* a very cold place?	○	○	○
2 ... *(eat)* a strange animal?	○	○	○
3 ... *(break)* his/her arm / leg?	○	○	○
4 ... *(sing)* a song in public?	○	○	○
5 ... *(visit)* a famous building?	○	○	○
6 ... *(cook)* a meal for more than six people?	○	○	○
7 ... *(meet)* a famous person?	○	○	○
8 ... *(learn)* more than three languages?	○	○	○
9 ... *(swim)* with sharks or dolphins?	○	○	○
10 ... *(see)* the Pacific ocean?	○	○	○
11 ... *(climb)* a volcano?	○	○	○
12 ... *(go)* scuba-diving?	○	○	○
13 ... *(live)* in another country?	○	○	○
14 ... *(watch)* an opera outdoors?	○	○	○
15 ... *(get)* lost in a city?	○	○	○
16 ... *(fly)* in a helicopter?	○	○	○
Total points:			

Fold

Answer key

0 – 4 points: *You've tried a few things in your life, but remember that the world is a big place, with lots of things to see. Perhaps you worry too much about the future. Take a few risks and enjoy life!*

5 – 16 points: *You've had quite an interesting life and have tried different things. You like having new experiences but at the same time you know when to be careful.*

16 + points: *Wow, you've experienced lots of different things, and are not afraid of danger. Be careful though, remember that sometimes you need to take things slowly!*

Role card 1A

You are Jack, and want to call Ben. If he's not there, then leave a message asking him to call you. Use the prompts to help you.

Hi, (your partner's name), it's (your name). / Ben there?

/ leave a message / him?

/ ask him / call me.

OK / 6479102.

No, 6479102.

Role card 1B

Jack is calling you and wants to speak to Ben. Ben isn't here at the moment, so take a message. You're not sure if Ben has Jack's number, so ask for it. Use the prompts to help you.

No / not here.

OK, no problem.

Could / give / number?

Let / check. 6479182?

9102. Ok, I'll ask him / call you. Bye.

Role card 2A

You are Susan Jones. Mr Right is calling you, but you are very busy at the moment. Ask him to call you back later, on your mobile, and give him the number. Use the prompts to help you.

This / Susan Jones. / very busy / moment. Could / ring back later on my mobile?

97824615.

No, 97824615

Bye.

Role card 2B

You are Mr Right, and want to speak to Susan Jones. She is very busy at the moment and asks you to call her later on her mobile. This is ok, but get the number. Use the prompts to help you.

Hello, this / Mr Right. / speak to Susan Jones?

No problem. What / number?

Let / check. 97825615?

4615. OK.

Bye.

Role card 3A

Call your friend, Owen. Ask him if he wants to go for a drink tonight.

Role card 3B

Your friend, Neil calls you. You're busy tonight but free tomorrow night, so suggest then.

Role card 4A

You are Mr Swift's secretary. He's in a meeting, so take a message.

Role card 4B

Call Mr Swift. If he's not there, leave your number and ask him to call you.

Unit 1

WHAT DO YOU NEED?

Materials: One copy of worksheet A and worksheet B per pair of students and one set of pictures per pair of students
Put Ss into pairs and distribute the A and B worksheets so each pair has one of each. Tell each pair to label all the objects in the picture with words from their lists, without showing their lists to their partners. This encourages Ss to share information verbally. N.B. in order to prevent Ss from comparing their worksheets, arrange the pairs so they are sitting face-to-face if possible.

> **Answers:**
>
> A a file   B a mobile phone   C a laptop   D an umbrella
> E a camera   F chewing gum   G batteries   H a watch
> I a sweater   J coins   K a dictionary   L sunglasses

Check answers to the first activity, putting the words on the board. Check for correct pronunciation.

Get Ss to take a minute to look at the pictures and then brainstorm what the situations are: on the beach/on holiday, in a classroom/at school, in town/out with friends. Then tell Ss that for each situation, they must choose five items from the whole group of words (no more and no less), and that they must try to agree. If time, pairs can compare their ideas with other pairs when they finish. If you have any early finishers, get them to think of two more objects they could take in each situation (they may need to check vocabulary with you). Elicit some answers from different pairs and give whole class feedback on errors/good language used.

MEET AND GREET

Materials: One role card per student
Distribute the role cards, one for each student. If you have more than twelve Ss, then make two copies and double-up on some of the roles. N.B. In the pairs of nationalities, the first card is a man's name and the second is a woman's name.

Get Ss to memorise their names and nationalities, and walk around the class introducing themselves until they find their 'partner' from the same country. Once they have found their partner, tell Ss to introduce themselves or each other to the other Ss in the class. Remind Ss of the language for greetings (*Nice to meet you. And you. How are you? Great, thanks. And you?*) and to use the verb 'be' in the present simple. (*I'm Japanese, we're Russia, etc.*).

When all the Ss have had a chance to introduce themselves, ask them to sit down with their 'partners' from the same countries. N.B. If you have an odd number of Ss, have the 'odd' student work with another pair in a group of three. Write the following useful language on the board for Ss to refer to, and drill pronunciation: *(Jack) is American. No, he isn't, he's British! Is (Andrea) Italian? Yes, she is.* Give them five minutes to remember as many names and nationalities as they can and write them in their notebooks.

Check answers and write them on the board. N.B. You could add a competitive element here by awarding points for the correct answers. The pair with the most correct answers wins!

WHOSE ARE THESE?

Materials: One picture per pair of students and one copy of worksheet A and worksheet B per pair of students
Show Ss the picture and ask them to study it for one minute, paying particular attention to who the objects belong to.

Cover or take away the picture, and distribute the A and B worksheets. Instruct Ss to work together to remember who owns each object and complete the sentences. Put the following sentences on the board for Ss reference: *This is Ben's laptop. Those are Manisha's sweaters. Is this Ben's hairbrush? No, it isn't. It's Manisha's Are those Manisha's photos? Yes, they are!* and demonstrate/model the activity. Give Ss five minutes to remember as many as they can.

Show the picture again for Ss to check their answers, and award points for correct answers. The pair with the most points wins!

> **Answers:**
>
> **Student A:** 1 They're Manisha's magazines.   2 It's Ben's laptop.   3 It's Ben's newspaper.   4 It's Manisha's passport.
> 5 It's Ben's camera.   6 They're Manisha's sweets.
> **Student B:** 1 They're Ben's keys.   2 They're Ben's tickets.
> 3 It's Manisha's hairbrush.   4 It's Manisha's MP3 player.
> 5 They're Manisha's sweaters.   6 It's Ben's mobile phone.

CAN I HAVE ONE …?

Materials: One role card per student
Explain to Ss that they are in a London train station, and have a few things to do before they catch their train. Choose four Ss (or ask them to choose) who will be 'employees' and give them their role cards. Arrange them around the class, so that they are sitting down in their 'shops', and ask them to write the names of their shops on pieces of paper in front of them, as 'signs'. Allow them a few minutes to review their information, then tell them to plan what they need to say.

Distribute the remaining 'customer' cards and allow Ss some time to prepare how they will ask for the things they want. N.B. if you have more than eight Ss, you will need to make two copies of the 'customer' cards and double up on some of the roles.

Check the phrases for making requests (*Can I have four of those batteries, please? Could I change 100 dollars, please?*) and for the employees (*That's two euros, please. Yes, here you are.*). Drill the phrases, making sure Ss sound polite.

Position the four 'employees' around the room and have the customers walk around and role-play the situations. Listen carefully for errors and good phrases, and give feedback on this at the end of the activity. If you have any *early finishers*, you could give them another role card and/or have them discuss possible solutions to the problems.

Unit 2

A GOOD JOB?

Materials: One grid per student and one set of cards per group

Prepare for this activity by cutting up the 'job' cards in section two. Arrange Ss in small groups and distribute one grid and one set of cards to each group.

In their groups, Ss discuss and match the jobs to the qualities in the grid. There are no 'correct' answers here, so Ss can give their opinions. Some jobs may also go in more than one category. As an extension, ask Ss to think of more jobs for each category.

ARE YOU TYPICAL?

Materials: One set of stereotypes and one set of responses per pair of students

Elicit/Explain 'national stereotype', and elicit some typical stereotypes for the country you are teaching in (if this is Brazil, then elicit some typical stereotypes about British/Americans). Explain to Ss that they need to read the stereotypes in the first part then guess which country it is in pairs. Also elicit some ideas as to how true they think each one is. (The country is Brazil.)

Direct Ss' attention to the responses, and explain they have come from Brazil. Instruct students to work in pairs to match the responses to the stereotypes given in the first part. Check answers with the class.

Answers:

1 E   2 D   3 C   4 A   5 F   6 B

Ss, working alone or in small groups of the same nationality, prepare sentences (some true, some false) about their own countries. Monitor carefully and check Ss are producing sentences correctly. Write the following prompts on the board to help them: *food, drink, sport, films/TV, music, any other ideas.*

Rearrange them in different pairs/small groups to then read out their sentences. The other Ss decide if they are true or false. For *monolingual classes* (and/or classes with Brazilian Ss), tell Ss to write about different areas in their country. Elicit any interesting facts for feedback.

WORKING 9 TO 5?

Materials: One role card per student

Write *Shop assistant* on the board. Go over some of the verbs to talk about daily routines from Unit 2.2, and elicit sentences from Ss to talk about a shop assistant's daily routine (e.g. *she gets up at 7.00, she starts work at 9.00, etc.*).

Arrange Ss into four groups and distribute a card to each student (Card A to Ss in group A, Card B to Ss in group B, etc.). Ask the Ss in each group to complete the sentences using the correct forms, then guess what the job is. N.B. Make it clear to Ss that they should <u>not</u> 'call out' the job, but write it down in the space provided.

Answers:

Student A: 1 gets up   2 starts   3 has, gets   4 has   5 doesn't go;   He is a sportsman.

Student B: 1 gets up   2 has, goes   3 starts   4 has   5 finishes, doesn't go;   He is a receptionist.

Student C: 1 gets up, doesn't have   2 starts   3 has   4 starts   5 gets, goes;   She is a businesswoman.

Student D: 1 gets up, doesn't have   2 starts   3 has   4 starts   5 goes, goes;   She is a nurse.

After you have checked answers with each group, rearrange Ss into small groups (ideally of Student A, B, C and D) and tell them to read out their sentences for their partners to guess the job.

When they have finished this, ask each pair/small group to choose a job and write 4–5 sentences about what the person's daily routine, as in the role cards. When they have finished, they can read out their sentences for other pairs/groups to guess the job.

TOUR OPERATORS

Materials: One worksheet per group

Preteach '*slogan*' by eliciting some famous examples (e.g. *Nike; 'Just do It'*). Write the following information on the board:

The (Name of you teaching institution) Tour

Slogan: Discover a world of English!

Starts at: 10.00

Leaves from: (the name of your class or room)

You will see: Lots of interesting people.

You will visit: Classes, reception and the teachers' room.

Finishes at: 12.00

It costs: 5.00

We accept credit cards.

Ask Ss if they would like to go on this tour, and elicit reasons why/why not.

Arrange the Ss into small groups, and explain that they are going to design their own tour, then try and 'sell' it to other Ss. Distribute the cards and get them to fill in the information, making sure they come up with a name and a simple slogan. Encourage Ss to be creative and come up with interesting tours (even if they are not physically possible!). Early finishers could add extra information about their tours.

When all the groups are ready, elicit/review the questions for asking about the tour information from Unit 2.3 (for weaker classes you could put the questions up on the board). Explain that one student from each group will stay where they are, with the tour information, and the other groups members will visit the other 'Tour Operators' and find out about the tours. As they are doing this, go round and listen, and note down any common errors/good language for later class feedback.

When the other group members have visited all the other 'Tour Operators', instruct them to go back to their original groups, share the information, and choose which tour they would like to go on and why. Conduct class feedback.

Unit 3

I'M FRIENDLY FRED!

Materials: One role card per student

Write *'I'm _____ Fred'* on the board, and elicit/write up the following sentences: *I always say hello to people I know. I usually make new friends. I hardly ever say bad things to people.* Elicit the missing adjective (*Friendly*).

Explain that Ss will receive a role card of a person. On the card there is the adjective describing the person and the name of the person. Tell Ss they must keep this adjective a secret. (It is there to help them write their sentences.) Tell Ss they must complete three sentences about that person on their own, then distribute the role cards. Monitor the Ss while they are working, and help if necessary. Early finishers could be asked to write more sentences, using different adverbs of frequency.

When Ss have their sentences ready, explain that they will have to go around the class, reading their sentences for the others to guess the adjective. For *weaker Ss*, you could explain that the adjectives and the names share the same first letter.

For feedback, elicit some of the answers and Ss' ideas.

LATE AGAIN!

Materials: One copy of the board and a coin per group and one counter per student

To prepare for this, distribute (or ask Ss to find) enough counters for each group, and each group will need a coin. Elicit 'heads' and 'tails'.

Write the sentences up on the board: *I watch TV in the morning. I have breakfast at home.* Insert the correct frequency adverb to make the sentences true for you, and elicit a few answers from Ss in the class. Then write the following adverbs on the board: *hardly ever, sometimes, often, usually, always* and remind Ss that the adverb comes after the verb 'be', and before other verbs.

Explain the rules. Each turn a student flips the coin – if it's heads they move their counter forward two squares, and if it's tails they move one. When they land on that square they have to say a true sentence for them, using the relevant frequency adverb. If they land on a 'star' square, they must complete the sentence in whatever way is true for them. Other Ss should listen and say if the sentence is grammatically correct or not. If they are not sure, and you are not available, then they can stay on the square, write the sentence down and check with you at the end.

While they are playing the game, go round and help Ss with sentences they are not sure about. Note down any common errors to work on at the end.

At the end of the activity, invite Ss to write the sentences they weren't sure about on the board, and go through them with the class. N.B. For *stronger classes/groups*, you could ask Ss to give some false sentences and ask other students in the group to guess if they are true or false.

HAVE YOU GOT IT?

Materials: One worksheet per student

Working alone, ask Ss to put a tick or cross next to each thing in the 'You' column. Don't get feedback here, but monitor Ss doing the task to check they've understood. Ask Ss to write two ___ ___ ___tions at the bottom to make the questionn___ ___ ___

Ask Ss to ___ ___ ___ ___ they will need i.e. *Have you ___ ___ ___ ___ d the class and find pe___ ___ ___ ___ hem, and write their na___ ___ ___ ___ es'. Demonstrate with a ___

Go th___ ___ ___ ___ ncouraging the use o___ ___ *new car, it's a Ford. Vane___ ___ ___ ___ ulia, etc.*

WHAT'S G___ ___ ___ ___ U?

Materials: One copy of role card A and role card B per pair of students and one set of role cards 1–3 per pair of students

Write on the board: *Making arrangements, Making suggestions, Responding to suggestions.* Elicit what phrases Ss can remember from Unit 3.3 of the **Students' book** and write them on the board. Alternatively, you could put Ss in 3 groups and assign one of the titles to each group. They brainstorm, then come and write their phrases on the board under each section.

Divide the class into pairs, and distribute copies of the A and B role cards. Make it clear that students <u>cannot</u> show their card to their partner. Demonstrate the activity with a stronger student, then get Ss to practice the dialogue in pairs. N.B. with weaker Ss, you could ask them to write out the phrases in full first from the prompts, then practice the dialogue. However, by this stage Ss should be able to use the prompts to say the phrases, allowing for freer practice. For early finishers, have them swap roles and practice again.

Once Ss have finished practicing their dialogue, have one pair perform it for the class. For further practice, give out the other cards in section 2 and have the pairs practice the dialogue again, using their A and B role cards as a model.

YOU'VE HIT MY TELEVISION!

Materials: A copy of worksheet A and worksheet B per pair of students

Explain and demonstrate the rules of the game, using a simple diagram on the board. Ss first secretly place their words wherever they like in the grid – horizontally (left to right), vertically (down) or diagonally (but not backwards). They can place words so that they share letters, if they want, and make this clear to the Ss. Ss A and Ss B have four different words, and stronger Ss could add two more of their own. When Ss have placed their words, they take it in turns to call out a square (e.g. *G3*). If this square is empty, the other student replies; *'miss'*. If it contains a letter, they say *'hit'* and which letter it is (e.g. *'hit, s'*).

If, during their turn, a student thinks they know the word, they can guess the whole word. If they are correct, the other student replies; *'you've hit my (armchair)'*. This counts as a turn.

THE IDEAL HOME

Materials: One worksheet per pair/group of students

Pre-teach 'ideal' and 'exhibition'. Introduce the activity by drawing a simple floor plan of your 'ideal home' on the board, and talking through the rooms and the furniture in them. Make sure you use *there is/are* and prepositions of place (e.g. *There is a TV in front of the sofa, etc.*). Ask Ss if they like your home.

Put Ss into pairs/small groups and distribute the worksheets. Instruct them to design their own 'ideal home', by answering the questions and drawing a simple outline. Give Ss 10 mins to do the outline, and tell them that they do not have to produce perfect pictures – only outlines! Tell Ss they have a maximum of four rooms, and each room only has three pieces of furniture, to avoid the pictures becoming too complicated. Make them aware that when they have finished each pair/group will present their home to the rest of the class. Allow Ss to be creative and add any 'extras' they want. Be on hand to help supply vocabulary for this.

When they have finished their designs, invite each pair/small groups to come to the front of the class and present their ideas. For larger classes, or if you are short of time, Ss could just present to the group next to them. In feedback, ask Ss to tell you which other designs they liked.

DO'S AND DON'TS

Materials: One worksheet per student

Review places in a town from Unit 4.2 by asking Ss what they can do in these places. Put them in pairs/small groups and distribute the quiz. Set a time limit and ask Ss to choose the correct option to make true sentences. Check answers and award points for correct guesses.

Answers:

1 can   2 can   3 can't (The sale of chewing gum has been banned since 1994.)   4 can   5 can't (You can only buy chicken burgers as Hindus don't eat beef and Muslims don't eat pork.)   6 can   7 can   8 can't (Unattended bags are destroyed in case they pose a terrorist risk.)   9 can't (In 1910, kissing was banned on French Railways, as it was said to cause delays.)   10 can

When they have finished, ask Ss to write some similar sentences about things they can do at different places in their countries/towns.

CAN I HELP YOU?

Materials: One copy of worksheet A and worksheet B per pair of students

Draw a three-column table on the board and add the following categories to the table: *Shop assistant, Customer, Saying 'no' politely*. Read out the following phrases and elicit which column they go under, then write them on the board: *No, it's not right. Thanks anyway. It's too big. Just a moment. Here you are. They're too small. Fine. No problem. I'll take it/them. It's not big enough. I'm not sure. I need to think about it. Sorry, we've only got … Can I help you? Have you got it/them in a larger size?*

When the phrases are up on the board, ask Ss to repeat them after you, and mark the stress (underlined above). Arrange Ss in pairs, and distribute the worksheets to Ss A and Ss B. Explain the first situation (sports shop) and demonstrate if necessary. Ss then practice the situations, swapping roles.

Unit 5

WELL, I LIKE IT!

Materials: One copy of worksheet A and worksheet B per pair of students

Check understanding of *dozen, healthy/unhealthy, sweet/savoury* and *breakfast*. Divide the class into half and hand out worksheet A to one half of the class and worksheet B to the other half. Give them time to complete their questions. You might want to refer them to the photo bank in the Ss' book to help with the names of food/drink.

Pair off Ss A and Ss B and explain the activity. Each student shares his/her list with the other student, and elicits ideas from their partner, and vice-versa. Conduct some class feedback at the end and elicit any interesting information the Ss found out. N.B. As an alternative with *monolingual classes*, you could distribute only the Student A worksheets. Ss then work on their own to complete the lists, before working with a partner to try and agree on common lists.

WHAT'S IN YOUR DISH?

Materials: One recipe card and one set of ingredients per pair of students

Introduce the topic by writing the ingredients of a simple dish you are familiar with on the board. Write countable nouns in a list on the left, and uncountable nouns in a list on the right. See if students can guess what the dish is. (e.g. *Tomato Soup. Left – some tomatoes, some herbs and spices, Right – some water*).

Pre-teach *Feta cheese, garlic, stock* and *coconut milk*. With weaker Ss, you could ask them to divide up the food/drink in the box into countable and uncountable first. Put the Ss in pairs/small groups and give a card to each, along with the list of ingredients. Explain that Ss need to decide which ingredients they need for their dish, with countable nouns on the left and uncountable nouns on the right. When they have finished, they can check answers with you.

Answers:

Spaghetti Bolognese (C): an onion, some tomatoes, some herbs (UC): some oil, some garlic, some beef, some pasta (Spaghetti)

Chicken Curry: (C): an onion, some herbs and spices (UC): an onion, some garlic, some chicken, some coconut milk, some rice

Greek Salad: (C): a lettuce, some olives, some tomatoes, a cucumber (UC): some oil, some cheese (Feta)

Prawn Paella: (C): an onion, some tomatoes, some prawns, some herbs and spices (UC): some oil, some garlic, some stock, some rice

When all the pairs/groups have finished, they can read out their lists of ingredients to other pairs/groups, who try to guess what the dish is.

As an extension, if any of the dishes here are popular in Ss' countries, you could ask them if they use any different ingredients. Refer them to the BBC website cooking section for ideas if necessary.

HOW MANY CALORIES?!

Materials: One chart per students and one set of nutrition cards per pair of students

Introduce the topic by discussing processed foods – how much they eat and what they usually contain. Give out the chart with the pictures, and ask Ss to match the pictures to the names of foods/containers along the top of the chart. Check answers and ask students how healthy they think each one is.

Put Ss in pairs and hand out the nutrition information cards. Model the activity with a stronger student by asking and answering some questions (e.g. *How many calories are in a bar of chocolate? How much saturated fat is in a can of baked beans? etc.*). Instruct Ss to mingle and find out the necessary information to complete their charts. Conduct feedback and elicit any surprising answers.

NOTE ON NUTRITIONAL INFORMATION

Although small amounts of each of these things are important in a balanced diet, it is generally agreed that it is healthier to limit the amount of saturated fat, salt and sugar in our diet. The UK Department of Health recommends an average daily calorie intake of 1,940 for women, and 2,550 for men. A calorie is the amount of energy needed to heat a litre of water by 1 degree Celcius.

TEA FOR TWO

Materials: One worksheet per student

Distribute one worksheet to each student in the class. Ask them to complete it with the names of dishes and two or three ingredients to go in the descriptions for each dish. The dishes could be traditional from their country or made-up dishes. They should also think of a name for their restaurant. Monitor and check spelling.

When the Ss have finished, arrange them in groups of three. One student will be the waiter (they should use their own menu), and the other two are diners. Instruct them to role-play ordering in a restaurant using the 'waiter's' menu, and refer them to Unit 5.5 of the student's book for useful language. Monitor closely and take notes on the Ss' language for later feedback/correction.

When they have finished, they can change roles using the new 'waiter's' menu. If your class does not divide into threes, they can do it in pairs instead.

Unit 6

WHEN WAS THE PARTY?

Materials: One copy of worksheet A and worksheet B per pair of students

Write on the board: *on _____, in _____, _____ago, last _____, yesterday ____*. Read out the following words and elicit which preposition they go with (or ask Ss to write them up): *23rd December (on), weekend (last), year (last), evening (yesterday), four hours (ago), 2009 (in), three days (ago), January (in), morning (yesterday), Tuesday (last)*

Arrange Ss in pairs and distribute the worksheets to Ss A and Ss B. Make sure the Ss are sitting opposite each other, so they can't see each other's calendars. Explain Ss need to ask when the activities on their list were, and mark them on their calendars. Encourage Ss to use different ways of saying when the things were, referring them to the board if necessary. For feedback, ask Ss to tell you when the things happened.

Possible answers:

Student A: 1 on the 1st January   2 Two weeks ago   3 yesterday   4 today   5 on the 22nd December   6 Three days ago   7 on the 24th December   8 in December, three weeks ago

Student B: 1 on the 21st December   2 on the 30th December   3 last weekend   4 four days ago   5 last Monday   6 three weeks ago   7 two Sundays ago   8 a fortnight ago

For early finishers, ask them to think of three more events and write them in their calendars. They then repeat the activity with their own events.

BEFORE THEY WERE FAMOUS

Materials: One copy of worksheet A and worksheet B per pair of students

Introduce the activity by writing '*Madonna*' and '*Dunkin Donuts*' *(a popular 'doughnut' fast-food chain in the US)* on the board. Ask students if they know how these two things are connected. Elicit some ideas, then tell them that before Madonna was famous, she was a waitress at Dunkin Donuts.

Distribute the Student A cards to half the class, and the Student B cards to the other half. Ss A work together, and Ss B, too, and match the famous people to what they were before they were famous, on the top part of their cards.

Don't give the answers, but pair off Ss A and Ss B. Model a few questions (e.g. *Was J. K. Rowling a waitress? No, she wasn't, etc.*), and then instruct pairs to do the same to check the rest of their answers. For feedback, elicit which answers were surprising and ask Ss if they know of any other 'before they were famous' stories.

SNAPPED!

Materials: One set of picture cards and one set of sentence cards per group

Introduce the topic with a short visualization activity. Ask Ss to close their eyes and imagine they are ten years old, and they are lying in bed at home. It is the first day of the summer holidays and they are feeling really about the start of the holidays. They should imagine what their bedroom looks like and what they are going to do during the holidays. Write on the board; *I liked…, I didn't like…, I had …,* and ask them to open their eyes and tell their partner about their life at that time by completing the sentences.

Arrange Ss in small groups and distribute one set of cards, face down in two piles to each group. Explain the game and demonstrate. One person from each group takes it in turns to turn over a card from each pile. When they have a match, the first person to say 'Snap!' wins that pair of cards. The student with the most sets at the end wins. When they have finished, check answers.

Answers:

1 L 2 K 3 A 4 G 5 F 6 C 7 H 8 B 9 J 10 D
11 I 12 E

In the same groups, Ss then tell each other if the sentences are true or false for when they were young. Encourage the other Ss to ask follow-up questions, and put the question frames on the board: *When did you…?, How many times did you…? How often did you…?* etc. Monitor and take notes on the Ss' language for later feedback. Round off the activity by asking Ss to tell you one interesting thing they learnt about their group members.

THE WEEKEND STARTED HERE

Materials: One set of cards per group

Arrange Ss into small groups. Distribute the cards to each group and tell Ss to place them in a pile face down in the middle. Write the following prompts on the board: ___/ have a good weekend? Where / go? Who / with? ___ / have a good time? What / weather like? What / eat? What / drink? How many people / there? What time / get home?

Elicit the full forms of the questions and drill them, but leave only the prompts on the board. Explain that each turn, a student picks up a card, and begins with *'Last weekend I had a great time'*. The other Ss must then use the prompts to ask questions, then guess which of the activities they did. Whoever guesses correctly first, gets to keep the card. The student with the most cards at the end wins.

Unit 7

LOST

Materials: One worksheet per student

Distribute the worksheet and ask Ss to match the names of the compass points to the picture. Check answers, drill the new words, and put them on the board for Ss to refer to.

Answers:

1 North 2 North East 3 East 4 South East 5 South
6 South West 7 West 8 North West

Instruct Ss to work alone, and choose six of the features to draw on their map. Tell them that they only need to be very simple drawings! *Early finishers* can add more features.

Demonstrate the activity with a simple outline of an island on the board. Instruct a couple of Ss to come up and draw a feature on the island, following your instructions (e.g. *There is a city in the North-West, etc.*). Arrange Ss in pairs, and make sure they sit face-to-face, so they can't see each other's pictures (N.B. it's a good idea to rearrange the Ss before you do this, so that they won't have seen their new partner's picture). Go over the following useful language: *There is a city in the South-West. There is a jungle in the North.* drill and write it on the board for Ss to refer to. Ss take it in turns to describe their 'islands' to their partner, who listens and draws it in their notebook or on the back of the worksheet. When they have both finished, they can look at each other's pictures to check. Monitor closely and take notes on their language/pronunciation for later feedback.

MY CAR'S BETTER!

Materials: One set of cards per pair of students

Introduce the activity by asking Ss about common forms of transport in their country/ies, and/or telling them about any unusual forms of transport you've used in the past.

Arrange the Ss into pairs, and give one set of cards to each pair, which they then divide up between them. They must not show their cards to their partner.

Demonstrate the activity with a stronger student. Each turn, a student picks a category and one of their forms of transport to compare. The other student then responds by saying the number of symbols they have. Whoever's number is highest must then form a comparative sentence in order to win both the cards selected (e.g. *The Becak is better for the environment than the Humvee.*). If the numbers are the same, then both Ss keep their cards. The winner is whoever gets all of the cards.

THE LONGEST JOURNEY

Materials: One copy of worksheet A and worksheet B per pair of students

Arrange the class in two groups: Ss A and Ss B. Distribute the worksheets and ask Ss to attempt to answer the questions, working together with other members of the same group.

When all Ss are ready, pair off Ss A and Ss B, and explain the activity. Ss ask each other the questions, then look down their list of facts to give the right answer. To round up, see how many they guessed correctly.

Answers:

Student A: 1 a) 2 c) 3 a) 4 c) 5 b)
Student B: 1 a) 2 c) 3 a) 4 a) 5 c)

At the end, if Ss want to devise some questions of their own, direct them to the Guinness world records online and tell them to look up more travel and transport facts.

AN ENGLISHMAN IN NEW YORK

Materials: One copy of worksheet A and map B per pair of students

Arrange Ss in pairs and distribute the worksheets to Ss A and Ss B. Demonstrate what Ss have to do. Each student reads out the directions below their map, while their partner follows the corresponding route on their map. The written directions are wrong, and while listening, their partner needs to check and correct them. Monitor carefully and take notes for later feedback/correction. When Ss have finished, they can check their answers by comparing maps.

Answers:

1 Take the fourth right, not the second.   2 Take the 3rd right, not the second.   3 It's on the right, not the left.
4 Turn left into 9th Street, not right.   5 Turn right, not left.
6 It's on the left, not right.   7 Go down 1st Avenue, not Lexington Avenue.   8 Take the second left, not the first.

Unit 8

WHAT DO THEY LOOK LIKE?

Materials: One worksheet per student

Distribute one copy of the worksheet to each student. Ask them to find the twelve words using the clues 1–12 and compare with a partner when they have finished. Go through the answers and check pronunciation.

Answers:

1 overweight   2 tall   3 slim   4 short   5 bald
6 curly hair   7 beard   8 moustache   9 make-up
10 in his thirties   11 nice smile   12 big eyes

I	N	H	I	N	F	W	F	H	J	E	E	T	I	E
D	I	N	H	I	S	T	H	I	R	T	I	E	S	S
S	I	D	T	C	E	Y	C	M	I	L	E	S	L	B
R	O	T	E	E	R	F	K	P	A	R	E	H	I	B
S	V	A	E	S	H	O	R	T	T	Q	E	R	M	I
W	E	R	T	M	J	R	S	D	S	E	G	H	W	G
S	R	E	O	I	K	M	E	F	S	E	H	J	F	E
E	W	S	I	L	L	A	E	G	D	R	H	M	W	Y
R	E	B	I	E	L	K	W	J	U	F	S	E	M	E
V	I	M	D	E	D	E	R	T	S	T	E	B	H	S
G	G	W	E	M	O	U	S	T	A	C	H	E	H	E
H	H	R	R	E	G	P	S	E	H	J	S	A	E	G
J	T	A	L	L	T	A	L	K	I	E	S	R	W	T
K	H	A	R	R	I	E	F	R	B	A	L	D	D	D
E	C	U	R	L	Y	H	A	I	R	B	A	L	L	S

Then arrange Ss in pairs or groups of three and tell them to look at part 2. Write the following prompts: *He's got (a beard). She's got (a nice smile). He's (tall and slim). She's a bit (overweight).* on the board and demonstrate the activity by describing someone you know. Monitor Ss carefully and note any common errors/good language use for later feedback and correction. Elicit a few descriptions for feedback, and find out if any of the Ss' descriptions of people were similar.

I'M ON THE PHONE!

Materials: One set of cards per pair of students

Introduce/model the activity by writing on the board: *At a _____, I'm singing 'My Way'. I'm feeling happy. Some people are dancing. My friends are singing, too.* Ask students where they think you are (*At a karaoke bar*).

Put Ss into pairs and give each pair one of the 'situation' cards. Explain that they have to put the verbs into the present continuous, and think of two more sentences to describe what is happening. When they have finished preparing, monitor to check they have formed the present continuous correctly (early finishers can add more sentences). Ss then read their sentences out to other pairs, who guess where they are.

WHAT DO YOU USUALLY DO?

Materials: One card and one chart per student.

Distribute one situation card to each student. If you have more than eight Ss divide the class into two and distribute a set of cards to each group. Instruct Ss to keep their sentences secret, and correct them if necessary so that they are true for the moment.

Distribute a chart to each student, and instruct them to mingle and share their true sentences, then ask follow up questions to find out when they usually do the activities and complete the chart with the information. Elicit a few answers for feedback and find out if any are surprising/unusual.

IT'S RECOMMENDED

Materials: One worksheet per student

Distribute the worksheets and check understanding of the 'film ingredients'. Instruct Ss to work in pairs and think of a film title for each type, preferably a film they've seen and enjoyed. Make sure both Ss in the pair complete their worksheets, as they will need them when they work with a different part later. Don't worry if the Ss don't know the names of the films in English, they can put them in their own language if necessary.

Rearrange the pairs so that Ss are working with different partners. Go through the following useful language: *What kind of films do you like? What can you recommend? What's it about? Where/when is it set? I think you'll like it.* checking understanding and drilling pronunciation. Write it on the board for Ss to refer to. Instruct them to find out what kind of films their partner likes, then recommend two of their titles. Monitor carefully and take notes on their language for later feedback/correction. If they're available, Ss could watch one for homework and tell you about it the following week!

Unit 9

FAST PLANES

Materials: One copy of worksheet A and worksheet B per pair of students

Introduce the topic by writing one of the adjectives on the board and eliciting two types of transport that could be described with it (e.g. *Fast – a train, a plane*).

Arrange Ss in two groups, Ss A and Ss B, and distribute the worksheets. Allow them time to write the names under the categories, working alone. There are no correct answers here as the Ss should be putting their opinions. Monitor and help with vocabulary and spelling.

When Ss have finished, pair off Ss A and Ss B and ask them to compare their adjectives and chosen types of transport, seeing if they agree. Feedback any interesting/overlapping answers.

As an extension, you could ask Ss if their answers are the same when talking about their own cities, or other countries.

THE TRAINS IN SPAIN …

Materials: One copy of the board and a coin per group and one counter per student

To prepare for this, distribute (or ask Ss to find) enough counters for each group, and each group will need a coin. Elicit 'heads' and 'tails'.

Write the sentence up on the board, and elicit the correct answer: *I don't like travelling by a/an/the/- bus.* The correct answer is -. Tell Ss if this is true for you or not, and elicit some of their preferences.

Explain the rules. Each turn a student flips the coin – if it's heads they move their counter forward two squares, and if it's tails they move one. When they land on that square they have to say the sentence with the correct article, and discuss the question. If they land on a 'star' square, they must complete the sentence in whatever way is true for them. Other Ss should listen and say if the sentence is grammatically correct or not. If they are not sure, and you are not available, then they can stay on the square, write the sentence down and check with you at the end.

While they are playing the game, go round and help Ss with sentences they are not sure about. Note down any common errors to work on at the end.

At the end of the activity, invite Ss to write the sentences they weren't sure about on the board, and go through them with the class. N.B. *For stronger classes/groups*, you could ask Ss to give some false sentences and ask other students in the group to guess if they are true or false.

Answers:

1 a   2 –, –   3 a   4 the, the   5 the   6 –   7 –, a   8 –
9 a   10 –   11 –   12 –, –   13 –   14 a   15 a   16 the

LAWS AROUND THE WORLD

Materials: One set of cards per group

Arrange Ss into pairs/small groups and distribute one set of cards per group, placing them in a pile face down in the centre. Write the example prompt on the board: *UK / have to / drive / left.* and elicit the sentence (*In the UK, you have to drive on the left*). Instruct Ss to take it in turns to pick a card and turn it over. The first student in the group to use the pictures and prompts to form a correct sentence wins the card. The student with the most cards at the end wins.

Answers:

1 Illinois, USA, you have to drive using a steering wheel.
2 In New York, USA, you don't have to wear a seatbelt to drive a car.   3 In San Francisco, USA, you can drive a car when you are eight years old.   4 In Brewton, USA, you can drive anyone's car. You don't have to have their permission.   5 In Thailand, you have to wear a shirt when you are driving.   6 In Alaska, USA, you can't look at a moose from a plane.   7 In Alabama, USA, you can't drive a car without wearing shoes.   8 In France, you can't kiss on a railway.   9 In Ontario, Canada, you can't take your friend to the airport in your car. You can only take them to work.   10 In Finland, if you break the law in your car, you have to pay a percentage of your salary.   11 In The Philippines, if your license plate ends with a 1 or 2, you can't drive your car on Monday.   12 In Memphis, Tennessee, a woman can't drive a car without a man walking in front.

When Ss have finished, tell them that two of the laws are not real, and have them turn over all the cards and decide together which two of the laws are false. As an extension, Ss could then discuss laws concerning transport in their own country/countries.

Answers:

The sentences about New York and San Francisco are false. The others are real laws!

WHAT HAPPENED WAS …

Materials: One set of cards per group

Make copies of the worksheet and cut up the cards. Arrange Ss in pairs and distribute one card to each pair, and explain that they are in the police station, having just been caught doing the action on their card. Working together, they must prepare an excuse as to why they were doing the action, in order for them not to be arrested. Refer them to the language in the **Language Bank 9.3** in the **Students' book** if necessary, and the following linkers: *first of all, and, but, so, because, then, after that, finally*

When Ss have their excuses ready, join them with another pair to explain the situation (or they could read them to the class), and vice-versa. For feedback, ask the other pairs if they accept the excuses.

Unit 10

THE BEST PLANS

Materials: One copy of crossword A and crossword B per pair of students

Write ___ *jogging* and ___ *to swim* on the board. Elicit which verbs we use with each one (*go* and *learn*). Arrange Ss into two large groups: Ss A and Ss B, and distribute the worksheets. Instruct Ss to write clues (or prompts if you think clues are too challenging) for the answers they have, working with other people in their group. Go round and check their answers before moving on to stage 2.

Pair off Ss into Ss A and Ss B and make sure they are sitting face-to-face, so that they can't see each other's answers. Ss take it in turns to say their clues (or prompts) for their partner to guess their missing phrases. Monitor and check spelling. When Ss have finished, they can check answers by looking at each other's worksheet.

As an extension, Ss can talk about which of the things they are going to or would like to do.

PLANNING AHEAD

Materials: One worksheet per student

Distribute the worksheets (one per student) and check understanding of the sentences.

Ask Ss to work alone and try to guess a sentence for each student in the class, writing their names next to the sentences (N.B. if you have less than 12 students, they can repeat names). It might be useful to write your Ss' names on the board before they do this (or ask them to).

Instruct Ss to find the people whose names they have written and ask a question to find out if their prediction is true. Model the question forms first with the class. Encourage Ss to ask follow up questions with correct predictions. When they've finished, elicit some correct answers from the class.

Put Ss in small groups to discuss which of the sentences are true for themselves.

THE FUTURE IS OURS TO SEE

Materials: One copy of worksheet A and worksheet B per pair of students

Arrange Ss into A and B pairs. Distribute the worksheets to Ss A and Ss B, and instruct Ss to work alone to complete the gaps in their sentences using *'ll, might* and *won't* to make true predictions.

When Ss have finished, pair them off and explain the activity. Each turn, a student reads out a prediction and asks if it's the same for their partner. Encourage Ss to ask follow-up questions and explain why think the predictions are true. If necessary, write some useful language on the board for doing this (e.g. *Why do you think so? What do you think will happen?* etc.) For feedback, elicit some interesting/surprising answers.

WHAT SHALL WE DO?

Materials: One copy of role cards A and role cards B per pair of students

Arrange Ss in pairs, and distribute the A/B role cards for the first situation, only. Give them time to read through their roles and check understanding. Review the language for making and responding to suggestion in unit 10. When Ss are ready, then can do the role-plays, making suggestions then agreeing on three ideas between them. When they have finished, elicit which ideas they agreed on.

When they are ready, distribute the second set of role cards, so Ss can start the activity again. As each pair finishes, you can then distribute the third and fourth set of role cards. For the fourth role-play, Ss will need time to plan their ideas before they begin.

Unit 11

NAME THAT ILLNESS!

Materials: One set of cards per group

Revise the vocabulary from Unit 11.1 of the **Student's book**. Arrange Ss in small groups and cut up one set of the cards for each group. Place the pile of cards face down in the centre of the group, and explain the rules. Each turn, one person turns over the top card for the rest of the group to see. The first person to name the illness correctly takes the cards. The student with the most cards at the end wins. At the end, check answers to make sure Ss named the pictures correctly.

> **Answers:**
>
> 1 He's got a stomach ache.   2 She's got a runny nose.
> 3 He's got a backache.   4 She's got a headache.   5 She's got a cough.   6 He's got a sore throat.   7 He's got a temperature.   8 He feels better.   9 He feels tired.   10 She's got an earache.   11 His arm hurts.   12 His foot hurts.

SPEED COUNSELLING

Materials: One set of cards per group and one advice form per student

Elicit/Check 'Speed Dating', (It's an event where potential 'couples' have 3 mins to talk to each other before a bell sounds and they have to move to the next person. They fill out a card as they go round, then decide at the end who they would like to meet again.) Explain that Ss are going to do 'Speed Counselling', and have to give each other advice.

Hand out a situations card and advice form to each and ask Ss to write their problems at the top of the form. Tell them they can't show their cards to each other. Model the activity by telling Ss; '*I've got a headache*' and elicit some advice, making sure Ss use *should/shouldn't* in their replies.

Arrange Ss into A and B pairs and tell Ss to explain their problems, give and receive advice, and write the advice they receive next to 'Advice 1'. When you clap your hands, Ss A move to the next student B and repeat the activity. Allow them three minutes with each partner. Monitor and encourage Ss to use *should/shouldn't* when giving advice.

When they have finished, put the Ss into different pairs and get them to share their situations and the advice they received, then together choose the 'best' piece of advice. Elicit some answers round the class.

THE MIME GAME

Materials: One set of verb phrase cards and adjective cards per group

Make one copy of the cards, cut them up and place face down in two piles. Check understanding of the verb phrases and the adjectives, and review how we form adverbs. Put Ss into two teams and explain the rules. Each turn, a student must secretly turn over a verb phrase and an adjective (e.g. *say the number 1–10 quickly*), and mime this action to their group, who must guess both by saying the verb phrase and the correctly formed adverb. Demonstrate with an example. (N.B. if you feel your class need more practice in forming adverbs before they do this, you could ask them to write out the adverbs from the adjectives given first)

Each team receives up to two points for each correct answer, one for guessing the verb phrase, and one for the correctly formed adverb.

LET ME HELP YOU!

Materials: One role card per student

Make one copy of the worksheet and cut up the role cards. Distribute one card to each student and explain that they will explain this situation to other students. (If there's more than eight Ss in the class, divide the class into 2 and distribute a set of role cards per group.) Give them a few minutes to think about how they will do this.

Review the language for offering to help, then ask Ss to stand up and walk around explaining their problems to other Ss, and offering to help. Monitor carefully and take notes on their language for later feedback/correction.

If you are short of preparation time, you could distribute copies of the whole worksheet to pairs, and ask them to discuss what they would say in each situation.

Unit 12

GET ME OUT OF HERE!

Materials: One copy of map A and map B per pair of students

Write up the following useful verbs and prepositions on the board, and elicit possible ways to finish them: *Start at …, Go down…, Go over…, Go though…, Go across…, Go up…, Go into…, Go towards…, Come out of…,.* Leave the completed expressions on the board for Ss to refer to while they do the activity.

Arrange Ss into 'A' and 'B' pairs, make sure they are sitting face-to-face, and distribute the worksheets accordingly. Model the activity by describing a route on the map (not either of the routes *A* or *B*) and asking Ss to tell you where you finish. Draw Ss' attention to the useful language below their map.

Ss describe their route to their partner, who must follow it and draw it on their map. When they have finished, they can look at each other's pictures to check.

Answers:

Route A: Go down the mountain, towards pollution city, over the bridge, towards Nice city.

Route B: Come out of New Town, go across the river, go through 'Happyland', go towards the forest.

Then ask Ss to work on their own and draw two more routes on their map. When they are ready, they can describe these for their partner to draw, as in the first two steps. Monitor and take notes for later feedback.

BEEN THERE, DONE THAT.

Materials: One worksheet per student

Arrange Ss in pairs and distribute one worksheet to each student. Drill and write the following useful language on the board: *Have you ever (eaten a strange animal)? No, I haven't./ Yes, I have. How many times have you (eaten a strange animal)? Once/twice/three times.* for Ss to refer to while they do the activity. Model the questions, and ask Ss to interview each other, ticking the chart according to their partner's answers. (N.B. with weaker groups you may want to give them time to work out the past participles first). Monitor carefully to check Ss are forming the questions correctly.

When Ss have finished, ask them to add up their partner's score and read the summary at the bottom of the page to see if they agree.

As an extension, Ss could devise their own, similar quiz and interview another student and/or talk about which of the things they would like to do.

I'VE DONE IT!

Materials: One set of cards per group.

Arrange Ss in small groups, and distribute one set of cards per group, in a pile face down in the middle. Demonstrate the activity. Each turn, a student picks up a card and tells the rest of the group he/she has done this activity, regardless of whether they actually have or not. The other Ss then ask him/ her questions in the past simple to find out the details. Write up some question words on the board (e.g. *When…? Why …?, Who…with?, etc.*) for Ss to refer to while they do this. Ss then decide if the one with the card is lying or telling the truth. Monitor carefully and take notes on their language use for later correction. For feedback, ask Ss to tell you what they found out about the other group member's experiences, using the 3rd person correctly.

As an extension, Ss could talk about some of the other activities they've experienced, truthfully!

CAN HE CALL ME?

Materials: One set of role-cards per student

Arrange Ss in pairs and distribute the role cards. Explain that they will have four telephone conversations, following the instructions on the cards. For the first two, they need to use the prompts to respond to their partner. With weaker Ss, ask them to write the sentences first. Monitor carefully and take notes on the Ss' language for later feedback/correction. N.B. *Early finishers* could write out one of the dialogues for conversations 3 and 4, then perform it to the class.

TESTS INDEX

LISTENING

1 ▶ 54 Listen and match speakers 1–3 with pictures A–C.

Speakers: 1 ____ 2 ____ 3 ____

A

window

| Shelves | armchair | | sofa |

TV

wardrobe

bed

B

window

| Table | | Plants | |

sofa

wardrobe

bed

TV

C

window

| Shelves | | sofa |

TV

bed | wardrobe

[6]

2 ▶ 55 Listen and complete the notes.

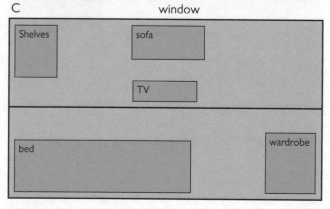

Sydney Bus Tours

Name of Tour:	1 _City Tour_
Starts at:	2 _____
Finishes at:	3 _____
Price per person:	$ 4 _____
Leaves from:	The Park 5 _____

[4]

PRONUNCIATION

3 ▶ 56 Listen and write the words you hear in the correct stress group.

Oo	Ooo
sometimes	_businessman_
oOo	ooO
museum	

[5]

VOCABULARY AND GRAMMAR

4 Add one more word from the box to each group.

~~hall~~ butcher's comb roll above gave
cabbage town hall serious carpet lawyer

1	stairs	kitchen	garage	_hall_
2	wallet	lighter	coins	_____
3	politician	sportsman	nurse	_____
4	rug	lamp	plant	_____
5	baker's	dry-cleaner's	chemist's	_____
6	prawns	lettuce	crisps	_____
7	kind	friendly	funny	_____
8	behind	between	next to	_____
9	health centre	theatre	museum	_____
10	can	packet	cup	_____
11	began	took	was	_____

[5]

5 Complete the sentences with a new form of the words in capitals.

1 She works as a _receptionist_ in a hotel. RECEPTION
2 She went to a very good _____ last week. HAIR
3 You can buy a lot of different things at a _____. NEWS
4 They usually buy their organic vegetables at the _____. GREEN
5 My son sat on the _____ in the bathroom and broke it! BASIN
6 Can you get my glasses, dear? I left them _____ in my bedroom. STAIRS

[5]

6 Complete the sentences with the correct form of the verbs in brackets.

1 Last night we _watched_ TV and _saw_ a film. (see / watch)

2 They usually _____ out and _____ to the cinema on Saturday night. (eat / go)

3 Peter _____ up at 7 and _____ home at 8. (get / leave)

4 Last Sunday I _____ the house and _____ for a walk. (clean / go)

5 I _____ going out with friends and _____ dinner. (love / have)

6 Lisa always _____ clubbing on Friday and _____ late on Saturday morning. (go / sleep)

☐ **5**

7 Write questions and short answers in the present or past tense.

1 you / born / in Scotland ? (–)
Were you born in Scotland?
No, I wasn't.

2 she / buy / any new clothes / yesterday? (+)
_____

_____

3 there / any milk / in the fridge now? (–)
_____

_____

4 you / can / buy / stamps / in the supermarket? (+)
_____

_____

5 he / always / go to bed / late? (–)
_____

_____

6 they / got / any children? (–)
_____

_____

☐ **5**

8 Write questions for the answers.

1 When _were you born?_____
I was born in 1985.

2 Where_____?
My parents were born in Canada.

3 How _____?
She's got two brothers and one sister.

4 When _____?
I saw him last weekend.

5 What time _____?
They start school at 8.45.

6 What _____?
We bought a new sofa.

☐ **5**

9 Underline the correct answer, a), b) or c).

1 There's a good ____ in her bathroom.
a) wardrobe   b) sofa   c) shower

2 They didn't have ____ interesting DVDs.
a) any   b) some   c) the

3 I ____ to my girlfriend three times.
a) saw   b) phoned   c) spoke

4 She doesn't go to work ____ the morning.
a) in   b) on   c) on

5 There isn't ____ rice in the cupboard.
a) many   b) some   c) much

6 I don't like yoghurt ____ I don't eat it.
a) because   b) so   c) some

7 He always parks his car ____ of my house.
a) in front   b) above   c) next

8 We ____ see a film because there isn't a cinema here.
a) can   b) often   c) can't

9 They ____ late because they ran.
a) were   b) weren't   c) wasn't

10 They ____ a lot in the USA on their holiday.
a) travelled   b) eat   c) walks

11 He usually ____ work at 5.30.
a) leaves to   b) leaves the   c) leaves

☐ **10**

10 Complete the second sentence using the information in the first sentence.

1 There aren't any plants in my house.
I haven't _got any plants in my house._

2 She never goes to bed early.
She always _____.

3 We haven't got any cheese.
There _____.

4 My husband works late every night.
Last night _____.

5 This is a very small town.
_____ people here.

6 They always have breakfast in a café.
Yesterday _____.

☐ **5**

11 Complete the text with one word in each gap.

I was ¹ _born_ in Boomtown ² _____ 1980. I loved it when I was a child. We lived in a quiet street and I ³ _____ lots of friends. There weren't many cars so ⁴ _____ played games in front of our house. My ⁵ _____ worked in the town hall and mum was a swimming teacher in the sports ⁶ _____. They didn't drive us ⁷ _____ school or meet us after parties and ⁸ _____ cinema – we always rode our bikes or walked. Now it's a ⁹ _____ different place. Children can't play in the streets or ride ¹⁰ _____ bikes because there ¹¹ _____ too many cars and buses.

`5`

READING

12 Read the article and underline the correct answer, a), b) or c).

Team GB – Olympic heroes

The year 2008 was a very special one for British sportsmen and women. Team GB (Great Britain) won a total of 47 medals at the Beijing Olympic Games: 19 gold, 13 silver and 15 bronze. This was Britain's best performance for one hundred years.

The two most popular heroes of the 2008 team were cyclist Chris Hoy and swimmer Rebecca Adlington. Chris won three gold medals in Beijing and Rebecca won two. Chris was already a world champion cyclist. Born in Edinburgh in 1976, he began cycling after he saw the Steven Spielberg film *E.T.* in 1982. He started winning races in 1999 and won his first Olympic gold medal at the Athens Olympics in 2004.

Rebecca is a new name on the Olympic gold medallist list. Born in 1989, she started swimming at the age of four and swam in her first race when she was ten. Only nine years later, she became world famous in Beijing. She broke the world record in the 800m final, and was the first British swimmer to win two Olympic gold medals since 1908.

When Team GB arrived back in Britain, there was a big welcome parade in London to celebrate their success. There were about 200,000 people in the streets. Then the team went to Buckingham Palace to meet the Queen. They're all now preparing for 2012 – the London Olympic Games. Will they repeat the successes of 2008?

1 Team GB was the Olympic team from _____.
   a) England   b) Beijing   c) Great Britain
2 Team GB won thirteen _____ medals.
   a) gold   b) silver   c) bronze
3 The last time Great Britain got more than 47 medals was in _____.
   a) 1908   b) 1958   c) 1998
4 Chris Hoy won his first Olympic gold medal in _____.
   a) Edinburgh   b) Athens   c) 2008
5 Rebecca broke the world record _____.
   a) in 1908   b) in the 400 metres
   c) when she was nineteen
6 The London Olympic Games are in _____.
   a) two hundred thousand
   b) nineteen hundred and eight
   c) two thousand and twelve

`5`

13 Read the notice and the message. Then complete the information in the notes.

Watermill's Bookshop
Author James Blake talks about his new book *Travels in Tibet.*
Friday 15th June at 7.00pm
Seats limited – please book early.   Price: £5

Helen,
James Blake just called. He's on the train. Can you meet him at the station at 6.30? Please bring him to the bookshop. There's some tea and biscuits for him in the kitchen. See you later.
Thanks,
Jane Watermill

Name of author:	¹ _James Blake_
Meet at:	² _____
Time:	³ _____
Take to:	⁴ _____
Name of book:	⁵ _____
Price of ticket:	⁶ _____

`5`

COMMUNICATION

14 Match sentences 1–6 with responses a)–f).

1 Could I have the roast chicken, please? __d__

2 How much is that black top, please? ____

3 Are you free on July 10th? ____

4 Where do you want to go tonight? ____

5 Would you like to order? ____

6 It isn't big enough. ____

a) It's £9.99.

b) How about a pizza at Mario's?

c) We've got it in large.

d) ~~Yes, of course. Would you like it with vegetables?~~

e) Yes, please. We'd like two beers, please.

f) Why? What do you want to do?

| | 5 |

15 Complete with conversation with the words from the box.

| ~~suit~~ got have small you enough in too that know much |

A: Look Jack. That's a nice ¹ ____suit____

B: I've got a suit!

A: Yes, but it's ² _____ small for you. You need a new one for Danny's wedding.

B: Yeah, you're right. How much is ³ _____ one?

A: I don't ⁴ _____. Ask the assistant.

C: Can I help you, sir?

B: Yes, how ⁵ _____ is that grey suit, please?

C: It's £89.

B: Have you ⁶ _____ it in medium?

C: Hold on. I'll check … Yes, here ⁷ _____ are.

A: That isn't big ⁸ _____.

B: Yes, it's very small. ⁹ _____ you got it ¹⁰ _____ large?

C: Sorry, sir. We've only got it in ¹¹ _____ and medium.

A: Oh, that's a shame.

B: It's OK. We can look again next week.

A: Jack!

| | 10 |

WRITING

16 Write the text again with the correct punctuation.

> my bedroom was my favourite place when i was fourteen i loved reading music and films so there were lots of books cds and dvds on the shelves my favourite stars were brad pitt and robbie williams i watched one of brads films fifty times and listened to robbies music for hours

My bedroom was my favourite place when I was fourteen. I ____

____

____

____

____

____

| | 5 |

17 Write *your* biography. Use the prompts to help you. Write 60–75 words.

Where you were born / live, your family

____

____

____

____

____

Education, work

____

____

____

____

Interests, likes, dislikes

____

____

____

____

Things you are happy about / want to change

____

____

____

____

| | 10 |

| **Total:** | 100 |

LISTENING

1 ▶ 54 Listen and match speakers 1–3 to pictures A–C.

Speakers: 1 ____ 2 ____ 3 ____

A

window

| Shelves | sofa |
| | TV |

bed   wardrobe

B

window

| armchair | sofa |
| | TV |

wardrobe

bed

C

window

| | Plants |
| Table | sofa |

wardrobe

bed

TV

☐ 5

2 ▶ 55 Listen and complete the notes.

Sydney Bus Tours

Name of Tour: ¹ _City Tour_

a.m or p.m: ² _____

Finishes at: ³ _____

Price for two $ ⁴ _____

Leaves from: The ⁵ _____ Hotel

☐ 5

PRONUNCIATION

3 ▶ 56 Listen and write the words you hear in the correct stress group.

Oo	oOo
sometimes	_museum_
Ooo	**ooO**
businessman	

☐ 5

VOCABULARY AND GRAMMAR

4 Add one more word from the box to each group.

~~hall~~ Korean baker's coins tube in front of brought grapes kind accountant hardly ever

1 stairs	kitchen	garage	_hall_
2 behind	above	next to	_____
3 sometimes	often	usually	_____
4 can	roll	cup	_____
5 began	took	were	_____
6 wallet	lighter	comb	_____
7 politician	sportsman	nurse	_____
8 Malaysian	Thai	Vietnamese	_____
9 butcher's	chemist's	dry-cleaner's	_____
10 prawns	lettuce	crisps	_____
11 serious	friendly	funny	_____

☐ 10

5 Complete the sentences with a new form of the words in capitals.

1 She works as a _receptionist_ in a hotel. RECEPTION

2 My mother and grandmother are _____. ACT

3 Can you get my book, dear? I left it _____ in my bedroom. STAIRS

4 She went to a very good _____ last week. HAIR

5 You can buy a lot of different things at a _____. NEWS

6 We usually buy our fruit and vegetables at the _____. SUPER

☐ 5

6 Complete the sentences with the correct form of the verbs in brackets.

1 Last night we _watched_ TV and _saw_ a film. (watch /see)

2 Yesterday she _____ the house and _____ to the gym. (clean / go)

3 We _____ going to the theatre and _____ dinner. (love / have)

4 I often _____ out and _____ to the cinema on Friday night. (eat / go)

5 David _____ up at 8 and _____ work at 9. (get / start)

6 Joe usually _____ late on Sunday because he _____ clubbing on Saturday night. (sleep / go)

[ ] 5

7 Write questions and short answers in the present or past tense.

1 you / born / in Scotland ? (–)
Were you born in Scotland?
No, I wasn't.

2 she / always / go to bed / early? (+)
_____
_____

3 he / got / any brothers? (–)
_____
_____

4 they / often / go / to the gym? (+)
_____
_____

5 there / any vegetables / in the fridge now? (–)
_____
_____

6 you / can / buy / newspapers / in the pharmacy? (–)
_____
_____

[ ] 5

8 Write questions for the answers.

1 When _were you born?_
I was born in 1985.

2 What time _____?
They have dinner at 8.

3 Where _____?
My grandparents were born in Spain.

4 How _____?
He's got a brother and three sisters.

5 When _____?
I saw her last night.

6 What _____?
We bought a new bed.

[ ] 5

9 Underline the correct answer, a), b) or c).

1 There's a good ____ in her bathroom.
  a) wardrobe   b) sofa   c) shower

2 They ____ often late for work.
  a) wasn't   b) weren't   c) was

3 He ____ a lot in the USA.
  a) walk   b) travelled   c) drink

4 I usually ____ work at 5.30.
  a) leave to   b) leave the   c) leave

5 They had ____ really interesting CDs.
  a) any   b) some   c) the

6 She ____ to her mother three times.
  a) speak   b) called   c) spoke

7 He always parks his car ____ of my house.
  a) in front   b) above   c) next

8 You ____ buy a book because there isn't a bookshop here.
  a) can   b) often   c) can't

9 I don't go to work ____ the afternoon.
  a) in   b) on   c) at

10 We haven't got ____ bread here.
  a) many   b) some   c) much

11 We don't eat fish ____ we don't like it.
  a) because   b) so   c) some

[ ] 10

10 Complete the second sentence using the information in the first sentence.

1 There aren't any plants in my house.
I haven't _got any plants in my house._

2 They didn't have any nice shoes in the shop.
There _____ _____.

3 We always have lunch in a café.
Yesterday _____.

4 He never goes to bed early.
He always _____.

5 We haven't got any butter.
There _____.

6 My son works late every night.
Last night _____.

[ ] 5

11 Complete the text with one word in each gap.

I was ¹__born__ in Boomtown in 1980. I loved it when I ²_____ a child. We lived in a quiet street and I had lots ³_____ friends. ⁴_____ weren't many cars so we played games in ⁵_____ of our house. My dad worked in the town hall and mum ⁶_____ a swimming teacher in the sports centre. They ⁷_____ drive us to school or meet us after parties and the cinema – we always ⁸_____ our bikes or walked. Now ⁹_____ is a very different place. Children can't ¹⁰_____ in the streets or ride their bikes ¹¹_____ there are too many cars and buses.

[ ] **10**

READING

12 Read the article and underline the correct answer, a), b) or c).

Team GB – Olympic heroes

he year 2008 was a very special one for British sportsmen and women. Team GB (Great Britain) won a total of 47 medals at the Beijing Olympic Games: 19 gold, 13 silver and 15 bronze. This was Britain's best performance for one hundred years.

The two most popular heroes of the 2008 team were cyclist Chris Hoy, and swimmer Rebecca Adlington. Chris won three gold medals in Beijing and Rebecca won two. Chris was already a world champion cyclist. Born in Edinburgh in 1976, he began cycling after he saw the Steven Spielberg film *E.T.* in 1982. He started winning races in 1999 and won his first Olympic gold medal at the Athens Olympics in 2004.

Rebecca is a new name on the Olympic gold medallist list. Born in 1989, she started swimming at the age of four and swam in her first race when she was ten. Only nine years later, she became world famous in Beijing. She broke the world record in the 800m final, and was the first British swimmer to win two Olympic gold medals since 1908.

When Team GB arrived back in Britain, there was a big welcome parade in London to celebrate their success. There were about 200,000 people in the streets. Then the team went to Buckingham Palace to meet the Queen. They're all now preparing for 2012 – the London Olympic Games. Will they repeat the successes of 2008?

1 Team GB was the Olympic team from ____.
   a) England   b) Beijing   c) Great Britain
2 Team GB won ____ medals in Beijing.
   a) nineteen   b) forty-seven   c) fifteen
3 Chris Hoy won ____ gold medals.
   a) three   b) two   c) one
4 Chris started cycling in ____.
   a) 1976   b) 1999   c) 1982
5 Rebecca broke the world record in ____.
   a) 1908   b) the 800 metres   c) 1999
6 The London Olympic Games are in ____.
   a) nineteen hundred and eight
   b) two thousand and twelve
   c) two hundred thousand

[ ] **5**

13 Read the notice and the message. Then complete the information in the notes.

The Town Library

Author Jennie Blair talks about her new book
Travels around China.
Friday 27ᵗʰ October at 6.30pm
Seats limited – please book early.   Price: £7

Helen,
Jennie Blair just called. She's on the train. Can you meet her at the station at 5.30? Please bring her to the library. There's some tea and biscuits for her in the kitchen.
See you later.
Thanks,
Janet

Name of author:	¹ Jennie Blair
Meet at:	²_____
Time:	³_____
Take to:	⁴_____
Talk begins:	⁵_____
Price of ticket:	⁶_____

[ ] **5**

COMMUNICATION

14 Match sentences 1–6 with responses a)–f).

1 Could I have the roast chicken, please? _b_

2 How was your weekend? ____

3 Can I have some batteries, please?

4 How about meeting in front of the cinema? ____

5 What time does the film start? ____

6 It's too small. ____

a) How many do you want? We've got packs of three or six.

b) ~~Yes, of course. Would you like it with vegetables?~~

c) At 6.30 and 8.45.

d) OK. About 7.15?

e) We've got it in medium.

f) Not bad. And yours?

| 5 |

15 Complete the conversation with the words from the box.

~~suit~~ that help large it that's
small on isn't right much

A: Look Jack. That's a nice ¹___suit.___

B: But I've got a suit!

A: Yes, but it's too ²_____ for you. You need a new one for Danny's wedding.

B: Yeah, you're ³_____. How ⁴_____ is that one?

A: I don't know. Ask the assistant.

C: Can I ⁵_____ you, sir?

B: Yes, how much is ⁶_____ grey suit, please?

C: It's £59.

B: Have you got ⁷_____ in medium?

C: Hold ⁸_____, I'll check …Yes, here you are.

A: That ⁹_____ big enough.

B: Right. It's very small. Have you got it in ¹⁰_____?

C: Sorry, sir. We've only got it in small and medium.

A: Oh,¹¹_____ a shame.

B: It's OK. We can look again next week.

A: Jack!

| 10 |

WRITING

16 Write the text again with the correct punctuation.

> my bedroom was my favourite place when i was fifteen i loved computers music and films so there were lots of computer games cds and dvds on the shelves my favourite stars were julia roberts and annie lennox i watched one of julia's films twenty times and listened to annies music for hours

My bedroom was my favourite place when I was fifteen. I _____

_____

_____

_____

_____

_____

| 5 |

17 Write *your* biography. Use the prompts to help you. Write 60–80 words.

Where you were born / live now, your family

_____

_____

_____

_____

Education, work

_____

_____

_____

Interests, likes, dislikes

_____

_____

_____

Things you are happy about / want to change

_____

_____

_____

| 10 |

| Total: | 100 |

LISTENING

1 ▶ 57 Listen and tick (✓) the correct answer, a), b) or c).

1 What time does Jim leave home?

a) ___   b) ✓   c) ___

2 What will the weather be like tomorrow?

| wet | dry | hot |

a) ___   b) ___   c) ___

3 How did the woman get to Washington?

| by train | by car | by plane |

a) ___   b) ___   c) ___

4 What has the boy got?

| headache | flu | stomach ache |

a) ___   b) ___   c) ___

5 Where can Sheila eat her sandwiches?

| office | staff room | park |

a) ___   b) ___   c) ___

6 What did the man lose?

| wallet | present | credit card |

a) ___   b) ___   c) ___

[ ] **5**

2 ▶ 58 Listen and write true or false next to each sentence.

1 Ben can't go to the theatre tonight. _T_

2 There's been a problem at the office. ___

3 Ben didn't have flu when he got up. ___

4 He took two aspirins because he had a sore throat. ___

5 Ben doesn't want to go home because he's got an important meeting. ___

6 He decides to take some flu medicine and stay at the office. ___

[ ] **5**

PRONUNCIATION

3 ▶ 59 Listen and write the verbs in the correct sound group.

/e/	/æ/
went	sang

/əʊ/	/eɪ/
wrote	paid

[ ] **5**

VOCABULARY AND GRAMMAR

4 Underline the wrong word in each group.

1 tram   <u>slow</u>   ferry   van
2 bank   lake   desert   jungle
3 socks   coat   back   skirt
4 safe   convenient easily   dangerous
5 sci-fi   horror   drama   straight
6 cough   bald   flu   sore throat
7 went   sung   seen   given
8 knee   toe   neck   shirt
9 slim   tall   foot   short
10 healthy   well   badly   quickly
11 excited   nervous   explore   proud

[ ] **10**

5 Circle the correct adverb or adjective.

1 I can't walk _fast_ / slowly. My feet are hurting a lot.

2 Why did she look at you so angrily / angry?

3 He lives opposite us but he's never said hello. He's a really strange / strangely man.

4 You have to be quietly / quiet. Your dad's on the phone.

5 We suddenly / sudden realised we were on the wrong train.

6 I'm feeling terrible / terribly. I have to go bed.

[ ] **5**

6 Complete the sentences with the correct form of the verbs from the box.

> hurt feel go (x5) get (x7) do (x2)
> stay explore fly read travel have

1 My back ___hurts.___ and I ___feel.___ sick.

2 He should _____ a course and _____ a job.

3 She'd like to _____ married and _____ four children.

4 John can't _____ swimming. He has to _____ in tonight.

5 Why don't you _____ to the clothes shop and _____ a new suit?

6 Let's _____ for a walk and _____ some shopping.

7 I've always wanted to _____ abroad and _____ new places.

8 We have to _____ off the bus here and _____ on a number 19.

9 We're going to _____ to China by train and then _____ back.

10 They can't _____ on safari alone. They'll _____ lost.

11 I'm _____ a book about climate change. I _____ it for £4 in the bookshop.

[10]

7 Complete the second sentence using the information in the first sentence.

1 It isn't a good idea to go out because it's too cold.
You _shouldn't go out because it's too cold._

2 It's 1.30, so she's having lunch.
_____ every day at 1.30.

3 The Trattoria is more expensive than Pizza House.
Pizza House _____.

4 I'd like to buy a new car. I'm not sure.
I might _____.

5 Mark's got a bad cold – he has to stay at home today.
_____ go to work today.

6 She doesn't have to get up early today.
_____ get up late today.

[5]

8 Underline the correct alternative.

1 I see / _saw_ / 've seen him at work yesterday.

2 We have to run or we _'ll_ / won't / can be late.

3 It was the good / worse / worst book I've ever read.

4 You can't / have to / shouldn't buy stamps in a pharmacy.

5 What are they do / doing / done?

6 You _'ll_ / have / can to wait here for the bus.

[5]

9 Underline the correct answer, a), b) or c).

1 We don't ___ eat out on Tuesday.
   a) easily   b) early   c) usually

2 This is the ___ city in the world.
   a) noisier   b) noisiest   c) more noisy

3 I'd like ___ bigger house.
   a) a   b) the   c) –

4 You ___ park here. It's for taxis.
   a) can't   b) can   c) should

5 ___ President has arrived at the airport.
   a) –   b) A   c) The

6 We ___ never win the lottery.
   a) will   b) won't   c) can't

7 I'm going to take my driving test ___ month.
   a) the next   b) next   c) last

8 He turned and walked ___ from me.
   a) across   b) away   c) towards

9 ___ we said goodbye and drove away.
   a) As well   b) Because   c) Finally

10 The bookshop in town sells ___ very interesting books.
   a) some   b) a   c) the

11 You ___ take the underground. It'll be quicker than a taxi.
   a) might   b) should   c) shouldn't

[10]

10 Complete the email with ONE word in each gap.

> Hi folks!
> We__'ve__ had a fantastic time in China. We've
> ² _____ to Beijing, seen the Great Wall and swum
> in ³ _____ Yangtze river. Now we're in Shanghai.
> We arrived late ⁴ _____ night after a sixteen-hour
> train journey! I feel really tired ⁵ _____ morning
> so I'm not going to do much – but Josh never stops!
> He's out taking photos of ⁶ _____ city. I can see
> it through my hotel window – it's amazingly modern
> ⁷ _____ beautiful. I might go and look around this
> evening. The temperature is 30°C ⁸ _____ the
> moment but it
> ⁹ _____ be hotter this afternoon. We're going to
> stay here for 2 days. Then we're flying to Hong Kong,
> and after ¹⁰ _____ we'll be in Singapore, our last
> stop. I hear you can do some very cheap shopping in
> these places so I'll ¹¹ _____ to be a careful! See
> you next week.
>
> Jess xx

[10]

11 Read the article and match sentences a)–f) with gaps 1–6.

Three things to do before you leave the planet!

① Visit Tuvalu

Tuvalu in the Pacific Ocean is the fourth-smallest country in the world. ¹*Sadly, it's also only 4 metres above sea level at its highest.* Because of the rise in sea levels, Tuvalu might be the first country to disappear under the waves. The islands are a paradise of beautiful tropical beaches and palm trees. ²_____ Take a plane from Fiji, stay in one of Tuvalu's four guest houses and have a drink in its one bar. Go now, before it dies.

② See the world's largest flower

Go to the jungles of Borneo or Sumatra and find the world's strangest plant, *Rafflesia*. For most of its life, the plant is invisible and hard to find. ³_____. It grows into the world's largest flower. And it smells terrible! ⁴_____. However, it only lasts a few days. You'll be lucky you saw one.

③ Find happiness

Why do some people live perfectly happy lives while others find life hard? The answer might be in our genes – some people are born happy. Lucky them, I hear you say! ⁵_____. Help other people, have lots of friends, change your job. ⁶_____ It's the only European country where people are happier than they were 30 years ago. Why? Go and find out!

a) It can be one metre across and weigh 10 kilos.

b) Why don't you go there before they disappear?

c) Or move to Denmark.

d) ~~Sadly, it's also only 4 metres above sea level at its highest.~~

e) Don't worry, there's still a lot you can do.

f) But if you do find it, you'll see something amazing.

[ ] | **5**

12 Read the article again. Tick (✓) the true sentences and cross (✗) the false ones.

1 Tuvalu is a country of islands. _✓._

2 There are lots of places where you can have a beer or a cola. ____

3 Rafflesia grows in dry places. ____

4 It isn't very easy to find. ____

5 You can't learn how to be happy. ____

6 People in Denmark were sadder thirty years ago. ____

[ ] | **5**

13 Match sentences 1–6 to six notices from A–H.

1 Children can swim for £1.50. _D._

2 It's cheaper to buy a shirt today. ____

3 You can't take your bags with you. ____

4 You don't have to pay for lunch for your five-year old son in the afternoons. ____

5 You have to stop here. ____

6 You aren't a doctor. You shouldn't park here. ____

A
**Lunch served
12.00 – 2.00**

B
Danger!
Do not swim here.

C
Parking
– Doctors only

D
Swimming Pool
Open evenings
Adults - £3.00
Children - £1.50

E
Stop!
Train crossing

F
**£5 each shirt.
ONE DAY ONLY**

G
**Please leave
bags at the
desk**

H
**Children under six eat free
2–6 p.m.**

[ ] | **5**

COMMUNICATION

14 Match sentences 1–11 with responses a)–f).

1 Can you tell me the way to the town hall, please? _d._
2 Let me open the jar for you. ____
3 I'm afraid I forgot to bring it. ____
4 Do you think I'd like this DVD? ____
5 Why don't we go to the zoo? ____
6 Can you ask him to call me? ____

a) That doesn't sound very interesting.
b) Of course, sir. What's your number?
c) No, I don't think it's your kind of film.
d) ~~Yes, straight on and second left.~~
e) Don't worry about it. Bring it tomorrow.
f) That's very kind of you.

5

15 Complete the conversation with the phrases from the box.

> ~~what about~~ who's it about they'll let's see
> what time's feel like do you think want to
> there's a should be

Woman: [1]_What about_ seeing a film tonight?
Man: Good idea. What do you [2]_____ see?
Woman: I don't know. What's on?
Man: [3]_____ brilliant new comedy with Mr Bean.
Woman: No thanks. I don't [4]_____ seeing him.
Man: How about the new Coen brothers' film?
Woman: What's [5]_____?
Man: It's a black comedy like all their films. It [6]_____ good.
Woman: [7]_____ in it?
Man: George Clooney and Brad Pitt.
Woman: Really? [8]_____ that then! [9]_____ it on?
Man: Hold on. I'll check on the computer.
Woman: [10]_____ we should phone and book tickets?
Man: Don't worry. [11]_____ have lots …

10

WRITING

16 Delete one mistake in lines 1–11 and write the correction in the right hand column.

1	One of the ~~most good~~ films	_best._
2	I've ever saw is *Fargo* by	_____
	the Coen brothers, Ethan	
3	and joel. It came out in 1996	_____
4	and was a big sucess.	_____
	Frances McDormand played	
5	the police officer in a film	_____
	and won the Oscar for Best	
6	Actress. She's married with	_____
7	Joel in real life and is made	_____
	six films with her husband.	
8	The Coens' more	_____
	successful film was *No Country*	
	for Old Men with	
9	the spanish actor Javier	_____
10	Bardem. It come out in 2007	_____
11	and wins four Oscars.	_____

10

17 Write a story beginning or ending with: *I'll never go there again.* Write 60–80 words.

_____
_____
_____
_____
_____
_____
_____
_____
_____
_____
_____

10

Total: **100**

LISTENING

1 ▶ 57 Listen and tick (✓) the correct answer, a), b) or c).

1 What time does Jim leave home?

9.15	8.15	7.00
a) ___	b) ✓.	c) ___

2 What would the man like to have this weekend?

picnic	barbecue	lunch
a) ___	b) ___	c) ___

3 How did the woman get to Florida?

by train	by plane	by car
a) ___	b) ___	c) ___

4 Where should the boy stay?

in bed	at work	at school
a) ___	b) ___	c) ___

5 Where's the coffee machine?

office	park	staff room
a) ___	b) ___	c) ___

6 How late was the man this morning?

14 minutes	an hour	40 minutes
a) ___	b) ___	c) ___

	5

2 ▶ 58 Listen and write true (T) or false (F) next to each sentence.

1 Ben can't go to the theatre tonight. _T_

2 Ben hasn't got a problem at work. ___

3 He started feeling ill in the car. ___

4 He doesn't have to go to the meeting. ___

5 Maggie thinks everybody in the office might get flu. ___

6 He's going to buy some flu medicine on his way home.

___

	5

PRONUNCIATION

3 ▶ 59 Listen and write the verbs in the correct sound group.

/e/	/eɪ/
went	paid
/æ/	/əʊ/
sang	wrote

	5

VOCABULARY AND GRAMMAR

4 Underline the wrong word in each group.

1	tram	slow	ferry	van
2	swum	been	saw	driven
3	knee	face	finger	shorts
4	tall	toe	short	bald
5	noisy	fast	well	easily
6	embarrassed	afraid	nervous	throat
7	bookshop	desert	lake	jungle
8	top	feet	coat	tie
9	comfortable	green	slowly	polluting
10	comedy	curly	horror	drama
11	straight	headache	flu	sore throat

	10

5 Circle the correct adverb or adjective.

1 I can't walk _fast_ / _slowly_. My feet are hurting a lot.

2 They _suddenly_ / _sudden_ realised they were at the wrong cinema.

3 She's feeling _terrible_ / _terribly_. She should see a doctor.

4 Why is he looking at you _angrily_ / _angry_?

5 She's a really _strange_ / _strangely_ woman. She never says hello.

6 Please talk _quietly_ / _quiet_. The baby's sleeping.

	5

6 Complete the sentences with the correct form of the verbs from the box.

~~hurt~~ *feel* go (x6) get (x7) do (x2)
stay explore fly read have come

1 My back ___*hurts.*___ and I ___*feel.*___ sick.
2 Let's _____ to the gym and _____ some exercise.
3 I've always wanted to _____ abroad and _____ new places.
4 You should _____ off the train here and _____ to platform 5.
5 We're going to _____ to Turkey and then _____ back by bus.
6 You can't _____ on safari alone. You'll _____ lost.
7 I'm _____ a book about the life of Henry VIII. I _____ it for my birthday.
8 She should _____ a course and _____ a better job.
9 They'd like to _____ married and _____ five children.
10 Joanna can't _____ running. She has to _____ in tonight.
11 Why don't you _____ to the shoe shop and _____ some new boots?

[ ] 10

7 Complete the second sentence using the information in the first sentence.

1 It isn't a good idea to go out – it's too cold.
   You *shouldn't go out because it's too cold.*
2 I want to buy a new car but I'm not sure.
   I might _____.
3 Greta's got a bad cold so she can't go to work today.
   _____ stay at home today.
4 He doesn't have to leave now.
   _____ leave later.
5 It's 10.30 so she's making coffee.
   _____ every day at 10.30.
6 The Trattoria is cheaper than the Pizza House.
   The Pizza House _____.

[ ] 5

8 Underline the correct alternative.

1 I *see* / *saw* / *'ve seen* him at work yesterday.
2 Where are you *go* / *going* / *gone*?
3 It's late. We *'ll* / *have* / *can* to go now.
4 Take an umbrella or you *'ll* / *won't* / *should* get wet.
5 It was the *good* / *worse* / *best* film I've ever seen.
6 You *can't* / *have to* / *should* buy stamps in a pharmacy.

[ ] 5

9 Underline the correct answer, a), b) or c).

1 We don't ____ eat out on Tuesday.
   a) easily   b) early   c) usually
2 I turned round and walked ____ from her.
   a) across   b) towards   c) away
3 ____ we said goodbye and drove away.
   a) Finally   b) As well   c) Because
4 The clothes shop in town sells ____ very cheap trousers.
   a) a   b) the   c) –
5 You ____ take a taxi. It'll be quicker to walk.
   a) might   b) shouldn't   c) should
6 This is the ____ city in the world.
   a) greater   b) greatest   c) more great
7 She'd like ____ bigger garden.
   a) a   b) the   c) –
8 You ____ park here. It's free.
   a) can't   b) can   c) shouldn't
9 ____ President has arrived in the USA.
   a) –   b) A   c) The
10 We ____ never be rich.
   a) 'll   b) won't   c) can't
11 I'm going to get married ____ year.
   a) next   b) the next   c) last

[ ] 10

10 Complete the email with ONE word in each gap.

Hi folks!

We ___*'ve*___ had a fantastic time in China. We've been to Beijing, seen [2]_____ Great Wall and swum in the Yangtze river. Now we're [3]_____ Shanghai. We arrived late last night after a sixteen–hour train journey! I feel really [4]_____ this morning so I'm [5]_____ going to do much – but Josh never stops! He's out taking photos of the city. I can [6]_____ it through my hotel window – it's amazingly modern and beautiful. I might go and look around [7]_____ evening. The temperature is 30°C at [8]_____ moment but it'll be hotter this afternoon. We're [9]_____ to stay here for 2 days. Then we're flying to Hong Kong, and [10]_____ that we'll be in Singapore. I hear you can do some very cheap shopping in these places, so I'll have to be careful! See you [11]_____ week.

Jess xx

[ ] 10

11 Read the article and match sentences a)–f) with gaps 1–6.

Three things to do before you leave the planet!

⊡ Visit Tuvalu

Tuvalu in the Pacific Ocean is the fourth-smallest country in the world. ¹*Sadly, it's also only 4 metres above sea level at its highest.* Because of the rise in sea levels, Tuvalu might be the first country to disappear under the waves. The islands are a paradise of beautiful tropical beaches and palm trees. ²_____ Take a plane from Fiji, stay in one of Tuvalu's four guest houses and have a drink in its one bar. Go now, before it dies.

⊡ See the world's largest flower

Go to the jungles of Borneo or Sumatra and find the world's strangest plant, *Rafflesia*. For most of its life, the plant is invisible and hard to find. ³_____. It grows into the world's largest flower. And it smells terrible! ⁴_____ _____. However, it only lasts a few days. You'll be lucky you saw one.

⊡ Find happiness

Why do some people live perfectly happy lives while others find life hard? The answer might be in our genes – some people are born happy. Lucky them, I hear you say! ⁵_____. Help other people, have lots of friends, change your job. ⁶_____ It's the only European country where people are happier than they were 30 years ago. Why? Go and find out!

a) ~~Sadly, it's also only 4 metres above sea level at its highest.~~
b) Don't worry, there's still a lot you can do.
c) It can be one metre across and weigh 10 kilos.
d) Or move to Denmark.
e) But if you do find it, you'll see something amazing.
f) Why don't you go there before they disappear?

| | 5 |

12 Read the article again. Tick (✓) the true sentences and cross (✗) the false ones.

1 Tuvalu is a country of islands. ✓.
2 There aren't many places where you can sleep. ____
3 Rafflesia grows in hot, wet places. ____
4 It's a very small plant. ____
5 You can learn how to be happy. ____
6 People in Denmark were happier thirty years ago. ____

| | 5 |

13 Match sentences 1–6 to six notices from A–H.

1 Children can swim here for £1.50. _e_
2 You have to stop here. ____
3 You're a nurse. You shouldn't park here. ____
4 It'll more expensive to buy a skirt next week.
5 You can't swim here. ____
6 You don't have to pay for your five-year old son's food in the evenings. ____

A
Lunch served
12.00 – 2.00

B
Please leave bags at the desk

C
Stop!
Train crossing

D
Skirts & tops £5
THIS WEEK ONLY

E
Swimming Pool
Open evenings
Adults - £3.00
Children - £1.50

F
Children under six eat free after 7 p.m.

G

Parking
– Doctors only

H
Danger!
Do not swim here.

| | 5 |

COMMUNICATION

14 Match sentences 1–11 with responses a)–f).

1 Can you tell me the way to the town hall, please? _b_
2 Let me open the jar for you.   ____
3 I'm afraid I forgot to bring it.   ____
4 Do you think I'd like this DVD?   ____
5 Why don't we go to the zoo?   ____
6 Can you ask him to call me?   ____

a) No, I don't think it's your kind of film.
b) ~~Yes, straight on and second left.~~
c) Don't worry about it. Bring it tomorrow.
d) That's very kind of you.
e) That doesn't sound very interesting.
f) Of course, sir. What's your number?

[ ] **5**

15 Complete the conversation with the phrases from the box.

> ~~what about~~   we should   it on   what's   in it   I'll check
> don't worry   good idea   what's on   seeing that
> how about

Woman: ¹_What about_____ seeing a film tonight?
Man: ²_____. What do you want to see?
Woman: I don't know. ³_____?
Man: There's a brilliant new comedy with Mr Bean.
Woman: No thanks. I don't feel like ⁴_____.
Man: Well, ⁵_____ the new Coen brothers' film?
Woman: ⁶_____ it about?
Man: It's a black comedy, like all their films. It should be good.
Woman: Who's ⁷_____?
Man: George Clooney and Brad Pitt.
Woman: Really? Let's see that then! What time's ⁸_____?
Man: Hold on. ⁹_____ on the computer.
Woman: Do you think ¹⁰_____ phone and book tickets?
Man: ¹¹_____. They'll have lots …

[ ] **10**

WRITING

16 Delete one mistake in lines 1–11 and write the correction in the right hand column.

1	One of the ~~most good~~ films I	_best._
2	has ever seen is *Fargo* by	_____
3	the Coen brothers, ethan	_____
	and Joel. It came out in	
4	1996 and was the big	_____
5	sucess. Frances	_____
	McDormand played the	
6	police officer on the film	_____
7	and has won the Oscar for	_____
	Best Actress. She's married	
	to Joel in real life and has	
8	made six films of her	_____
9	husband. The Coens' more	_____
	successful film was *No*	
	Country for Old Men with	
10	the Spanish Actor Javier	_____
11	Bardem. It came out on	_____
	2007 and won four Oscars.	

[ ] **10**

17 Write a story beginning or ending with: *I'll never go there again.* Write 60–80 words.

| Total: | 100 |

219

Mid-course Test A

LISTENING

1

Audioscript

1

A: My flat's not bad, I suppose. It's quite cheap – and near the train station – so I can get to work in about 30 minutes. That's really good for London. It's only got one bedroom – but the living room's quite big and it gets a lot of light from the large window. I haven't got much there – a sofa, a table, some plants next to the window … I put my TV in the bedroom. I love watching TV in bed – it helps me sleep.

2

B: I don't like my flat very much. It's not very big – but flats with two bedrooms are too expensive in this area. I work in a restaurant in the day – and study at night – so I haven't got much money. And I haven't got much furniture either. Some friends gave me their old bed and wardrobe – that's in the bedroom. In the living room, there's an old sofa under the window – and a TV I had when I was 14. My mum bought me some shelves for my music equipment and CDs – that's what I love most – listening to music.

3

C: I love my flat! It isn't very big but it's really comfortable. The kitchen and bathroom are fine – at least everything works! The kitchen's a bit on the small side but I don't like cooking very much– so it's big enough for me. We – my husband Freddy and I – like watching DVDs so we've got a big sofa and an even bigger TV! The TV's on the right, by the window and there's an armchair on the left. I sit on the sofa!

1 B   2 C   3 A

2

Audioscript

A=Wife   B=Husband   C=Travel agent

A: So what do you think? A City tour? The Sydney Opera House?

B: Oh, a City tour I think. It's a lovely day for sightseeing – and we can see a lot of places in a short time.

A: Yes, we've only got four days in Sydney so we can see all the main places from the bus today– and if we want to see them again, we can go back tomorrow!

B: Exactly honey … Come on – let's buy the tickets.

A: OK, you just go ahead.

B: Hi there! We'd like to take the City Tour, please.

C: Yes, sir. Do you want the morning or afternoon tour?

B: What do you think?

A: Well, it's 9.15 now. (to the assistant) What time does the morning tour start?

C: At 9.30 ma'am.

A: Oh, perfect! So we can go now!

B: And what time does it finish?

C: The bus gets back here at quarter to one. Or you can take the full day tour with lunch included.

B: How much is that?

C: It's $150 dollars per person.

B: $150?? So that's $300 for two. Umm, no, I think we'll take the morning tour thanks.

C: Right sir. Two tickets? That's $150 dollars.

B: Excuse me? 150? But …

C: That's for two people, sir. £75 dollars each.

B: Oh…do you take credit cards?

C: Of course, sir.

B: Here you are.

A: And where do we get the bus?

C: Over there ma'am. In front of the hotel.

A: Which hotel?

C: The Park Hotel, ma'am. Look, it's over there.

A: Oh yes! I see it …

2   nine thirty / 9.30
3   twelve forty-five / 12.45
4   $75 / seventy-five dollars   5 Hotel

PRONUNCIATION

3

Oo listened, chicken, headphones
Ooo vegetables, foreigner,
oOo bananas, assistant, umbrella
ooO souvenir, Japanese

VOCABULARY AND GRAMMAR

4

2   comb   3 lawyer   4 carpet
5   butcher's   6 cabbage   7 serious
8   above   9 town hall   10 roll   11 gave

5

2   hairdresser / 's   3 newsagent's
4   greengrocer's   5 washbasin   6 upstairs

6

2   eat, go   3 got, left   4 cleaned, went
5   love, having   6 goes, sleeps

7

2   Did she buy any new clothes yesterday?
      Yes, she did.
3   Is there any milk in the fridge now? No, there isn't.
4   Can you buy stamps in the supermarket?
      Yes, you can.
5   Does he always go to bed late? No, he doesn't.
6   Have they got any children? No, they haven't.

8

2   were your parents born
3   many brothers and sisters has she got
4   did you see him   5 do they start school
6   did you buy

9

2 a   3 c   4 a   5 c   6 b   7 a   8 c
9 b   10 a   11 c

10

2   goes to bed late   3 isn't any cheese
4   my husband worked late
5   There aren't many
6   they had breakfast in a café

11

2   in   3 had   4 we   5 dad   6 centre
7   to   8 the   9 very   10 their   11 are

READING

12

2 b   3 a   4 b   5 c   6 c

13

2   the station   3 6.30   4 the bookshop
5   Travels in Tibet   6 £5

COMMUNICATION

14

2 a   3 f   4 b   5 e   6 c

15

2   too   3 that   4 know   5 much   6 got
7   you   8 enough   9 Have   10 in
11   small

WRITING

16

My bedroom was my favourite place when I was fourteen. I loved reading, music and films so there were lots of books, CDs and DVDs on the shelves. My favourite stars were Brad Pitt and Robbie Williams. I watched one of Brad's films fifty times and listened to Robbie's music for hours.

17 (sample answer)

I was born in São Paulo, Brazil in 1990. My mum's from Sao Paulo but my dad's from Rio de Janeiro. I've got one brother called Guillerme – he's 17.

I went to school in São Paulo but when I was 18 we moved to Brasilia. Now I go to university here. I want to be a lawyer.

I don't have much free time but I enjoy playing football at the weekend.

I'm very happy with my life but want to live in Rio when I finish university.

Mid-course Test B

LISTENING

1

Audioscript

See test A.
1 C 2 A 3 B

2

Audioscript

See test A.
2 a.m / morning 3 twelve forty-five / 12.45
4 $150 / one hundred and fifty dollars
5 Park

PRONUNCIATION

3

Oo listened, chicken, headphones
oOo bananas, assistant, umbrella
Ooo vegetables, foreigner
ooO souvenir, Japanese

VOCABULARY AND GRAMMAR

4

2 in front of 3 hardly ever 4 tube
5 brought 6 coins 7 accountant
8 Korean 9 baker's 10 grapes 11 kind

5

2 actresses 3 upstairs.
4 hairdresser / 's. 5 newsagent's
6 supermarket

6

2 cleaned, went 3 love, having
4 eat, go 5 gets, starts 6 sleeps, goes

7

2 Does she always go to bed early? Yes, she does.
3 Has he got any brothers? No, he hasn't.
4 Do they often go to the gym? Yes, they do.
5 Are there any vegetables in the fridge now? No, there aren't.
6 Can you buy newspapers in the pharmacy? No, you can't.

8

2 do they have dinner
3 were your grandparents born
4 many brothers and sisters has he got
5 did you see her 6 did you buy

9

2 b 3 b 4 c 5 b 6 c 7 a 8 c
9 a 10 c 11 a

10

2 weren't any nice shoes in the shop.
3 we had lunch in a café.
4 goes to bed late. 5 isn't any butter.
6 my son worked late.

11

2 was 3 of 4 There 5 front 6 was
7 didn't 8 rode 9 it /Boomtown
10 play 11 because

READING

12

2 b 3 a 4 c 5 b 6 b

13

2 the station 3 5.30 / half past five
4 the library 5 6.30 / half past six
6 £7 / seven pounds

COMMUNICATION

14

2 f 3 a 4 d 5 c 6 e

15

2 small 3 right 4 much 5 help
6 that 7 it 8 on 9 isn't 10 large
11 that's

WRITING

16

My bedroom was my favourite place when I was fifteen. I loved computers, music and films so there were lots of computer games, CDs and DVDs on the shelves. My favourite stars were Julia Roberts and Annie Lennox. I watched one of Julia's films twenty times and listened to Annie's music for hours.

17

See sample answer in Test A.

End of Course Test A

LISTENING

1

Audioscript

1

A: Do you get up early, Jim?

B: Yes, at half past seven. Then I have a cup of coffee and a quick shower.

A: What time do you start work?

B: At quarter past nine. I leave home at about eight fifteen.

2

A: What are you going to do this weekend, Steve?

B: I'm not sure. My brother's going to come for the weekend. I haven't seen him for ages.

A: It'll be good to see him then.

B: Yes. We might have a barbecue in the garden tomorrow.

A: Mmm, I don't think so. The weather forecast says it'll rain this weekend…and it won't be very warm!

B: Oh no! Typical! Oh well, we can go out for lunch then…

3

A: Hi Fiona! How was your holiday?

B: Oh, fantastic!

A: Where did you go finally?

B: Well, we flew to New York first and stayed there for three days.

A: How marvellous! I love New York!

B: Me, too! Then we took a train to Washington.

A: How long did you stay there?

B: Three days. Then we rented a car and drove down to Florida. It was wonderful. We got back last night.

4

A: Mum, I can't go to school today.

B: Why? What's wrong?

A: I feel terrible. My back hurts and I've got stomach ache.

B: Have you eaten any strange food?

A: No, I don't think so. I had dinner with you and dad last night – we ate the same things.

B: All right. You should stay in bed and I'll call the doctor.

A: OK Mum, thanks.

5

A: It's lunch-time, Sheila. Shall I show you where the staff restaurant is?

B: Oh no, no thanks Mr James. I've brought some sandwiches. I'll eat at my desk.

A: Oh sorry Sheila. I'm afraid you can't eat in the office – company rules, you know.

B: Oh, really? Oh, well then…um, do I have to go out and eat in the park?

A: Oh, no, nothing like that! Anyway, it's raining! No, you can eat in the staff room.

B: Is there a coffee machine there?

A: Yes – and a fridge! Let me show you …

6

A: Hello, my dear. How was your day?

B: Not bad. But you don't look very happy.

A: No, I've had the most awful day.

B: Why? Did you have problems at the office?

A: No, nothing like that. No, first of all it was the morning train…

B: Was it late?

A: No, it broke down – so I was forty minutes late for work!

B: Oh dear, those trains are too much.

A: And then … I went out to buy you a birthday present … but when I looked in my wallet, my credit card wasn't there! I lost it!

B: Oh no! That's terrible. Come on, let's have a cup of tea, or would you prefer something else…

2 a 3 a 4 c 5 b 6 c

2

Audioscript

A=Ben B=Maggie

A: Hi Maggie – it's Ben.

B: Oh hi, Ben. What's up?

A: I'm sorry Maggie but I don't think I can go to the theatre tonight.

B: Why? Is there a problem at work? You don't sound too good.

A: No, works fine. But I think I might have flu.

B: Flu? Oh no! But you were fine this morning.

A: Yes, I felt OK when I got up. But I started to feel strange on the bus on the way to work. I think I've got a temperature now.

B: Oh dear. Have you got a sore throat?

A: No, but I've got a terrible headache. I took two aspirins an hour ago but it hasn't helped.

B: Do your arms and legs hurt?

A: Yes, my whole body hurts!

B: Right. You have to come home immediately.

A: I can't! We're going to have a very important meeting in 10 minutes. I can't miss it!

B: Oh come on, Ben. Yes, you can. You'll give flu to everybody at the office if you stay at work!

A: Yes, I suppose you're right Maggie. I should come home and go to bed.

B: Exactly. That's the best thing to do. I'll go to the chemist's on my way home and get you some flu medicine.

A: Thanks a lot Maggie. I'll see you later.

2 F 3 T 4 F 5 T 6 F

PRONUNCIATION

3

/e/ met, read, /a/ sat, had, swam,

/ow/ spoke, flown

/ei/ made, played, gave

VOCABULARY AND GRAMMAR

4

2 bank 3 back 4 easily 5 straight
6 bald 7 went 8 shirt 9 foot
10 healthy 11 explore

5

2 angrily 3 strange 4 quiet
5 suddenly 6 terrible

6

2 do / get 3 get / have 4 go / stay
5 go / get 6 go / do 7 go / explore
8 get / get 9 travel / fly 10 go / get
11 reading / got

7

2 She has lunch
3 is cheaper than the Trattoria
4 buy a new car 5 Mark can't
6 She can

8

2 'll 3 worst 4 can't 5 doing
6 have

9

2 b 3 a 4 a 5 c 6 a 7 b 8 b
9 c 10 a 11 b

10

2 been 3 the 4 last 5 this 6 the
7 and 8 at 9 will 10 that 11 have

READING

11

2 b 3 f 4 a 5 e 6 c

12

2 ✗ 3 ✗ 4 ✓ 5 ✗ 6 ✓

13

2 F 3 G 4 H 5 E 6 C

COMMUNICATION

14

2 f 3 e 4 c 5 a 6 b

15

2 want to 3 There's a 4 feel like
5 it about 6 should be 7 Who's
8 Let's see 9 What time's
10 Do you think 11 They'll

WRITING

16

2 seen 3 Joel 4 success 5 the 6 to
7 has 8 most 9 Spanish 10 came
11 won

17 *(sample answer)*

Last summer I went to Wales on holiday with a couple of friends. We wanted to go walking in the mountains. We booked a room in a small hotel and arrived there on Saturday. The sun was shining and it was quite hot.

We didn't see the sun again. It started raining on Saturday night and didn't stop – it rained and rained. We played cards but we were very bored. Finally, we decided to leave Wales and go home early. *I'll never go there again.*

End of Course Test B

LISTENING

1

Audioscript

See test A.

2 b 3 c 4 a 5 c 6 c

2

Audioscript

See test A.

2 T 3 F 4 F 5 T 6 F

PRONUNCIATION

3

/e/: met, read; /eɪ/: made, played, gave;

/æ/: sat, had, swam; /əʊ/; spoke, flown

VOCABULARY AND GRAMMAR

4

2 saw 3 shorts 4 toe 5 noisy
6 throat 7 bookshop 8 feet 9 slowly
10 curly 11 straight

5

2 suddenly 3 terrible 4 angrily
5 strange 6 quietly

6

2 go / do 3 go / explore 4 get / go
5 fly / come 6 go / get 7 reading / got
8 do / get 9 get / have 10 go / stay
11 go / get

7

2 buy a new car 3 Greta has to
4 He can 5 She makes coffee
6 is more expensive than the Trattoria

8

2 going 3 have 4 'll 5 best 6 can't

9

2 c 3 a 4 c 5 b 6 b 7 a 8 b
9 c 10 a 11 b

10

2 the 3 in 4 tired 5 not 6 see
7 this 8 the 9 going 10 after
11 next

READING

11

2 f 3 e 4 c 5 b 6 d

12

2 ✓ 3 ✓ 4 ✗ 5 ✓ 6 ✗

13

2 C 3 G 4 D 5 H 6 F

COMMUNICATION

14

2 d 3 c 4 a 5 e 6 f

15

2 Good idea 3 What's on 4 seeing that
5 how about 6 What's 7 in it 8 it on
9 I'll check 10 we should
11 Don't worry

WRITING

16

2 have 3 Ethan 4 a 5 success 6 in
7 won 8 with 9 most 10 actor
11 in

17

See sample answer in Test A.

Pearson Education Limited
Edinburgh Gate
Harlow
Essex CM20 2JE
England
and Associated Companies throughout the world.

www.pearsonelt.com

First published 2011

Fourth impression 2013

ISBN: 978-1-4082-1655-2

Set in Gill Sans Book 9.75/11.5

Printed in Malaysia (CTP-PJB)

Illustrated by Eric Smith

Photo acknowledgements: The publisher would like to thank the following for their kind permission to reproduce their photographs:

(Key: b-bottom; c-centre; l-left; r-right; t-top)

iStockphoto: 152bc, 177 (car), Mark Atkins 170 (microlite), Craig DeBourbon 170tc, John Guard 170bl, Tinglei Guo 170br, Gary Martin 152tl, Bridget McGill 170bc, Aleksandr Popov 170 (ski-doo), Peter Spiro 152tc; **Pearson Education Ltd:** Jules Selmes 177 (bus); **Rex Features:** 152br; **Thinkstock:** Comstock 152bl, 177 (helicopter), Digital Vision 177 (train), Photos.com 177 (pedestrian), Stockxpert 152tr, 170 (gondola), 170 (junk), 170 (tram), 170 (tuk-tuk), 170tl, 170tr, 177 (bicycle), 177 (horse), 177 (motorbike), 177 (plane)

All other images © Pearson Education

Every effort has been made to trace the copyright holders and we apologise in advance for any unintentional omissions. We would be pleased to insert the appropriate acknowledgement in any subsequent edition of this publication.